PRAISE FOR *ENDLESS FEASTS*

"From the editor in chief [of *Gourmet*] comes the food magazine's tastiest morsels."
—*Entertainment Weekly*

"*Endless Feasts* brims with the joy of discovery, and the pleasure of good food and good company. And perhaps the best company here are these fine writers who couldn't be more varied, but who have collectively given *Gourmet* a tradition of excellence. This is a feast to which you'll happily return."
—*The Oregonian*

"If food can be culture, identity and art, then it follows that writing about food has no limits as literature. . . . This [is the] cream of gastronomic prose."
—*Newsday*

"For *Endless Feasts: Sixty Years of Writing from Gourmet,* Ruth Reichl (*Comfort Me with Apples*) serves a banquet of portraits and reminiscences, from eminent writers such as Anita Loos, James Beard, M.F.K. Fisher, Madhur Jaffrey and Laurie Colwin. William Hamilton's childhood encounter with betrayal, in which jellied consommé is promised as a reward to the unsuspecting, and Paul Theroux's blissful journey from Denver to San Francisco by luxury railcar will entertain and refresh."
—*Publishers Weekly*

"[*Gourmet*] is the standard against which all other food and travel magazines are measured. . . . This anthology, compiled by *Gourmet*'s newest editor, Ruth Reichl, offers some of the highlights of past issues. For biographical excellence, little surpasses Jay Jacobs's two-part treatment of the rise of James Beard."
—*Booklist*

"Contributors include some of the leading culinary writers of the twentieth century such as M.F.K. Fisher and Elizabeth David, and the range of subjects explored is quite diverse. . . . From the graceful simplicity of Laurie Colwin's prose to Ruth Harkness's evocative descriptions of living and eating in a Tibetan lamasery, there is a remarkable bounty of riches awaiting readers in this soon-to-be classic collection of culinary writings. . . . This is a book worth savoring."
—*Library Journal*

ALSO FROM THE MODERN LIBRARY FOOD SERIES

Life à la Henri by Henri Charpentier and Boyden Sparkes

Clémentine in the Kitchen by Samuel Chamberlain

Perfection Salad: Women and Cooking at the Turn of the Century
by Laura Shapiro

Cooking with Pomiane by Edouard de Pomiane

High Bonnet: A Novel of Epicurean Adventures by Idwal Jones

Katish: Our Russian Cook by Wanda L. Frolov

The Supper of the Lamb by Robert Farrar Capon

The Passionate Epicure by Marcel Rouff

ENDLESS FEASTS

ENDLESS FEASTS

SIXTY YEARS OF WRITING
FROM *GOURMET*

Edited and with an Introduction
by Ruth Reichl

THE MODERN LIBRARY

NEW YORK

Library of Congress Cataloging-in-Publication Data

Endless feasts : sixty years of writing from Gourmet / edited and with an
introduction by Ruth Reichl.
    p.   cm.—(Modern Library food)
         ISBN 0-375-75992-1 (pbk.)
1. Cookery. 2. Cookery, American. 3. Cookery, International. I. Reichl, Ruth.
II. Gourmet. III. Series.
         TX652.9 .E53   2002
         641.5—dc21
         2001051404

CONTENTS

PERSONALITIES OF *GOURMET*

MATTERS OF TASTE

ON FOODS AND COOKING

Introduction

Ruth Reichl

America's greatest writer on the subject of food once described her own work as being about "eating and what to eat and people who eat." The careful reader will note that this left her an enormous amount of room to turn around in.

It is also a perfect description of *Gourmet* magazine in its early years. When M.F.K. Fisher talked about her chosen subject, she was staking out territory, declaring her intention to write about much more than what was on the table. *Gourmet,* at its inception, demanded the same latitude. There was almost nothing that the editors considered outside the magazine's purview, no voice that could not be heard within its pages. The largeness of this vision was due entirely to its founder, Earle MacAusland, a man who saw nothing strange about inaugurating a "magazine of good living" just as the world was on the brink of war. He wanted to make his mark, declare his belief in the importance of living well even in the face of disaster. Bringing his magazine into the world was a decidedly optimistic act, an impulsive vote for the triumph of good sense and the value of good taste.

MacAusland lived large, and in conceiving America's first epicurean magazine, he thought big. In a time when food was not considered a serious subject, he believed it was the only one. To him food included hunting and fishing, history and science, politics, anthropology, and fiction. It certainly included drink. Refusing to limit his imagination, he invented a food magazine that roamed the world long before it had been shrunk to its current size by the speed of jets.

He encouraged *Gourmet*'s writers to venture far and send back reports from the front. They went by rail, by bus, and by ship, and they covered every continent. Sometimes they brought back recipes; often they did not. In later years food magazines would come to rely on recipes, but in MacAusland's *Gourmet,* they did not hold pride of place. In looking back, what stands out is the breadth of the coverage and the quality of the writing.

And so we have Ruth Harkness deciding, one cold New York morning, to pull up stakes and take her Siamese cat to Mexico. When the bus dumps them—unceremoniously—in the village of Tamazanchale (the name, she notes, sounds just like a Manhattan speakeasy), they decide to stay because Wha Lin (the cat) likes the food. Meanwhile, another Ruth is actually in Siam (sans cat), feasting on Japanese fare. Their personalities could not have been more different, but each had a wonderful way with words, an adventurous spirit, and a unique way of looking at the world.

Joseph Wechsberg, one of America's best (and most underappreciated) writers, found a home at *Gourmet* for almost forty years. He cast his affectionate, intelligent eye on everything from bootlegged booze to swinging London, and it breaks my heart that we had room to include only two of his stories in this anthology.

One of MacAusland's greatest notions was to ask writers to cover the United States as if it were a foreign land. Robert P. Tristram Coffin, poet and Pulitzer Prize winner, roamed the countryside of his native Maine and wrote as if he were introducing it to us for the first time. His tales of tracking deer, robbing lobster pots, and eating off the land seem very long ago and almost impossibly romantic.

It was MacAusland's *Gourmet* that published E. Annie Proulx's first short story, William Hamilton's early cartoons, and the story that would grow into Ray Bradbury's novel *Dandelion Wine.* In later years the magazine would give Laurie Colwin a place to write about the pleasures of home cooking and would encourage writers like Madhur Jaffrey, Anita Loos, and Claudia Roden to look back at the way they once were.

Gourmet recognized that the strength of American cooking lies in its diversity, and its editors understood that a truly great magazine had to reflect that. By allowing its writers to follow their own appetites, by refusing to force them into a format, *Gourmet* became a true mirror of American taste.

In this anthology we have tried to chronicle eating and what people ate and who they were over the past sixty years. *Endless Feasts* is just a little snack, a sample tidbit of the many riches still hidden in the archives of the magazine. American food is a constantly changing representation of who we are, and what you will find in these pages is an ongoing history of our national adventures at the table.

A note about the recipes:

Gourmet inaugurated its test kitchens in 1965. We now scrupulously test, and retest, every recipe in the magazine. But in the early years the editors assumed that readers (or in many cases their cooks) could fend for themselves in the kitchen.

In many cases they had to. When testing recipes for the sixtieth-anniversary issue of the magazine, we discovered many that were not to modern tastes, some that did not work with modern ingredients, and a few that simply didn't work. In that anniversary issue of the magazine, we changed the recipes to meet the times. But when putting this book together, we decided, in the interest of historical accuracy, to run the recipes as printed. I'm tempted to tell you that when I make Laurie Colwin's chicken recipe, for instance, I don't cook it for the two hours she specifies because I don't like my chicken falling off the bone. But I've decided to keep my opinions to myself. In other words, you're on your own.

GOURMET TRAVELS

Three Swiss Inns

M.F.K. Fisher

I remember three restaurants in Switzerland with a special clearness: one on the lake near Lausanne, another behind it in the high hills toward Berne, and the last on the road to Lucerne, in German speaking country.

When we went back, in June of 1939, to pack our furniture and bolt the shutters, we could not believe our friends were right to make us do it. All of Europe stretched and sang under a warm sun; the crops were good; people walked about and ate and drank and smiled dreamily, like drugged cancer sufferers. Everyone was kind to us, not consciously thinking that we might never meet again, but actually knowing that it was so.

We drove toward Lucerne one day. Children were selling the first early Alpine roses along the roads—tight ugly posies, the same color as the mottled purple that the little girls' cheeks had.

At Malters, one of the few villages of that part of the country not almost overpoweringly quaint and pretty, we stopped at the *Gasthaus zum Kreuz*. We wondered if Frau Weber would remember us, and if her neurasthenic daughter Anneli would be yearning still to be a chambermaid in London, and if—most important—if there would still be trout swimming in the little tank of icy water that stood in the dining room.

Frau Weber, looking more than ever like a virile Queen Victoria, did indeed remember us, discreetly, at first, and then with floods of questions and handshakings and general delight. Anneli was there, fat, pale, still yearning, but this time for Croydon, where she hoped to exchange her Cockney accent for a more refined one. And the trout still darted behind glass in the bubbling water.

We stayed there for many hours, eating and drinking and remembering incredulously that once we had almost driven past the *Kreuz* without stopping.

That incident was several years ago, when my husband and I were roaming about the country with my parents. The chauffeur was sleepy after a night spent in a hotel filled with unusually pretty kitchen maids, and he lost the way. We went along roads, mazily, that led where we did not want to go at all; and we all got very hungry and perhaps a little too polite.

Finally we said to stop at the first *gasthaus*, no matter what it looked like. We could certainly count on beer and cheese, at the least.

Pierre stifled a yawn, and his neck got a little pinker; and in perhaps a minute we had come to an impressive stop in front of one of the least attractive buildings of German Switzerland, in the tight village of Malters.

The place had a sharp peaked roof and many little windows; but there were no flowers on the wooden ledges, and a smell of blood came from the sausage shop on the ground floor. Dark stairs led up from the street through a forbidding hallway.

We wanted to go on. It was late, though; and we were hungry and cramped and full of latent snarls. I told Pierre to see what the place looked like.

He yawned again, painfully, and went with false briskness up the dour, dark stairs. Soon he was back, beaming, no longer sleepy. We crawled out, not caring how many pretty girls he had found if there was something in their kitchen for us, too.

Soon life looked better. Frau Weber herself had led us solicitously to ancient but sparkling toilets, and we had washed in a porcelain bowl enameled with swans and lavender chrysanthemums, and were all met again in a little piney honey-colored room full of family photographs. There was a long table with chairs primly about it, and cupboards and a beautiful rococo couch. We felt happy, and toasted one another with small glasses of a strange, potent bitters.

"Whatever you have," we said to Frau Weber, and sat back complacently waiting for some sausage from her shop and maybe a salad. We watched the trout swimming in a tank by one of the windows, and thought them an odd, enormous decoration.

Anneli came in. She was pretty, in a discontented way; and we knew Pierre would have a pleasant lunch. We talked to her about England, which she apparently loved as some women love men or some men the bottle. She set the table, and then came back with a net and a platter. She swooped up a trout, held it by the tail, and before we could close our ears or even wince, had cracked its skull smartly on the sideboard.

My mother lay back farther on the couch and gulped wanly at her bitters; and Father muttered with a kind of sick admiration, "That's the way! By George, that's the way!" as Anneli whacked the brains loose in some ten trout.

She smiled and said, "You 'aven't long to wite naow," and hurried from the room.

By then we were eating slices of various strange sausages, surprisingly delicate, and drinking cold, thin white wine of the country. Nothing else much mattered.

Frau Weber and her daughter came in carrying a long shallow copper pan between them. They set it down carefully; and Anneli stood back puffing while the older woman lifted the lid, her white hair bristling upward in a regal pompadour, and her face flushed and dewy.

The trout lay staring up at us, their eyes hard and yet somehow benevolent. Our heads drew nearer to the pan, willy-nilly, pulled by one of the finest smells we had ever met. We sniffed and murmured. Frau Weber beamed. Then she scolded at the girl, who ran from the room for little white potatoes and a great bowl of hot buttered peas from the garden. The mother served the fish herself, and then disappeared proudly.

It was, of course, the most delicious dish that we had ever eaten. We

knew that we were hungry, and that even if it had been bad it would
have been good ... but we knew, too, that nevertheless it was one of the
subtlest, rarest things that had ever come our way. It was incredibly
delicate, as fresh as clover.

We talked about it later, and Frau Weber told us willingly about it,
but in such a vague way that all I can remember now is hot unsalted
butter, herbs left in for a few seconds, cream, a shallot flicked over, the
fish laid in, the cover put on. I can almost see it, smell it, taste it now;
but I know that I could never copy it, nor could anyone alive, probably.

Finally we were eating large, fragrant strawberries and drinking
quite a lot more wine. It amused Anneli that we wanted our coffee in
the tall porcelain goblets we saw in the cupboard. But it is the trout
that really mattered. They were more important than getting to
Lucerne, or than the pride of Frau Weber, or than the girl Anneli, frus-
trated and yearning. They were, we felt, important like a *grisaille* window or the coming of Spring.

And we went back many times to the *Kreuz,* and the trout were
always that way ... important.

The second restaurant I remember now was near our old home in
Châtel St. Denis, where the army used to send its ski-learners to use
the fine, easy slopes all around. It was called the *Hôtel des XIII Cantons.*

We knew Mademoiselle Berthe there. Tall, she had a thin, spirited
face; and her dark hair was rolled in odd corkscrews behind each ear,
in the disappearing fashion of her village. She had hips that were wide
and firm, hung low on her legs; and her feet, on which she always wore
exotic beach sandals, were very long and flat. She flapped about on
them, and was the best waitress that I have ever known, in Europe or
America.

The upstairs room held perhaps fifty people on market days and
times like Easter; yet Berthe was always alone and always unruffled.
Sometimes in winter, when army officers were there, teasing and flirt-
ing and barking, she got more taciturn than usual. But no matter what
kind of people she served, she was always skillful and the most impersonal woman I have ever watched.

She never made mistakes; and no matter how many people were
tapping their empty glasses and calling, she would always see that

plates were hot and platters properly bubbling above her innumerable alcohol lamps before she left one table for another. She sped about, flat-footed, heavy-hipped, unruffled, waiting for the day when her mother would die and she could renounce the dining room for the glories of the kitchen.

In the meantime, Madame reigned on the other side of the wide stairs which led to the square pine dining room with its mirrors and white linen curtains and window ledges heavy with hideous, meaty begonias.

Madame Mossu was famous for her trout, her frogs' legs, and her shrimps. I have eaten them all many times. Some sticklers for gastronomic etiquette have criticized what she called *truites meunières* because the fish were always curled like *truites au bleu*. Once I asked Berthe why that was. She shrugged and said, "What of it? A trout dead not a minute curls with agony in hot butter. One can flatten him: I admit it. But Maman prefers to let him be as comfortable as possible." There was nothing more that one could say.

The season for shrimps is short, and Madame Mossu paid well for all the boys and old men could find in their hundred icy streams. But there were never enough; so diplomats from Geneva and Bernese politicians and horny shepherds on their annual gastronomic bender in Châtel would make appointments in advance for cold shrimps in their shells, or in a *court-bouillon*.

There was a general who always had to unbutton his tunic, and at the bottom of the table a lieutenant with a gleam in his eye that meant, by God, some day he, too, would be a general. Once, on All Saints' Day, there were three peasants in full black linen smocks, and two sat smiling quietly while the third stood up and sang a little mountain song. None of us listened, and yet we all heard; and probably we all remember his serious, still face flushed with feast day drinking, and the way he sat down after the song, and wiped his lips and put a piece of trout between them with complete un-self-consciousness. Then, besides all the diplomats and such, there were *pensionnaires;* a tall, beautiful girl dressed like a Paris mannequin, who played cards every night with the butcher and young Mossu, and then went away without a word; the lame pharmacist, who had widowed himself four times by his own vitality; a dried, mean, sad old woman who might have been the librarian if there had been a library.

One night a little woman with a black wig came in. She went straight to the long table usually reserved for the military and seated herself. Then a strange party of domestics sat down facing her. One was a woman who looked as though she took dictation daily from 10 until 2. Her hair was like mud, and she was probably a "companion." One was a flirtatious man with a mouth too terribly sensitive; two others were poor, beaten-down maids with mean eyes and stringy skins; and last was a young, healthy, arrogant chauffeur. Berthe scuttled with her usual dexterity around this motley table. First of all, as if she well knew what to do, she brought one glass and a large dusty bottle of the finest Cognac to the old woman, who poured it out hastily for herself, all her dirty diamonds a-tremble. Then Berthe brought cheap wine for the others, who did not speak, but drank thirstily without looking at their mistress.

An enormous platter of twisted trout Berthe carried in next and put down before the old woman, who drained her glass for the fifth or sixth time and started shoveling fish onto the plates the others held out to her. While we all tried not to watch, the poor souls slashed and poked at the fish until each plate held its neat pile, with bones tidily put on a side dish. The clatter stopped.

Old Wig lifted her glass again, and tossed the brandy down. The servants stood up; and she looked at each plate with its heap of the best trout in Switzerland, boneless and delicate. She nodded finally; and the companion, the weak-mouthed secretary, the two maids, the chauffeur picked up their plates obediently and went out the door and down the stone stairs.

Berthe's long face was expressionless, but her little ear-curls vibrated gently.

"Curiosity grips my bowels ... excuse me," my husband said. In a few minutes he was back, full of news: the five servants, solemnly, as though they were serving some obscene Mass, had filed out into the little square before the Soldiers' Monument, and had stopped by three immense and antiquated limousines. In each car were three or four tiny feeble Mexican dogs, the shuddering hairless kind, yapping almost silently at the windows. The humans fed them, and then stood in the cold thin air for a minute, silent.

They came back to the dining room and ate well. The secretary flirted dispassionately with the companion and the less dreary of the maids, and the chauffeur stared arrogantly about. Old Wig ate little; but as the evening went on and the brandy warmed her, she smiled occasionally, and spoke to Berthe once about how cold she had been for the thirty years since she left Guatemala.

She makes me think of Fritz Kuhn's sister, in the last of the three Swiss restaurants I remember so well.

Monsieur Kuhn ran the Hôtel du Ville et du Raisin at Cully, near Lausanne on the lake. He was quiet, with sad eyes and a long face. The only things in the world he cared about were fishing for perch and cooking his haul.

The inn itself was strange and secretive, like its keeper, with cold, high halls, dank air, and an enormous kitchen which never showed anything like a live fire or a sign of bustle. There was a gaunt dining room, always empty, and the café where we sat, a long, queer room with a big stove in the middle, local wine advertisements on the murky walls, and a paper rose in the vase that topped the elaborate coffee machine.

From that dead kitchen into that bleak, smoky room Monsieur Kuhn would send his wonderful filets. He ripped them from the live, stunned fish, as they were ordered. The filets were perhaps three inches long, always with a little crisp point of the tail left on.

Monsieur Kuhn would creep shyly into the dining room, after we had come to his café for a year or more, and bow and shake hands and smile painfully when we thanked him. His long, lined face was always sad and remote and we felt that we were wrong to distract him.

His sister and his wife were different, and grew to like us almost too much. At first we thought they were blood sisters: they both looked so virginal that we could not believe that one of them was married to Fritz Kuhn, even though he himself looked quite beyond such bothers as cohabitation. It took us some time to learn that the taller of the two women was his wife.

She was very thin, and something about her was out of a drawing, out of an El Greco. Her eyes were bigger than human eyes, and slipped upwards and sideways; and her mouth was pale and beautiful. She was shadowy—a bad liver probably—but mysterious-looking. She wore black always, and her long hands picked up sizzling platters as if they were distasteful leaves from a tree. She had a light voice; and there was something good and fine about her, so that I always warmed to her.

Her husband's sister was quite different. She was short; and although she had a thin face, she looked puffy, with a white, thick skin, the kind that would bend a hypodermic needle. She wore her mole-colored hair in an elaborate girlish mass of curls, and her hands were small and pretty. She, too, dressed in black; but her sweaters had gold threads in them, and her skirts were broadcloth.

Madame Kuhn adored her more plainly than is often seen, and saved all the easy work for her, and did all the ugly jobs herself.

One time we took Michel to the Raisin. He was the kind of short, virile, fox-like Frenchman who seems to have been born in a beret, the kind who is equally ready to shoot a wild boar, make love, or say something which seems witty until you think about it. He was unconscious of Mademoiselle Kuhn.

She, on the other hand, was completely upset by him. She sidled and cooed, and put down our plate of bread as such a thing had never been put down before, and smiled again.

We finished our celestial filets, and drank more wine. Madame Kuhn hovered in the cold darkness near the kitchen, agonizing with her great dark eyes for the poor tortured sister. We paid the bill, cruel and wrapped in our own lives.

As we got into the car, Mademoiselle ran out with a knot of the first wild narcissuses, and thrust them loosely into Michel's hand.

"Some are for you, Madame," she cried, but she looked only at him, and his neat aristocratic bones and the power in his flesh. Then she ran back into the cold glare of the doorway and stood close against the stone, saying, "Oh, you are adorable, adorable ..." in her bad Swiss-French.

Michel suddenly broke into a sweat, and wiped the flowers across his forehead. *"Mon dieu!"* he cried.

We drove away as fast as we could, leaving the poor soul there against the stone, with Madame watching her through the colored glass door, and the smell of the little filets all around.

But when we went back, that June of 1939, things were changed. Madame stood with a plate of bread in her long hands, and tears ran down her face. Mitzi was in a clinic. "Ah, she is not the same. My little dear will never be so sweet, so innocent again," the woman said. And her eyes, as dead and haunted as something from a Spanish portrait, stared at the wine posters on the murky walls. "Nothing is the same. Nothing will ever be the same."

She walked toward the cold, dank kitchen, truly grief-stricken; and we, sitting there in the café, felt lonely and afraid. The filets, though, were the same as always; and when Monsieur Kuhn came from the kitchen and smiled proudly at us, we forgot his foolish sister and why we were there at all, and remembered only that some dishes and some humans live forever—remembered it thankfully, as we do now.

September 1941

IN A TIBETAN LAMASERY

Ruth Harkness

During the course of several Asiatic expeditions, it has been my good fortune to have had many adventures in eating. There have been highly "civilized" ones, such as shark's-fin soup at the fashionable Hotel Cathay in Shanghai, *rijsttafel* at the Raffles in Singapore, and many less formal ones, in the way of raw fish with strange sauces and fried lotus root in a tiny Japanese inn, old eggs in a Chinese temple, and, once, fried cucumbers and coagulated chicken blood for breakfast in a cave on the Tibetan border.

I think that in all my explorations of eating by far the most extravagant was the winter in which I ate an estimated ten thousand dollars' worth of rare pheasants. At least, after the expression of astonishment finally faded from the face of Robert Bean, curator of birds and mammals for the Chicago Zoological Society, when I told him about the tragopans, Lady Amhersts, and impeyans, and others the names of which I did not know, that had been served to me by my Chinese cook, he said, "Well, if they could have been brought to Chicago, I think ten thousand would have been a modest price for them."

But of that there could have been no possibility, because the scene of my solitary banqueting was in far Western China in the Tibetan foothills, where I spent a winter in a crumbling old lamasery from which all the monks had fled during the rout of the defeated Chinese Communist armies. And war raged over China, so that travel with or without pheasants was well-nigh impossible. Besides which, any fancier of pheasants will tell you that these birds, which live at altitudes of 8,000 feet and more, are most difficult to transport alive from their mountains.

An expedition had taken me to Western China for the second time, and because of the war I could find only my former Chinese cook to accompany me; my Chinese guide and interpreter had disappeared, so I was at the mercy of fat old Wang, who regulated my life as well as the expedition. It was he who decided that we should camp in the lamasery, who chose the least ruined room for my living quarters, told me when I should call on the local mandarin and the native Prince of the district (making sure that I took my Chinese calling cards with me), gave me Tiger Balm when I had a cold, advice as to what to buy from the Tibetans who offered me coral and turquoise jewelry, and what to pay.

Outside the cubicle which was my bedroom, living room, and dining room, was a great open terrace that overlooked a wild valley through which rushed an icy aquamarine river. In one corner of the terrace was a tiny enclosure which had been a shrine of some sort, and Wang decided it would serve very well for the kitchen. There were painted gods of many varieties on the walls, and an ancient, spicy odor of incense. High up in a niche reposed what surely was not meant to be the god of my kitchen. When I asked Wang what it contained, he said tersely, "Tiger bones, goodee joss, Master."

As I had left the war-torn city of Shanghai more or less as a refugee, with only two small suitcases and a typewriter, there was no question of taking anything in the way of tinned or preserved American food, as I had previously done. It would have been utterly out of the question on the long detour through French Indo-China and into the western hills, as transportation, to say the least, was varied, precarious, and very scarce. The only commodity we bought in the far city of Chengtu was dried milk; so we "lived on the country"—and very good living it was, too, both on the caravan journey and for the duration of the expedition conducted from the lamasery, which was headquarters for my hunters.

These hardy little hunters of the hills ... my chief hunter was no bigger than a boy and was also the local priest ... have never ceased to be a matter of wonder to me. In the preparations for the long trips which they made for me high into the snows of the mountains, sometimes to be gone for a week or ten days, they took with them as their only rations a homespun bag containing perhaps eight or nine pounds of corn meal, a lump of grey rock salt, perhaps a few bunches of *bei-tsai,* which is a Chinese green like a cross between romaine and cabbage, a *lobo* or two—reminiscent of both radish and turnip—and, if they could get it, a piece of fat salt pork. In the hills, rice is very dear and very scarce; so the staple food is good Indian maize.

Many, many times I have watched the hunters, in camp after a long day's trudging up and down mountains, prepare their corn meal over a tiny blaze under an improvised shelter of bamboo. Not only did these people travel lightly as to food, but most of them carried no blankets, sleeping close to the fire on snowy nights. Not one had a pair of socks, only straw sandals and thin blue cotton trousers and jackets.

One method of cooking their maize was to make a dough of it with water in which a lump of rock salt had been soaked, knead it into little balls, and cook it as a sort of dumpling with a few leaves of *bei-tsai* and a tiny piece of fat pork. Another was to bake it in a shallow, curved iron pan in the ashes of the camp fire until it was like hardtack, and hence would keep for many days and obviate the necessity for cooking on the trail.

In the lamasery, Wang cooked the meal into pancakes for me, or into "johnnycake" with native baking powder made up in the hills, or into mush with coarse brown sugar, or into dessert with eggs, walnut meats, and dried milk. We even had a version of Scottish scones which Wang called "skonks."

The oven in which he turned out these delicacies was a little gem that had been lovingly and artistically made from a ten-gallon Socony gasoline tin. It had a tiny door and a rack, and it could bake to perfection over the little brazier which was Wang's stove, and by which he squatted by the hour, his long blue gown tucked up under his knees, stirring some delicious mess with a pair of chopsticks. His fuel was charcoal, or sticks and twigs.

Meat was very scarce in that far and almost uninhabited country; there was only a tiny collection of huts at the base of the rambling old lamasery, and the people were very poor. Wang, however, could usually manage a chicken every few days, a few eggs, dried bamboo shoots, and a casual roundup of odds and ends that he could always put together and make a delicious meal. There were chestnuts and walnuts (the walnuts had the deeper flavor of black walnuts rather than that of the English) from the surrounding hills which he served with chicken, and a little *bei-tsai* seasoned with soya sauce until it was fit for a king. Soy beans are one of the commonest of Chinese products and are used in many ways, including the delicious salty sauce universally known.

As news of the foreigner living in the lamasery spread, nearly every day saw a few picturesque tribespeople straggling down the valley with something edible to sell. A Jarung man would put his hand into an inner pocket of his long homespun robe and proudly produce a packet of wild honey wrapped in leaves. Or a Chang woman, smiling shyly at me from tilted eyes, brought out from the pack on her back (in which she also carried her sloe-eyed baby) a kind of strange squash that I had never seen before, which was mine for a few cents. These women always worked as they toiled up and down the mountain trails. A little basket of raw wool hung from their belts, and deftly they shredded and twisted it into yarn, which, with a flip of the wrist, wound itself on the spindle that hung dangling and swinging rhythmically.

There was, of course, always tea, delicious pale Chinese tea, and I was seldom without a bowl of it. To drink unboiled water is an invitation to disease; so one becomes accustomed to tea instead of water. The Chinese country people make their tea differently from the way the city people do, and I think I prefer the peasant way that you see in the village tea shops all over China. These shops are usually open to the street, and are the common meeting place for exchange of news and local gossip. The tea bowls in no matter how poor a place are always pretty, even though much mended (and to see an old Chinese carefully tying the broken pieces of a delicate bowl in place, and then riveting them together with tiny copper clips is an unforgettable experience). A pinch of tea is put in the bowl and boiling water poured over it.

In our kitchen in the lamasery shrine there was always tea for the "neighbors," for the tribespeople who came drifting in, or for any chance traveler. Never a day passed that my kitchen was not enlivened by the hum of Chinese talk over tea.

The feasting really began with the return of the hunters from their first forays in the hills. They brought me slabs of wild boar, venison, sometimes coral, which is a species of wild sheep, and partridge and pheasant. This border country between China and Tibet is sometimes called the "lost triangle of the world," and abounds in strange animals that are to be found no place else on earth. Within a week's march of the lamasery could be found giant panda, the little panda which the Chinese call "fire fox," takin, the goat-antelope creature, serow, coral, the tiny musk deer, blue sheep, Ovis ammon and Ovis poli, rare species of mountain sheep. There are also sambur deer, tufted deer, black bear, and several species of small wildcats, as well as the beautiful snow leopard.

Pheasants abound in the bamboo jungles and are of many varieties—blood pheasants, white pheasants, Lady Amhersts, Tibetan white-eared, impeyans, tragopans. My larder was never without dozens of these extravagant birds, including partridge, but by far the most plentiful were the beautiful tragopans. The plumage of the male is a scintillating symphony of color, orange and gold speckled with brown and black, and then generously dusted with silver, star-like markings. The hens, by comparison, are modest little birds with brown coats, but possessed of a valiant spirit.

Sometimes the hunters carried them in by the dozen packed in bamboo baskets, but at other times they brought them in alive tied up in empty corn meal bags. Wang made a pen for them near the kitchen, where he kept them well fed and watered until needed for the pot.

As they were usually brought in in pairs, it was interesting to watch the pride with which the brilliant male stood over the little female, guarding her, with a belligerent ruffling of feathers for anyone who approached, while she crouched at his feet. But the "female of the species" always survived longer than the male; for several times when

I went to look at them in the morning, the male lay dead beside the sad little hen. Wang explained that the male's pride was so great that he died of shame in captivity, leaving a bereft wife who seemed to be able "to take it." After that, I gave instructions never to bring them in alive.

In spite of the fact that I watched Wang dozens of times in his preparation of pheasants, I am sure I could not duplicate any of the ways in which he served them ... not even if I could get the birds in New York, and had the finest of kitchens and equipment with which to work. And Wang had only two small covered pots and an open fire to manage his culinary masterpieces, for the little oven was not big enough to hold a pheasant.

One of his methods was to brown the whole bird very carefully in hot fat, add a very small amount of water, and leave it nearly all day over the very slow charcoal fire. At intervals he basted it with a mixture of rice wine, soya sauce, and a hot, red pepper condiment, but how the bird ever acquired that shiny, lacquered look with the skin oven-crisp by dinner time, I never knew.

Another way of serving was to cut the cold breast of pheasant into fine, thin strips which he added to *lobo* and *bei-tsai* which had been lightly fried in hot fat so that they did not lose their crispness; then he seasoned the whole with soya sauce and sprinkled it with chopped walnuts. Or he varied this procedure by using, with boiled chestnuts, whatever bit of vegetable he might have on hand at the moment.

When Wang served food in his own way, he called it "Chinee speakin' chow;" when he served me a whole pheasant with corn meal bread, he called it "Englis' speakin' chow," which was, to say the least, imaginative, and might be almost any way.

As winter progressed in the lamasery, I sorely missed fresh food, for there was no fruit of any kind and vegetables were limited. Although the latitude of that country is subtropical, the altitude of the mountains makes green vegetation the year 'round impossible. I began to long for the luscious tangerines and fruit that grew on the plains about five days' journey away. So Wang and I consulted, and decided to send two of the hunters on the ten-day journey.

Besides the fruit for me, there were a couple of things that Wang wanted ... to send messages to his family, and a few odds and ends of shopping that would be possible in the plains village. He suggested, too, that we might not have made sufficient joss to the gods of the mountains for the success of the expedition, and he thought it would be wise to buy in the little town of Kwanhsien a certain kind of red cock to sacrifice to them. Also wine for libations to the gods of the earth, and, of course, plenty of incense and paper money, all of which I agreed to as being very wise.

In those days of the hunters' absence, I believe that my mind dwelt unduly upon the thought of a luscious fresh tangerine and other delicacies that they might have found, and it was with disappointment that the tenth day went by and they did not return.

Just at dusk of the eleventh they straggled up the crumbling, steep stone staircase of the lamasery (its age was estimated in the neighborhood of seven centuries) with all sorts of strange bundles in the baskets strapped to their backs, and the sacrificial cock—a magnificent one—tied on top. There were rice and ginger, a bit of dried sea food for Wang, shrimps and sea slugs; they had replenished our supply of coarse brown sugar and Chinese spices and condiments; there were the golden tangerines and, unexpectedly, sweet potatoes. They brought also a tin of kerosene for our lantern and some hard green pears. I could hardly wait for dinner.

But Wang, who was not only managing the expedition, but practically every detail of my life, said that first we must sacrifice the cock, because Whang Tan Hsin, my chief hunter and the local priest, was leaving early in the morning for the mountains. So as darkness deepened, Wang, Whang, several hunters, and I all trooped down from the lamasery, past the huddled huts at its base and up a steep mountain trail, our way lighted by a flickering torch.

We came to a sort of grotto overhung by a forbidding, fire-blackened rock painted with cabalistic signs, with a sort of crude wooden altar before it. The torches cast weird shadows on the dark faces of the men and gleamed in their slanting, inscrutable eyes; the scene might have been something from an age gone and forgotten a thousand years. Whang of the gentle face and thin drooping moustache held the cock; he repeated certain phrases in a language that was not Chinese three times before the burning incense on the altar. He stamped first one foot and then the other three times. Then he stabbed the cock in the neck three times and allowed the blood to drip on the ground. Three tufts of the cock's feathers were pasted with blood to the altar, and we poured three libations of wine to the gods of earth on the ground. Then we made little piles of paper money which were burned, and set off the firecrackers, and, the ceremony finished, we all trooped back through the darkness to the lamasery.

Wang had put two sweet potatoes in the ashes to bake before we left, so that, what with cold Lady Amherst pheasant, the potatoes, tangerines, and nuts, I should dine like a queen. After weeks of pheasant (even for breakfast), the thought of new food was exciting.

I broke open a potato and sprinkled it with coarse, unbleached salt (I hadn't seen any butter for many a long month), and with expectations high, took a bite of it which I promptly spat out, choking. It reeked of kerosene.

And for dessert I had a tangerine which, in spite of its Standard Oil flavor, I managed to eat.

It wasn't long after, that the expedition came to its successful conclusion (I still think the red cock did the trick), and there was all the excitement of packing for the long journey back to the great plains city of Chengtu and the 2,000 miles more to Hong Kong and Shanghai. As presents for my friends in Chengtu, I had nearly fifty rare pheasants, which required three men to carry them.

In Chengtu I reveled in the luxury of a hot bath, coffee, and buttered toast for breakfast, and a clean dress instead of dirty, ragged trousers. I dispatched Wang with the pheasants, and he returned with dinner invitations. And that night I again dined on tragopans, but in the beautifully appointed home of my American hostess, whose table gleamed with snowy linen and beautiful silver, and whose guests wore dinner clothes. There were delicate goblets with white wine, and the table was strewn with pink camellias, although it was still winter.

Since that night I have not eaten pheasant of any kind, and I doubt certainly that I shall ever again have the opportunity of eating ten thousand dollars' worth in the course of a few months' time.

March 1944

Mexican Mornings

Ruth Harkness

All winter long, everywhere you went—whether it was at a cocktail party or just walking up Fifth Avenue—you heard and saw nothing but Mexico. People had just come home from Mexico—people were just going. Shop windows were full of Mexican embroideries, pottery, *huaraches*, and gaudy travel posters. Certain people who had always been addicted to the European scene spoke of Mexico as the Last Refuge.

It was, I think, the morning when the radiators were stone-cold, when the cupboard was bare of butter, bacon, and coffee that I spoke seriously to Wha Lin, the blue-eyed Siamese, about going to Mexico, too.

She sat on the kitchen table, her tail carefully curled about her paws, gazing into space. I privately believe that she is the reincarnation of an ancient Delphic oracle, and when her cerulean eyes go suddenly crossed—it is a portent.

In less time than it takes to tell, our Chelsea apartment had been snapped up by an eager friend, a carpenter had made a commodious traveling box for her Siamese Highness, and we had tickets to Mexico.

We crossed the border at Laredo, Texas, not without some difficulty with the Mexican customs officials. The first questions were: what kind of *animalito* was Wha Lin, and was she dangerous?

"She is," I told our inspector, "a nondangerous Oriental cat from Siam."

"But," explained the official patiently, "the cats never have the blue eyes." Before I could think of an answer to that, he was pawing through my luggage.

"What is this?" he asked suspiciously.

"That," I replied, "is a book."

He ruffled the pages; it was a volume of the poetry of Li Po, and the margins were well decorated with Chinese characters.

"They are not Japanese," I added firmly. "They are Chinese." His heavy eyebrows went up into black and sinister arches. He continued his explorations into the very bowels of my suitcase.

"And these?" he inquired, after he had made my underthings look like a mess of Italian spaghetti.

He held up gingerly an embroidered mandarin coat as though it might explode, and my very old and treasured address book. I explained what both articles were. He thoughtfully tugged at his black moustaches, his brows beetled threateningly, and he walked off down the platform to consult with other powers. I could see him gesticulating mightily to an interested group; it was only a little over an hour when he returned, with an almost amiable smile.

All difficulties, he assured me, had been overcome; he'd keep only the volume of Li Po and the address book. I could even take the animal and the coat with me. It was as though he were bestowing an honorary university degree upon me.

I was tired from the long journey and I stormed angrily, or as angrily as I could in Spanish, which was not very well. My address book I considered highly personal and, to me, valuable property. His tacit but knowing attitude suggested that he was indeed a very clever fellow who knew more than one way of catching a possible spy. I even wept a little, but my address book is still in Mexico, and I believe to this day many of my friends think because of my unbroken silence, I was probably murdered there.

Mexico is a land of sharp contrasts—high, snow-covered mountains and volcanoes, and tropical, palm-fringed beaches—gay cosmopolitan cities and Indian towns. We decided on an old Aztec village called Tamazanchale, which because it's pronounced like Thomas and Charlie, you'd think ought to be on West 52nd Street, instead of in subtropical Mexico. The night the bus dumped us off unceremoniously in front of the little Tamazanchale Inn, and fat Don Esteban Montemayor rolled out onto the dining veranda to greet us, we felt we had temporarily reached journey's end.

That feeling was pleasantly intensified the next morning on the bougainvillea-draped terrace where breakfast waited: strong coffee with hot milk, piles of smoking yellow *tortillas,* and a Mexican omelette whose exotic fragrance rose magnificently on the morning air. Don Esteban slip-slapped down the veranda on flat *huaraches,* bearing a plate which he set on the table with a flourish.

"Very good days to you, Señora. I hope you have rested well? This *platito* is for La Siamese; it is fresh fried *robalo* fish which came up from Vera Cruz this morning ..."

"It smells as delicious," I answered, "as the omelette I've just eaten—although my tongue still burns a bit."

Don Esteban smiled—the man had a lazy, indefinable charm—showing his gold teeth, and said, "You find the Mexican food *muy bravo,* no? That sauce it is the invention of my wife; it is *chile verde,* but my wife she is not Mexican, she is Chinese so she add the herbs—coriander and *oregano.*"

Later, when I became sufficiently familiar with the inn to be accepted by its Oriental mistress, the Indian cook, and the barefoot, brown-skinned girls who pat-patted *tortillas* in the dim Mexican kitchen, I was permitted to witness the mysteries and rites that produced the tongue-tingling *salsas de chile* to which our commercial chili sauce is a very pale cousin.

Whether the *salsas* were the hot green kind or the hot red kind, the pepper pods were always roasted in a medium hot oven until they seemed about to burst. Then they were wrapped in a damp cloth and allowed to steam for a few minutes. Brown hands slowly and carefully peeled them, removed stems and seeds, cut them into small pieces. For a moderate amount of the sauce, six or seven pods were crushed in the *molcojete,* the corrugated clay mortar, with the *mano,* the small stone pestle, along with two or three cloves of garlic and salt. Then a small handful of fresh coriander leaves from the garden, along with another of *oregano,* either dried or fresh, were macerated in a separate mortar and then blended with approximately half a cup of lime water; the whole was mixed until smooth. The lime water is the kind used for babies; this, they said, made the hot mixture completely digestible. Whether this was so or not, I do not know, but I came to eat it with true Latin gusto—rolled in *tortillas,* compounded with dried jerked meat, or in sauce for *chile con carne.*

Mexico, besides being a land of infinite variety, is also a land of infinite leisure—the Land of Tomorrow. A wit has remarked that in Mexico tomorrow is the busiest day of the week. He might have added that the first lesson Americans should learn south of the border is that haste—even promptness—is in the nature of a vice; that the first essential Spanish phrases to learn are: *mañana*—which may be any indefinite future tense; *mas o menos*—more or less; *todavia,* which the dictionary defines as "yet," but which invariably means "not yet"; and *poco a poco*—little by little.

Wha Lin took to the lotus-eating atmosphere as any Oriental would; she spent long hours on the purple bougainvillea arbor which became her blonde blue-eyed beauty outrageously, while I managed to spend hours strolling the banks of the Moctezuma which ran lazily blue through the valley where sprawled the village. The jagged emerald hills rose steeply on either side, their crowns in places dotted with flowering trees of a breathless pink. On the banks knelt the dark women beating their washing clean on the rocks, then hanging it on the low shrubs to dry as they have done since long before the time of the Indian emperor whose name the river bore. Small naked boys splashed and swam, their bronze bodies flashing in the brazen sunlight.

It was one of these small carefree persons who had observed my walks on the river path and attached himself to me one morning. He solemnly announced that his name was Napoleon de Jesus Benavides and was *"a su servicio"*—at my service. His charm was proportionate to his name. He wore a ragged little white shirt and seemed not at all embarrassed that his brown bottom was clearly visible through a large rent in the seat of his diminutive pants.

He offered me fascinating bits of information as we strolled along. The man who lived in that hut, he said, was now in the *carcel* because he had murdered his wife. When I asked why he had, Napoleon gave me the vague answer one everlastingly encounters in Mexico. *¿Quien sabe?* Who knows? He pointed out a haunted house, and a cave high in a mountain where lived a *bruja*—a very dangerous witch.

As we reached the end of the path on the way back, we passed a white stucco building, the most imposing in the village, which bore the legend Hotel Cadillac.

"*Muy elegante,*" murmured Napoleon. "Why does not the Señora eat her *lonche* here? Don Federico, who owns this magnificence, is *Americano.*"

This proved to be only the first of a long series of advice that I ultimately accepted from Napoleon, who squatted down in the portico to wait for me.

The dining room was deserted; obviously it was a place designed to catch the passing tourist trade—and just then there was none. A small malarial-looking man, scant of hair, sardonic of face, was the only person in sight. Obviously an American who had spent too many years in the tropics, he sluffed across the floor and handed me a menu.

"Since American fried chicken," I said, "seems to be your specialty, I'll have that."

"Yes," he replied in a voice that managed to be at once weary, but faintly sarcastic, "fried chicken *is* our specialty, but today there is none. You will soon discover, Señora, that Mexico is the land of '*no hay, no hay,*' which is," he added, "a very impersonal verb meaning 'there is not, there is not....'"

"Well, then," I said brightly, "I'll find something else on the menu, but could I have a cocktail first?"

"I'm sorry," he answered, "times are so bad, what with the war, that I have no license, but if I may offer you my *aguardiente* with lime and fresh pineapple juice....?"

It was only natural that one should ask Don Federico to share his own hospitality. As he poured the two cocktails a not unattractive Mexican woman clicked across the room on high heels, passing close to the table. She paused imperceptibly to give her husband a sidelong venomous glance, another withering one at me, before she went out and slammed the door. We could hear her voice raised in sharp, imperious Spanish, berating an Indian servant.

The situation, I reflected a little sadly, was not a new or unusual one: the *mestizo* woman who had raised her social standing by marrying the *Americano,* and who then despised her own kind, who considered the pure Indian a species of slave, and whose resentment against the whites and their superiority, assumed or actual, filled her body and soul with a poison for which there is no antidote.

"The Easter festivities are soon due," remarked Don Federico in his dry, toneless voice. "The Governor of San Luis Potosi will be here the Saturday before to campaign for reelection and there will be Indian dances in his honor. It's all old stuff to me," he said in a contemptuous tone, "Indians hopping up and down—but it might amuse you. And the usual bombastic and rotten Mexican politics." He smiled faintly, showing yellow teeth. "There might be some fireworks as there's a pretty bitter opposition faction in the village."

It occurred to me then that Don Federico was in almost as unhappy and anomalous a position as his wife: the man who'd lived so long in Mexico that he had nothing but withering contempt for his adopted land. And yet the sort of man who, when he went home, was unhappy until he found someone to whom he could talk, with brooding sarcasm, of things Mexican. And underneath it all he'd have disdain for the unadventurous stay-at-home. It was obvious that Don Federico considered himself a somewhat daring and unusual man.

He went on about the Governor. "There is to be a banquet here in his honor. Why don't you come? You'll get a laugh or two...."

Days, even weeks, went by uncounted, unnoticed. Wha Lin explored the small jungle behind the inn and caught lizards until her plaintive indigestion was such that she had to be shut in my room. Whenever I went in the village, Napoleon appeared out of nowhere to escort me and carry my purse and bundles. He became known among the merchants as my *pistolero,* my bodyguard. On *Viernes Santo,* Good Friday, Napoleon appeared on the terrace while I was having breakfast.

"Señora," he announced, "you must hurry. Today they carry *El*

Cristo around the patio of *el templo* in his coffin, and you must see him. He is *muy bonito.*"

I went to get my hat and purse and was followed back by Wha Lin, who surreptitiously had watched her chance of escape. Napoleon, catching sight of her, stared with open mouth; he hadn't seen her before—or anything like her.

"Mother of God," he finally breathed, "can it be real?" He touched her beige silky fur reverently and looked up at me, his black, tip-tilted eyes shining with an almost holy fervor. "She is," he murmured, "even more beautiful than *el bebe Jesus.* May we not take her with us to the church?"

I finally convinced Napoleon that I thought Wha Lin would not particularly care to go, and diverted his attention on the way by buying him a *palito,* a sort of frozen ice on a stick.

The church was the scene of considerable confusion; *El Cristo* had just been taken down from the cross and was being deposited in a glass-topped coffin. The cheap plaster figure was like no other I had ever seen; the sallow face was weak and chinless, well smeared with gore. The body was clothed in what looked like a tea gown of purple velvet.

Old Indian women knelt by the coffin, arranging the velvet folds, while other old women moved seats, mopped the floors, lighted candles, and arranged flowers. Young mothers squatted everywhere with nursing babies, while through the crush puppies and children wandered at will. Bronzed, intense young Indian men knelt motionless, hands outstretched before them, their faces mirrored in dark rapture.

Napoleon and I followed the procession which took the casket into the courtyard to march solemnly around and around. In one shaded corner a group of hill Indians—all young men and boys wearing elaborate headdresses of feathers, tinsel, and bright cloth sewed with tiny mirrors—were performing an intricate and beautiful dance to the monotonous but strangely haunting music of Indian violins, shaken gourds, and drums.

After we had watched until both dances and the procession were finished and were again on our way back to the inn, Napoleon, still bemused and ecstatic, said, "Tomorrow, Señora, *El Cristo* goes to Heaven. I will come and get you when it is time to go."

El Sabado de Gloria was also the day of the Governor's banquet; the streets were decorated with extravagant floral arches and gay with the town's citizenry dressed in their best. The broad roadway in front of the Hotel Cadillac was lined with milling throngs, while the thoroughfare itself was the scene of dozens of groups of Indian dancers from the hills. Each group had its distinctive and often beautiful costume, with music and intricate dance steps peculiarly its own.

The hour came and went for the Governor's appearance. An occasional cry went up, *"Viene, viene,"* but when it was proved false the Indian men went on tirelessly hour after hour in the broiling sun with their dancing and music.

Inside the hotel Don Federico hovered nervously over the long tables, supervising the flower arrangement, giving his servants directions. Earlier I had seen his *mestizo* wife, dressed in her most elegant, haughtily surveying the hoi polloi from the solitary seclusion of the hotel roof.

The great kitchen basement that opened onto a patio was alive with the activities of the Governor's servants and cooks, as he had provided everything for the banquet. There were mountains of steamed chickens and turkeys, with iron caldrons of rich red *molé* sauce to pour over them; platoons of *tortillas,* both golden and white; huge platters of *albondigas,* the delicious pork dumplings in the traditional style of San Luis Potosi, *tamales* steaming in their corn husks, squash cooked with pineapple and bananas, great baskets of mangoes. There looked to be enough food to feed the entire village.

At last there were wild yells and shouts from the roadway; the Governor had finally appeared. The feminine elite of the village made a welcoming committee, their arms laden with gardenias, orchids, roses, and lilies. The Governor, who was a city man, and I suspect not too well versed in the more Indian ways of the villages, made a flowery speech. It was another full hour before he had greeted all the local dignitaries from the *Presidente* down to the minor judges, and mopping a very damp brow, he entered the dining room and signaled that now the banquet could proceed.

Tequila, mescal, aguardiente, pulque, and beer flowed freely, as well as *habanero,* Mexican whisky. The assembled hundred or so guests, mostly men wearing fancy boots, tight velvet pants with bright satin shirts, broad sombreros, and very efficient-looking silver- or pearl-handled pistols, stood on no ceremony with the food and drink. There were intermissions when guitars were strummed and lusty male voices soared in rollicking Mexican lyrics; then the feasting and drinking started all over again.

It was about dusk when the Governor, looking tired and a little confused, rose to make his campaigning speech. He began with a very florid tribute to the noble town of Tamazanchale and its citizens who down to the last man were *culto y correcto*. He was launching into a paean of praise on its elegant institutions, when from the distance came a volley of shots, wild shouts, and more shooting. The Governor paled, and looked about for his bodyguards—huge, bewhiskered gentlemen whose pistols had earlier been much in evidence. But these gentlemen, replete with turkey and *tequila*, were slumped over the banquet table, fast asleep. If this were the opposition party announcing its arrival, it looked as though the Governor might be in a very tight spot.

At that moment the door burst open and in flew the small ragged figure of Napoleon. He caught sight of me and rushed to my chair. Silence had fallen over the room.

"Señora, come!" he urged. "You may yet be in time."

"In time for what?" I asked.

"Did you not hear the shooting?" he inquired impatiently. "It is at the church to make holes in the sky, because it is time for *El Cristo* to go to Heaven. If we hurry we may yet see Him go."

I rose from the table to go with Napoleon, then remembering, turned to say at least *adios* to my host, the Governor.

He stood, still quite pale but thoughtful, at the head of the banquet board. Then he smiled, a rather sad and charming smile. He held out his hand and said, "*Asi es Mejico*—thus is Mexico—is it not, Señora?"

February 1947

Paris Report

Don Dresden

Returning to live in Paris again is a strange mingling of impressions: memories of prewar days when France was a soft and lovely place where everything abounded; crowding thoughts of first seeing Paris at an age when foreign capitals took on an added glamour and charm; recollections with a touch of knight-in-shining-armor feeling when returning with the invasion forces; reminiscences of the incomparable enthusiasm and joy of Parisians on their day of liberation when the capital was short of food but long on goodwill, and when old bottles hidden during the occupation were brought out in celebration.

All those thoughts of days gone by tumbled over one another when I first returned. I found myself looking for things I had remembered so fondly and discovering that more than one might normally expect were still in their places from prewar and war days. Yet Paris was a place of strange contrasts during the first winter.

Out of the fairyland dream that is Paris for so many who come just to see it and end up loving it, resolves a very real kind of being when one comes to the city to live again after several months' absence. Even the weather seems to contrive to be different from how it was remembered, and everywhere one hears the natives remark, "Well, it has never been like this before."

Most days during the winter have been rainy with a tomblike sky shrouding the city. The streets have looked black and wet from the moisture in the wood or stone blocks, and footsteps were muffled in the damp air. There have been bright days when the thin winter sun with its lemon rays burned off the nighttime mist, and the spires of churches and the outlines of the classical architecture slowly lifted as though they were being pushed up and out by an invisible hand for everyone to see. Waves of cold have hit the capital. The Siberian blasts have frozen the pavement, turned the dark streets white and sparkling. The heels of pedestrians clicked in a high, hollow sound as people hurried to warm themselves in the nearest heated place, a search not always fruitful. On such days and nights, the people who always have looked less cold and forlorn than the average person seemed unchanged: the news vendors, the roasters of chestnuts, the ticket collectors on the busses. But their apparent acclimatization had nothing to do with avoiding the penetrating kind of cold that seeped into every cell of the softened American and made him want to run for copious libations of hot grog. Luckily there were days when the temperature lifted, and the snow fell softly as though designed for a city with lovely lines on which to shed its grace. People were happy, for *le grand froid* was temporarily at an end; children romped in *la neige* that for them is a rarity. All these meterological variations have been striking.

So it has been with gastronomy—stark contrasts.

Disregarding such exigencies, it is possible to find a sound and most pleasant meal, provided one is well heeled and knows his way around. As has always been the case, refreshing one's gastronomical lore about this center of eating is a pleasant process. It is possible that one might contract gout in searching for new taste sensations or in trying to recapture old ones, but the odds are that he won't. Moreover, there is a better than even chance that the waistline will go down.

Before starting on a tour of the city's restaurants, one must prepare for changes, the first and most important of which is monetary. Without mixing finances and gastronomy too much, the franc today is worth about eight-tenths of a cent in contrast to about three cents just before the war. A bistro meal without anything to drink, an unsatisfactory way to eat, costs about 120 francs or $1 today. Before the war it was common to find the equivalent for a tenth that price, *vin compris.* At the other end of the scale, the average check at Maxim's is about 2,000 francs or $16. Between those extremes are many small restaurants where prices range from 350 to 700 francs ($2.80 to $5.60) with a moderately good half-bottle of wine.

The next most striking change from prewar days is the lack of butter and other dairy products. This scarcity makes cooking with butter a rarity, a cream sauce practically unheard of, and also keeps one from bulging out at the middle. Chefs in some of the more *bon ton* spots refuse to have anything to do with substitutes for the real products with which they practice their craft. Like artists who don't have the proper paint with which to do a scene, they refuse to attempt dishes that were common in happier days when there was plenty of everything.

There is still another change. Good drinking has always been a part of good eating in France. It has meant the effervescent joy of champagne, the light white wines of Alsace kept in their long-necked bottles and served in long-stemmed glasses, the deep body and bouquet of a fine Burgundy, the delicate color and lovely aftertaste of an excellent Bordeaux. It has also meant the honest *vin rouge* and *vin blanc ordinaire* served for free in carafes with meals all over the nation. As this article is being written, the ration for two months ago has not yet been distributed; there have been scandals in many departments of distribution, including wine.

A reasonable amount of good wine can be found in most restaurants, but often it is young and unmarked except for the region of its birth. The price is approximately ten times as high as it was before the war. Famous cellars such as Maxim's which were moved to the country just before the green wave hit Paris in June 1940 have been retained intact with their magnificent selections. The value of such stocks has jumped many times over; the owners are unwilling to predict what prices might be for their bottles several months hence. In a nation where prices have gone up at least ten times over prewar levels, it is understandable that dealers, distributors, and patrons should want to hang on to their tangibles (in this case potables) as they see their balance of francs diminish in value.

Throughout this past winter, during the seemingly endless crises in the distribution of meat, it was common to find much more of the insides of the animal on the menu, such as heart, liver, brains, and sweetbreads, than the steaks and chops and roasts which had been sold in the black market or were being held under the counter in reserve for regular customers.

Restaurants which before the war would have offered seven or eight entrées could muster only two or three, and often the choicest items were quickly exhausted by hungry and wise patrons who came early.

Lastly, there are many little things that one misses in the cuisine such as the variety of cakes and tarts now restricted because of flour and sugar shortages and the scarcity of lemons that always were linked with oysters, *bis,* and a good glass of *vin blanc.* It is possible to find the lemon at times, the *bis* at others, but rarely both together. Real coffee is scarce; the *café national* is a mélange of real coffee with a high percentage of some strange roasted thing.

Lest all these changes give the impression that dining out in Paris is so different that it is no longer enjoyable, the returnee to this land of the table can be assured that he will get full measure for his time and money. One of the best indications of the restaurant situation is the fact that a mess for newspaper correspondents and businessmen closed because members found other places to eat more interesting and not too expensive.

My gastronomical wandering started from the Rue Cassette, which is on the Left Bank in the Sixth Arrondissement. I walked along the Rue de Vaugirard that skirts the Luxemburg Gardens, somber in winter, gay in spring and summer, past the Rue Servandoni which tilts and winds and where the houses for centuries have leaned out and bulged over the street like portly gentlemen in suits made for them long before they have partaken so heartily of the table. My path took me past the Senate where nearby Foyot stood for years as a landmark of excellent food and service. I was headed for the Place de l'Odéon where one can always find a good restaurant open, for hard by each other are the Mediterranée and the Restaurant Voltaire, while Au Cochon de Lait in the Rue Corneille is nearby—no suckling pig at the last visit, but promised soon.

The oyster boxes with their bits of green seaweed bursting from the covers were stacked in front of nearly every place, but especially the Mediterranée which specializes in sea food and has, among many delightful dishes, a fine *soupe aux poissons,* a kind of bouillabaisse.

I remembered the Restaurant Voltaire particularly from the days following the liberation of Paris, for it was there that I had my first meal outside an army mess. That day ended with much celebration in nearby haunts of the *Résistance.* The first time I went back this winter it looked just the same; the precise waiter who had served me three years ago and demanded ration tickets repeated himself. This time I had the tickets. The food was excellent: *fine de claire* oysters, cold and filled with juice, a tender *poulet rôti cresson* with French fried potatoes, tiny peas, a *tarte aux cerises,* all helped down with refreshing Riesling and topped with passable coffee. The atmosphere was as French as the tricolor: the polite yet not obsequious waiter, the center serving table on which the oyster sauces and cheese are kept, the hissing of steam through coffee as it was freshly prepared, the view toward the columns of the old Odéon Théâtre through the falling rain.

After that first lunch, I wandered about a great deal renewing acquaintances with big and little places on the Left Bank. The Restaurant Polidor at 40 Rue Monsieur le Prince seemed the same; so did the genial patron and his kitchen-handy wife whose combined arts have apparently meant a prosperous business, for there is little modernization compared to the days when the restaurant was largely a hangout at mealtime for ex-French Forces of the Interior. It provides honest food and drink for a relatively small price to habitués of the *quartier.* The Restaurant des Arts in the Rue de Seine is operating under normal management and provides its usual inexpensive fare. About halfway down the serpentine Rue St. André des Arts is Chez Vincent, long known to most Left-Bankers, and others too, as one of the soundest establishments where one can satisfy an appetite for excellent cuisine. It hasn't changed, luckily.

Eventually one gets around to those places he remembers among the first he saw years ago. For me the Coupole on the Boulevard du

Montparnasse was one, for it was there that I was taken for an introduction to the Left Bank, and especially to French oysters. I remember how frightened I was of *la Portugaise verte,* the green oyster, unadorned except for a dash of lemon juice, I who had been brought up on the standard tomato catsup sauce with oysters in America. Later I became a devotee of French oysters and longed for them when I was away from France.

The Coupole is a disarming establishment, for outwardly it isn't the kind of place in which one would expect to find such excellent cooking. It is a large, airy place with something of the mood of the Left Bank; an artist with long flowing hair is often seated at a table sketching a client; M. Lop, the perennial and strange candidate for the presidency, pops in to make a quick and fiery speech. But most of the customers are interested mainly in food. They are ably cared for under the personal direction of Messrs. Fraux and Lafon, who keep a very close watch on their establishment during lunch and dinner.

Oysters come to the Coupole directly from Brittany, the wines are purchased directly from the producers. Beer has always been famed here: today French, Danish, and the renowned Pilsen from Czechoslovakia are on draught; it must be admitted that the latter is not up to its prewar standard. English stout and ale used to be additional choices.

On the other side of the river at 3 Rue Royale is one of the restaurants best known all over the world for years—Maxim's. Going there today is like turning the clock back for as many years as one can remember, for outwardly it seems to have changed so little.

At first the restaurant seems to be closed, for the steel shutters are down and only a tiny light shows through the doors, like an imperfect wartime blackout. Inside, Albert the maître d'hôtel stands Buddha-like at the entry to greet the clientele, just as he has stood for years. The deep red carpet, the polished bar out of another age, the regiment of waiters, the faultlessly laundered linen, the flowers on the tables, the polished glassware—everything is complete and exactly as it has been for years. M. Vaudable, formerly at LaRue up the street, is manager today.

Every place that has a name with a glamorous past—Maxim's has gone through a series of lives since its birth in 1893—is certain to attract foreigners. The crop of natives who patronize it changes with the winds. Today it is easy to distinguish many of the Americans even without their uniforms, for they can be heard across the room. The English are conspicuous more from their choice of food, for they come from an austerity country where the counterpart of a menu like Maxim's is just about unknown. There are a few of the old-guard French with sufficient cash to take the check without whimpering, although their currency has been cut to less than a twentieth of its value of a quarter of a century ago. And there are *nouveaux riches* whose bulging billfolds can take an inordinate amount of punishment.

The most striking differences between a menu at Maxim's last winter and its counterpart of the early thirties are, first, the number of dishes, reduced by about half; second, the prices, which have gone up about ten times; and third, the complete lack of meat on the menu except young wild boar, during part of the winter of scarcities. There was plenty to eat—fish, chicken, duckling, pheasant, venison, all beautifully prepared—but to find Maxim's without meat on the menu is an indication of the times in France.

The time might come again when Maxim's will offer *truite vivante au bleu, gratin queues d'écrevisses, basrond d'agneau de Pauillac persillé pommes Maxim's, médaillon de ris de veau Grand Duc, coeur de filet bordelaise,* and such things. M. Vaudable and his chef, M. Barthe, say that there is no *grande cuisine* today because of the lack of butter and cream. Until such things return one will be able to get along adequately, and the lack of such products makes unnecessary the only really efficacious waist-reducing exercise: pushing yourself away from the table.

June 1947

FOOD WITHOUT WORDS

Ruth Kim Hai

Siam is a wonderful country. I was wakened from a sound sleep at five o'clock on a sticky December morning and shoved out of a comfortable Pan American airliner into a mosquito-infested customs shed all because I wanted to visit Bangkok, and I still love Siam. So it must be a wonderful country.

I began to appreciate Siam as we bumped along eighteen miles of it between the airport and Bangkok in the Siamese Airways Company's ancient bus. The other PAA passengers had gone unadventurously on to Manila, and we shared the bus only with the driver and our own luggage. The sun was coming up on the left, its level rays gilding the surface of canal and flooded ricefield, silhouetting murderously horned black buffalo and shaggy thatched houses on stilts. Women squatting on front porches over the water fanned their charcoal burners as they cooked breakfast; fishermen in dugouts too small to sit down in cast their nets into canals narrow enough to jump across; families of children took their baths under little bridges arched over the water. And all down the road toward us, singly and in groups, came shaven-headed *bonzes* in saffron robes, their begging bowls swinging empty at their sides until they stopped to pray before a peasant's house and to accept his gift of rice.

"What do you suppose *we*'ll get for breakfast?" I asked my husband, suddenly aware that it was after six o'clock and that I'd been awake for a long time without food.

"Rice."

"Oh, not for breakfast! I'll settle for tea but not for rice."

It turned out he was wrong. The Suriyanond was a hotel in the best English tradition and sent up an early morning tea with fruit and toast to our room. I had hoped for green China tea, which I dearly love, but the tea was in the best English tradition, too, black as ink, quite similar in taste, and designed to be diluted with milk and sugar.

When we had unpacked summarily and gone downstairs, we found that all the Suriyanond's cuisine was European. This, for two gourmets on an international bender, was unthinkable. "We'll go out for breakfast," said Hai.

"But we just had breakfast."

"That was early morning tea. I'm hungry again." So out to breakfast we went.

We didn't have far to go. The Suriyanond Hotel is on the grandest avenue in Bangkok, where the royal architect has decreed that space be left between the buildings. Pleasantly tucked into the grass plot between the hotel and the next building was an ambulating kitchen. Later we found that there was a similar kitchen tucked into every available inch of Bangkok, but this one was our first, and we fell on it with all the joy of novices.

The young proprietor smiled at us over the caldron of boiling broth on his soup wagon and asked us something politely in Siamese. We shook our heads and tried English. He shook his head and tried something we took for Chinese. We shook our heads and tried French. Then we all tried combinations of everything all at once and got nowhere.

There was only one solution. We looked at what the other customers, seated on stools at low wooden tables grouped around the kitchen, were eating and made our choice. Pointing impolitely, we indicated to the cook that we would like some of that. With a comprehending grin he took up a ladleful of raw noodles and dunked them in the boiling broth. From a little glass case—something like the one on a peanut roaster—he selected a reddish piece of pork such as you see in New York's Chinatown and expertly hacked thin slices off it with a cleaver big enough to dissect an elephant. Scallions and mushrooms followed the fate of the pork, and all of them got dumped in the bowl with the noodles, to be moistened with a spoonful of broth.

The bowl was placed on the bare wood of our table, and the cook motioned his ten-year-old assistant to bring the sauces and implements. Of sauces there were several bottles: the familiar soy sauce, the less familiar fish sauce which seems peculiar to the Indo-Chinese peninsula, and a pepper so hot I gave it up after the first try. Of implements there was a choice, too, and the little boy hesitated between Chinese and Siamese cutlery, not sure that we were used to either. We helped him out of his dilemma by choosing our own: I settled for a fork and an enameled spoon (the unbreakable counterpart of the Chinese porcelain one), and Hai atavistically picked up a pair of chopsticks, with a spoon for gravy insurance.

In spite of our willing cooperation, the little boy still seemed disturbed. He addressed us earnestly in Siamese and held out his hand. Were customers supposed to pay extra for cutlery? Hai fished in his pocket and offered the child a *baht* note; the child laughed and gave it back, then firmly grasped the chopsticks and spoons to take them away from us.

A grown man can't fight with a ten-year-old child over a pair of chopsticks. Hai gave up, and we surrendered all our eating implements with a sense of complete futility. The little boy dashed away with them, dipped them lingeringly in a ten-gallon tin of boiling water, placed them across a saucer, and brought them dripping back to the table.

"And they always told me the Orient was dirty," I said in an awed whisper.

The pork and noodles were first-rate. While we enjoyed them, the little boy and the customers enjoyed us. We were evidently a novelty to the ambulating kitchen trade, but a novelty accepted with open curiosity and friendly tolerance. The news spread, and the tricycle boys stationed in front of the hotel strolled down our way, pushing their tricycles to join the audience.

The tricycle boy is not what the name conjures up in my American mind—a youngster of five scooting along the sidewalk and upsetting pedestrians with his little vehicle. In Siam, the tricycle boy may be anywhere from sixteen to sixty, and his leg muscles are lean and hard from pedaling a bicycle the back wheel of which has been replaced by a two-wheeled buggy for passengers. There is much to be said for tricycling as a profession; you may never earn a fortune, but while you are waiting for trade, you have a comfortable place to sit. The half-dozen boys who considered the Suriyanond their particular beat spent most of their time lolling luxuriously on the back seats of their tricycles with the folding tops raised to shield them from the sun.

Our noodles finished, we looked around for means of obtaining tea and dessert. The idea of tea I gave up immediately when I saw that it was served in tall glasses with milk and sugar already added. The dessert idea I gave up more lingeringly while I looked over the case of cakes. There were a few iced monstrosities covered with violent pink curlicues and flat, stonelike cookies of a poisonous yellow. Neither variety looked edible. "Don't you have any fruit?" I asked of no one in particular, sure that no one would understand me.

"Fruit?" A tall, brown tricycle boy had wandered closer to observe us and, wonder of wonders, had understood me. "Fruit, you like?" he repeated. "I take you," and he motioned to his tricycle at the curb. "Come on."

"Can you take us where we can buy fruit?"

"Yes. Market. Plenty fruit. I take you; you buy." The effort of speaking English wiped the grin momentarily from his friendly, sunburned face, but once the agony was over, the grin came back like the sun out of a cloud. He stood before us expectantly, radiating goodwill and helpfulness.

"But there are two of us," Hai said.

"Never mind." The grin broadened. "I strong. You little. I take you both."

We paid our bill by holding out a handful of Siamese banknotes and letting the proprietor choose what we owed him. He took the equivalent of twenty cents and gave us back three cents in coppers, so we were fairly sure we were not being cheated. Then we wedged ourselves into the little buggy, and our horse-and-guide pulled us away from the curb to the accompaniment of encouraging remarks from his competitors.

Going anywhere in Bangkok is a lesson in international confidence. You whiz through narrow streets lined with open-front shops where not only the names but the numbers are in Siamese, which you can't read; you turn corners at all angles to lose yourself in the maze of streets; your driver toils over steeply arched bridges to cross and re-cross the same canal—or is it another canal? You have no idea where you are or how to get back to where you were; without perfect confidence in your guide, you are a lost man.

Our confidence was well placed. After ten minutes of dodging cars, little wagons drawn by little horses the size of calves, and other tricy-cles, we conquered the arch of one last bridge and coasted down a street full of fruit-sellers. Our boy drew up to the curb beside a line of waiting tricycles, and we got out before an open market building full of shouting women.

We must have looked bewildered. Our boy said something to the tricycle boy alongside, indicating his machine with a backward jerk of his head, and followed us toward the market house. "Never mind. I show you," he grinned.

And he showed us. Strange apple-green grooved fruits that give a star-shaped cross section and have a crisp, refreshing flesh that is translucent; fruits that look like little red apples and taste like flowers; fruits that look like overgrown hedgehogs and have inside delicious, apricot-colored sections carefully packed in their own home-grown excelsior; bananas as short as your finger and as delicious as anything you ever tasted; grapefruit as big as melons and as sweet as oranges.

After a prolonged fruit course, I ate my first lotus seeds in syrup, served in a saucer by a street vendor. He carried his jar of lotus seeds and his supply of saucers and spoons in a tray suspended from one end of his shoulder yoke; in the tray that balanced it was a pot of water boiling over a little charcoal burner, so that he could sterilize his uten-sils. I ate slices of candied yam sold by a little girl sitting cross-legged on the ground with her woven grass tray of merchandise on her knees. And at every purchase it was our tricycle boy who interpreted, who told us if we were being charged too much, who pointed out to us all the new and fabulous things we didn't see at first glance. By this time we had nicknamed him Never Mind.

We wandered through the market, down a market street, over a bridge, and down a narrow alley lined with shops where everything from dress goods to bicycles was for sale. The alley was full of people buying, bargaining, and just looking, and to fill it even more, there was a row of merchants down the middle, their wares displayed on push-carts or on the ground itself. Beautiful garlands of flowers like Hawaiian *leis* were cheek by jowl with terra-cotta pots and charcoal burners; a Chinese jewelry store full of red-gold chains and rings was wedged between a show store full of rubber sandals from Shanghai and a dry-goods store overflowing with printed rayons from America.

By the time we got to the end of the alley and out into a completely different street, my mind was so battered by new impressions and my body so battered by fighting through the alley full of humanity that I wanted to sit down on the curb to rest. Our boy noticed my pitiable state. "Never mind," he said. "You eat," and he indicated an open-faced restaurant behind us. "I bring tricycle. Yes?"

We weren't hungry, but there were chairs in the restaurant, so we said yes. Since we hadn't yet paid the boy, we were sure he would come back to rescue us, and in the event he couldn't find us (which seemed highly probable to me), there were other tricycles and their boys who must know the way to the big hotels. Besides, the restaurant looked clean and smelled delicious and had a huge refrigerator practically on the sidewalk.

At a table in the middle of the room, a group of Siamese were having their lunch. A terra-cotta charcoal burner sat in the middle of their table, and atop it a pot was bubbling. From plates of green vegetables and fresh meat, the diners were constantly adding to the contents of the pot, and everyone dipped merrily in with his chopsticks or spoon.

We sniffed appreciatively as we went by and when a waiter came to our table, we asked him what was in the pot. But our waiter understood no English. Neither did the other waiter, nor yet the customers. We reverted to sign language and eventually got charcoal burner, pot, and ingredients of our own. Obviously suspecting that we didn't know how to cook, the waiter insisted on doing our cooking for us. When the broth in the pot was boiling, he broke the greens (rather like mustard greens and scallions) into appropriate lengths and tossed them in. After them went a generous handful of transparent vermicelli. Next came the meat, not chopped in a grinder but with a knife. It was part lean beef and part liver, and an egg had been broken over it. The waiter mixed meat and egg together with a pair of chopsticks and dropped lumps of the mixture into the pot. As a last thought, he shoved in a few squares of *tofu*, that Chinese cream cheese made of beans instead of milk. Making signs that we were not yet to serve ourselves, he went back to the kitchen to get our bowls of rice and a series of little saucers which served their true etymological purpose of holding sauces. There was an extremely peppery sauce and a sweetish sauce that turned out to be peppery, too, once you had it in your mouth. Hai looked around for his native fish sauce and successfully explained what he wanted by drawing a map of Indo-China and indicating that he came from Saigon. Everyone in Bangkok knows that the Saigonese put fish sauce on everything: he got his *nuóc-mám*.

Now we were allowed to eat. The waiter served us each a bowl of his concoction, which Hai ate properly, dipping each morsel with his chopsticks in one of the sauces and lapping up a bit of rice after it. But I believe in simplification and was still a little uncertain with chopsticks. I dumped a little of each sauce into my bowl and ate happily if unorthodoxically with my spoon. It couldn't have tasted better.

There were still greens and meat waiting to be cooked. When the waiter had turned his back and we had emptied our bowls, Hai rose to the occasion and did the cooking himself. The result was authentic, and we licked up the whole pot of food without ever knowing what it was.

While we were having our cigarettes and tea—real China tea this time—Hai drew a picture of the burner and the pot and passed his pen to the waiter with the hope that he would write the name of the dish. Proud to have understood our request, the boy painstakingly wrote out the word in Siamese and beneath it an English transliteration. It was *suyiyake*. Allowing for culinary and linguistic variations, it was good old *sukiyaki*, just what we used to eat in Miyako's in New York!

"There's nothing new under the sun," Hai complained.

"It was good, anyway; I like it better than the Japanese variety. And I think there's something old and faithful out there under the sun, even if there's nothing new. Isn't that Never Mind waiting at the curb for us?"

Never Mind rose and dusted off the buggy seat when he saw us coming. His unfailing grin shone upon us. "You eat good?" he asked.

We assured him we had.

"Now go hotel, sleep," he advised us. "Too hot now; ride no good." And he trundled us briskly back to the Suriyanond.

That evening, Somkid Suntharothok, a young Siamese diplomat we had met in Paris the month before, came to take us to dinner. "Have you eaten any Siamese food since you got here?" he asked us.

"We meant to. But one meal we had around the corner was like Chinese pork noodles, and the other was like Japanese *sukiyaki*. So maybe we haven't."

"Of course you haven't. There are only four really Siamese restaurants in town. Almost all the merchants and restaurateurs in Bangkok are Chinese, so you've been eating Chinese. Now I'll take you to a real Siamese dinner."

He did. But that is another story.

June 1950

DEMEL'S

Joseph Wechsberg

Once I called Demel's in Vienna "the world's greatest pastry shop." That was an understatement; Demel's is much more. It is one of the world's last great institutions, one that somehow manages to fit into modern times without losing the glories of the past. At Demel's one doesn't talk about tradition; it's taken for granted. Demel's is the Rolls-Royce of *la grande pâtisserie*, the Cartier of the *crème du jour*. The loudest sound you hear at Demel's is the breaking of the crisp strudel dough.

The Viennese have shown Demel's their reverence and affection by calling the pastry shop, like a human being, "*der* Demel." When they love and admire somebody, they replace the first name with the article: *der* Kennedy, *der* Bernstein, *der* Caruso, *die* Lehmann (Lotte, of course).

The best times to go there, as they say in the guidebooks, are Saturdays and especially Sundays, around noon. However, no guidebook mentions Demel's under "What to See in Vienna," although it ranks with Saint Stephen's, the Opera House, the Brueghels, Schönbrunn Palace, and the not-so-blue Danube as one of the city's great sights. On Sundays after church, one goes to Demel's. "One" are the members of the Austrian aristocracy. Officially, hereditary titles are outlawed in Austria, but Demel's remains a noble enclave inside the democratic Republic of Austria. The Emperor was a good customer, and so, too, is the President of Austria, a Socialist.

On Saturdays and Sundays the Liechtensteins, Lobkowitzes, Palffys, Schwarzenbergs, et al. drop in—to have a glass of Sherry, to taste the saddle of venison or a tiny asparagus sandwich, to buy a small candy box (a more elegant gift than flowers), or just to see who is there. It may be a great actor, a prima donna, a couple of ambassadors, a famous tax evader, a ski champion, or a millionaire. Demel's is the local oasis of refinement in a desert of faceless inelegance, of mass travel and *Sozial-tourismus*. At Demel's, people are still what they once were—not what they want to be.

The "abbesses" are the guardians of tradition at Demel's. They are the older waitresses who came to Demel's forty or fifty years ago straight from convent school. Only a few of them are left. Nowadays the pretty young waitresses arrive via the modern route, from the *Arbeitsamt* (labor office). But they have to comply if they want to stay. At Demel's one takes a dim view of lipstick, makeup, and red fingernails. That's all right for an espresso waitress, but not for a Demel's girl.

The waitresses, like famous artists, are sometimes known under pseudonyms. "Frau Paula," for instance, is really Hélène, but when she was hired, long ago, there was already a "Frau Hélène," and there couldn't be two. When a real Paula arrived a few years later, she was renamed "Frau Grete" by order of Frau Demel, the owner, though this Paula would have preferred to be called "Agnes." (Even her husband now calls her "Grete.")

The waitresses use an archaic idiom, never addressing their customers directly as *"Sie"* (you) but in the third person plural. *"Wurden schon bedient?"* ("Have they already ordered?") the "abbess" may ask, referring to you alone. If the ordinary customer has been promoted to *Stammgast* (habitué) by the top-secret councils at Demel's, which may take nineteen years or longer, a "von" may be bestowed. All this is done matter-of-factly, with no trace of snobbism. Unlike many Americans, the "abbesses" at Demel's are totally unimpressed by aristocratic titles, although they never confuse a count with a duke, or a baron with a prince. They are impressed only by Demel's. If they want to express their highest approval they say, "It's Demelish." In their considered opinion Demel's is the only great place on earth. It's only fitting that the assorted highnesses pay their respects to the Institution, as they always have since Demel's was founded in 1786.

The founder was one Ludwig Dehne, sugar baker's apprentice from Württemberg. His sugar bakery was located across from the stage door of the old Burgtheater, which was close to the Imperial Palace. Naturally, Dehne's sugar bakery became popular with the people from both the Burgtheater and the Imperial Palace. In Vienna, the stage and the aristocracy have often been linked by romantic legends, and the sugar bakery was obviously in the middle. The most famous legend is the bittersweet story of Katharina Schratt, the Burgtheater actress, and Emperor Franz Joseph I, who considered Frau Schratt's homemade *Gugelhupf* the finest in Vienna. No one but an emperor could get away with that heretical statement; at Demel's everybody knows that their own *Gugelhupf* is the finest.

How did Dehne's become Demel's? Well, after Dehne's death in 1799 his widow, Antonia, was appointed court caterer, and the sugar bakery's name was changed to Kaiser-und-Königliche Hofzuckerbäckerei. The name changed again when a Dehne grandson sold the shop in 1857 to his first assistant, Christian Demel. When the old Burgtheater was torn down in 1887, the pastry shop was moved to its present location at Kohlmarkt 14. Today the firm's name, gold-lettered above the entrance and flanked on each side by three gold medals, is "Ch. Demel's Söhne, Zuckerbäckerei." The Court is gone now, but Demel's is still there.

At Demel's the pastry is the quintessence of a sweet (Demelish) way of life. Some people (such as this writer) occasionally go there without ordering anything, just to walk between the shelves and tables laden with *Salzgebäck, Torten,* petits fours and *crèmes,* and to know that Demel's is still there.

As you enter the *"Gewölbe"* (vault), you are in an Edwardian world, a fairy-tale kingdom of sweets, chocolates, candies, brioches, *Striezl;* dark colors, a laden buffet, the etched yellow glass bowls of the chandelier that have to be specially made now. The dark *Rauchsalon* (smoking salon) is in the rear. Habitués know that smoking is not *verboten* elsewhere, but also not encouraged. To the right of the entrance are the first and the second salons, in Regency style, with many mirrors. No checkroom for your topcoat. Keep it on your knees. At Demel's you are not supposed to be comfortable; you should be glad to be there.

A memory of the past are the old-fashioned containers for ice cream and parfait with the numbers of certain boxes at the Burgtheater. Boxholders would order their parfait ahead, to be delivered during intermission with a bottle of Champagne. A numbered Demel's container was a great status symbol in nineteenth-century Vienna.

The anachronistic Demel's décor has become very fashionable nowadays; in Paris some of the new pseudodrugstores have similar glass bowls over their light bulbs. Demel's is again popular with the *jeunesse dorée* of Vienna, whose great-great-grandmothers fell in love there.

It must have been nice around the *fin de siècle* when Demel's was the rendezvous of slim-waisted countesses and dashing officers, archdukes and courtiers, and spies and statesmen from the nearby Ballhausplatz where Austria's foreign policies and intrigues were woven. Many romances—one thinks of Arthur Schnitzler's *Liebelei* and *Anatol* and his *Reigen,* better known as *La Ronde*—began and ended at Demel's over the *crème du jour* that changed every day, as it still does. One day it is *crème Grenoble* (vanilla and coffee with curaçao plums) and the next it is *crème délicieuse* (chocolate with pineapple and raspberries).

In the refined ambience of Demel's an archduchess might not have noticed that she was rubbing her gloved upper arm with that of a *grande cocotte.* The famous *Kokettentisch* (the cocottes' table), as it was known among the pious "abbesses," stood in the rear of the establishment where today the *Salzbäckerei* is arranged on a large table. Alas, the *grandes cocottes* are a thing of the past, as are the dashing archdukes. They are no longer dashing, but probably selling cars to make a living, and the countesses are working in boutiques.

The cocottes' table was presided over by Madame B., who commuted between Demel's in Vienna, Maxim's in Paris, and, in summertime, the Casino in Deauville, which will give you the idea. Madame B. bought her dresses at Paquin and later at Chanel; she was easily the most elegant woman at Demel's, admired by archdukes, tenors, and

Burgtheater actors. She arrived in her tonneau, a smart two-wheel vehicle drawn by a pair of gray horses, with the lackey standing behind her. She would leave the tonneau with Demel's doorman, an imposing character who wore a long coat with, in winter, a dark gray fur collar. Alas, he is no longer there; parking is not permitted in the area now. Madame B.'s choice of headquarters was obvious; after all, the nicest men were not only married, but always seen at Demel's. Evidently this is still true; Anita Loos once told a friend of mine that the best-looking men in Vienna were at Demel's around noon.

Twice a year, before New Year's and Easter, Demel's "went to court." Christian Demel, dressed in white tie, like an ambassador about to be received in audience, went across Michaeler Square to the Imperial Palace with a collection of Demel's candy boxes. The hand-painted boxes, filled with delicious candies, would be arranged on two long tables. Emperor Franz Joseph would appear, accompanied by his court caterer, and walk past the tables to review Demel's latest creations. Then the Emperor would graciously select gifts for members of the Imperial House and for other monarchs.

Demel's also delivered thousands of *Hof-Devisen*, or court devices, for the official court balls. These favors consisted of a wrapped Demel bonbon fastened to a lace ornament, with a tiny, framed photograph of the Emperor or the Empress or the guest of honor. Every guest received one, and many tried to steal a few more.

Empress Elisabeth was another good Demel's customer. Before she rode out in the *Prater* about five in the morning, she would order coffee to be sent from Demel's. Perhaps she liked it better than the coffee from the palace kitchen. Some very old employees at Demel's still remember the beautiful, slim Empress who wanted to be even slimmer, and every morning was literally stitched into her riding costume.

People often speak about "the sweet secrets of Demel's" as if the establishment had top-secret recipes. But their only secret is quality. Today as before, they use only the finest ingredients, and they work a little harder than everybody else.

"We simply make everything as it should be made," one of the old pastry chefs says. "The finest butter. The freshest eggs. The best ingredients. No artificial flavorings or colorings. Everything genuine, and very hard work. Look at our *fragilités*." He showed me the crisp, thin hazelnut wafers filled with a chocolate-hazelnut cream. "Other people make them too but never as fine as ours. It's not easy. No one at Demel's takes it easy."

Demel's imports special spices, fruits, coffee beans. They make their own chocolates, using old French *conches* with marble wheels. They bake their own sandwich bread. They make little marvels of salt-and-cheese savories that are understandably the envy of their competitors.

There are twenty-two *Posten* (stations) in the high, old kitchens, where specialists make sandwiches, *Torten,* puff paste, strudel, *Teebäckerei,* ice creams, and so on. All pastry chefs are men, though there is an old superstition in Vienna that *Hausmehlspeisen*—homemade desserts such as *Streuselkuchen* or *Milchrahmstrudel*—are best made by the tender hands of a robust woman. The fact is that few women could top Demel's *Streuselkuchen* or the special strudel filled with cream and raisins that many connoisseurs prefer to the better-known *Apfelstrudel.*

Demel's repertory is more fascinating, more varied, and more reliable than the State Opera's. They have recipes for over a hundred *Torten* and hundreds of other pastries. A general staff selects the ones that are best for the season and are the most popular. Certain heavy winter pastries are not made in summer. And popular taste changes; people now prefer the lighter *Torten* to the ones filled with heavy, rich creams. Best sellers among the *Torten* are the relatively new *Döry-Torte,* a thin, elegant, light chocolate cream *Torte;* the *Demel-Torte,* crisp short pastry with nuts, filled with fruit *grillage;* the three-layer *Hochzeits-Torte* (wedding); and the nine-layer *Dobosch-Torte;* the *Zigeuner-Torte;* the *Punsch-Torte;* and the different *Linzer-Torten* (the "dark," the "light," and "the third one").

All year round they make *Potizen,* a Yugoslav invention similar to a *Gugelhupf,* but never covered with sugar, and filled either with ground nuts, poppy seeds, chocolate, or raisins that have been soaked in rum for two days; *Nuss-Schnitten* and *Linzer-Schnitten; Butterteigscheneckerln* (puff paste filled with ground nuts and raisins); *Bienenstich* (a yeast cake filled with vanilla cream, covered with sugared almonds); the famous *Crème-Schnitten,* either regular or "very thin"; *Jubilaeumskrapfen* (a biscuit dough filled with a vanilla-raspberry cream, covered with raspberry *gelée* and ground almonds); nut or poppy seed strudel made with yeast; pineapple *bombes* (*biscuit* with a pineapple cream, a piece of pineapple on top, and a finishing glaze); *Zitronentörtchen* (a sponge mix with lemon icing); *Kärntner Reindling* (a yeast cake filled with raisins and nuts); *Nussbeugerln* and *Mohnbeugerln* (crescents filled with poppy seeds or ground walnuts, honey, and cinnamon—they remind history-minded connoisseurs of the Turkish siege in 1683); and always a *bavaroise,* a different flavor every day.

The first kitchen specialists are at their posts about 5 A.M. when the brioches, *Potizen, Gugelhupf,* and the *Jourgebäck* are made. Many *Torten,* made the previous day and left overnight in the refrigerators, are being glazed and made ready. By 9 A.M., when the pastry shop opens and the first customers appear, the shelves are covered with many delicate things. Demel's closes at 7 P.M., and people coming late often find the shelves empty. There is a fairy tale in Vienna that Demel's employees are the best-fed people in town because they take home whatever perishable delicacies remain unsold. Actually, almost everything is sold, but the approximately one hundred employees don't exactly starve.

If there exists a nicer sight then Demel's pastry it is Demel's famous buffet. The word "buffet" might be misleading; Demel's is no rush-hour cafeteria. Demel's buffet offers probably the most elegant lunch in Vienna. There is always a consommé, and there are warm dishes—fine things made of chicken or sweetbreads, vegetables au gratin, a marvelous spinach *Torte* (with freshly cooked ham, on a short-dough crust), and Demel's *Schinkenfleckerl,* known as the *spécialité* of the *spécialités*—boiled pasta in squares, covered with butter, egg yolks, and minced ham, topped with bread crumbs and melted butter, and baked to perfection. Various cold salads with beef, with curry, with vegetables; *boeuf à la mode;* saddle of venison; Italian veal with tuna fish mayonnaise (*vitello tonnato*); *Butterteighendel,* small chickens made of puff paste filled with a chicken pâté; *Schinkenkipfel,* brioches filled with chopped ham; and in season there are goose liver dishes, crayfish, and lobster.

People don't eat much nowadays, and the men whose business it is to run nations eat even less. The menus for state affairs used to go on for pages, but at a recent working lunch for visiting statesmen at the nearby Ballhausplatz, Demel's delivered clear asparagus broth, trout filets, ham braised with Madeira sauce, various vegetables, and small pastries and fruit salad. When Austria's president had Marshal Tito for lunch on February 13, 1967, the menu began with cold trout in aspic with *sauce verte;* continued with beef broth made with Port; stuffed saddle of veal with rice, carrots, cauliflower, and tomatoes; green salad; and ended with fruit salad and mocha. The Marshal, who eats little and wisely, was delighted.

Among the many state dinners catered by Demel's there is one of which they are especially proud. The menu is dated June 2, 1961, Schönbrunn Palace. That night Austria's president had President Kennedy and Premier Khrushchev as his guests, as well as several hundred people. Demel's had prepared the following menu: *consommé printanier;* asparagus tips in *tartelettes;* perch in white wine; small steaks with mushrooms; stuffed peppers; *crème Vindobona;* and mocha.

Two Austrian wines were served, a white Loibner Kaiserwein, and a red Oggauer Blaufränkisch. The Kaiserwein was not the only imperial touch. There was the precious Habsburg china and silver, and there was, above all, Schönbrunn Palace, completed in 1750 after the plans of Fischer von Erlach, the great Viennese architect. The Vienna Philharmonic, whose beginnings go back to Emperor Leopold's Baroque Hofkapelle in the seventeenth century, contributed the musical entertainment. The Demel's people, themselves members of a somewhat neo-Baroque institution, felt very much at home that night in Schönbrunn. So did President Kennedy and Premier Khrushchev, according to all reports.

A while ago, an American tourist who had lunched at Demel's every day during his stay in Vienna and often came again in late afternoon for some pastry, said good-by to the "abbess" who had served him.

"I'm going back home," he said. "It was wonderful. Even the water is better at Demel's than elsewhere."

The "abbess" wasn't surprised. "Of course," she said.

October 1967

An Indian Reminiscence

Madhur Jaffrey

My first taste, my mother later informed me, was that of honey. It is the custom in my community in North India for the eldest woman of the house to preside at all births. Since I was born in my grandfather's house, it was natural that the mantle of presider was assumed by my grandmother. It was her job to supervise my first bath and then to clothe me in a vest and *kurta,* hand sewn and embroidered by an aunt. Next I was swaddled in shawls. At this point I was considered ready to participate in my first ceremony, which my grandmother performed by dipping her right forefinger in a bowl of honey and writing *Om* (I am) with it on my tongue. My mother's memory about the exact details of my birth was always rather hazy (I was her fifth child), but what she did remember was that I completely missed the religious and philosophical significance of this act and that after tasting the honey I just licked my lips and opened my mouth for more.

I continued to nurture a bent for sweets for the next six years. At the age of three my favorite drink was a carbonated lemonade sold by an old gentleman in a fez who would arrive in the evenings in his horse cart with wooden crates of bottles rattling behind him. The bottles were made of a rough blue-green glass and had a marble in their necks, and the only way to get at the lemonade was with the aid of an opener that pushed down the obstructing marble. The sweet lemonade was tinted green, yellow, and red to entice susceptible youngsters like myself. After dispensing it the salesman would urge his horse on to the next house, and we could hear him calling from a distance, "Lemonadewallah, lemonadewallah...."

By the age of five I had acquired a little more sophistication. The lemonade wasn't exactly discarded but allowances were made for the attractions of other treats. My mother's toffee, for instance. It was prepared by crushing several "rocks" of *gur* or jaggery, a sort of rock molasses, melting them slowly, and then boiling the syrup. Meanwhile peanuts were roasted and shelled, and a large metal tray was rubbed with shortening. The syrup was then poured into the tray, and the nuts were scattered on top. As the toffee hardened, the caramel-like aroma of jaggery filled the kitchen. We could have our toffee thin or thick, brittle or chewy. My mother had so mastered the art of making it that she could produce it any way we requested. We children liked it best thick, slightly sticky, and *very* chewy, and it was sometimes a good five minutes before we could separate our teeth again after the first mouthful.

We also savored my mother's *pooas,* little deep-fried whole wheat balls, somewhat like Italian *zeppole.* Unfortunately they were prepared only once a year for Karvachauth, a religious festival. This was the day my mother fasted and prayed for health and longevity of my father. She was not allowed to eat from sunrise until the first appearance of the moon, and when she broke her fast it was with *pooas.* After the *pooas* had been used in the religious ceremony they were distributed to all members of the household as holy food. How I loved them! I would go from one relative to the next asking, "Who doesn't want all their *pooas?*" My father usually nibbled at one and passed on the rest to me, and occasionally someone else would give up a few. I would collect the loot in a bag and then ration it out to myself over the next twenty-four hours.

As I grew older my passion for sweets gave way to a passion for salty, sour, and hot foods. I first discovered the joys of unsweet fare one day when our gardener offered me some of his lunch—thick whole wheat *chapati* (flat, unleavened bread) with slices of raw onion. I was converted instantly. As for sour food, we had a huge tamarind tree in front of the garage, and as children we would bring down the green tamarinds with sticks and stones and then climb to the roof to eat them.

I grew up in a large family, where my grandfather presided over about forty people. There were his sons and their wives and children. There were his unmarried or widowed daughters, and there was always one family of visiting relatives. Then every weekend and vacation his married daughters showed up with their husbands and children. Needless to say my grandfather had designed his house with these numbers in mind. The house stood by the Yamuna River in Delhi, its long veranda graced by Grecian pillars, its rooms sized to function either as Brobdingnagian parlors or as dormitories for the smaller folk. Forming a veritable maze around it were its numerous annexes—the servants' annex, the kitchen and dining room annex, the annex for private offices and legal books, an annex of extra bathrooms for use at large gatherings, the garage annex, an annex for my middle uncle, and the shed for my grandfather's cows.

On cold winter evenings a wood fire was lighted in the drawing room, where three upholstered benches encircled the fireplace. Here the children—about two dozen of us—would sit, munching freshly fried puffed lotus seeds, cashew nuts, and Kashmirian walnuts (which we were *never* allowed to eat without raisins, as this, we were told, would give us the sorest throats imaginable). Occasionally my grandmother would send over from the kitchen various kinds of *pakoris,* crisp fritters made by coating cut vegetables in a thin batter of chick-pea flour and water, deep-frying them, and then dipping them in Chinese parsley and mint chutney.

Behind the benches for the children there was another semicircle, composed of overstuffed chairs. One was reserved for my grandfather, and there he would sit every night puffing on his hookah, the tall water pipe that his servant filled with his special tobacco. Below him, on a dark red Persian carpet, two ladies, often my mother and an aunt, would sit playing *chaupat,* a game rather like Parcheesi. My grandfather would puff his hookah, sip a Scotch and soda, and imperiously direct them as to their next moves.

Once dinner was announced, Grandfather, accompanied by the ladies, would amble slowly toward the dining annex, and as soon as he had left the drawing room we children would line up behind the hookah. Each of us would take a quick puff, look around furtively, and move on until Grandfather's servant heard the gurgling of the pipe and rushed in to shoo us away.

In order to accommodate our large number, the dining room contained three long tables that had been joined together. My grandfather sat at the head with my grandmother to his left. Then came my aunts and uncles and the other grown-ups. Straight-backed chairs lined half the length of the tables and then gave way to plain benches. (I think that my grandfather's energy or patience probably wore out at some point and that instead of buying more chairs at the auctions, where he bought most of his furniture, he just ordered the local carpenter to make long benches to seat his growing family.)

During the cold winter days, my favorite food was game: black deer meatballs, roasted wild Siberian goose (a bird that flies all the way to India in the winter), and stuffed duck or quail cooked with cardamom, cinnamon, cloves, bay leaves, and nutmeg. We ate the game with either an aromatic rice or *roomali roti* (handkerchief bread), flat whole wheat bread as fine, soft, and large as a man's handkerchief. Another specialty was something called *daulat-ki-chat* (the snack made out of wealth), a rare treat that was served at breakfast. Early in the morning an old lady in an immaculate ankle-length skirt and a well-starched white muslin bodice and head covering appeared at our gate. On her head she carried an enormous brass tray, and on the tray were *mutkanas,* partially baked red clay cups containing the frothy ambrosia. The recipe was— and always has been—a mystery. I remember cornering the lady in white at about age eleven and begging her to tell me how she made it, but she shook her head, saying, "Oh, child, I am the only woman left in the whole city of Delhi who can make this. I am so old and it is such hard work that I only go to all the trouble because your grandmother and I have known each other for so many years. How do I make it? It needs all the right conditions. First I take milk and add dried sea foam to it. Then I pour the mixture into clay cups. I have to climb up to the roof and leave the cups there overnight in the chill air. Now the most important ingredient is the dew. If there is no dew, the froth will not foam. If there is too much dew, that is also bad. The dew you have to leave to the gods. In the early morning, if the froth is good, I sprinkle the cups with *khurchan* [milk that is boiled until all the liquid has evaporated and the sweetened solids peel off in thin layers]. Then I sprinkle pistachio nuts over that."

The lady in white is gone now, as is her recipe, but the taste of that cold *daulat-ki-chat* lingers still. The cups were placed in front of us at breakfast-time, and instead of spoons we were given flat pieces of bamboo. Each "spoonful" consisted of a heavenly froth dotted with bits of *khurchan* and pistachio nuts. The aroma held the scent of clay and freshly cut bamboo and gave hint of what food angels might consume.

The beginning of summer inevitably meant the coming of examination time, a period that fell, inexorably, during late April and early May. This was when the hot *loo* winds blew with the ferocity of furnaces gone wild, picking up sand from the deserts of Central India and scattering it over North Indian cities. We would sit up late studying about Mogul architecture or about Tudor intransigence. Early in the morning before we left to take our exams, my mother would appear with a plate of *badam-ki-golis,* small balls of almonds made by soaking the nuts overnight, then grinding them with sugar and cardamom seeds, and finally covering them with silver *varak,* real silver tissue. My mother firmly believed that almonds were brain food and that any child sent off to write two examination papers for six hours unfortified with almond balls was surely suffering from the grossest form of neglect. I would take a bite of the *goli* and savor it on my tongue. Meanwhile my busy mind would be reviewing the facts and figures about the Taj Mahal.

We would return from our ordeal hot, our tired fingers stained with royal-blue ink, and either irritable or ecstatic, depending on how we thought we had fared. We would walk straight to the refrigerator, where enormous jugs of buttermilk spiced with salt, pepper, and ground roasted cumin sat ready to provide restoration and refreshment.

The end of the examination period was celebrated by going to the river for a swim. But swimming was actually only half the purpose. Across the river there were vast watermelon fields, and the real fun lay in picking large watermelons, rolling them to the water's edge, and then swimming across the river with them tucked under our chins. The watermelons would act as floats. We would paddle vigorously, racing each other to the shore. Once on the other side of the river the floating melons turned into the loads of Atlas. It took two or three of us to lift each fruit, and, huffing and puffing, carry it back to the house. Once there, the melons were cooled, and that night we would carry slices to the roof to be savored under the twinkling stars.

The end of exams also meant an increase in our moviegoing. We saw many, many films—American, English, and, of course, Indian. The Indian movies were the most conducive to whetting one's appetite. They generally lasted about four hours, and whole families, including infants, would come to view the mythological-historical-tragicomic musicals. There was a great deal of yelling, crying, getting up, singing along, and sitting down in the audience throughout the show, and certainly no one minded the noisy unwrapping of paper cones, favored snacks that contained puréed chick-peas to which cumin, red pepper, sour mango powder, and black salt had been added. We would munch the cones while we watched Hanuman, the monkey god, fly across an indigo sky dotted equidistantly with hundreds of five-pointed stars, all cut from the same stencil. During the long intermissions we would exit to buy potato patties from the vendors who generally posted themselves just outside the cinema door. Each vendor carried a small charcoal stove on which an iron griddle was set. The patties were shaped from mashed potatoes, stuffed with spicy lentil dough, then flattened and browned slowly in just a few tablespoons of oil. Once they were golden and crisp on both sides they were lifted onto a clean, round leaf, smothered in dark tamarind chutney, and sold. We would carry these patties back into the cinema and eat them in the dark while we watched Hanuman try to rescue Sita, the good queen, from the clutches of the ten-headed demon from Ceylon.

Summer vacations saw us in the Himalayas, where the British, during their three hundred years of colonial rule, had built hill stations. My grandfather was a great believer in the health of his children and grandchildren, and he insisted on making this long journey every year. All relatives would meet in Delhi, and half a train would be booked to take us from Delhi to the foothills of the towering mountains. A fleet of cars was hired to transport us from there to six, seven, or eight thousand feet above sea level, where several houses were rented to accommodate us.

Once settled, we were left pretty much to ourselves: The only organized activity was the picnic. For this event preparations were begun several weeks in advance, with rickshaws or palanquins arranged for the old and the infirm and horses for the riders. The ladies of the house, as well as numerous servants, spent many days preparing the food. Baskets of mangoes were ordered from various North Indian cities: *langras* from Varanasi for those who liked their mangoes tart; *dussehris* from Lucknow for those who liked them sweet and smooth; and *chusnis*, small sucking mangoes, for those who preferred not to eat the fruit but rather to suck the juice straight from the skin. Litchis, those succulent fruits with sweet white flesh, were sent from Dehra Dun. Most of the packing, including pots and pans, the kettle to make Darjeeling tea, portable charcoal stoves, charcoal, disposable earthenware cups, cotton rugs, blankets, towels, serving spoons, and plates, was done the night before, and at sunrise, when the mountains were still shrouded in an icy mist, porters, rickshaws, palanquins, and horses were all assembled. First the porters were loaded with baskets of food and sent off with a party of servants. The walkers, led by my middle uncle, who had a passion for hiking, were the next lot. Third were those who rode in the rickshaws and palanquins, and the last group consisted of those on horseback.

The picnic site was carefully chosen weeks in advance—by the same middle uncle, who also acted as majordomo. Sometimes it was a distant mountain peak several ranges away; at other times it was a thunderous waterfall; once it was a mountain stream rushing through a remote gorge. (Ordinary picnic spots, where most mortals went, were never considered good enough.) Our spots were picked not only for their grandeur but for their inaccessibility in terms of distance or the climbing required.

Clad in heavy sweaters, mufflers, and shawls, our large party moved slowly, making numerous stops along the way. If we passed an orchard, a halt would be called and the farmer was asked if, for a certain sum, we might pick plums or apricots. My favorite groves were those of almond trees. I loved the green almonds, slit open and robbed of their tender white flesh.

We would generally arrive at our picnic spot around midday. If it was beside a waterfall or stream, the children were permitted to swim while lunch was unpacked. The mangoes were placed in the stream to cool, fires were lighted to heat certain dishes (and also to warm the children when they emerged from the freezing water), and a large cotton rug was spread on the ground. Arrayed on the rug were meatballs stuffed with raisins and mint leaves; potatoes cooked with whole fennel and cumin and fenugreek seeds; chopped goat meat cooked with peas; chick-peas tossed with raw onions, ginger, and green chilies; green beans seasoned with cuminseed, garlic, and lemon; chicken with almonds and yogurt; cauliflower flavored with ginger and Chinese parsley; spiced *pooris* (puffy, deep-fried breads); sour carrot pickles; hot green mango pickles; and spiced cucumbers. The meal was eaten to the accompaniment of tales of adventure and hilarious stories about our ancestors.

After lunch, the older folk would rest, napping on the rug or leaning against rocks and gossiping, and the children would disappear in various directions, fishing, hunting wild berries, or sliding on beds of pine needles. At about four o'clock we would all reassemble for tea. Served in disposable earthenware cups, it was accompanied by *mutthris* (biscuits) and my grandmother's thick, sweet tomato chutney.

Then the fires were put out, the rugs and utensils were packed, and the whole party would begin the long trek home.

The following recipes are for some of the specialties of North India, such as those served at the sumptuous picnic described above.

KOFTA
(*Meatballs with Raisins and Mint*)

In a bowl soak ⅔ cup golden raisins in 1 cup hot water for 2 hours. Drain and chop the raisins and combine them with 2 tablespoons minced mint leaves.

In a large bowl combine 2½ pounds lean lamb shoulder, ground twice, 2 garlic cloves, crushed, 2 teaspoons *garam masala*, 1 teaspoon salt, and ⅛ teaspoon pepper. Turn the mixture out onto a smooth surface and knead it for 5 minutes. Divide the mixture into eighths and divide each eighth into 5 parts. Flatten each part into a round and put ½ teaspoon of the raisin mixture in the center of each round. Lift the edges to enclose the filling and roll each round into a firm smooth ball.

In a large heavy skillet heat ½ cup vegetable oil over moderately high heat until it is very hot. Add 4 cardamom pods, crushed, and stir-fry them for 2 or 3 seconds. Add the meatballs in batches and brown them, transferring them with a slotted spoon to a dish as they brown and reserving them. Transfer the cardamom pods to the dish, reserving them, and set the pan aside, reserving the oil.

In a small heavy skillet combine 2 tablespoons ground coriander, 2 teaspoons ground cumin, and ¼ teaspoon ground mace, heat the spices over moderate heat, stirring constantly, for 3 to 4 minutes, or until they darken, and transfer the mixture to a dish. Wipe the pan with a paper towel, add 12 cloves, 1 tablespoon each of slivered blanched almonds and grated fresh coconut, and ½ teaspoon each of peppercorns and cardamom seed, and cook the mixture over moderately low heat until the almonds are golden. Transfer the mixture to a blender, add ⅓ cup water, 12 garlic cloves, chopped, and a 1-inch piece of fresh gingerroot, peeled and chopped, and blend the mixture until it is smooth.

In the reserved oil sauté 3 onions, minced, until they are golden. Reduce the heat to low, add the spice mixture and the garlic paste, and cook the mixture, stirring, for 1 minute. Add ½ cup plain yogurt, 1 tablespoon at a time, blending in each addition before adding more. Blend in ¼ cup tomato purée and cook the mixture, stirring, for 5 minutes. Add 1½ cups water, ½ teaspoon salt, ¼ teaspoon cinnamon, and ⅛ teaspoon each of nutmeg and cayenne, bring the liquid to a boil, and simmer the mixture, covered, over low heat, stirring occasionally, for 30 minutes. Add the reserved meatballs and cardamom pods and stir them to coat them with the sauce. Bring the sauce to a boil and simmer the mixture, covered, over low heat, stirring occasionally, for 30 minutes. Skim off the fat and remove and discard the cardamom pods. Transfer ⅓ cup of the sauce to a small bowl and combine it with 2 tablespoons sour cream. Stir the mixture into the sauce, transfer the meatballs and sauce to a serving dish, and garnish the dish with 1 tablespoon minced mint leaves. Serves 8.

GARAM MASALA
(*Indian Mixed Spice*)

In a spice grinder pulverize 1 tablespoon cardamom seed, a 2-inch piece of cinnamon stick, broken into pieces, 1 teaspoon each of cuminseed, cloves, and peppercorns, and ¼ whole nutmeg. Store the spice in an airtight container. Keeps for 2 to 3 weeks. Makes about 3 tablespoons.

DELHI CHICK-PEAS

In a large deep skillet sauté 3 onions, minced, in ⅓ cup vegetable oil until they are golden. Add 3 tomatoes, peeled, seeded, and chopped, and cook the mixture, stirring, for 10 minutes, or until all the liquid has evaporated. Add 1 tablespoon ground coriander, 2 teaspoons ground cumin, and ½ teaspoon turmeric and sauté the mixture for 1 minute.

Drain three 20-ounce tins chick-peas, reserving 1 cup of the liquid, and add the chick-peas and the reserved liquid to the pan with 1 tablespoon lemon juice, 2 teaspoons *garam masala,* and 1½ teaspoons salt. Bring the liquid to a boil over moderate heat, stirring, reduce the heat to low, and simmer the mixture, covered, for

10 minutes. Remove the pan from the heat and add 1½ tablespoons lemon juice, 1 tablespoon grated peeled fresh gingerroot, and 1 small fresh green hot chili pepper, seeded and minced. Serve the chick-peas hot or at room temperature. Serves 6 to 8.

PAKORIS
(*Spiced Vegetable Fritters*)

Trim the ends from 1 small eggplant and halve the eggplant lengthwise. Cut each half crosswise into ¼-inch slices, sprinkle the slices with salt, and let them drain on paper towels for 30 minutes. Press any remaining moisture from the eggplant. Cut 1 small green pepper into ¾-inch strips. Wash and trim ¼ pound spinach, halving the larger leaves. Peel and slice thinly 1 small potato.

In a bowl combine 2 cups sifted chick-pea flour (available at specialty food shops) and 1¾ cups water, or enough to make a thick batter, and stir in ½ teaspoon each of salt, turmeric, ground cumin, and baking soda, ¼ teaspoon pepper, and cayenne to taste. Coat the vegetables with the batter and in a deep fryer fry them, in batches just large enough to fit in one layer in the frying basket, in hot deep oil (350° F.), turning them occasionally, for 8 minutes, or until they are browned. Drain the vegetables on paper towels and sprinkle them with salt.

INDIAN BAKED RICE

In a bowl cover 3 cups long-grain rice with cold water and rub the grains with the hands. Drain the rice in a sieve, return it to the bowl, and wash it in the same manner 4 or 5 more times, or until the water is no longer cloudy. Let the rice drain in the sieve for 10 minutes. In the bowl soak the rice in 4½ cups cold water for 30 minutes and drain it in the sieve.

In a 1½-quart flameproof baking dish with a tight-fitting lid sauté 1 tablespoon slivered blanched almonds in 5 tablespoons vegetable oil until they are golden. Transfer them with a slotted spoon to paper towels and reserve them. Add to the dish 1 onion, halved lengthwise and cut into thin crosswise slices, and sauté it until it is golden. Add the rice, 1 garlic clove, minced, 1 tablespoon thinly sliced fresh green hot chili pepper, seeded, and 1 teaspoon each of *garum masala*, grated peeled fresh gingerroot, and salt and cook the mixture, stirring, for 8 minutes. Add 4 cups chicken broth, heated, and cook the mixture, stirring, for 5 minutes, or until the top of the rice looks dry. Transfer the dish to a preheated moderately slow oven (325° F.) and bake it, covered, for 20 minutes, or until the rice is tender and all the liquid has been absorbed. Let the rice stand, covered, for 15 minutes, transfer it to a serving dish, and garnish it with the reserved sautéed almonds. Serves 8.

INDIAN SPICED GREEN BEANS

Trim 1½ pounds green beans and cut them into ¼-inch slices. In a small ceramic or glass bowl combine ⅓ cup water, 5 garlic cloves, crushed, 1 tablespoon lemon juice, 1 teaspoon salt, and cayenne to taste. In a 10-inch enamel skillet cook ½ teaspoon cuminseed in ⅓ cup vegetable oil over moderately high heat for 3 or 4 seconds. Add the beans and sauté them for 1 minute. Stir in the garlic mixture, reduce the heat to low, and cook the beans, covered, stirring occasionally, for 20 minutes, or until they are just tender. Increase the heat to high and cook the beans, uncovered, stirring constantly, until the liquid has evaporated.

POORIS
(*Indian Fried Breads*)

Into a bowl sift together ½ cup each of whole wheat flour, unbleached white flour, and semolina flour. Add ½ teaspoon each of celery seed and salt and 1 tablespoon softened butter, blending the mixture until it resembles meal. Add 1 tablespoon plain yogurt and combine the mixture well. Blend in ½ cup water, or enough to make a firm dough, turn the dough out on a lightly floured surface, and knead it for 10 minutes. Form the dough into a ball, rub it all over with ½ teaspoon vegetable oil, and let it rest in a plastic bag for at least 2 hours. (The dough can be kept as long as 48 hours, chilled.)

Shape the dough into 18 balls and return all but 1 ball to the plastic bag. Roll the ball into a 3½-inch round on a lightly floured surface. In a *wok* or a deep skillet fry the round in 1½ inches very hot vegetable oil (400° F.), pushing it gently into the oil with a slotted spoon to keep it submerged. Turn the round over quickly when it begins to puff and fry it for 30 seconds more. Transfer the *poori* to a paper towel to drain and continue to make *pooris* with the remaining dough in the same manner. Makes 18 *pooris.*

October 1974

The Arabian Picnic

Claudia Roden

There is very little in the English picnic lunch repertory that fills the gap between Fortnum & Mason's hampers and the familiar trimmed triangular sandwiches that emerge timidly from tidily packed lunch boxes. Limp slices of roast beef or chicken have prompted some of us to adopt the French *casse-croûte* for a day in the country. But however full of *saucisson à l'ail* or *pâté de foie gras,* our baguettes are never quite as good as those found across the Channel. The last glorious English summer inspired me to introduce picnic fare quite different from the habitual Western kind—that of the Middle East.

Certainly, there are sandwiches in the Levant. Pouches of soft round bread hold kebabs, *falafel* (bean patties), or brown beans topped with mixed salads of finely chopped cucumber, tomato, lettuce, and scallion. But that is not all. For an area that harbors many of nomadic ancestry and over which the sun shines constantly, eating outdoors is a way of life. What one eats, as an enthusiast put it, is "anything without a sauce, that is easily transportable, that can be eaten cold, or that is not too difficult to heat up." And that, I assure you, does not leave very much out, for the open-air epicures, armed with giant pans and Primus stoves, will stop at nothing to take their beloved food on picnic.

A thirteenth-century Arab scholar gives an account of a pie "... fit to be put before kings and wealthy persons when they go hunting far from home or take part in pleasures in far off places ... easy to transport ... pleasing to the sight, satisfying to the taste, and keeps hot a very long time." A dough is made and divided into two parts, then "... they arrange on the dough three roasted lambs stuffed with chopped meats fried in sesame oil, crushed pistachios, various hot and aromatic spices like pepper, ginger, cloves, lentisk, coriander, caraway, cardamom, nuts and others. They sprinkle rose water, in which they have infused musk, over all." In the spaces left they put "a score of fowls, as many pullets, and fifty small birds, some roasted and stuffed with eggs, others stuffed with meat, others fried in the juice of sour grapes or lemon or some other similar liquor. They put above them pastry, and little boxes filled, some with the meat, some with sugar and sweetmeats. If one would add one lamb more, cut into morsels, it would not be out of place, and one could also add fried cheese." Twentieth-century zeal may not go quite as far, but the spirit of outdoor reveling remains the same.

In the Levant a picnic is not for the silent enjoyment of nature. One is too busy and too merry to contemplate the sea, the mountain, or the riverbank. The rule is the larger the group the better the picnic—the more for backgammon and cards, the more to tell jokes, to sing and dance, and to gossip. And the more dishes from which to choose.

Few occasions satisfy better the convivial Arab spirit and the legendary hospitality than a picnic. One becomes generous host and joyous guest at the same time. Intricacies of the intensely social Middle Eastern character are revealed in the warmth of personal contact and cheerful company. The ultimate aim, to please, is artfully achieved in choosing and preparing the contents of the picnic basket.

Relatives, friends, and neighbors are invited to join the party. Each family announces what it will contribute. Generosity is boundless; one's honor is at stake. Even those who live frugally surpass themselves in preparing a variety of delicacies. There are the traditional specialties, the seaside favorites, and the desert favorites. There are those foods taken to festivals and official occasions at public gardens, shrines, tombs of saints, or burial grounds. And there are the very simple preparations for casual, spontaneous affairs.

Bedouin and peasant dishes rub shoulders with dishes straight out of *The Arabian Nights.* Persian delicacies savored in the seventh century under the Sassanids are unwrapped side by side with dishes, elaborated by the Omayyads and later the Abbasids, that reached the height of magnificence at the banquets of the caliphs of Baghdad. Everything is spread on rugs specially woven for the purpose.

My favorite picnic as a child in Egypt was on the dunes of Agami in Alexandria. It was timed to coincide with the arrival of migrating quails. The birds fell, exhausted, to be caught in large nets and collected in baskets. They were cleaned and marinated in a rich cumin and coriander sauce and grilled on the beach. Fresh Arab bread was bought from the vendors who hawked their wares and played "odd or even" for a handful of pistachios or peanuts. The hollow rounds of bread were cut in half, opened, and placed beneath the birds to catch their flavorful juices; then the quail were gathered in them to be eaten as a sandwich. Watermelons and pieces of coconut and sweet nutty pastries, also bought from the vendors, ended the meal.

Another popular picnic spot was near a dam. With a smaller party we would bring quantities of *ful medames* (Egyptian brown beans) in saucepans, on top of which were embedded shelled *hamine* eggs (eggs boiled with onion until they become light brown and the yolks are creamy). A large box lined with foil held a vegetable and herb salad. The beans were warmed over a Primus stove while we unrolled our rugs and settled down in expectation of the *gala-gala*, a magician who invariably produced baby chicks out of metal cups and eggs out of noses.

Ceremoniously we filled a pouch of bread with the beans and sprinkled the beans with olive oil and a squeeze of lemon. Some liked to add a crushed garlic clove. We then put a quartered egg in each portion, pressed down the beans, and topped them with the salad. A basket of fruit was followed by pastries filled with pistachios, almonds, walnuts, and dates and scented lightly with rose water and orange flower water.

More often and in a larger group the variety of dishes was stunning. Set out on a tablecloth or on the traditional rug, plates vied for space. Numerous pies were invariably represented: *sanbusak,* pastry crescents filled with spicy meat or sharp cheese; *phyllo*, paper-thin dough, wrapped into little packets around fillings of spinach or cheese or fried minced meat with pine nuts; and the Sephardic *pasteles*, small pies filled with *handrajo*, similar to *ratatouille*. *Kibbeh* was always a favorite, its outer shell of lamb and cracked wheat holding the traditional fried minced meat with onions and pine nuts, all delicately seasoned with spices. Rice-stuffed vine leaves were almost always offered as well as stuffed tomatoes, zucchini, small eggplants, onions, and peppers. The rice was partnered with chopped tomato, onion, garlic, a great deal of parsley, and occasionally other herbs, such as fresh coriander leaves and mint. Quite popular was *blehat lahma* (meat loaf), holding such surprises as apricots and hard-boiled eggs, differing according to the family that produced it. Cold chicken was juicy from being cooked with oil and a little water, sharply lemony with a taste of garlic and cardamom and yellow with turmeric. Otherwise, cooked chicken was minced, mixed with veal and pistachios, and patted into balls or shaped as a loaf and cooked again. Fish usually made an appearance as *blehat samak*, fish balls flavored with cumin.

Salads, simple and unpretentious or rich and exotic, were always present. Vegetables, raw or cooked, cracked wheat, and even cheese were usually dressed with olive oil and lemon. Another dish always encountered was *eggah*, a Spanish-style omelet, thick with vegetables or minced meat and excellent cold, accompanied by a bowl of yogurt.

And for the sweet-toothed, as most of us were, there was always *baklava* or *konafa*, wafers of crisp *phyllo* filled with chopped pistachios, and *basbousa*, a cream pudding with coconut, all soused with a slightly lemony sugar syrup perfumed with orange flower water. For those who did not like sticky fingers, desserts might be *ma'amoul*, tartlets filled with date paste, or *assabih bi loz*, almond fingers, or petits fours made with almond paste or caramelized nuts, dried apricots, and dates.

Everything was carefully prepared and presented in a manner pleasing to the eye. Parsley, colorful pickles, some pink from beets, and olives were liberally used as garnishes. Cayenne was mixed with oil and dribbled on *tahini*, the ever popular sesame paste, in a crisscross pattern.

It must be said that Arabian picnics do not take place only in the

Middle East. I have come across them on Hampstead Heath in London, in the Bois de Boulogne in Paris, and on a beach in Forte dei Marmi in Italy. One needn't be an Arab to participate; one need only be addicted to a rich and delightful habit of an ancient way of life.

An outdoor Arabian feast can be conjured up with the following tempting dishes.

SANBUSAK
(*Middle Eastern Lamb Turnovers*)

Makes about 45 pastries

FOR YOGURT DOUGH

2¾ cups all-purpose flour plus additional for rolling
1½ teaspoons salt
2 sticks (1 cup) unsalted butter, softened
1 cup plain whole-milk yogurt

FOR FILLING

1 medium onion, finely chopped
2 tablespoons olive oil
1 lb ground lamb shoulder (not lean)
2 tablespoons tomato paste
¼ teaspoon cayenne
1¼ teaspoons salt
¼ teaspoon black pepper
½ cup minced fresh parsley
2 tablespoons minced fresh cilantro
¼ cup pine nuts, toasted
1½ tablespoons fresh lemon juice

FOR EGG WASH

1 large egg
1 tablespoon water

Special equipment: a 3-inch round cookie cutter

MAKE DOUGH:

Whisk together flour and salt in a small bowl. Beat together butter and yogurt in a large bowl, with an electric mixer at medium-high speed until well combined. Mix in flour at low speed until incorporated (dough will be sticky).

Halve dough and shape each half into a disk. Dust disks with flour, then chill, wrapped in plastic wrap, at least 3 hours.

MAKE FILLING:

Cook onion in oil in a 12-inch heavy skillet over moderate heat, stirring often, until softened. Add lamb and cook, stirring frequently and breaking up lumps, until no longer pink, about 3 minutes. Stir in tomato paste, cayenne, salt, and pepper, then transfer to a large bowl. Stir in remaining filling ingredients and cool.

MAKE TURNOVERS:

Preheat oven to 400°F. Roll out 1 piece of dough (keep other piece chilled) into an 8-inch round (⅛ inch thick) on a well-floured surface and cut out rounds with cutter. Center 1 teaspoon filling on each round, then brush edges of rounds with water and fold dough in half over filling. Pinch edges together to seal, then curve slightly to form crescents and arrange on a baking sheet. If rounds become too soft, chill on a lightly floured baking sheet.

Reroll scraps and make more turnovers. Chill turnovers while making more with dough and filling.

MAKE EGG WASH AND BAKE TURNOVERS:

Whisk egg with water and brush over tops of chilled turnovers. Make 1 slit (as a vent) in center of each turnover and bake, 1 sheet at a time, in middle of oven until tops are golden, 18 to 22 minutes. Transfer to a rack and cool 10 minutes. Serve turnovers warm or at room temperature.

ROAST CHICKEN WITH DATES

Serves 4

1 chicken weighing about 3½ to 4 pounds
2 tablespoons mild extra-virgin olive oil
Juice of 1 lemon
Salt and pepper
2 garlic cloves, crushed
1 teaspoon ground cinnamon

1 tablespoon honey

10 ounces dates, pitted (Tunisian or California dates)

Preheat oven to 350°F. Rub the chicken with a mixture of the olive oil, half the lemon juice, salt, pepper, and garlic. Put it breast side down in a roasting pan so that the fat runs down and prevents the breast from drying out.

Roast for about 1½ hours, until well browned, turning the chicken breast side up about midway through. Test for doneness by piercing the thigh with a pointed knife. The juices should run clear, not pink.

Put the dates in a pan and only just cover with water. Add the cinnamon, honey, and the remaining lemon juice, and cook for 10 minutes or until the dates are soft and have absorbed the flavors.

Cut the chicken into serving pieces and cover with the dates.

ROASTED RED PEPPERS WITH PRESERVED LEMON AND CAPERS

Serves 4

4 fleshy red bell peppers

2–3 tablespoons argan or extra-virgin olive oil

Salt

Peel of 1 preserved lemon, cut into small pieces, to garnish

2 tablespoons capers to garnish

Roast, seed, and peel the peppers and cut them into strips about ⅔ inch wide. Dress with argan or olive oil and very little salt, and garnish with the preserved lemon and capers.

ISPANAKLI PILAV
(*Rice with Spinach*)

1 pound fresh spinach

1 large onion, chopped

4 tablespoons extra-virgin olive oil or vegetable oil

1½ cups long-grain rice

2¼ cups water or chicken stock (or you may use a boullion cube)

Salt and pepper

Wash and drain the spinach, and remove only tough stems. Cut it coarsely or leave it whole.

Fry the onion in 2 tablespoons of the oil in a large pan till soft.

Add the rice and stir well. Then add the water or stock, salt and pepper, and the spinach. Stir and cook, covered, on very low heat for about 18–20 minutes, or until the rice is tender. Stir in the remaining oil.

Serve hot or cold. Accompany with yogurt, beaten, if you like, with crushed garlic.

April 1978

Shanghai: The Vintage Years

Irene Corbally Kuhn

Shanghai—once known as the Paris of the Orient—has persisted in the Western imagination as the essence of exoticism, excitement, color, and vitality through wars, revolutions, and decades of isolation. But vintage Shanghai, the city that epitomized these qualities, actually existed in all its extraordinary variety and complexity for only a very short span of time: during the years between the end of World War I and the capture of the Chinese part of the city by the Japanese in 1937.

In those days the great port, which lies about thirteen miles above the mouth of the Whangpoo river, a small tributary of the mighty Yangtze near its estuary, was a city unlike any other, a place so cosmopolitan that sizable colonies of some thirty nationalities lived and worked there in amiable juxtaposition. Westerners who were drawn to Shanghai at that time, whether led by fate or by choice, were generally free spirits—adventurous and enterprising—or soon became so in order to survive. The British were the dominant group, although for them Shanghai was a seven-week journey by sea, half the world away from home. But when their ship dropped anchor alongside the Bund, the long, curving waterfront street that was a main thoroughfare of the city, they found much that was familiar in a strange setting. Decades before, under the terms of the Treaty of Nanking, which ended the first Opium War in 1842, British merchants were given permission to set up permanent trading establishments and residences in Shanghai as well as in other Chinese cities. The French and then the Americans followed shortly after the British, and other nationalities were not far behind. Within a few years Shanghai's International Settlement, a mere nine square miles and entirely unique, came into being.

The International Settlement was almost a city-state. It observed its own code of law; was governed by its own municipal council, composed of all resident nationalities; had its own police force of tall, straight-spined, turbaned Sikhs, its own customs authorities, courts, currency, and even its own language—the delightfully flexible, easily acquired Pidgin English. Much of Shanghai's foreign population (along with numerous wealthy Chinese) maintained spacious, airy European-style houses set in large, tree-shaded gardens in the French Concession. Here Annamese from the French Colonial Service kept order in place of the Sikhs, and the streets bore such names as Avenue Joffre and Rue Massenet.

But it was the surrounding Chinese city, noisy and noisome, vast and vibrant, filled with teeming life, constant motion, and daily drama, that claimed the heart of every Westerner fortunate enough to know Shanghai in that brief, suspended time between the wars.

I was one of those venturers to vintage Shanghai in the twenties. Young and innocent, I arrived on a Japanese freighter after a six-week voyage from Marseilles to find a place where everything was strange, nothing was surprising, and anything seemed possible. My limited experience as a journalist in New York and Paris proved sufficient to get me on the staff of *The China Press,* an American-edited, English-language newspaper that ran brisk competition to the staid, hundred-year-old, English-edited *North China Daily News,* sometimes called the Old Lady of the Bund as much for its editorial views as for its location.

The owner of *The China Press* was a Mesopotamian (he would be called an Iraqi now) who had made an early fortune in the opium trade and then had turned respectable. An indulgent and appreciative man, he rewarded his staff not just with sturdy salaries but with rent-free lodgings in a large and comfortably appointed house in the French Concession. Thus, *The China Press* Mess was established, a common living arrangement for the unmarried employees of many Western enterprises. As I was to be the only single woman living there with six male newspaper colleagues, a housekeeper-chaperone was required, and an American woman with long experience in running a household in China was engaged. From her I learned about the elaborate rituals of domestic life in Shanghai so that when, in several months' time, I was married to a fellow journalist and we moved into our own home, organizing a domestic staff held no terrors for me. Wages were so low that one could afford a houseful of servants on even the most modest of incomes. And, indeed, one was expected to. For there was always Chinese custom to consider, custom born of the pressures of over-population and expressed in the saying: One does not break another man's rice bowl. In other words, the available work was extended to provide as many jobs as possible, and the subsequent divisions of responsibility were punctiliously observed.

The standard requirements of a small household of a Westerner then consisted of a "Number One Boy," a "Number One Cook" (and, if there was to be a lot of entertaining, a "Small Cook" as well), a coolie, a "Wash Amah," a gardener, and a jinrikisha (more commonly shortened to rickshaw) coolie, who came complete with his vehicle. This was the minimum. For larger families assistants proliferated, and where there were children a "Baby Amah" was installed to wash them, feed them, dress them, and take them on outings to the French Park, an enclave of green, shaded gardens surrounding the French Club.

The place of the "Number One Boy," I soon discovered, corresponded to that of the butler in a large English household. He served as general factotum, ran the rest of the staff, and, in addition, had certain specific duties such as serving drinks, waiting table, and answering the door. He consulted with "Missy" daily for his marching orders, and he was charged with keeping the household books. The accounts were divided among three large ledgers: one for the comprador, who supplied staples as well as wine and spirits; one for the butcher, who also served as the fishmonger; and the third for purveyors of fresh produce and sundries. At the end of every month there would be a reckoning with "Missy"; she would pay the "Number One Boy," and he in turn would pay the suppliers. As a matter of course the "Number One Boy" collected cumshaw, a commission from the shopkeepers for bringing them his household's business; this sum was built into the prices so scrupulously noted in the ledgers. He also collected a small slice of the wages of each of the servants under him in the household. There was never any protest or complaint, because it was all part of a complex code. More important, it worked.

There was an easy mixing among the nationalities composing Shanghai's foreign population, and social life involved a great variety of activities. The most common was the dinner party, followed by an evening of dancing at the French Club, the Carlton Café, the Cathay or Astor House hotels, or in one of the seemingly hundreds of small nightclubs that stayed open all night all over the city. Dinner, served at nine o'clock, was as a rule a fairly formal meal at which one might encounter any of a number of cuisines, for each national group taught its Chinese cooks all manner of regional specialties. One's choice of menu as a hostess, however, was not unlimited; it was constrained by primitive refrigeration and the uncertain origin of much that appeared in the markets. Still, ships calling at Shanghai regularly brought lamb and butter from New Zealand, beef and citrus fruit from Australia. The Dollar Line ships from San Francisco and Honolulu were an occasional source of expensive fresh green vegetables bought from the ship's stores. I recall with painful vividness one of the few times I availed myself of this possibility and paid a dollar (at least ten dollars in today's terms) for a head of lettuce. I took it to our cook with an equally expensive bunch of celery and explained that each had to be washed carefully in water that had been boiled and then allowed to cool. I knew I risked losing our cook if I caused him to lose face by appearing in the kitchen to see if instructions were being followed, but these greens were too precious to sacrifice to indifferent handling. Imagine my horror when I stopped by later to find the cook washing the greens in cooled boiled water, all right, but also carefully scrubbing the celery with a toothbrush that had decidedly seen better days.

"No, no!" I exclaimed. "No brush!"

"*Maskee* [never mind], Missy. No belong yours, belong my!"

It took me no time at all to decide to take the incident in stride, and all ended well. Nobody got sick, and, in fact, it was one of our better dinner parties.

Restaurants have always been a feature of life in any big Chinese city, as much for the Chinese themselves as for foreigners, and Shanghai in those days was no exception. We had a dazzling array of choices, for restaurants abounded and ranged from the elegant formality of the St. Petersburg, owned and managed by a former White Russian cavalry officer, to the small, dark, and steamy noodle shops of the old Chinese walled city. The two leading Chinese department stores, Wing On's and Sincere's, specialized in banquets of Chinese food where serving five hundred was commonplace. Their boast was that they could manage to provide for any number up to two thousand, and they occasionally made good on the claim. All the large, luxurious hotels, but notably the Cathay, took justified pride in the quality of their European cuisine. As one might have supposed, however, the finest table in Shanghai, by general agreement, was that of the French Club.

Clubs were the hub of much of our social life, and there were, it seemed, an infinite number of them, centered on nationalities, sports, professions, hobbies, and any number of indeterminate interests. Whereas some of them were sternly exclusive, there was much cross-membership and much reciprocal entertaining. The four annual productions of the Shanghai Amateur Dramatic Club, for example, were invariably sold out; concerts by visiting musical notables were often the occasion for splendid receptions at the appropriate club; and every national holiday from Saint Andrew's Day to the Fourth of July was observed with gay celebrations to which everyone was invited. How else, we joked fondly, could the Scots dispose of all that haggis?

Amid all this conviviality, the all-male Shanghai Club stood staunch and foursquare in an imposing pillared stone building at Number One the Bund. Inside, beyond the spacious, two-storey lobby, was the renowned Long Bar. More than one hundred feet of dark, polished mahogany, it was said to be the longest in the world. A wide bay window in the barroom overlooked the frenzied harbor traffic. Tables there were commonly reserved for that colorful breed, the Yangtze river pilots, the men who negotiated the tricky passage through shoals and sandbars from the estuary to Shanghai and beyond. Protocol also dictated the locations where others positioned themselves to sip slings and down pink gins. By silent agreement the bank managers sorted themselves out from the trading tycoons, the lawyers from the engineers. And many a deal was done over steak-and-kidney pie at tiffin (luncheon) in the Shanghai Club.

A mile to the north at the far end of the long sweep of the Bund stood the British Consulate, set in a handsome square of lawn as carefully cultivated as a golf tee. It was one of the few green spots in the concentration of gray stone and red brick that was the International Settlement, for land was generally too expensive and scarce to give over to gardens or even to trees. Nearby, just across the graceful Garden Bridge, which spanned the Soochow Creek, was the American Consulate. In between these two structures and the Shanghai Club, at the southern end of the Bund, were ranged all the city's great commercial houses, the offices, the banks, and many of the hotels, all with spectacular views of the harbor. To travel the length of the Bund, or even a small section of it, was to encounter Shanghai at its rawest and most vibrant. And, no matter how often I did it, it was a trip I never tired of, for there was always something new to see. Traffic was indescribably dense, and the air was thick with bells, horns, shouts, and cries. Rickshaws, carts, bicycles, motorcycles, and an occasional car or truck fought for space with hurrying coolies bent under the weight of massive loads balanced in baskets at the ends of bamboo poles or with others trotting behind barrows piled with vegetables, furniture, pieces of machinery, or mysterious crates. Anything that could be transported by human muscle power was, as well as much that it seemed couldn't possibly have been.

More orderly but duplicating the traffic of the Bund in destiny and noise was the constant flow of river life, where every kind of vessel made its way and whole families sometimes spent all their lives. Ocean liners and coastal ships were moored at the jetties or stood a little downstream awaiting space; junks, heavily carved and garishly painted, sampans, barges, and tenders nosed restlessly among them.

The gray bulk of battleships of the Royal Navy or the U.S. Pacific Fleet was constantly visible, and the number-one buoy in the Whangpoo by long custom was always occupied by the flagship of whatever contingent of the British navy happened to be in port. Always, that is, until 1946 and the end of World War II, when, in a subtle nod to history, the number-one buoy was yielded to the flagship of the U.S. Seventh Fleet.

Other fixtures along the Bund, as well as elsewhere in Shanghai, were the professional beggars. They were dispatched daily from the old walled city to ply their trade by the King of the Beggars, who was the rough equivalent of a labor union boss. He gave them their training, provided food and shelter, settled territorial disputes, and commanded a share of their proceeds. Two in particular usually divided the sidewalk outside the Palace Hotel at the intersection of Nanking Road and the Bund. One was known as "Light in the Head" because he appeared to have driven a nail into the top of his shaven skull, a nail that then served as a holder for a candle whose flame cast a flickering light over his thin, piteous face. The other, a woman, was called "the Weeping Wonder" for her ability to cry ceaselessly and silently in such quantities that her tears formed small pools around her hunched form. And though the tourists might stand and gawk at Shanghai's professional beggars, for those of us who lived there even the professionals were regarded as painful reminders of a poverty so profound and so prevalent as to seem beyond rational remedy. One did what one could, but realistically it could never be enough to make a noticeable difference.

The main artery westward from the Bund was Nanking Road; it was also the direct road to the Race Course, where amateur jockeys, young tea traders, and perhaps bankers would race speedy Manchurian ponies while Chinese and foreigners alike would bet on their favorites. So popular was this pastime that, during one period I recall, the foreign-owned firms would simply close down for a race week every spring and fall.

Nanking Road was also one of Shanghai's principal shopping streets, lined on both sides by Chinese and foreign-owned stores. The Chinese shops, often open-fronted and always inviting, could be identified by wooden signs inscribed with outsized characters painted in red and gold, by pungent fragrances, and by the *click-click-click* of the abacus, a sound so distinctive it could be heard over almost any competing noise. Bargaining was expected in the Chinese shops; for both buyer and seller it was more than half the fun of shopping. Here on Nanking Road stood one of the most famous shops of its day in all Asia, the great silk house of Lao K'ai Fook. Nothing was sold here but silk in every imaginable form, from shimmering chiffons to the heaviest of brocades, and in every conceivable color and pattern, all from long bolts stored on shelves that went from floor to ceiling. Dealers in antiques, porcelains, curios, and wood carvings had shops along here, too; the British department store of Whiteaway and Laidlaw was nearby; not far was the Chocolate Shop, where, improbably, American ice-cream sodas were a specialty; and farther on at Kelly and Walsh, the bookseller and publisher, almost any current book in English could be bought or ordered.

Indeed, before I had been in Shanghai a year I was convinced that, despite its remoteness and the slow pace of transport, almost anything one could need or wish for (apart from certain foods) could sooner or later be found there. And what could not be found already made could always be copied. Usually, the copy proved to be better than the original, for the industry, ingenuity, and artistry of the Chinese artisan were prodigious. Among these craftsmen the most talented and versatile was the Shanghai tailor, a formidable and wonderful institution. Each one had his speciality, from lingerie to ball gowns for women, linen suits to overcoats for men. The Shanghai tailor could—and did—copy anything requested. Men usually went to the tailor's shop to select materials and be measured for their clothes. But the tailors who specialized in women's garments customarily came to a client's home, often bringing the latest issue of *Vogue* or *Harper's Bazaar*. After a choice had been made, there might be a fitting or two, and within days as a rule the new clothes were delivered, beautifully finished and perfect fits. Moreover, because almost no shops stocked Western-style shoes for women, handmade ones were also commonplace, made of fine leather or silk with the same meticulous workmanship as was lavished on the clothes.

Work apart—and we did work hard—such was life for the Westerner once privileged to call himself a Shanghailander. Small wonder that for each of us who knew them those days will always be different from any others in our lives, no matter how full and satisfying those others may have been. As I look back down the corridor of years, it was a time apart, a time when it seemed as if nothing had ever been different and thus never would be. In some measure this state of mind was induced by China itself. Even though the tremors of approaching violent change were occasionally felt, it seemed that the land was too vast, the civilization, the people, and their ways too ancient, for change ever to be successful. And yet, even as we lived those days, somewhere deep below our consciousness we sensed this was a life that would never exist again. Perhaps that, more than anything else, was what made that brief, bright span Shanghai's vintage years.

January 1986

THE ROMANCE OF UMBRIA

Pat Conroy

"Tell about Italy," my wife says, her voice sugared with her deep Alabama accent. "Tell me what you loved the most." I tell her two stories:

In the house I once rented on the Via dei Foraggi in Rome, my landlord stood beneath a painting of St. Sebastian.

I asked the man, "This house I'm renting, is it very old?"

"No, no, no, no," he said quickly. "You Americans love the old things, but this house is not even 500 years."

Stunned, I said, "It was built before Columbus set sail."

"Yes," my landlord said. "But you don't understand. In Rome, she is a baby."

That is how Italy taught me about time.

Then I tell my wife of the morning I left Rome to return to the South to help my mother fight the cancer that would kill her. I walked to the small piazza where my family did its shopping to say good-bye. My infant daughter, Susannah, was radiant in her stroller, and everyone in the piazza knew *la famiglia americana* was leaving their city forever. When I rolled Susannah to the center of the piazza, all the shopkeepers boiled out onto the cobblestones. One woman scooped

Susannah into her arms and cried out, "You cannot take Susannah *tutta panna* from us. She was born here. She is a *romanina*. She belongs to Rome!"

The women passed the baby back and forth, smothering her with tearful kisses. Adele, the vegetable lady, in a mournful, ancient voice, said through tears, "We did not do our jobs. We did not love your family enough. If we had done our jobs better, you could never leave us. You would be Romans forever."

Then the wine man handed me a bottle of Frascati for the journey, and the cheese lady cut off an enormous wedge of Parmigiano-Reggiano. Sausages and loaves of bread, *pizza bianca*, fragrant mozzarella, bunches of grapes and olives: Every shopkeeper in that piazza came forward bearing gifts, generous as Magi.

I always compare this completely unexpected scene with the time I was moving to Rome and shopped in Atlanta's Kroger for the last time. For ten years I had shopped there and nowhere else in my hometown. I did not know the name or face of a single sourpuss employee in that store, and not one knew mine.

That is how Italy taught me about being alive.

After I told my wife these two stories, she said, "A honeymoon in Italy. It has a ring to it, southern boy."

Since I met Sandra King Ray of Pinckard, Alabama, daughter of a peanut farmer who once walked from Alabama to Miami looking for work during the Depression, I am finally living the life I think I was meant to live. I had no idea that a man in his fifties could fall in love with a woman in her fifties and that they could teach each other things about love and ecstasy and wonder, things I have tried to infuse in the secret corners of my novels but have rarely encountered in real life. Because our nation is stupid and Hollywood is coarse, there is no one to tell us of the deep and extraordinary beauty of older women. I now see them all around me and am filled with a fierce joy that one of them has come to live in my house.

The president of the College of Charleston, Alex Sanders, married us in the gardens surrounding his lovely eighteenth-century mansion, where John James Audubon once taught a class in ornithology. My father had just died, and our children from various marriages over the course of our sloppily lived lives were visiting our island house for their summertime breaks. There was no time even to think about a honeymoon. Our lives were busy, disquieted, American. No one told my generation that none of our children would ever grow up, that they would swarm around us, forever discontented, underemployed, and woebegone. We share nine children and four grandchildren between us, and our hands are constantly full. Still, Sandra deserved a honeymoon, and we began a long dialogue about where it should be.

It amazed me that she had never seen the Pacific Ocean and, though she had traveled to London twice, had never drifted over to continental Europe, where our language is put out to pasture. Not to have traveled widely seemed unlucky to me, but not to have seen Italy was heartbreaking and unimaginable. My own heart has been shaped like a boot since I lived in the city of Rome for three years in the faraway eighties. If you cannot find happiness in Italy, I told Sandra, then I do not think you can find it in Eden.

We plan our honeymoon in Umbria, a part of Italy where I have never spent a night, and on the flight over, I fear I have erred greatly, and perhaps tragically. I keep telling Sandra endless variations of the same baffled theme. I tell her I should have taken her to Venice, that gondola-blessed city that looks as if it were carved by swans from ice. If not Venice, then immovable, Tiber-cut Rome, which I could move through blindfolded—I know those beloved and noisy streets so well. Then there is the incomparable Amalfi coast. And how could I leave out Florence or unknowable Siena or the Alpine majesty of Lake Como? Then I relax and put my trust in the simple mystery that Italy has never let me down, never refused to lay its dazzling treasures at my feet.

Umbria. The shuttered beauty of the very name strikes me as luscious as a pear, as dark as the boars that roam her mountains, gorging themselves on wild chestnuts. This is a place where the centuries give up their stories at their own pace.

You go to Tuscany because you must; you go to Umbria because you can. It is the province in Italy you travel to when you want the country itself to enter the pores of your skin after you have grown weary with sites and endless churches and surly crowds moving through the taut, sovereign air of museums. Umbria is Italy turned inward, its prayer to itself.

We stay at the Palazzo Terranova, a sublime eighteenth-century restoration, recently opened, that looks like the castle you always hoped Cinderella got to live in with the prince. It is a hill town unto itself. A British couple, Sarah and Johnny Townsend, runs the palazzo, which I predict will soon be famous all over the world. Above the hotel, a footpath cut into the crest of the mountain by the Etruscans themselves winds its way to a small hill town three miles away. The walk is breathtaking. Sandra and I tell each other we are in the best place in the world to be on a honeymoon.

The view from our room, which looks down on time-shaped olive groves, three lakes nestled like freshwater pearls in the landscape, and a ruin that makes the vineyards near the village of Ronti seem noble and necessary, appears as an untroubled dream that one mountain had of many others, as though time itself could come to rest in these valleys.

Since Sandra has never seen an olive tree, we walk the precipitous road that winds its banked way from the palazzo to the village. Halfway down the mountain, we hear a car coming from behind at warp speed. I turn to Sandra and say, "I haven't told you about Italian drivers yet, have I?"

"Better do it quick," she says, and suddenly the small car is over the blind ridge that separates us. Sandra and I hug against an outcropping of rock. The driver sees us and squeals to a dramatic stop. The woman who brought our breakfast that morning, Piera Menardi, leaps out of the car: "Oh, Mister Johnny and Miss Sarah will not like that I have killed two of our guests. This is for sure."

Earlier that morning, I observed a scene that made me fall madly in love with the richly good-humored Piera. To get a recalcitrant worker to help her with some heavy lifting, she pulled out a picture of herself in a bikini on an Adriatic beach in 1967. She showed him the picture. She showed me the picture. It is almost a pleasure to be run off the road by such a woman thirty-two years later, her beauty still a pleasant, inmost thing.

Piera drives off, imperiling every living creature she encounters, and we descend toward the olive groves and approach a marvelous ruin of a farming village, where remnants of tobacco-curing sheds remind us both of our own deep roots in the Deep South. I gaze at olive trees hundreds of years old, loving the silver-headed shimmer of their wind-tossed branches, and think to myself, what is more beautiful or useful than an olive tree? What is prettier than a bowl of green olives or the molten green of the first pressing of extra-virgin olive oil looking, in cut-glass cruets, like watered-down jade? For a souvenir of our honeymoon, we take a single small branch as both memento and pledge to each other, then walk back to the hotel, perched above us like a bird of prey the color of fire.

The next day, the hotel's chef, Patrizio Cesarini, offers to give us a tour of his hometown, Città di Castello. As we board the chef's little Fiat, I tell Sandra that she is lucky she has relatives who are native to Talladega, Alabama, where one of the most famous Nascar racetracks is located, for she is about to feel like a Nascar racer herself.

Then Patrizio is off, careening down the mountain at such a precipitous rate it makes Piera look like a high school driving instructor. We travel at cheetahlike speeds even through small medieval alleyways. When he hits the *autostrada,* it simply feels like space travel. When we reach Patrizio's hometown, Sandra, ashen and shaken, says that she thought she had never traveled at such speed, even in an airplane. I say, "He was slow. Wait until we ride with a Calabrian. They get faster as you move south in Italy."

Patrizio now walks us languorously through the ancient, hidden-away parts of his town, leading the way in a happy bracelet of *"ciaos,"* for he knows almost everyone he passes. When I ask him to tell us the differences, if there are any, between Umbrians and Tuscans, he answers cheerfully, "It is very easy. We are the best. They are the worst," summing up admirably why we are at the tail end of the bloodiest, most chillingly fratricidal century in the history of mankind.

Once we reach the market, Patrizio moves through it like a perfumer gathering wildflowers in a bee-struck field. Sandra moves through it with the astonished, mouthwatering appreciation of a rookie in the folkways of Italy.

At an outdoor *salumeria,* Patrizio orders prosciutto for the meal that night. "See the motion," he tells us as a young man cuts razor-thin slices from the top of the cured ham. "That is called 'playing the violin.' It is very difficult to master. I have mastered it." The young man lifts a piece of meat in the air to let us see the sunlight flow through it like some odd and flawless merger of paper and flesh.

We wander from stall to stall, the food so fresh that the smell of the earth itself is the strongest, most assertive odor in the marketplace until we pass the store that specializes in the sale of local white truffles. The odor of truffle is as distinctive as the giveaway scent of marijuana. It enlarges the air around itself and gives you some idea of what a tree must smell like to itself. I have never quite forgiven America for its shameless inability to produce truffles. When I see Patrizio enter the shop and purchase a small, knobby truffle for that night's pasta, I want to kiss him on the lips but hesitate for fear the gesture may be misinterpreted.

It is a pleasure to watch a southern farm girl wander about an Italian food market, stunned by the profligate abundance taken from the countryside. I follow as Patrizio and Sandra inspect great albino-faced cauliflowers, eggplant displays that look like a rack of bowling balls, *porcini* mushrooms the size of kittens, the cool anise-smelling fennels that always look like failed cacti to me, and the mounds of huge, brilliantly yellow peppers that make their space look like the entrance to a gold mine. Blood-red oranges from Sicily are sliced open to reveal exactly what shade of dripping scarlet is inside. When I reach to taste a sprig of mint, a fierce old Italian woman, who probably was part of the crowd that murdered Mussolini, slaps my hand firmly and wags a gnarled finger at me. Her finger looks truffly, which somehow pleases me.

Sandra tastes grapes, arugula, oregano, spring onions, plum tomatoes, every time turning to me and shaking her head. I do not have to ask what she is thinking. It is this: Food tastes better in Italy than anywhere else in the world.

As we leave this deep-throated market, its musk a nosegay of aromas, we pause at the fishmonger's, where Patrizio studies a tank of slithering freshwater eels netted that same morning from Lake Trasimeno. More amazing still, the woman behind the counter prods one of the ocean-going crustaceans that the Italians call *"canocchie,"* tasty creatures that appear to be a cross between a shrimp and a praying mantis. She prods it again, and it moves—in landlocked Umbria, it moves. Among Italians, the love of freshness is a form of both spontaneity and discipline.

But bold Patrizio is in a hurry now, and he marches us past an ancient tower that is made of stacked stone with no cement at all. It is called the Torre Rotonda and is the pride of Città di Castello. Patrizio tells me that he feels like he owns the tower. He does now, but Sandra and I know that the Torre Rotonda will wait him out and one day reclaim its title from Patrizio. We *"ciao"* our way back through the old city, then rocket our way back into the green hills of Umbria for what will be one of the best meals of our lives. Sandra, in utter terror, does not open her eyes a single time on the trip back to the hotel.

Over the next few days, Sandra and I drift through hill towns we had never heard of. In the lentil-happy town of Monterchi, Italy reaches up, striking quick as an adder, and grabs us by the throat. In what looks like a minor chapel serving a monastery across the street, we encounter Piero della Francesca's breathtaking painting *Madonna del Parto,* the famous "Pregnant Madonna." I had read about it in art history books but could not believe such a masterpiece had not been relocated to one of the grander Italian cities. It is the most serene portrait of Mary I have ever seen, granting new meaning to the very idea of serenity. Its discovery, in the tomb of a nobleman a long time after its rendering, has brought pride and joy and many art lovers to this town. Years later, the painting still shimmers with the genius of the artist. As I stand before it, I think of what it must have been like to be a man of genius, God-struck in his native Umbria, painting a portrait of the woman he considered the mother of God, carrying that God inside her. This is what art should do.

"This," I say to Sandra, "is your honeymoon gift."

From our hotel, we walk through the rain along the Etruscan ridge to an exquisite hill town called Monte Santa Maria Tiberina and try to put the unstressed, unpurchasable beauty of this place into words. Both of us are novelists and believe that words can do anything. The stones from which the town's houses are built have had their color bled out from them by time itself. Sandra says that the town is so lovely, its residents should only be allowed to make music boxes or perfume bottles. When it begins to rain, we seek shelter in Oscari, the only bar or store in town. Oscari himself, a man of grace and elegance, serves us cappuccino. Preparing it, he looks like a priest at Mass. There are pictures of his son, a soccer star, on the walls, the taste of that cappuccino ... *perfetto.* That taste is Italy in a cup. My honeymoon in a cup, at Oscari in a hill town in the rain.

We have come to our last hill town, and our honeymoon nears its end in the piazza in the gemlike town of Citerna. We have said the things to each other that we needed to say, made all the promises we needed to make. But we stand overlooking a valley with farmhouses and palazzi of infinite age staring coldly back at us. This town seems conceived by waterless Venetians driven out of their city and forced to seek refuge in the hills. The colors of the stones puzzle because age has formed them and we have no equivalent in our American vocabulary to name them; our culture is still so new and shiny. These stones are the color of bruised fruit, I begin, or the shade of some rough white wines. But another house is darker, an amber bracelet, perhaps, or maybe the shade of palominos or horseshoe crabs. I catch myself writing again instead of living at the moment of sunset in the Umbrian hills on the last day of the first honeymoon I have ever taken. And so I turn to Sandra.

Holding her hand, I say, "Sandra, it doesn't get any better than this."

In that piazza in Citerna, our honeymoon ended and our accidental life together had its Umbrian beginning.

September 1999

THE GHOSTS OF TASTE: RECAPTURING THE FLAVORS OF CHILDHOOD

Edna O'Brien

Food begins with Mother, and our relationship with it and her remains strategic, running the gamut of taste, distaste, appetite, nausea, fastidiousness, and good old-fashioned guilt. "We are what we eat," the proverb says, but this is only half true. In some sense we remain hungry even when sated, because food is an emotional trigger to things long forgotten, trapped in memory.

The addictions start in childhood. Our likes, our dislikes, and that gnaw that we never quite outgrow. I recall a biscuit tin with a delectable picture of each biscuit. I would study the pictures, deliberate on them, and wait for that blissful moment when a grown-up would open the lid and say "Have one." The biscuit I always coveted, and sometimes got, was a pink wafer with a pink filling as sturdy as putty.

Another grail in those times was the glass-fronted casket in the town shop, filled with Irish diamonds—actually small diamond-shaped biscuits with various colored icings. The shopkeeper sat behind the counter from nine in the morning until six in the evening knitting, and moving only to serve biscuits, bags of toffees, bars of chocolate, and licorice sticks that were pipe-shaped and had pink crusting on the end to simulate a lit tip. To look at these dainties, to long for them, was to luxuriate on them in the mind. Eating them was a far more hurried and unrecollectable thing.

Baudelaire said that touch has a memory, but taste has more so. If I taste orange cake, it is never simply the one I am eating; it is the cake my mother made when things were relatively buoyant. To test the cake, she would put a knitting needle into the center, then allow me to lick the moist crumbs that had congealed around it. I taste it at odd moments, that and sliced beetroot put to cool in a glass bowl and seasoned with chives. I think of these not as food but as something more: the summation of a time, a place, of sunshine or rain, of happiness or strife—our little histories, and always, at least in those childhood days, a hunch that something extraordinary was about to happen.

Food was pleasure, food was reward, and food was substitute for something other, possibly love. To deny oneself was the path to sanctity, and I would set days of the week in which I would not eat this or that. But, of course, the cravings persisted. Caught out in these fasts, I would be made to eat porridge or slices of bread and butter and inwardly wished that it could be bread and jam, especially black-currant jam, which gave a puce dye to the lips and the fingers and which was beautifully tart.

In those days I did not care for bacon and cabbage, thinking it too agricultural, but things have changed. Last winter, in the gravid sanctum of the Four Courts in Dublin, I smelled cabbage on a landing and was surprised that the judges were serving something so humble to their visitors. And all of a sudden I could see the cabbages growing in the kitchen garden at home; drills of it, the green leaves a strange, haunting shade of blue, our workman cutting a few heads for the Sunday dinner, the stumps thrown onto the ash pit, where the dogs sniffed at them. And in the kitchen, the bacon and cabbage water boiling over and my mother running to wipe it up. I remembered, too, a coy verse that girls put in each other's autograph books:

> *My body is but a cabbage.*
> *The leaves I give to others,*
> *But the heart I give to you.*

Next came the cookery books. There were a couple of very old ones in which the authors were prodigal with their recipes—extravagances such as little quails to stuff larger birds; two dozen eggs for a custard galantine; menus that included soup, lobster, chicken cutlets, oysters, artichokes, partridges, charlottes, and puddings—all at one sitting. I would pore over the pictures, the jellies, the trifles, the molds of carrageen moss, their surfaces dimpled from the wedged glass in which they had been put to set. And while my mother was heroic enough and daring enough to try some of these confections, it always seemed that the ones in *Mrs. Beeton* were more celestial.

Sometimes when I would gorge myself reading page after page of recipes, I would not feel hungry at all. It was one way of not eating. The other was that much mused-upon state of vertigo known as falling in love. To eat in front of a boyfriend or a lover was an impropriety and lessened the intensity of the love. But with heartbreak would come a bout of gluttony. In the convent to which I was dispatched at the age of 11, the love of food disappeared completely. Girls carried little parcels of meat and potatoes under their gym frocks to dump in the lake on their afternoon walk. I would put Vicks VapoRub on the back of my tongue to quell my hunger and was certain that I would not ever have an appetite again. However, with freedom came the old longings, and the Italian ice-cream parlors in Dublin were palaces that I stared into.

True to the notion of Victorian heroines (my reading matter at the time), I eloped at a young age and in an isolated country house taught myself to cook. The book I bought was by Elizabeth David, who not only gave recipes but took one, as it were, on a "grand tour." I went to different regions of sunny Italy, reading of the Venetian traders who brought cane sugar back from the East to make sweetmeats or the *pan-forte* of Siena, cousin to plum pudding. I wondered if it was like the plum pudding in James Joyce's *Portrait of the Artist*, "studded with peeled almonds and sprigs of holly, bluish fire running around it." She wrote of white truffles in Tuscany, hunted by specially trained dogs, and of Catherine de Médicis taking her own pastry cooks to the French courts in 1533 because the French were behind in culinary knowledge. It was like literature. In Tolstoy I would come to read of banquets where the sated nobility were given sorbet between courses to revive their appetites, but in Elizabeth David I learned how to make the sorbet. And making it was as exciting (or more so) as eating it.

There are meals we never forget for the sheer delight, the astonishment, the novelty, of them. I knew a shy woman in the west of Ireland who lived by the sea and when the tide was out stuck a gorse bush into the sand to collect a few oysters. The oysters in her kitchen tasted better than any, tasted of the Atlantic, and maybe that was because there were so few and she was so proud to serve them. In the early '60s I was sent to Cuba by a newspaper to report on the life there, and I will not forget the long queues for even the simplest staple. I remember being brought once to a villa where all was spartan until, in a moment of inspiration, one of the sisters reached into the sideboard and hauled out a pot of greengage jam. She scraped the mold off the top, put spoons out, and we ate it as if it were a compote.

Oh, such feasts—meals in distant places, vegetables never before tasted, soufflés that literally took one's breath away, and yet there is always a meal that one wants to repeat. For me, it is an impromptu lunch at Darina Allen's cookery school in County Cork. I was staying with Myrtle, Darina's mother-in-law, in Ballymaloe House, once the seat of the Geraldines of Munster. There were Jack Yeats paintings on the walls, a library of the very books one wants to read, a turf fire, and, through the long Georgian windows, a vista of rolling fields stretching to bluish hills that went off into sky.

Myrtle suggested we walk the couple of miles to the school, and maybe it was the fresh air or the sight of so many eager white-coated students bustling about, but I felt ravenous when we arrived and welcomed the invitation to stay to lunch. We had Irish stew, followed by a soufflé-omelet. The lamb was from the local butcher, a Mr. Cuddigan, who prided himself on grazing his lambs on old pasture that hadn't been plowed in living memory.

The atmosphere was spontaneous and jocular. Soon some of the students were up whisking the eggs for the soufflé-omelet, and when it was cooked and puffy, they added fresh cream and raspberries, folded the omelets, and turned portions onto our plates.

I remember asking Darina what her favorite foods were. "The first, rhubarb," she said excitedly, as if she were about to pick the young pink stalks and poach them on top of the Aga. Rhubarb, she thought, was for the blood, and fish roe for the brain. "And for the heart?" I asked. "Bread and butter pudding, because it is 'mother' food."

Back to Mother and that first bite.

BALLYMALOE IRISH STEW

Edna O'Brien recalls the locally raised lamb that made the Irish stew at Bally-maloe especially memorable. And Darina Allen—whose recipe for this dish, from The Complete Book of Irish Country Cooking, *we adapted— likes to use fresh, organic produce. We agree that these things can't be beat. But even with supermarket ingredients, this stew is delicious.*

Serves 4 to 6
Active time: 30 min Start to finish: 1¾ hr

  3 lb shoulder lamb chops (1 to 2 inches thick)
  1 lb small onions, peeled and root ends trimmed
  1 lb carrots, cut into 2-inch pieces
  2½ cups lamb stock or chicken broth
  1 fresh thyme sprig
  2 lb small boiling potatoes, peeled and, if desired, halved
  1½ tablespoons unsalted butter
  2 tablespoons all-purpose flour
  2 tablespoons chopped fresh flat-leaf parsley
  2 tablespoons chopped fresh chives

  Preheat oven to 350°F.

Cut chops in half lengthwise and trim off, but don't discard, excess fat. Cook fat in a large heavy skillet over low heat, stirring occasionally, until fat is rendered, about 10 minutes. Discard solid bits.

Pat chops dry and season with salt and pepper. Brown chops in fat in 2 batches over moderately high heat and transfer to a dish. Sauté onions and carrots in fat, tossing to coat, 1 minute, and remove skillet from heat.

Arrange half of lamb in an ovenproof 4-quart heavy pot and top with onions and carrots, then remaining lamb, seasoning each layer with salt and pepper. Put stock in skillet and bring to a boil, scraping up brown bits. Pour stock into pot and add thyme.

Arrange potatoes on top and season with salt and pepper. Bring liquid to a simmer and cover pot. Transfer pot to middle of oven and cook until meat is tender and vegetables are cooked through, 1 to 1¼ hours. (Alternatively, stew may be simmered gently on stove.)

Holding back solids with lid, pour liquid from stew into a bowl and let stand 5 minutes. Spoon off and discard fat.

Melt butter in a small heavy saucepan over moderate heat and add flour. Cook, stirring, 2 minutes. Whisk in hot liquid and simmer until slightly thickened, about 5 minutes. Stir in parsley and chives. Pour liquid back into stew and reheat.

Stew is best made a day ahead and can be made up to 2 days in advance. Cool completely, uncovered, before chilling, covered.

November 1999

THE AMERICAN SCENE

AMERICAN NAMES FOR AMERICAN WINES

Frank Schoonmaker

When the New Year came in with a hurrah (and confetti) and a huzzah (with horns) the average American wine producer was not out celebrating. He probably heaved a sigh of relief as we shut the door on 1940—his seventh lean year was over and done with, and it looked as if a few fat years—perhaps seven, certainly two or three—were on their way. Wine consumption, at long last, is on its way up in the United States, and people as a whole are beginning to show a genuine interest in American wine.

Seven years ago, at the time of Repeal, American wine producers had a chance such as few ever get: this country had no drinking habits worthy of the name, people were favorably disposed toward wine, ready to try anything and, after the Prohibition years, to accept anything good.

American vintners proceeded to muff the chance, miss the boat. This was largely their fault, but as we look back on December, 1933, across the intervening years, we can see pretty clearly why the muff was made, why it was more or less inevitable, and why the United States did not become overnight (as a good many people rashly predicted it would) at least as much of a wine-drinking country as Argentina or Chile.

First, there were, in 1933, scarcely a dozen fine vineyards in North America. Plenty of raisin grapes, plenty of table grapes, but a pitifully few thousand acres of wine grapes. A good many California producers had torn up their superior vines during Prohibition and planted in their place the tough, common, heavy-bearing varieties then in demand as "juice grapes" for the home wine maker. A certain number of good vineyards had been simply abandoned.

Second, at the time of Repeal there was only an infinitesimal amount of good, properly aged, American wine on hand. But most American producers, underfinanced if not in actual financial straits, had to sell what they had available, good or bad, mature or fresh from the fermenting vat. And they did.

Third, instead of explaining, to a public then definitely sympathetic, their problems and plans and hopes, American vintners, with a few notable exceptions, decided to brazen the thing out. They announced that their wines were quite as good as the better vintages of Germany and France and Spain—but any beginner with a couple of dollars in his pocket could buy two bottles and find out that this was not by any means true.

Fourth, American vintners insisted on selling their wines under European names to which these wines had no moral and precious little commercial right—St. Julien, Château Yquem, Pommard, Chablis. The Government finally stepped in and stopped the worst of these abuses; meanwhile American growers had, by inference, admitted that their wines were imitations and invited the public to compare the imitation with the original. The public did, and for the next two or three years almost all of the American wines sold were sold on a price basis.

Fifth, and this is not the fault of the vintners, there appeared, with Repeal, a collection of self-styled connoisseurs, most of them quite as ignorant as the public they pretended to instruct, who published, generally with the imprimatur of some wine merchant, enormously complicated vintage and service charts which baffled and embarrassed the average housewife—anyone was a barbarian to serve a '24 Claret after a '29; an average Sunday dinner required three wines, none of which,

The Vine Dies Hard

Frank Schoonmaker

It could hardly be expected that a part of the United States which has had as fantastic and extraordinary a history as California, would be anything but extraordinary as far as the history of its viticulture is concerned. A state in which a Mexican general, born a Spaniard, received as his guest a Russian princess who had arrived in America by way of Siberia and Alaska, and protected this Russian princess from the amorous advances of an Indian chief, is no ordinary state. The treatment which the vine has received in California has been exactly as fantastic and as extraordinary as that story, and involves an even greater array of nationalities and events tragic and comic.

In California was planted the largest vineyard in the world, 3,060,000 vines that never produced anything worth drinking. California also boasted the largest small vineyard, a single vine planted in 1783 by a Mexican woman named Maria Marcelina Feliz, and known to have yielded upward of five tons of grapes. The European vine was introduced into California in 1770 by Franciscan missionaries, who brought over with them what were supposed to be Malaga cuttings and planted them around their missions from San Diego up the old

in the majority of cases, the local liquor store carried; good wine should not be served to those who smoked, when all of one's friends smoked.

Faced with all this, after one or two unfortunate experiences with widely advertised domestic wines, the American housewife decided to concentrate on Martinis or Manhattans and highballs, and I can only praise her good sense.

American wine will never take the place which it deserves on America's dinner tables until it is honestly presented to the American public, and by "honestly" I mean under American names. California and New York and Ohio have now, after seven years, the vineyards to produce good wine, and considerable and fairly adequate stocks of good wine laid by. In justice to the wine and to ourselves, this ought to be sold for what it is. Let us look into this subject.

What is a French Chablis or a French Sauternes? And what is a California "Chablis" or a California "Sauternes"? Well, a French Chablis (unless shipped by a downright thief) is a wine made from Pinot Chardonnay grapes, incidentally one of the four or five best white-wine grapes in the world, either in the township of Chablis itself or in one of nineteen adjoining townships which enjoy the same climatic conditions and have pretty much the same type of soil. A French Sauternes is a wine produced in a delimited district about one-fourth as big as a California county, from Sauvignon, Sémillon, and Muscat grapes. Well, what is a California "Chablis"? Legally, it is any white California wine which the producer (who has probably never tasted a good French Chablis in his life) thinks tastes like Chablis. It can be made from Pinot Chardonnay grapes or from culls thrown out by raisin pickers, in the best viticultural district of California or the worst. A California "Sauternes" can be made anywhere in a state nearly as large as the wine-producing area of France, and it can be made of any kind of grape that the wine maker happens to have or cares to buy, including Tokays, Muscats, and Concords. Actually, I do not believe there are five thousand acres of true Sauternes grapes in California, and I am certain there are not three hundred acres of Pinot Chardonnays.

The trouble, therefore, with European names for California wines is not primarily that they are wrong or dishonest: it is simply that they mean absolutely nothing, that they give the consumer no idea what he is buying, no guarantee, and no information; that they give the producer of superior grapes and the owner of superior vineyards no advantage and no higher prices; that to the merchant they mean endless complaints and explanations. No two American "Sauternes" taste exactly alike.

Despite this lack of standards, these foreign type names, as Harold J. Grossman says, in his excellent *Guide to Wines, Spirits, and Beers,* "are more appropriate when applied to California wines than to American wines, as they do bear some resemblance to the originals, which is not true of the Eastern types."

Wine, it is important to remember, is not a manufactured article but a farm product, and its excellence or mediocrity is primarily the result of the soil on which the grapes were grown and of the grape variety which the producer chose to plant. Thus, in all of the great wine-producing countries of the world the local wines take their names from the factors which make them what they are—the place from which they come, the grapes from which they are made. We have our full share of pleasant and picturesque place names in this country, and there is no reason why we should be unwilling or reluctant to use them. A few progressive wine growers have already started using them, and the public response has been overwhelmingly favorable.

Away, then, with California "Moselle," New York State "Burgundy," and the whole crew of hyphenated Americans. The fine vineyard districts of the United States are these: the Napa Valley, the Sonoma Valley, the Livermore Valley, and the foothills of the Santa Cruz Mountains in Santa Clara County, California; the Lake Erie Islands off Sandusky, Ohio; the Finger Lake district of New York State, especially the shores of Lake Canandaigua and Lake Keuka. Other districts will, no doubt, soon come into production, and some of them may prove every bit as good as those already known.

The fine wine grapes grown in this country are, in California, the Pinot (from Burgundy), the Cabernet (from Bordeaux), the Gamay (from the Beaujolais), the Riesling, Sylvaner, and Traminer (from the Rhine and Alsace), the Folle Blanche (from the Cognac country), the

Sauvignon and Sémillon (from the Graves and Sauternes distric the East the grapes are native grapes, and the best of them, all of yield white wine, are the Delaware, the Elvira, Moore's Diamon Catawba, the Diana, the Duchess.

These, then are the names one should look for on American v the names of the American districts in which the wines were and the names of the grapes from which they came.

March

Camino Real as far as Monterey and Sonoma. But the grapes they planted were not of any very good variety, and the wine they made was nothing to boast about.

We can safely say that when the Forty-niners arrived on the coast, they found no very good wine awaiting them. People of almost every nationality made a contribution of some sort to early California wine making. A Hungarian nobleman and a Finn were leading pioneers; Chinese labor was used almost exclusively in the vineyards until 1890; a member of the Japanese royal house was, for several decades, the owner of one of the state's best vineyards; German emigrants became wine makers; a score of leading Frenchmen planted vines and gave their vineyards French names; and a large part of California's present wine production is in the hands of Italians. Thus a sort of viticultural League of Nations has existed in the state, with almost every race that played a part in the building of America contributing its penny's worth to the creation of California's vineyards and wines.

Among these strangers who appeared on the scene was a remarkable individual who came as Count Agaston Haraszthy, but presently had Americanized himself into plain Colonel Haraszthy. He introduced, it is said, the Zinfandel grape; and the cuttings of this variety, carried off and planted all over the state, undoubtedly changed the whole trend of California viticulture. It became an industry and began to grow like the prairie towns of the same period. California made up its collective mind to "go places," and the familiar American cycle of boom-and-bust was under way.

The "bust" was due to perfectly evident causes. The first boom lasted a little more than ten years. Most of the get-rich-quick planters knew very little about grape varieties, and still less about wine. Huge crops were harvested, but the wine was poorly made, and found no ready market. Then, to cap the evil days, the phylloxera arrived, that parasite which devours the roots of grape vines. The disastrous effects it had on the vineyards of California were hardly less than those it wrought a few years later on the vineyards of France. Whole vineyards were wiped out and abandoned; all conceivable remedies, from those of science to those of witchcraft, were tried, with little or no success.

But the vine dies hard. By 1876 in California it was on its way back.

The resurrection was due largely to the efforts of two individuals, Professor George Husmann and Charles A. Wetmore. Professor Husmann was America's first wine technician of real consequence, and did more than any other person in this country to develop the phylloxera-resistant roots on which not only all California wine grapes, but virtually all European wine grapes as well, are now grafted.

Mr. Wetmore's contribution to the second boom now about to begin was that of a vast enthusiasm and a better knowledge of grape varieties which he had acquired on his pilgrimage through European vinelands. Returning from that tour, he labored to impart this enthusiasm and this knowledge to the wine producers of California. Those whose interest in vineyard culture was not altogether speculative soon began to plant good grape varieties. There were also people of independent means who began to produce fine wine as gentlemen wine-growers; and thanks to the cheap Chinese labor which was then available, acre after acre along the steep slopes overlooking the Sonoma, Napa, and Santa Clara valleys was cleared of brush, plowed, and planted in vines. Storage cellars were dug back into the hills; and big, cool, thick-walled stone wineries began to spring up all over northern California. A good many of these carried simply the names of their owners; others were given classical or purely fanciful or foreign names.

There must have been a hundred such vineyards, within fifty or sixty miles of San Francisco Bay, that were relatively famous in 1890, and even more famous at the turn of the century. Some had changed hands, but most of them were going their sound and prosperous way in 1910. A decade later, the cultivation of a fine vineyard had become a millionaire's or a bankrupt's occupation; and all but a pitiful few of the great wine names of California had disappeared.

It is difficult, across the chasm of twenty-five years, to see National Prohibition as the better California vintners saw it. One of the principal arguments of the Prohibitionists was that essential foodstuffs were being diverted by the liquor industry; but wine grapes are not raisin or table grapes, and what could the growers do with wine grapes except make wine? Good wine grapes are grown on hillsides where little else, least of all cereals, will grow; then why were vines torn up which had taken a decade or more to come into full production? The wine growers of California had seen their fathers make wine, and their friends and their fathers' friends drink it without drunkenness, and with real enjoyment. It is not a pleasant thing to be told, when you have loyally and honestly pursued an occupation which has been honorably regarded since the beginnings of human literacy, an occupation which your father and grandfather pursued before you, that your occupation is criminal. But that was the law. So the upland vineyards were uprooted, and the equipment and the cellars were allowed to fall in disrepair.

It looked at first as though Prohibition meant the end of the wine-grape industry in California—but not for long. California farmers actually found it profitable between 1915 and 1934 to plant 100,000 acres of red wine grapes.

Now a word about the grapes that were planted during this period. The public in the East wanted and demanded what were euphemistically described as "juice grapes," and was prepared to pay fancy prices for them. These home wine makers knew little about wine and less about grapes. As it happens, almost all of the fine wine grapes of the world are small, thin-skinned, fragile, and not particularly prepossessing. They ship poorly. On the other hand, the thick-skinned, tough, common varieties—Alicante Bouschet, Mataro, Carignane—travel well; and it was these which the wine makers of New York, Philadelphia, and Boston wanted and secured. As a result, hundreds of acres of superior wine grapes in California were torn up and replanted in these varieties, which never could yield, even under the best conditions, anything but mediocre wine.

The damage Prohibition did to California is not likely to be repaired for another fifteen or twenty years. With a few notable exceptions, those who had created the traditions of wine producing in California, and had maintained its standards, did not survive Prohibition. The industry fell inevitably into less scrupulous hands. The decline in the quality of California table wine is partially due to this. Also, let it be remembered, the poor-quality grapes that were planted during the Prohibition era to satisfy the demand of the home wine makers are still there, still producing.

How long it will take for the wine industry of California to recover from Prohibition and its succeeding evils is difficult to estimate. This hoped-for recovery has been further delayed by the mistaken policy which many of the wine-growers adopted after Repeal. Instead of frankly admitting at that time that there was almost no sound, well-aged wine on hand in this country, California's wine industry decided to brazen it out; no more dishonest and disastrous policy was ever adopted by a major industry. Wines that were poor, unsound, artificially "aged," artificially flavored, misrepresented, and mislabeled became the rule rather than the exception on the American market. It is to our everlasting credit that we recognized these for the frauds they were, and turned instead to cocktails and highballs. California wine producers have gone through difficult years since the end of Prohibition, but most of the difficulties were very largely of their own making.

Since 1936 and 1937 the situation has changed remarkably and for the better. The intelligent producers of California have begun to plant fine wine grapes, to make their wine with vastly more attention and care, and to put out wines which are quite able to hold their own against all but the really great wines of Europe.

This country for just and valid reasons condemned the California wines that were being marketed in 1934 and 1935. For no less just and valid reasons, we should now welcome with open arms the excellent California wines which are being produced today; for the vine, at long last, is beginning to receive in the better California vineyards the respect and study and loving care which it deserves, and which it can so richly reward.

April 1941

NIGHT OF LOBSTER

Robert P. Coffin

It is a pleasant thing to spend a night with a Maine lobstering man. It is especially pleasant when the man is deep in lobsters. I spent a night with one just this fall. It was a night I shall always remember.

A friend of mine and I went along together. This friend is a most particular one. He hails from Oregon and the other coast. But that is nothing against him. With his attainment of maturity, he has adopted Maine as his proper place. He is one of the thousands of artists who have recently done so. Artists are wise people. They know which side their bread is buttered on. This friend of mine makes the loveliest handmade books this side of the fourteenth century. Just to make sure the whole of his creation is good, he writes the prose and poetry that go into his hand-tooled covers. He is one of the best poets alive now.

This man is also an Old Blue of Oxford. In case you do not know what an Old Blue is, I can say he is just a half step down from one of the major gods on Olympus. He is one who wears the dark blue of Oxford University for having represented the University against Cambridge in an athletic contest. This friend made his Blue in that peculiarly American and Indian game from up Wisconsin way, part mere massacre, part pure brain, part sword-dance, and good part poetry, which is played at its most spectacular best in England—lacrosse. The man has an international standing in this sport.

This friend is also, in odd moments, an excavator of English abbeys and human nature, friend of British prime ministers and artists. He is also an authority on most medieval arts and crafts, on the great medieval church, on carving and stained glass—which he can make in the medieval manner—on tennis and an excellent player at it, on Herrick, and on Maine quahaugs. He also happens to be one of the best storytellers living. But he wasn't telling stories this evening. He was eating lobsters, with this lobstering man I speak of, and with me.

This lobsterman is probably my friend's sole rival in that ancient art of storytelling. He is one of the few survivors of that race of oral storymakers who used to live along the Maine coast. I believe he is one of the best of the race. He is, like most Maine coast men and my friend, the Old Blue poet, a decidedly all-round man. Besides catching lobsters, he paints in oils and water colors, does wood carving with his jackknife. His dolphins and mermaids, both single-tailed and double, his full-rigged ships, anchors and rope, carved on pine sea chests, have made him well known and taken his name over New England. A master storyteller he is. But this evening he wasn't telling stories, either. He was after lobsters. He was purely and simply a fisher and an eater of them. So he kept quiet, like my friend, the poet. They both kept quiet.

The fisherman, I noticed, brought along a huge tomato-can he had put a bail in, when he came down to his dory. What was that for? Oh, he guessed we might have use for it. We got in and pushed off.

We rowed down the long bay I used to row as a boy on my saltwater farm—or rather, the lobsterman rowed. He was fishing his string of traps tonight by oar-power. It was four miles he rowed, steady as a clock, quiet. I wanted to spell him on the oars. The poet wanted to. We had both pulled a fair oar on our college crew at Oxford. But this lobstering man would not let us. This was our vacation. We should rest. The man rowed as he breathed, without effort. He had just finished an eight-hour shift at the Bath Iron Works, making destroyers for the American Navy. This was his way of resting.

The herons were taking their stations for the night, indistinct on the mud flats. It gloamed and darkened. The mighty two-hundred-foot cliffs of the shore faded into the few bright stars. Other stars came out, blurry with September softness, over the jagged spruce skyline along each side of us. I could see nothing at last but the glow of my friend's and the lobsterman's cigarettes. The tide, as it rose, made dim and sweet sounds around us. We moved gently on through whispers like eternity. The oars creaked in the tholepins. The oar sounds and the tide's sounds went beautifully together. A fresh little night breeze came up from nowhere and lapped us round. The fragrance of the balsams on the shore mingled in with the smell of the sea. We floated gently on.

All at once, the lobstering man backed water hard and shipped his oars. He put out his hand into pitch-black night, took in a lobster-buoy, stood up in the boat without tipping it the slightest bit out of plumb, and started pulling. It was his first trap. He could have found it with his eyes closed in all that vast bay. Maybe his eyes *were* closed. I could not see. The trap came in over the side. Things fluttered and clapped in it like wet wings. The man put in his hand among unseen scissors of claws. He started taking things out. A crab. A crab. A crab. They splashed over the side and sank in the water.

A pause. "He's too small." It was a lobster, but it was a "short." Overboard it went. Another followed it. Another. It was dark. No warden could have seen if we had taken a lobster of illegal length.

"A 'count!'"

A lobster hit the dory's bottom and flapped in a fury. More crabs went over. Another "count" lobster came skidding against my shoe. Another. Three good ones. Still another. And another. This was remarkable. Five good lobsters in one trap! Seemed like a record. The trap was baited up in the dark, slid over the gunwale, was gone.

The rower put out his oars and went on to the next buoy. It was like clockwork. He found it, pulled, and the ritual of falling lobsters began again. Four "counters" this time. The lobsterman rowed on and picked up the next trap just where it should be. More good ones. Clockwork it was. The sound of the oars in the tholepins made it more that way.

The sky was stars all over it now, and it had lifted up millions of miles high, the way September skies do when it gets late. It had got lighter. I could see things dim on the bay now, but no buoys. But the rower could see them, coming up on them backwards, too. He could see them through the back of his head. Or feel them. The way bats feel door-casings when they fly in the dark, by radar. See them or feel them—it was all the same to the lobstering man. He came up on them back-to, and he never missed one or fumbled for one. That was the kind of lobsterman he was. If he ever goes blind, this lobstering man can go right on fishing. It won't hamper him in the least.

The man got every one of his string of thirty-two traps, without turning his head in the night. He must have been using a good "ripe" bait, too. The boat's bottom was alive with lobsters. They were up to our ankles.

The fisherman rowed to the dim shore. It looked all like an entire mountain to me, high on the stars, but we slid gracefully into a deep little cove hardly wider than our boat. We grounded on a beach where I should have said there was nothing but ledges. The lobsterman took out the killick and went up with it and put it down on the turf he knew would be there. We were anchored. The man disappeared into the woods for just a moment. He was back almost before he was gone; he had an armful of bone-dry spruce brush, he threw it down, touched a match to it. A vast blaze like a section of the Milky Way shot up against the night that was already sprinkled with stars. The poet and I had to back away from the light and heat. The bronze face of the lobstering man loomed smiling in the firelight. The brush crackled, and all three of our shadows danced up high upon the wall of silent woods above us.

The man of lobsters went down to the boat, took out the tomato-can pail, dipped some of the bay in it, and crowded it full of lobsters. He came back and set the pail on his fire, with a green fir-bole he had picked up Lord knows where strung through the bail and resting, each end of it, on two jutting rocks that seemed just to have happened to be there, one on each side of the fire he had laid in the dark. The man lit his pipe up and settled back on his calves. We all lit up. It was quiet. Our fire made the only sound there was in the night. But soon the pail of lobsters began to sing low, too.

The fire burned down to red coals. Suddenly the lobsters boiled over. Hiss! The gush of water put out part of the embers. The lobster-man shoved more brush on from somewhere with his toe. The flames leaped up again. The lobsters started to boil over again. But this time the man raised the fir-bole a bit, pail and all, stopped the boil, put the fir-bole back on the two rocks. The pail boiled over fiercely for the third time. This time the lobsterman let it boil. Then he poured the lobsters out bright red in the glow of what coals were left. He kicked on a whole new heap of brush. The fire danced up, sprinkling the night with wild stars. It was as light as day. Our shadows wavered enormous on the high wall of night.

We took the hot lobsters, tossed them from hand to hand to keep them from scalding us, and broke them in two. We ate the hot green tomalley right out of the back-shells. We broke off the large claws, put the broken end to our mouths, tipped back our heads, worked the jaws of the claws like scissors, and let the scalding hot juice spurt down our throats. I did not have to show the Old Blue of Oxford how to do it. He knew how. He had eaten Maine lobsters before. His Oxonian chin dripped just as much in the firelight as the lobsterman's and mine did.

We fractured the thick claws in our teeth and got the sweet red meat out whole. We put the flanged tailpieces between our two palms, clasped our hands as if at prayer, cracked inward, cracked outward, laid the flanges wide, broken open clean as a whistle, lifted out a column of meat as large as a tholepin, stripped off the top strip, and took out the dark thread of the colon. Then we shoved the whole delectable busi-ness into our mouths. Tears came into our eyes from the heat and taste of the lobsters. But we chewed and swallowed through our tears. We knew just how to eat the crustaceans. We were old hands at eating them, all three of us. We regaled ourselves on meat as hot as a spruce bonfire and sweet as a boy's first love.

My Oregonian-Oxonian friend is a poet, I say. He knows a poem when he sees one. He knows a poem when he is sitting in the middle of one. He knew he was right smack in the midst of a fine poem this night with the lobsterman. He hoed in. He got a lobster ahead of me. He got half a lobster ahead of the lobsterman. And that, let me tell you, is lobster-eating!

Before we knew it, we had run out of lobsters. The fisherman went back to the boat for another pailful. He breezed up our fire, and he set the new lobsters on. They boiled over in about ten minutes' time. The fragrance of hot lobsters spiced the whole night. Qwoks went over duskily like ghosts and cried at the sight of our fire, and at being kept from their feeding grounds and the small fish crowding the edge of the rising tide where we were sitting. We ate some more lobster claws, rested, and talked. We didn't talk much. We were too happy to find much to say. But we felt a lot. We dozed off, watched the stars, ate another claw, thought long, long thoughts. We dozed off, singly, then together. We woke together, stirred the fire, and basked in happiness again. We heard small waves lapping somewhere. The tide was getting well up.

Suddenly our boat loomed huge right beside us, on a level with our firelight. There was a hiss. The edge of high tide was licking our embers. But it did not put them out. It just kissed the outer coals. Our lobsterman had known to an inch where this particular September high tide would come when he kicked up his fire.

We lost all track of time. The spell of the lobsters was upon us deep. We thought and dozed, dozed and thought. We threw on more fragrant spruce brush. The night was turning colder. The fire licked our faces and made them feel good. Little waves lapped about our toes. Our boat leaned on us and on our fire. All three of us got to feeling how this night and the stars of this night and we were brothers. We got to feeling as the ancient Indians, the Abenaki, must have felt in this same little cove here on some September night like this a thousand years ago, and for thousands of years together in this cove, as they ate their lobsters over their sprucewood coals just the way we had eaten the same Maine lobsters now. The three of us merged with the tide and the soft sounds of life it made around us along the shore.

The morning star was burning big on the horizon when we pushed off our boat. The lobstering man rowed us home through the cool and widening dawn.

It was a night like a night of marriage. I shall remember it all my days. I hope I shall remember it, too, beyond even those.

September 1946

NIGHT OF VENISON

Robert P. Coffin

I don't suppose such a night could have happened anywhere but on the coast of Maine. The parts of it could not have been these parts, nor could they have added up to this effect.

To begin with, the three of us had been hunting for our dinner miles away from where we found it. We had walked, I don't know how many miles, looking for a nice plump buck-deer for our roast. We must have covered three townships easily, townships mostly alder thickets and spruce swamps. We had walked one whole day and part of a night, through bogs and gullies, through junipers and blackberry hells. We were pincushioned with thorns. It had rained, then stiffened up and hailed, sleeted, snowed, then moderated again, and rained upon us. We were plastered with mud. We had worn ourselves through to our uppers. Not a deer had we seen. We gave up the idea of a venison dinner. We would roast hot dogs. We came on home.

My friend from Virginia, who is probably America's foremost woodcut artist, maybe the world's, now on his first trip to Maine, made slighting remarks about Maine as the deer-hunter's paradise it is reported to be. I think he was beginning to doubt if the state that sends to the outside alone, each year, over 75,000 velvety bundles of forest-fed meat—and goodness knows how many more to Maine woodsheds to hang half the winter—had any deer in it at all.

So J. J. and I gave up life in the rough, scrubbed up, and went to a professor's home for luncheon. I think it was sweetbreads or kidneys on toast, or some such suave and civilized meat. Anyway, it was philosophy and art and music. My friend J. J. discovered with some surprise that we raised these down in Maine even if we didn't raise deer. Later on, he was to discover, with still more surprise, that a Maine lobster-man knew Gerrish's *Anatomy* by heart and all about the layers of different ancient red men who lived and ate their clams where the lobsterman digs his clams now.

While we were eating our sweetbreads and talking art, the weather outside took one of those headers it can take only in Maine in November. The thermometer fell from forty-two above to three below zero. When we came out of the house, the wet world had hardened up so it rattled like broken glass when we stepped on it.

And then we got word to come down to the bay for our venison dinner after all. The third man of our hunting party, who is a bay man and an old friend of mine, and who felt, as I did, that our state's hunting reputation had been maligned, had gone home and found a four-pronged buck eating the late zinnias out of the dory-flowerbed in his own front dooryard. Maine is like that. The best deer in the woods often comes down Main Street and goes into Senter's Dry Goods Store, to be there when you get back from a two-hundred-mile jaunt after him up in the wilderness of Piscataquis County.

It was a set-up of a shot. My friend brought the buck down at the top of his bound over the outside cellar-door, startling his wife so she dropped her cake on the floor and marked it for life. He skinned him, dressed him, and hung him up in the woodshed on his way in to lunch. Now, with this change in weather, the deer was properly frozen and ready to eat. Our bay friend sent us the word. He also ordered his wife to run up a batch of cream-o'-tartar biscuits and to draw on the crock of butter she had laid down, for the biscuits and the deer. He got the dishes ready, and three quarts of Scotch. Considering the weather, that was the absolute minimum for three men. We must hurry right down.

We did. We came on two wheels around the road bends, with the choker right out.

It was our bay friend's idea to cook our supper out on the bay and eat it in the light of the full moon. He had arranged it so from the beginning. He had counted on that moon all the time we had been slopping through the damps and the fogs. Here it had gone and cleared off nicely. And here was the moon. Now that it had gone below zero and was still falling, J. J. and I thought the bay might be a dubious place to sit by and eat. Fred's warm kitchen looked pretty good to us.

No, Fred was set on the moon. We would have a big bonfire. We could keep warm all right. Fred hustled all the gear, almost a quarter of the deer—in case we got very hungry—and the Scotch, into his cart. We would ride down to the bay in style. It was about two miles down there where he had set his heart on eating in the open. It was right on the tip of everything, next to the open Atlantic, where they used to launch the square-rigged ships in the old days, right where the ocean around us would be good and wise. Fred, being a Maine man, loved to have elbow room.

We ought to have some coots and black-duck for hors d'oeuvres, Fred insisted. So he threw in a lot of shotguns. While he was building the fire, the woodcut man and I could go along the bay and shoot us some ducks to roast. It seemed to me sort of cold to handle a shotgun. And it was getting much too dark to shoot ducks well. And anyway, said I, brightening, the sun had gone down, and there was a law against shooting ducks after sunset. Oh, piped up Fred, that didn't matter a bit. There was going to be a bright moon, said the bay man, and that law was a Maine law. People in Maine didn't begrudge a man's shooting himself a few ducks when he was hungry, at any time. Fred was hungry. So it was all right. And Fred was also the warden. The shotguns went along.

There was a good cartload of us and the deer meat and the guns and other gear. I figured we had about enough deer along for ten men, but with this cold weather we might need it all. Fred had tried to persuade his wife to join her biscuits and us. But no go. She was a wise woman. We could save her a little tidbit from the buck's flank. Anyway, she had to run up a crazy-quilt, hook a rug, and also wash the kitchen floor, she remembered, this very night. She sent us off well fortified by biscuits, wrapped deep in turkish towels to keep the heat of the oven in them— a huge batch of browned beauties. Fred said, good, and told his wife not to count on any biscuits coming back.

When we came out around the corner of the barn, the full moon met us face to face. It was just coming up in front of my own summer home over the way. The moon was half as big as my five-horse, twelve-cow barn, and more silvery than I had ever known a moon, even in Maine, to be. It was hoary with frost. Maybe it was partly the Scotch. For we had taken a pretty large slug of it before we opened the door and went out into the Frigid Zone. But that moon *was* peculiar, Scotch couldn't have made it that silvery. I hoped the bay was freezing the ducks right into itself, so we wouldn't be able to shoot them on the wing.

It was colder than three below now. I knew it in my bones. It was ten below zero. The vast moon rolled right along with us as we drove out and jounced along the frozen ruts. Our shadow went off west across the world like a long-legged camel with a high hump. The hump was the Virginian and me. Fred had put us on top of the deer and the biscuits, in the back of the cart, to hold everything down. Our eyeteeth rattled with the ruts so we couldn't talk. I felt my hands freezing. My back was warm, though. It was up against the biscuits. We made a sound of thunder as we rolled on that iron world.

Fred cracked at the horse with his whip, to hurry him on. The horse was surprised. He fetched a leap like a jack rabbit. The cart bounced high, the kingpin came out. J. J. and I went down in a heap in the road and bit our tongues. Everything came down on us, biscuits, deer, Scotch, and guns. Fred went away from us in the moonlight on his front wheels.

When I could get my tongue out from between my frozen lips so I could shout, I shouted hard. My voice boomed and bounced around the startled bays.

Fred had missed us, anyway. He came bouncing back for us, standing up on his two wheels like a Roman charioteer. He looked like a Roman in the face, too, in the moonlight, with all that Scotch in him.

It was all right, Fred said. He scraped us all up in no time, got under the cart body, lifted it on the wings of Scotch with his narrow back, slipped the kingpin in, jumped back to his place, opened up his quart of Scotch, took a drink, gave us one, fetched the horse a crack, and away we went, jolting from one side of the road to the other. The iron world sent out sparks under us. The whisky began to work in us. The big moon rolled along with us. We all burst into song.

We came to the point, and Fred drove right down over the cliffs and onto the beach. He tethered the horse to an overhanging spruce, cut down a dead spruce, touched it afire, and unloaded us in a cloud of sparks which showered up fragrantly from the crackling pyre. Fred had down a dozen other dead spruces with his axe before we could limber up, piled them up, set them aflame, and had a fire that lit up half the universe, standing thirty feet up into the night. He thawed the Virginian and me out.

"Now you boys go and get them ducks, and I will start the meat. Here! Have something to keep the cold out!" He tossed us the Scotch.

Fred cut a long green spruce bough, cut a large hunk of the deer meat into thirds, and skewered the pieces on his bough. He stuck the spruce skewer right into his flames.

The Virginian and I picked up the shotguns and shells. We started off towards the water. The ducks were flying all right. We could hear plenty of them. We could see long chevrons of them crisscrossing the big moon. Ducks were all over the bay. But they seemed to be all converging way out. We could never get out there where they were.

Couldn't we!

We discovered a remarkable thing. It was dead-low tide—the deadest low-run tide I ever did see. The ocean must have been halfway over to Spain. There were miles of mudflats before us. And, by George Keezer!—hadn't it got so cold that the mud had frozen hard as a ballroom floor. We could run right out on it without a speck of mud on us.

We ran. It was like nothing I had ever known in Maine before. We ran for miles, from island to island. I think we sang. And the full moon ran along with us and threw our shadows out long beside us, with flying daddy-long-legs' limbs. We found we could run, then pull our feet together, and slide for yards. We did it over and over. We had to run anyway, to keep from freezing solid. But the surprise and exhilaration at such a vast marble floor, which no human feet had ever touched before, made us run wild.

The ducks slanted by the hundreds across the moon. The ducks were surprised, too, at this strange, hard, bright world. They got exhilarated with the thing also. They quacked and squawked in amazement. In our elation we up and let go at them. The orange fire rocketed out of our guns. There wasn't a chance in a million of hitting the ducks. They were too high, too excited, and going much too fast. But it was fun shooting. Our guns echoed and re-echoed around those lonely distant shores like rolling thunder. The ducks appreciated the fun and quacked louder. We yelled. Our voices came back to us from six or seven shores in succession.

To run dry-shod on places where only water and waves belonged, where I had only rowed before, without being slowed up by soft footing, to run wild under a wild full moon in a night far, far below zero— this was a thing once in a lifetime, a once-and-for-all joy. So run we did and fired, fired and ran, through this unreal, silvered world. The iron-paved bay rang with us. The ducks quacked quick and loud overhead and laced the sky with excitement. We were like boys, in a world no boys ever knew. Oh, I tell you it wasn't just the Scotch in us, either!

We had run miles. Now, as we turned back at last, we could see the tall tower of Fred's fire. It seemed half the world away. The nearest shore was low down on the rim of the great silver world we were in. The mud had turned to sheer and shining ice under the cold and the moon. We stood and shouted, and our voices went away over this level universe and bounced, long afterwards, on the distant shores.

In the midst of our echoes, we heard another. We listened. It was Fred. Far away, he was calling us. Supper was ready.

We wanted to stay out there in the wonder. But we were good and hungry now. Our running had shaken all the sweetbreads down into our shoes. We started running homewards. Fred's fire sent out a long pathway and yellow light towards us, and we ran along that yellow path through the wild white night. And the white moon was on our shoulder.

From Plato to a path of fire on bay ice. From a tame indoors meal to a wild outdoors one, in the matter of three hours, a few miles. Maine is like that. A man can run from one kind of goodness to another at the other end of the world in a moment.

Our bay friend was waiting for us, as we came off our sheet of silver, with the Scotch. And the deer was ready. The three steaks were smoking on the ledge. Fred had kept the biscuits hot by burying them, pan and all, in the hot spruce ashes. Now he excavated them, pulled them out, blew them off, and set the pan before us. He tossed us the butter. Knives and forks. To each man his bottle of Scotch.

We threw knives and forks aside, seized the meat up in our hands, and bit into it. Charred black on its crust, it was tender and juicy inside. And Fred had thought to upholster it with strips of bacon. We ate like three wolves. It must have been hard on towards midnight now. We were starving. We smeared the butter over the hot biscuits, bit into them. It must have been twelve below zero. First a mouthful of meat, then a mouthful of biscuit that melted like warm snow, then the third mouthful, the whisky. We ate, ate, drank; ate, ate, drank. It was the sweetest eating I have done, maybe, in my life.

And the moon climbed and reached the top of the world's ceiling above us. The cold grew colder. The earth cracked and boomed with the frost. But our faces and lips were full of the fire of the spruce logs, and our insides were the fires of sweet roasted venison and fine Scotch.

The three hunks of meat were gone at last. The biscuit pan was naked and empty. So were the three bottles. All good things must have an end.

We tipped our heads back and sang. J. J.'s voice is none too sweet, but out there under the moon it was convincing. Fred is no operatic baritone, but with all that silver space around him he sounded noble that night. And I was, as usual, superb. Our song was doubled and quadrupled by the echoes around us. The far-away sea rose and came in with a silver rush, and the hard floor we had danced on was gone all at once. All at once the whole ocean was at our heels. It licked our hissing embers. The ducks out on the bay missed us and quacked mournfully for us to come back and be insane with them once more. But the ocean was there now, there was no going back. There is no going back to boyhood and once-in-a-lifetime wonder. The fringe of the sprucewoods above us stood out fiery with our fire and the moonfire.

The world was so quiet, we noticed it and fell quiet, too. We sat there together, hot and alive in the midst of the vast, cold death of sky and night, and the cold, vast death of the ocean touched our feet, but could not touch us at all.

Night of twelve below zero, night on the ocean's edge, of venison and hot biscuits, night of a full moon making night into day! O night I will recall to the end!

November 1946

Down East Breakfast

Robert P. Coffin

Weather, mother of good poetry, is also mother of good breakfasts. The solider the weather, the solider the meal. The sharper the air, the sharper the appetite. Maine runs to fine breakfasts as it runs to fine poetry. The world's biggest breakfast, which was the old-time Maine farm meal of the morning, could never have originated and developed south of the halfway mark from the equator to the North Pole. It took a lot of hardy subarctic cold and sting and bite to the air to bring out its very substantial contours.

Like the American tea of a century ago, which faded out into our modern supper, the American farm breakfast of the north was a whole three-ring meal, maybe one of the only two meals a man was going to get; and so it was built with strong buttresses, to buttress him about for a hard day's work, in the sprucewoods, on the Fundy swells, in snow up to his middle, in nor'easters and sou'westers he had to lean on to keep standing.

Unless a man had a lot of ballast at his middle, he might never go through the day and come home to his loved ones at sundown. The few old-timers who, for dyspepsia or love or other reasons, ate light in the morning, never came home from a heavy spell of weather to beget their kind. They blew away. The heavy-breakfasters begot heavy heirs, and they stayed put.

It was a pioneer meal, that ancient breakfast, a meal for men who were carving a nation out of forests and earth and mountains. It was a prelude to the two-bladed axe, the cant dog, the crowbar, the scythe, or the adz. It was the only proper breakfast for the man with fists like mauls and thighs like young oak trees.

It still is, in Maine. The present-day Maine outdoors man is built on the same solid foundations as his pioneer grandfather, and he sticks close to his cordwood or his lobster traps because he is hefted down to stay with several pounds of solid breakfast. Our best citizens are still mostly farmers and fishermen, outdoors men, and the standard Maine breakfast is cut even now to fit such men's jobs. It cannot be a pindling, indoors sort of thing. The Maine man has to do his day's work in weather like the edge on a crosscut saw, like a breeze in Baffin Land, like an Old Home Week among the icebergs. So he better eat hearty, or he won't last the day's weather out.

The Maine morning meal is like a tune on the bagpipes which calls the stouthearted Scot to war. It is something that must strengthen him deep to his marrow, and only the masculine and downright victuals will do. The ordinary American breakfast, with its precooked and predigested cereals, its hummingbird nectar of citrus, butterflies of bacon, and anemias of eggs, is as much out of place in Maine as a sarong, as a French breakfast of a dry roll and *chocolat chaud* would be to an Eskimo of Greenland. It would be an insult to his oily manhood. Fat is the foe of weather, and fat is the making of Maine's first meal.

The *habitant* breakfast of the Province of Quebec is a brawny brother to the Maine one. Good reason why: it is a doughnut bronzed in the same fat. The French-Canadian has ten-twelve hours of work ahead of him, out in the blue blazes of winter sun, weather, and water, and it behooves him to put a hefty, hot, bronzed breakfast under his belt if he is going to stand up to the tough logs and tough codfish of the day's job.

The basic principle of this northern North American, Laurentian, or Kennebecan breakfast is that it must stick by the ribs for a long time. It must stay put and generate heat. It must be food that takes a long time to get digested, that keeps—to quote a Maine man— "a-nourishing and a-nourishing ye for nine-ten hours." It must have rich, fattened, and oiled doughnuts to it, heavy pies and pancakes, to keep the stomach busy, to keep the blood away from a man's brain, where it can only do mischief, to keep his blood in his arms and thighs where a good woodchopper's or smelt-fisherman's blood belongs. It should have bulk enough to keep the inner man busy for ten-twelve hours, say. For few farmers or fishermen I know would ever dream of coming home at midday. It would be like telling stories in haying-time, making love in a dance hall. It would be like whaling out on a job, it would be like a strong man putting on skirts.

The Maine breakfast is a hefty meal for hefty he-men.

The Down East breakfast is concocted under the sign of the frying pan. Hot fat is at its heart. It begins with a seething and bubbling of pork fat in the skillet or spider. Fat salt pork in chunks, not lean and feminine bacon rashers, is its base.

The flapjack is the wrapper to all the solid foods the working man gets outside of, once he gets inside his pants, starts weathering up against the weather, and begins the day's work by working four-five pounds of flour, fat, meat, and pie into him as his first job. For this breakfast is a job, and only the brawny can bring it off with a flourish. And the flapjack is a rather solid wrapper to wrap all this substance in.

The Down East farm flapjack is the outdoors, masculine, New-World *crêpe Suzette*. It is about as much like its relative in Paris, in London, or in our own sunny South, as an All-American tackle is like a boy in pants six inches long playing with a ten-cent-store football. It is the same fruit, but grown up and with great strength upon it. It is just the size of the whole spider it is cooked in.

The flapjack cook gives her creation the works. She uses no prepared and effete pancake mix. She uses plain buckwheat or wheat flour, sour milk, salt, two even teaspoons of cream-o'-tartar, one of saleratus, a tablespoon of sugar, elbow grease, a tablespoon of shortening, a large duck's egg, and vigor to mix it up. She pours it out of a gallon pitcher into an old-fashioned, thick iron frying pan, sending up volcanoes of blue smoke from its sizzling pork fat, and she fills the spider full of her dough from rim to rim. She sears her dough-flap brown on its port side, as she can tell when it begins to bubble over all its continental width, tosses it high in the air, big as the frying pan itself, catches it exquisitely as it comes hurtling down, on the horizontal, without smearing on the rim of her pan, catches it squarely on its starboard, sears it, this side, to a light mahogany, and tosses it tablewards to her hungering man. The parade of flying flapjacks is continuous. The good cook keeps the kitchen air full of them, being flapped over the fat or over to the table.

These flapjacks are a steady procession of wrappings for the more substantial victuals the man is stowing away meantime. The man wraps up each cod steak or pork chop or beefsteak in one of these hot blankets of dough as he downs it. A good man can get outside of six or seven of these wrappers.

These main dishes of Maine are of many solid kinds. But all are hefty. The ideal breakfast will include three or four or five of them. Here is a list of the more pronounced ones of the lot.

Hulled corn (hominy to the less husky eaters of Wisconsin and Minnesota) washed down cold in thick, hot molasses is a pretty fair dish. Cold pig's-feet standing up in the jelly of the cooled broth they were cooked in are always in good taste. A beefsteak thick and wide enough to fill up the spider from side to side—fried till it is charred almost black on the outside and gets light brown only after you get two inches in—that is a dish always current. Or a man might hanker for a little of last night's corn meal mush, and his wife will slice a big bowlful of it into thick slabs and sear it brown in her frying pan, and he will eat the slabs with a pint of red-hot maple syrup from his own maples up back of the henhouse.

A man may choose between the hulled corn and the mush and take only the steak and pass the pig's-feet-in-jelly. But he will probably take the two kinds of fish. Smothered eels and fried cod steaks, both. The basis of both is pork. The eels are stewed slowly in a thickened pork gravy. The cod is fried with hunks of pork the size of a man's thumb, so crisp that they melt away in the mouth. The man eats maybe a sixth of a pound of pork along with his well-browned cod and his hot jellied eels without conscious effort, without noticing anything but the flavor of it. It is easy eating.

In any case, there must be the cheese. And when I say cheese, I don't mean something that starts out as a mollycoddle of a food for babies, like milk. I mean cheese with meat to it. A solid phalanx of fat, lean, gristle, embedded in a firm, delectable jelly the meats themselves have made. I mean calf's-head cheese or pig's-head cheese. I mean meat. I mean the meat that has been boiled off a calf's head or a pig's, until the skull bones are bare and taken out, the meat chopped finely with a chopper, sage and bayberry sprinkled in, salted and peppered, poured back into the broth, and the whole business left to settle and grow wise. As it cools, the dish composes itself into a massy continent which has to be cut with the butcher knife. This is strenuous and fine eating, and it makes a "stick-by-the-ribs-Billy" dish that will take a man straight through three cords of beechwood or the whole length of a string of a hundred lobster traps without a rest and with a song in the mouth.

The hog's-head cheese of Maine is one of this unhappy world's happiest dishes. It contains the jowls and muscles, those delicious pockets of lean along the brows, the half-fat, half-lean tissues over the cheek bones, the half-marrow, half-heaven of the juices inside the porous head bones, the toothsome tough fabric of the resilient skin-rind. It is jellied in its own savory jelly.

Of course, the pig's head frightens most people away from its nectarean hulk. But the tastiest part of your pig is his head, as it is with the cod. The Maine farmer alone has kept this meat for kings, the boar's head, still on the democratic table, to the delight and strength of men.

One of the secrets of this dish—which I ought to be ostracized for letting out of the bag this way to the other states west and south—is the deer meat in it. For the wise Maine wife chops in with the pig's meat strings from the deer hung in the woodshed, and this lean wild venison points up the tame gelatinous pig meat till it tastes exactly as lusty and intoxicating as the meat of the wild boar of the Middle Ages.

Naturally—and this breakfast is all nature and good-natured eating—there is a liquid constantly drunk to float all these ships of heavy meats and fish and wheat or buckwheat on. It is tea. It is scalding hot tea that fills the farmer's eyes with unsorrowful tears till they drip from his moustache or chin. It is the color of Javanese mahogany. It is as black as your hat. It is about as near to the tea drunk at tea parties by women and womanish men as the male in three-cornered pants is to the adult one in overalls that can stand by themselves. The spoon can nearly stand in this tea. This brew has been steeping in a teapot the size of the teakettle. It has been boiled right up and down for lo these many days. It comes from the teapot that steams forever on the back of the Maine stove, in season and out, replenished and freshened with fistfuls of fresh tea leaves every other day or so.

Five cupfuls of this liquid iron, of this red-hot brew, is the minimum to float the average breakfast. Some of the older men a bit past their full bloom, or some younger ones not yet come to theirs and having peach fuzz instead of whiskers on their cheeks, dilute this tea with sugar and milk. But the middle and powerful males take its tannin into themselves neat. It galvanizes their "innerds," they say, against the damp and cold. *Yerba maté!*—Hunh! That is pink lemonade beside this whisky of the north that keeps the lumberjack and the lobsterman going strong.

Fat pork and strong tea. That is the Maine proverb for a good standard breakfast. Another wise saying is that tea is tea only when it puts whiskers on the soles of your feet. Maine men's feet have hair on their bottoms so they can cling to their dories and rolling logs.

And so, solidly, we come to dessert. For dessert is one of the two substantial meals of the Maine day one must have. Sugar is a fuel for the working man, and it cannot be left out of his morning menu. Of course, he has already got some sweetness into himself in the honey, maple sugar, or molasses he has had on his corn meal and flapjacks. But that was merely an accompaniment of sweetness. He must take it pure and unadulterated at the close of his breakfast.

So the wise woman of the house trots out her pies, hot and cold, custard, cream, cranberry, mince, apple, cherry, squash, punkin, blueberry, huckleberry, lemon, or vinegar. Maybe four or five of this lot if she has them. And the smart wife usually does have at least three kinds on her pantry shelves. A man that is a man can generally take care of four-five pieces of pie. And a piece of pie, in Maine, means usually a quarter, for most housewives cut but two diameters when they take a pie apart.

And when the man lets out his belt finally to the last notch, brushes the piecrust off his vest, and gets up to get going at his saw, his axe, his gas engine, or his plow, he goes out of his home with the wifely kiss on his lips, and her blessing for the day, with two hands of doughnuts. That is, he has a doughnut, from the four-gallon stone crock which is always within arm's length of the breakfast table, on each one of the fingers on his two hands.

"Eiah," as Maine man says when he is feeling in the affirmative, the Maine breakfast is the keystone, the cornerstone of the whole day's work. It is the first and biggest meal. It is a symphony concert of the north, the proper prelude to manhood, a three-ring circus of dough, of meat, of sweet, of fat. It is a square meal, *up and down the center, all promenade, and eight hands around! Swing your partner!*

The Down East breakfast is the strong meal of strong men.

January 1949

THE RITZ IN RETROSPECT

Louis Diat

On December 15, 1910, the *New York Times* announced: "The first dinner at the new Ritz-Carlton Hotel, Forty-sixth Street and Madison Avenue, was served last night to 120 newspaper men and friends of the management." The speeches were quoted, the distinguished guests, international as well as New York celebrities, were listed, and the following menu appeared:

Caviar d'Astrakhan

Blinis à la Russe

Tortue Verte en Tasse

Stichy à la Polonaise

Mousseline de Homard au Chablis

Crevettes Rosés à l'Américaine

Velouté Duchesse

Selle d'Agneau à la Broche

Pommes Mireilles   Flageolets au Beurre

Neige au Clicquot

Cailles de New York sur Croustades

Salade Japonaise
Parfait de Foie Gras au Porto
Soufflé Walkyrie
Feuilles Viennoises Mignardises
Corbeilles de Fruits

Amontillado Dry
Saarburger Moselle Extra
Pontet Canet 1900
Giesler Brut 1904
Martinez Old Port
Denis Mounié 1865
Grandes Liqueurs

That was on the fourteenth. On the fifteenth, the Oval Room, resplendent with its mirrors, soft green walls, and decorations in the architectural style of the Adams Brothers, served its first dinner to the public. Every table had been reserved months in advance; the long menu and carefully selected wine list left nothing to be desired. This was a gala night for the globe-trotting elite who now had one of their beloved Ritz Hotels in New York.

Few men, I suppose, have the opportunity of living through the entire life, from its very beginning to the final end, of a celebrated establishment. But when the Ritz-Carlton in New York closes its famous doors—as it will shortly—that will be my status. I am the only department head who has remained steadily at his post during all those forty crowded years. Older men, for the most part, guided the early days and, one by one, have passed on or retired to quieter ways of living. But I was pretty young in 1910, the youngest chef, they told me, ever to be handed such responsibility.

Anyone who has ever prepared to move into smaller quarters by clearing out the attic of a big house where the family was raised will understand how I feel. Familiar objects, now that they will be dispersed this way and that, evoke reminiscences, amusing, wistful, often sad, that are suddenly etched on the mind as sharply as a photograph. My memories of the Ritz are involved, as you might expect, with cooking and menus, with recipes and eating customs, but also with how they reflect the changing scene in New York and in the world. The unhurried elegance before World War I, the years of riotous spending after it, the Depression years, Prohibition and the lowered standards of eating and drinking that it brought about, the rationing of World War II—all bring back their own pictures that lead from an era of fine food leisurely enjoyed to the quickened meal tempo and the don't-waste-time-on-cooking ideas that are so prevalent today.

When the closing was announced some months ago, a gasp went around the circle of Ritz devotees. This couldn't be, they said. What would New York be without the Ritz? It was to them an institution, not just a hotel. The news made many stop to wonder how the Ritz had achieved this intangible but very definite connotation which makes even the word itself or any of its colloquial forms—Ritzy, *à la Ritz*, putting on the Ritz—a symbol of luxury and sophistication. To understand this, you have to understand the philosophy and ideals of one man, César Ritz.

Ritz dreamed of a hotel, duplicated in important world centers, that would offer the ultimate in fine living to those who could afford and appreciate such luxury. Beautiful surroundings, unexcelled and unusual service, unsurpassed food and wine regardless of the cost in time, effort, and money, anticipation of the whims of the fortunate guests as well as satisfaction, an uncommonly careful selection and training of staff to give meticulous attention to the smallest details. All these ideals formed the keystone of the Ritz tradition of elegance and quality. César Ritz, of course, had no monopoly on dreams or ideas but he was unique because he managed to bring them to such splendid fruition.

It was Mr. Robert Walton Goelet, because he so appreciated the Ritz Hotels in Europe, who decided to give his own New York the last word in this type of luxury establishment. He and his friend Mr. William Harris, the president of the London Ritz and Carlton Hotels, later president of the New York Ritz-Carlton, put their heads together on plans for the new hotel. Fortunately, Mr. Whitney Warren, America's great architect, whose firm built the Grand Central Station and many buildings in that area, was an uncle of Mr. Goelet. So when his services were obtained, he took a personal as well as a professional interest in the project.

Mr. Goelet spared no expense on the construction, equipment, and furnishings, and during the ensuing years made every change and addition required for the needs of the growing establishment. For example, by 1912 it became obvious that the important social functions were all coming to the Ritz, which had been designed not so much for large functions as for serving a very restricted clientele. So the Crystal Room and Ballroom were added in such a way that a wall composed of doors could be opened at one end of the Oval Room onto a wide, curving staircase down to the Crystal Room and up to the Ballroom, making a tremendously impressive setting for any huge affair. I remember that when Queen Marie of Rumania visited this country in the twenties, she said on seeing it, "Why, this is as beautiful as my palace."

Mr. Goelet still wasn't satisfied. It bothered him that we had nothing comparable to the French *terrasse,* the outdoor or garden spot where Parisians love to sip their vermouth cassis or have a light meal. Busy and dusty, Madison Avenue certainly offered no suitable place for this. But Mr. Warren found a solution. He designed a garden for outdoor eating in the space between the Ritz Hotel and Carlton House, which is the connecting building of huge apartments served by the Ritz. The *décor* was Japanese, tables ranged under pagodalike awnings along a winding, rock-strewn stream with tiny islands, gold fish darted through the water, and bird cages hung from trees. The whole effect was one of exquisite charm.

But Mr. Goelet felt we needed still another eating place, for evening dinners in summer. And again, Mr. Warren found an answer; this time he arranged a Roof Garden Restaurant in the space which opened off the fourth floor over the newly completed ballroom addition. No high buildings interfered, there were only private houses on the side streets off Madison Avenue. When they did rear up and overshadow our Roof Garden, we closed it.

I worked directly with Mr. Albert Keller, the general manager who eventually followed Mr. Duncan Harris as president of the Ritz-Carlton, and I considered myself very fortunate. Trained by César Ritz himself, Mr. Keller had already made a reputation as a manager and as an international gourmet before coming to this country. To me, who knew the Paris and London hotels so well, he had the genuine Ritz touch. The guests loved his graciousness, and the employees were devoted to him. A typical gesture was the one he made when he received the *Légion d'honneur* decoration for the contribution he had made to French culinary art. He ordered case upon case of champagne sent to the kitchen and then came down and treated everyone right down to the Senegalese who mopped the floors—at least a hundred chefs and other help.

The food served at the Ritz, and that has been my responsibility, has always been of prime importance. Mr. Goelet, Mr. Harris, and Mr. Keller each made it very clear to me that our cuisine could not be second to any in the world. And they all enjoyed a world-wide experience in fine food. Money was no object; leave it to the wine cellar to show the profit—or to the rooms. I was even scolded once by Mr. Harris for making too much money on the kitchen. He thought I was not giving the guests the best that the market offered. I had to convince him that efficient management and elimination of waste could be the cause of profit. When I showed the Board of Directors that it was impossible to serve the perfect meals of a Ritz cuisine in a Roof Garden five flights from the kitchen and on the other side of the building, they never questioned it but gave me a free hand to plan and equip a kitchen near the Garden to take care of dishes that must be cooked immediately before being served and must be brought to the table without any delay.

Our food facilities were as complete as we could make them. Many were unusual. For example, we bought green coffee, roasted it daily, and ground it before each meal. The blend was decided on by coffee connoisseurs—twelve pounds of Maracaibo, eighteen of Mocha, and thirty of Java. I recall Frank Munsey, who was most particular about coffee, saying that there was no cup of coffee so good as ours no matter where he went.

We made the finest chocolates and bonbons in our own confectionery kitchen and packed them in very beautiful imported boxes. None of them was for sale, however, but were gifts for our guests. Everyone living in the hotel received a beautiful box on Christmas morning—unless Mr. Keller knew that a jar of Strasbourg *pâté de foie gras* would be preferred. Every lady in the dining room was given a box on the opening night of the Horse Show, and it was specially designed for the occasion, sometimes in the shape of a horseshoe.

We had a *chef charcutier* in charge of making all the pork sausages, headcheese, *pâtés* and so on that we used for *hors-d'oeuvre*. The ice-cream plant was large enough to take care of freezing many differently flavored ice creams and all the special frozen desserts, sometimes thousands of individual molds, and also included equipment for making the large decorative forms of ice that are lighted up and displayed at banquets. Smaller forms were made daily because we always served melon in a molded piece of ice.

There was a tank for keeping fish, especially trout, so fresh that they could literally jump from water to stove. And an oyster bar was set up in the kitchen to take care of guests who were oyster fanciers and liked to eat them the instant they were opened—and keep on eating them, too, beyond the usual mere six. Every evening there was a group of *bons vivants* in evening clothes, tails and high hats, crowding around the oyster bar.

When the Volstead Act sneaked onto the scene, it didn't take long, however, for the trend to start away from fine cooking and gracious dining. Who is interested in the nuances of flavors if the palate has been dulled with bathtub gin? Or why should restaurants vie with each other to attract gourmets when everyone was being taken in by speak-easies? The Ritz-Carlton was more fortunate than many places because our guests continued to travel abroad and so kept the spark of the *haute cuisine* alive in this country. But fine cooking slipped badly during Prohibition, mainly because the dining room was suddenly on its own and had to make a profit. No longer could the kitchen count on the bar and the wine cellar to supplement its earning. The lush years up to 1929 were able to carry us through this difficult period because people had so much money to spend, but when the crash came, even we found it rough going until Repeal gave us a new lease. Again the Ritz-Carlton was more fortunate than many hotels in having most of its older men, who had come originally from the Ritz Hotels of Paris and London, still on hand to help restore the old standards. Dozens of my chefs had never worked anywhere else. Even now I have a *chef boucher,* Henri Baritaud, who has been with me since the opening, and a first assistant, Louis Magnin, who has seen thirty-eight years in our kitchens.

The pride that men of this type have in their work and in maintaining the Ritz tradition of perfection is not found too often in this day and age. For instance, last year during the shad season I was showing the kitchens to a guest who became intrigued watching the fish chef bone a shad, a very complicated boning job which he can do in almost the twinkling of an eye. "Do you ever leave a bone in?" she asked. He looked horrified when he replied, "Then I would no longer work at the Ritz, madame."

The changes, when watched from day to day, are almost imperceptible. But when I compare the meals of 1910 and 1911 with those of 1950, the difference is startling. It's many a year since we have served one meal of sixteen courses. Our kitchens were then staffed with one hundred twenty to one hundred fifty chefs and helpers to take care of the dining rooms and prepare the banquets, even when we had a fifteen- or sixteen-hour day and a seven-day week. Long and hard ones, too. I recall that the chef who made the *blinis à la Russe* for that opening dinner in 1910 fainted from the fatigue and heat of standing over the range turning out almost two thousand *blinis.*

But maybe some of the changes are for the better. Our chefs no longer work until they faint. One of the first suggestions I made to Mr. Keller was to reduce the hours of work and the days per week for the help in our kitchens; I believe that the Ritz was the first of the New York hotels to do this. The trend toward simpler eating during recent years is undoubtedly a good thing, too. But mind you, by simpler I do not mean indifferent or hurried eating, with which I have no patience. Certainly fewer of our guests make the yearly trek to the spas of Europe for the gout cure, however, and fewer have trouble with their waistlines.

The mementos of four decades seem endless: books of recipes, many of which came with me on the old "Amerika" in October, 1910; stacks of menus—the records of banquets given either by or for royalty, diplomats, financiers, singers, actors, and actresses; letters of appreciation from plain John Doe and society leaders; an old box that held cigars that "even the Kaiser (a great cigar connoisseur) couldn't buy," given me long ago by a well-known ambassador; a valuable sapphire stickpin from Mr. Harris. Some will be saved, many tossed out. But remaining forever will be my memory of the skills of the hands and the lore of a great cuisine gained from forty years at the Ritz.

Of all the Ritz *spécialités* that I have originated, it seems to me *vichyssoise* was really the one that most thoroughly captured the fancy of Americans from coast to coast. But there have been many others which were equally popular with our own guests. Filet of sea bass Pershing, for example, has been a favorite ever since it was first served at the banquet given at the Ritz for General Pershing after World War I. And one of my favorite chicken dishes has been *poulet sauté Gloria Swanson,* which I concocted especially for the well-known actress and which I prepared for her recently on her television program.

FILET OF SEA BASS PERSHING

Spread 1½ tablespoons butter in a shallow pan and sprinkle over it 3 shallots, finely chopped, and 1 teaspoon finely chopped parsley. Season 6 filets of sea bass with salt and a little white pepper and arrange them in the pan. Add about ⅓ cup white wine and 1 cup fish stock. Bring to a boil, cover the pan, and simmer slowly for 10 to 12 minutes. Add 12 oysters and cook for 2 or 3 minutes. Remove the filets and oysters to a heated serving dish and put with them 12 cooked shrimp and 12 cooked mushrooms. Arrange small cooked potato balls around the fish.

Cook the liquid remaining in the pan until it is reduced to about ½ its original quantity. Thicken it with 3 tablespoons cream sauce and add 1½ tablespoons butter. When the butter is just melted, fold in 3 tablespoons cream, whipped. Correct the seasoning and pour the sauce over the fish and its *garniture* of oysters, shrimp, and mushrooms. Set under a hot broiler flame until golden-brown.

POULET SAUTÉ GLORIA SWANSON

Cut 2 young chickens, each weighing about 2½ to 3 pounds, into pieces for frying. Season the chicken with salt and a little white pepper. Melt 2 tablespoons butter in a shallow pan and cook the chicken in it until it begins to turn golden-brown. Add 12 mushrooms, cleaned and peeled, and cook for another 5 minutes. Add 2 shallots or ¼ onion, finely chopped, to the fat in the pan and sprinkle in 1 tablespoon flour. Add ½ cup white wine and a faggot made by tying together 1 stalk of celery, 2 sprigs of parsley, a small piece of bay leaf, and a little thyme. Cover the pan partially and cook slowly for 30 to 35 minutes, or until the chicken is done. Discard the faggot.

Mix 1 egg yolk with ¼ cup cream and add to this some of the liquid from the pan, combining it gradually. Turn off the heat under the chicken and carefully pour the egg yolk–cream mixture into the pan liquid, blending it by shaking and rotating the pan. Correct the seasoning with salt. Arrange the chicken on a heated platter and pour the sauce over.

While the chicken is cooking, prepare the following garnish: Pack cooked rice in 6 demitasse cups to make attractive molds. Sauté 6 peeled tomato halves in butter. Alternate the rice molds and the tomato halves around the chicken. Place a slice of truffle on each rice mold and put a little sauce and some chopped parsley on each tomato.

Coeur flottant à la Ritz has probably been served at more famous Ritz dinners than any other dessert. It is a praline-flavored mousse served with a vanilla sauce and decorated with chocolate leaves. We had hundreds of the heart-shaped forms in which it was molded, and these were frozen in ice and salt. It can be frozen, although less successfully, in the freezing unit of an automatic refrigerator.

COEUR FLOTTANT À LA RITZ

To make a *pâté à bombe*, combine in the top of a double boiler 5 egg yolks, a piece of vanilla bean, and a syrup made by cooking 3 cups sugar and 1½ cups water for 7 minutes. Cook over simmering water until the batter becomes lukewarm, beating it with a whip all the time. Remove from the hot water and continue beating it until cool. Remove the vanilla bean. Chill the batter and add ½ cup almond praline (see below). Fold in 2 cups cream, whipped, to make the mousse.

Soak a few dice of spongecake in any liqueur and put in the center of a heart-shaped mold or individual molds. Fill with the mousse and place in the freezing unit of the refrigerator.

When ready to serve, invert the mousse on a serving dish and surround with vanilla sauce combined with a few pieces of fruit. Scatter chocolate leaves and trimmings around. The whole dish then may be masked in spun sugar.

Almond Praline

Mix equal quantities of blanched almonds and sugar in a very heavy frying pan and add a few drops of vanilla extract. Cook until it becomes well caramelized, stirring all the time. Turn the praline out on a buttered marble slab or into a cold heavy pan to cool. Chop it for garnishing or crush for mixing with ice cream and mousses.

January 1951

Dandelion Wine

Ray Bradbury

On this one special afternoon in the great oasis of summer, the dandelions flooded the world, dripped off lawns into brick streets, tapped softly at crystal cellar windows, blew and agitated themselves so that on every side lay this green lake, dazzling and glittering with molten sun.

The boys picked the golden flowers.

"I encourage them," Grandfather said. "For two weeks at the very heart of summer, the lawn mower is banished. Let the dandelions *run,* I say! Run amuck, like a herd of African lions in the yard. A beautiful flower. So common, however, that we have forgotten how beautiful it is. Why, look right at it and it'll burn a hole in your eye."

Plucked tenderly, one by one, the dandelions, in sacks, pots, and pans, were carried to the cellar. In great buckets of sunshine they arrived. The cellar glowed with them.

The wine press opened. A golden bushel of flowers poured in. The press, replaced with the large rotating screw, personally twirled and twisted by Grandfather, gently squeezed upon the harvest. "There," he murmured. "So."

And before long, the golden tide, the essence of wild summer, of the good fair months, trickled and then ran and then rushed from the spout below. A clear essence like a breath of July, the color of stars on August nights gathered to be crocked and waited on, to be worked, to be skimmed of ferment, to be bottled in crystal and cut glass and shelved and ranked in glittering rows in cellar gloom.

Dandelion wine.

The words were summer on the tongue. The wine was summer in a bottle. It was all the warm afternoons and the cloudless skies, stoppered tight; to be opened, said the label, on a January day with snow falling fast. To be drunk, was the intimation, when the sun had gone unseen in thirty-nine days. Then let those who seek after summer tiptoe with stealth into the dim twilight nether world of the cellar and put up a hand.

There row upon row, with the soft gleam of flowers open at morning, with the light of a June sun glowing through a faint skin of dust, lies the dandelion wine. Uncork it, hold it up, peer through it at the wintry day. The snow is melted to grass, the trees are reinhabited with bird, leaf, and blossom, like a continent of butterflies breathing on the air. The sky is colored from gray to blue. Take a great sniff of the wine and change the season in your veins by the simple expedient of raising the glass to your lips and tilting summer in.

"All right, now, to the rain barrel!"

Nothing else in the world would do but the rare waters which had been summoned from the sweet lakes far away and the sweet fields of grassy dew on early mornings, lifted to the open sky, carried in laundered clusters nine hundred miles, brushed with wind, electrified with high voltage, and condensed upon cool air. This water, falling through space, gathered still more of the heavens in its crystals. Taking something of the east wind and the west wind and the north wind and the south, the water made rain and the rain would soon be well on its way to wine.

Douglas ran with the dipper. He plunged it deep in the rain barrel. This water must be carried in dipper and bucket down to the cellar, there to be ladled in freshets, in mountain streams, upon the dandelion harvest.

Even Grandma, when snow was whirling fast, dizzying the world, blinding windows, stealing breath from gasping mouths, even Grandma, one day in February, would vanish to the cellar.

Above, in the vast house, there would be coughings, sneezings, wheezings, and groans, childish fevers, throats raw as butcher's meat, noses like bottled cherries, the stealthy microbe everywhere.

Then, rising from the cellar like a June goddess, Grandma would come, something hidden but obvious under her knitted shawl. This, carried to every miserable room upstairs and down, would be dispensed with aroma and clarity into neat glasses, to be swigged neatly. The medicines of another time, the balm of sun and idle August afternoons, a wind from the Hebrides, the faintly heard sounds of ice wagons passing on brick avenues, the rush of silver skyrockets and the fountaining of lawn mowers moving through ant countries, all these, all these in a glass.

Yes, even Grandma, drawn to the cellar of winter for a June adventure, to stand alone and quietly, in secret conclave with her own soul and spirit, as did Grandfather and Father and Uncle Bert, or some of the boarders, communing with a last touch of a calendar long departed, with the picnics and the warm rains and the smell of fields of wheat and new popcorn and bending hay. Even Grandma, repeating and repeating the fine and golden words, even as they were said now in this moment when the flowers were dropped into the press, as they would be repeated every winter for all the winters in time. Saying them over and over on the lips, like a smile, like a sudden patch of sunlight in the dark.

Dandelion wine. Dandelion wine. Dandelion wine.

June 1953

The Fly Is Cast

A. J. McClane

When people ask me why I like to fish, they are, in effect, asking a man why he enjoys breathing, when he really has no choice but to wonder at the fact of it.

I could tell them how April begins the season on a trout stream. The May flies break from the dull folds of their nymphal robes and flutter over the water, dancing on finely etched wings, while clumsy caddis flies flop mothlike among their more delicate cousins. As the white lamp of spring approaches, the trout roll faster. The audible ripple of their steady rising counterpoints the drumming of a partridge, the vibrant eye-opening call of a whippoorwill, and the toneless growl of current beating against rock.

And there, balanced in air-clear water, is the fish you came for, a great heavy-mouthed brown trout who takes each May fly in quick turns, marking the surface with flicks of his tail. You have one, or possibly two, casts to make and the game will be over. If the fish is an experienced rogue who has been worked in days and years past, the taking of him is a sequence of movements as stylized as the art of fencing. The final turn of your wrist must place the line softly on the river, for the slightest splash or shadow would send him dashing for cover; the nearly invisible leader must swing the floating fly around and within a few inches of the trout without a hint of artifice. The trout sees the feathers as a wavering, blurred image and pin points of light: the same delicate impressions made by the legs of a May fly reach his lidless eyes. To bring him up in an exploding rise and know his silver-strong leaps would seemingly be the end of angling, and all that could be said. Yet I know that catching fish is but a small part of why I am an angler.

There are tidal marks in the development of an angler. In the beginning, when one is very young and inexperienced, fish are measured in quantity. After a while, only size and quality are important. Then even record fish lose their significance unless they are of a particular species, and ultimately the size doesn't matter, provided the species is difficult to catch. The difficulty is created in two ways—by using the lightest possible tackle or by fishing the places that are natural cul-de-sacs. When we fished the Andelle River, a French chalk stream, the trout generally weighed about a pound, but they were the most demanding kind. Chalk-stream water is diamond smooth, and the fish instantly vanish under the cress beds at the shadow of a passing bird or the glint of sun against a rod. You must work with a cobweb-thin leader and have enough control to drop your fly in a teacup at seventy feet. Bedell Smith once took a two-and-a-half-pound trout there during the May-fly season, and even now, when we talk about the old days, we speak of that fish reverently.

Each April, Albert Godard would come down from Belgium and old Dr. Tixier would come from Paris, and some of the best casters from England and America would come also, to stay at the little farmhouse below the convent and test themselves against the Andelle trout. Godard worked like a sensitive artist on canvas, feeling the effect of each stroke against his hand. He could cast a gossamer silk line to a hundred and thirty-five feet—a talent that once earned him a great deal of money as a demonstrator on royal rivers. Tixier, crooked forefinger braced along the rod grip, could put a dry fly on quick-rising trout before they turned downward. Seventy years of casting have greatly enlarged the joint and knuckle on his finger. But the man I enjoyed watching most was Charles Ritz. If the wind shifted, he could change hands in the middle of a long cast without losing line speed. This is comparable to a pitcher following through by throwing a fast ball with his left hand after putting his weight into the beginning of a fast right-hand delivery.

We never caught many trout on the Andelle; I think my best day after the May-fly season was the one when I caught five fish. That is what makes it a classic river. I often wonder if there was more talent on the river or around the old wood stove. We had simple meals, but perfect ones—*écrevisses à la crème, truite au bleu,* or *matelote à la normande,* and a young wine from a nearby *auberge.* All the emotional dividends are not measured in the Andelle logbook. Even now, the breath of drying waders hung from the rafters comes back like the wool smell of comrades in war.

Sitting around the wooden table after dinner, we would listen to Pierre Coulin tell about the old days and how impossible the trout were around Saint-Malo. I could only remember Saint-Malo the way it looked in the summer of 1944, but Pierre saw crumbling thatched-roof mills hidden behind chestnut and beech trees and limpid waters running among irises and water lilies. The trout rose in tricky places along the plants and between pockets of water cress. Pierre claimed that you had to use midge hooks for consistent fishing, which is like shooting elephants with an air rifle. He would tell us fascinating stories of the local history; this was his Brittany, *ses châtaignes, son cidre doux.*

And there was Jean Pollet, always with the cold stub of a Gauloise stuck to his lower lip, who measured his days against some very difficult trout in Corsica. In the early twenties, you could take a steamer from Marseille to Ajaccio and go by rail to the Gravona, the Travo, and the Golo. The Golo flows through a granite gorge known as the Scala della Regina, and in the bottom of the gorge where the sunshine never reached, one could catch small black trout—important for no other reason than that they had survived centuries of poaching and had become flighty bundles of conditioned reflexes.

The anomaly of angling was embodied at the Andelle table. More than forty world records and a million fish taken in waters around the globe were represented. Yet over coffee and brandy, no one ever mentioned the size of his fish, except perhaps as an incidental piece of information.

People often ask me about the biggest fish I ever caught, and I answer them the way they want me to. I tell them about the marlin I caught that weighed five hundred and sixty pounds and taped twelve feet long. Yet subconsciously I find myself measuring him from the brows of white marble clouds down to the sandy floor of the Gulf Stream plain. Figures mean little when you have worked for a month to raise one blue marlin, and then perhaps didn't take him or he got bill-wrapped or gut-hooked and you had to start all over again. Even in season the fish is not abundant; in the south equatorial current you can raise five blues in one day, but few people have fished there. It is easier to work from Bimini or Havana or San Juan before the sea turns to molten glass and the winds ki-yi north from Trinidad like the flailing of a crazy broom.

During April in the Islands, the morning calm turns sullen; a jet-black cloud passes low on the horizon, and the wind blows scud over the sea. There is an hour when you can't keep your bait on the water. The deck heaves, and under the outriggers, as you look back toward El Yunque, a silver rain spout spins menacingly at Morro Castle. The hull creaks as the ship strains to the wind, and over the hot cough of the engine the frigate birds scream. They tell of marlin down below. The ship lurches over the choppy sea with her screws biting air as you make the half-circle to bait the fish and take a following sea. You pitch and feel the bow fall when the engine slows to trolling speed. The baits bounce—*skitter flap, skitter flap*—and the exhaust sucks through the cockpit until you come about at full throttle, throwing a white rooster tail across the horizon.

Three times you pass the marlin and three times you check the drag. Then, with a sound like the snap of a pistol shot, white linen whips from your port outrigger and for one long minute the reel spool is a whizzing blur. Back you strike, five, six, seven times, and out comes the marlin in the ageless walking leap that thrills every marlin fisherman. The mate clears the flat lines and the starboard outrigger and you are left to subdue a quarter ton of shoulder-rocking fury. If you do the job right, the skipper weaves back through the island rigs coming from the harbor with a pennant fluttering overhead, while the beer and sweaters are passed topside. You can almost taste that first Planter's Punch and the big red *langosta* swimming in melted butter. Afterward there will be steaks from a baby hawksbill turtle or from a young green turtle weighing about thirty-five pounds.

To the angler, geography is an inexhaustible subject with remote beginnings and no definitive end. There is a sense of continuity in finding that the Beaverkill flows to the East Branch, the East joins the West Branch to form the Big Delaware; the Madison, Jefferson, and Gallatin meet to form the Missouri; the Snake and Deschutes flow to the Columbia. Through deserts and mountains the rivers course like the veins in the hand of a man who has gripped a rod all his life. There is a deep sense of movement. New Brunswick salmon have been caught in Norway and Irish salmon in Greenland; albacore travel from Japan to California; giant tuna pass the coast of South America and turn north into their great circle, edging Cuba to reach Nova Scotia. Through all the world men follow fish in their seasons.

I could tell the people who ask me why I like to fish how it used to be when I was a boy, how toward the end of summer the river pools shrank and how the enamel-finned brook trout pushed against the whispering current, seeking the icy water of the spring at the head of our brook. The big-eyed parr sucked at frail waltzing midges, the bees' humming became soft as they worked to cool their hives, and the hot night air fell silent. The cows abandoned their dry pasture to wander up the coarse bottom land, grubbing pye weed out of the damp parts of the stream bed. And then one morning, when the earth seemed a furnace, a strong wind sent dry limbs clattering one against the other and the gentle wet hand of rain rubbed life into our valley and flooded the barren brook bed. Far above the reawakening valley there was an eagle on the wind who saw beyond the saber-edged rim of our horizon, but he spiraled out of sight. Trout appeared again one by one and gave the water life.

These are some of the reasons that fishing is as much a part of my life as breathing.

April 1958

The Garlic War

E. Annie Proulx

Sometime back in the early thirties my uncle Hubert finished his internship at one of the smaller hospitals in Poughkeepsie, New York, took a pretty young wife, Sophia, and set up practice in his mother-in-law's rambling house on Garvin Street. His mother-in-law, whom everybody called Auntie Bella, was a formidable woman. She was, in the first place, large—not merely plump, not fat only, but tall, large-boned, and heavy-fleshed. She had a booming bass voice with which she sounded all her opinions to anyone who would listen. If no one would, she told her marvelous tales of the evil eye and of the time her cousin Giuseppe was robbed by bandits to the four cats who were constantly stalking in and out of the kitchen. The cats were swollen with pride and with tasty tidbits that Auntie Bella was always feeding them—a little dab of chicken cooked in a red sauce, for instance. "Here, Cat...good, no?" And the cat would purr, gobble down the last shred, and stare greedily into the empty dish.

The cats were not the only fortunate ones to taste Auntie Bella's savory sauces and delicate pasties. All day long she urged cups of steaming minestrone on the mailman, tortoni on the milkman, a golden slice of sweet bread, *pandoro di Verona,* on the grocery delivery boy, little anise cookies on any child within hailing range. And when mealtime finally arrived, the table, far from being diminished by her generous taste-givings, was laden with so many steaming, fragrant dishes that we could heap out oversized plates full and still not have sampled everything that was on the table.

Uncle Hubert was a spare eater, and the sight of those groaning tables thrice daily made him uneasy. In the days when he was courting Sophia, Auntie Bella urged the streaming dishes on him; he would take only a tiny portion, and she would snatch the ladle from his reluctant hand and heap his plate ever higher, until the lake of spaghetti sauce threatened to overflow onto the snowy tablecloth. But Uncle Hubert was a stubborn man, and he lectured Auntie Bella on the dangers of overeating, and the strain on the heart from excess weight. Auntie Bella thundered back at him the longevity tables of her entire family for three generations. She told him all her relatives lived to be at least eighty-seven, and any one of the four huge meals a day that they ate made her table look like a snack for gnats. But Hubert ate only as much as he wanted and then sat quietly thinking of the day when he would be married to Sophia and be master in the house; the huge meals would certainly stop. Auntie Bella's thoughts ran along rather different lines. Daily she told the cats how she would fatten Hubert up when he and Sophia were married, and that once he fell under the spell of her rich cooking there would be an end to this quibbling over meals.

The day of the wedding came, and late that evening, as Hubert and his bride were leaving for Niagara Falls, he looked at his mother-in-law in a masterful manner and said, "When Sophia and I come back, we will eat simple, small meals, and there will be no rich sauces. And one thing more: there is never, never, *never* to be any garlic in my food. I have my patients to think of, and I can't go about reeking of garlic. So, *no garlic!*" And he glared sternly at Auntie Bella, who was standing slack-jawed at this traitorous speech.

The moment the door closed behind Hubert and Sophia, Auntie Bella melted into a river of laughter that sent the cats flying behind the velvet drapes. No garlic! Garlic was more often used in Auntie Bella's kitchen than salt—than water, even. To do without garlic? Impossible! Impossible and mad.

The great purple strings of fragrant garlic that festooned Auntie Bella's kitchen were more than seasoning and piquant touches to otherwise dull sauces. Garlic was the mainstay, the rock upon which her cooking was founded. And then, too, any fool knew the other properties of garlic. Garlic was a sovereign remedy for all sorts of ailments: garlic warded off the evil eye; garlic at the foot of the bed of a newly wedded couple ensured a son for the firstborn. With this thought Auntie Bella was off to tie garlic cloves to the springs of her new son-in-law's marriage bed. Underneath so he wouldn't see them.

Two weeks later Hubert and Sophia were back. Hubert, after a hasty peck at the garlic-flavored cheek of his mother-in-law, went at once to his office where he arranged all the waiting-room chairs, hung a fresh sign in his window announcing visiting hours, and retired to his inner office to smoke a cigar and await the patients. Dusk was falling when Sophia came down and told him that dinner was ready. As they started up the stairway toward the living quarters, the fragrant aroma of garlic smote Hubert's nostrils, and his eyes flashed wildly for a moment, but he drew a deep breath and went into the dining room. The table was loaded more than usual, for was this not a homecoming feast? Platters of fried zucchini, spinach pie, ravioli, pompano, and *garmugia* (a beef stew) crowded each other. Huge bowls of eggplant with Parmesan cheese, red spaghetti sauce, white clam sauce, and shrimp *buongusto* sent up a heavy mist of steam. And over the table like a palpable cloud hung the heavy, pervasive aroma of garlic. Auntie Bella had outdone herself. Hubert took several shallow breaths and abruptly excused himself. The front door quivered as it slammed, and Sophia burst into tears. Auntie Bella sat her daughter down at the table, filled her plate, and commanded her to eat, but Sophia cried salty tears into the zucchini for ten minutes.

Then they both heard the door downstairs open and close. Footsteps came up the stairway. Hubert appeared in the doorway, slightly flushed and bearing in his hand a limp white package wrapped in butcher's paper. He went directly to the kitchen, found a frying pan, and brought it to Auntie Bella. "I will have these two chops cooked without garlic, if you please." Muttering, Auntie Bella cooked the chops, spitefully burning one of them on the edge, but Uncle Hubert ate them with relish and recommended them to his two dining companions. Aside from the crunching of chop bones and the salty plop of tears into the zucchini, dinner was a silent affair, for Auntie Bella sat deep in thought, plotting. The idea of garlicless meals filled her with a despair that soon gave way to the urge to battle. Waving an invisible banner painted with garlic cloves, she decided on a daring plan.

The next evening found the table lean and spare with two lonely chops adorning each of the three plates. In the center of the table, as a concession to a possible ravenous appetite, nine tomato slices lay on a gigantic white platter. Uncle Hubert bolted his chops down, ate one tomato slice, rose, bowed to the ladies, and excused himself from the table. As he left the room, he kissed Auntie Bella's cheek and murmured, "Very good dinner, Mother." Again Sophia burst into tears, and then, obviously emotionally upset from hunger, she bolted the remaining eight tomato slices and rushed out of the room. The next night the same dinner appeared, and the next, and the next. For three weeks the chops came to the table accompanied by the nine lonely tomato slices; for Sunday dinner there were twelve tomato slices.

As the flow of wonderful samples and mouth-watering tidbits stopped, so did the long kitchen visits from the mailman, the delivery boys, and the neighborhood children, who all sagged from wistful hope to mournful resignation as the weeks went by. Auntie Bella and Sophia grew as thin and sallow and nervous as the now-lean cats. Uncle Hubert remained as hearty as ever, and if he ever tired of lamb chops and tomato slices, he never said a word.

But as the fourth week began Auntie Bella's watchful eye detected a look of desperation on Hubert's face as she brought in the eternal platter of chops. Quickly, that afternoon, she went to the kitchen and locked the door. Then she took one of the forbidden garlic cloves from under the sink, their home of exile, carefully peeled it, and sliced off a tiny quarter, which she dropped into a cup of water. She let the garlic sliver sit in the water for a scant five minutes. Then she removed the pearly little fragment and tossed it to the cats. It was snatched up by Measles, who crunched it with pleasure and fell into a purring fit.

That evening Auntie Bella broiled six mushroom caps to arrange on the platter beside the tomato slices. In the privacy of her kitchen she brushed the caps with the garlic water several times, then dotted them with butter, and put them to broil. The chops received a drop or two of the garlic water, but the tomatoes were left unseasoned.

Uncle Hubert came into the dining room, somewhat reluctantly, but when he saw the mushroom caps a broad smile shone from his face, and he rubbed his hands in anticipation. "Well, well! A special treat, eh, Mother?" he boomed, genuinely pleased.

Uncle Hubert ate all six of the mushroom caps, remarking loudly on their extreme tastiness, succulence, and remarkable flavor. He finished his chops in jig time and cast his glance around the table as though looking for more. When his eye fell on the tomato slices, however, he rose from his chair and excused himself.

That night Auntie Bella received two kisses from her son-in-law. She smiled grimly. The plan was working. For three nights the mushroom cap tactic was repeated. Then, on Saturday at noon, she soaked half a clove of garlic in melted butter for twenty seconds. Next she injected the faintly garlicky butter into four plump baked potatoes, which accompanied the mushroom caps and the tomatoes. The chops were skillfully created in a like manner.

Uncle Hubert fairly fell upon the baked potatoes. He became expansive after the third one had disappeared and his vest was bulging comfortably. "Those were the finest potatoes I have ever tasted, I want you to know. There was something to the flavor ..." Words failed him. "Something familiar, but I can't quite put my finger on it. Mother, you're turning into a wonderful cook!" Having delivered this high accolade, Uncle Hubert speared the last potato and fell to.

Daily Auntie Bella increased the garlic dose, slipping it slyly into a green salad, smuggling a tiny pinch into a creamy tomato soup, swinging a clove of garlic on a string through a simmering sauce, and Uncle Hubert's appetite increased with the garlic dosage. He began to come to the dining room half an hour before dinner, and he would twiddle with his water glass and wonder impatiently when the food would be ready. His vests began to strain tightly across his stomach, and he occasionally told amusing stories to his mother-in-law and wife.

Auntie Bella worked with infinite caution. Never once in six months was the garlic flavor so strong that anyone possessing even the most delicate palate could announce triumphantly, "You've put garlic into this!" Just the subtlest hint, the faintest fragrance, the merest whiff, the tiniest sliver came from the kitchen. The plump garlic bulbs themselves still remained hidden under the sink, and Auntie Bella's garlic patch flourished unnoticed in the flower garden behind a thick forest of purposely neglected rambler roses. She gathered her harvests in the moonlight under the pretense of "taking a little walk."

After nearly a year of painstaking care, Auntie Bella's cooking was nearly up to the old pre-Hubert garlic standards, and the garlic bulbs themselves came out from under the sink and hung once again from the beams, sending a faint but constant reminder of their existence throughout the kitchen.

Uncle Hubert, who was not stupid and who had learned to love his meals and his mother-in-law's robust cooking, noticed them swinging gently from the beams one winter evening and remarked, "Mother, those garlic bulbs give a very quaint, old-fashioned touch to the kitchen, but watch out they don't come in contact with any of my dinner!" And he laughed uproariously and winked.

Finally Auntie Bella was quite happy because she knew the garlic had made a stubborn, bad-tempered man into a genial, good-natured one. And then, too, Sophia had given birth to twin boys almost exactly a year after the marriage—something Auntie Bella attributed solely to the garlic clusters dangling in the bedsprings. And Uncle Hubert's practice grew fat, as did he. He was constantly immersed in a mild effluvium of garlic vapors. His examinations and advice to his patients left them gasping a bit, but lonely for that little extra something they couldn't quite identify as they sat over their flavorless chops that evening.

February 1964

Cocktail Parties of the Twenties

Anita Loos

New York City provides the cosiest setting in the world for cocktail parties. It is not only the world's smallest big city, but the swinging New Yorker occupies that fairly limited area of it called Manhattan. Few citizens of any other borough ever find their way into a chic New York cocktail party. It is almost unthinkable to import a guest from Yonkers, the Bronx, or even Brooklyn. Whereas this might result in monotony, at the same time it makes for very fast communication.

The above statements were just as true in the twenties as they are today, but in the twenties a hostess had a more vital force of celebrities on which to draw. An average guest list might include Scott and Zelda Fitzgerald, who would always compete with each other in bloodcurdling misbehavior; if Scott was inspired to climb out on a high window ledge, Zelda could always find some excuse to take off her clothes, thus diverting attention from her husband. For in those days it was quite uncommon to be bare in public.

Then there was H. L. Mencken, whose behavior might be impeccable, but whose vocabulary exploded with scurrilous terms of his own manufacture. One subject on which Mencken held forth bitterly was the "boob mentality" of our South; he designated the state of Arkansas as "the Sahara of the Bozarts" (meaning Beaux Arts). It was at a cocktail party that Menck gave me the idea of choosing Little Rock as the proper birthplace for the idiotic blonde whose story I was writing. George Jean Nathan, the theater critic, always provided something dramatic in the way of a flapper; the fact that George was smallish required her to be smaller; she might be an Oriental. Sometimes he brought Florence Mills from Harlem. Frequently another famous George showed up and took to the piano, and we would find ourselves listening to Florence Mills sing Gershwin accompanied by Georgie himself, which was a carnival for the ears such as seldom occurs at cocktail parties anymore.

No party got into full swing until Tallulah arrived to put her particular type of zizz into it. She was always courteous to the unassuming but her gravel-voiced bitchiness would be unleashed without mercy on someone like Zelda who was foolish enough to lay herself open. One time, as an excuse for undressing, Zelda pouted, "Oh dear, my slip is showing!" "You mean your show is slipping, don't you darling?" barked Tallulah.

Another asset to any party was Tallulah's brunette sister, Jean [Eugenia], who had a *beauté du diable* that caused even more havoc among the males than the classic features of Tallulah. Jean was as irresponsible as any hippie, but with one big difference: Her behavior resulted in action instead of apathy. Jean could bring out a man's most violent behavior patterns. On one occasion a young suitor jumped off a pier in an effort to swim after the *Ile de France*, which was bearing Jean across the sea. Jean's swain didn't get very far, but he did get sober.

Every proper guest list of the twenties included the publisher Horace Liveright. Although his catalog listed all the best-selling authors in America, Horace's most cherished asset was a little black book with the most comprehensive list of telephone numbers in New York. Horace's associate publisher, Tommy Smith, made the scene of every cocktail party, from sundown to sunup. Looking like a youthful Mr. Magoo, Tommy always seemed to be half asleep, but he never went to bed. He was on intimate terms with everyone from Texas Guinan on up to Mrs. August Belmont. Toddling about Manhattan, he wove a connecting web that made us all understand and appreciate each other. Although not involved romantically with girls, Tommy was a storehouse of comfort; other men might get us into trouble, but Tommy then took over and straightened things out. He could provide solace for any girl's indiscretions and at the same time take responsibility off the shoulders of a seducer, allowing both of them to go on, carefree, to any further misconduct.

Every cocktail party boasted oodles and oodles of flappers and equal oodles of college men down from Harvard and Yale or up from Princeton, all of them available for marriage. I can remember only one fashion designer who ever got asked around. His name was Nate Clark and he provided a definite allure to New York's indoor scenery. Nate felt a responsibility toward his clientele that no longer exists. His creations added to a girl's charm instead of taking it away, and he strove to disguise our bad points instead of showing them up.

The conversation at a twenties cocktail party was largely informative, and one departed with the inner tingle of taking away something worthwhile. The homemaker could learn new recipes for synthetic gin or the needling of near beer. Names and telephone numbers of reliable bootleggers were swapped, and one was informed of the password to use at Lüchow's in order to get the real beer that was smuggled in from Munich and served in teacups. There was information regarding the opening of any new speakeasy, such as the one run by Reine Davies, the elder sister of Marion, who held forth in an Eastside cellar that she called Reine Davies' Country Club.

The love affairs of those days were romantic instead of clinical. We hadn't yet heard of that old Viennese spoilsport Sigmund Freud. A chance encounter at any cocktail party might well develop into the love of a lifetime; it did in the case of blonde little Marion and the powerful Mr. Hearst. The Mayor of New York himself was having an idealistic relationship with a chorus cutie. She looked, talked, dressed, and deported herself exactly like thousands of other New York cuties, but Jimmy's feelings for her were strong enough to recompense for the loss of his career. A stock question at cocktail parties used to be, "What *is* it that Betty's got?" The answer to which was, "She's got His Honor!"

The fact that I can't remember the food served at those parties must mean that it was a minor part of the entertainment. Because of Prohibition, people's minds were naturally obsessed by drink, with gin occupying the place now held by vodka. However, I do remember the introduction of one sensational new libation. It had been invented in Florida, the discovery of the founding father of Palm Beach, Addison Mizner. It appeared that one day Addison, in the throes of a hangover, had an inspiration for something to replace the time-honored prairie oyster and he forthwith ordered his butler to serve him the juice of some tomatoes. The butler obeyed the barbaric order with distaste, little realizing that he was on the threshold of a discovery that would one day affect the mores of much of the civilized world.

At first tomato juice took no part in the early phases of a cocktail party, and only came into use the morning after when, spiked with Worcestershire sauce, cayenne, and any other counterirritant this side of ground glass, it would make one forget the agony of being rent asunder by bathtub gin. Then, however, some genius went to work on Addison's discovery, introduced tomato juice to gin, and gave it dignity as an integral element of the party itself. And thus was born the Bloody Mary.

One main difference between parties of the past and those of today is that the former were marked by an ambiance of great virility. As a rule this stemmed from the fact that a party inevitably ran out of liquor and the hostess had to send in a hurry for the nearest friendly bootlegger. He was welcome first of all as a lifesaver and then, being a man of important social connections, he frequently remained as a guest. Sometimes the liquor again ran low and he had to send for a confrere to bolster the supply. This situation might repeat itself over and over again until the most entrancing bevy of square-shooting male sexpots would recharge a party with enough electricity to make it go on for a week.

However, even this did not exhaust the supply of males who were brothers-under-the-skin of James Cagney and Humphrey Bogart. Complaints about the noise would eventually start up from neighborhood tenants. Then some would-be killjoy might call for the police. This brought in another body of men of a virility seldom encountered in the upper echelons of Park Avenue society. They might enter with a rather rough admonition of, "What do youse guys think you're up to anyhow?" This, however, was merely to alibi the fact that they were crashing. One look at Zelda Fitzgerald in the buff was all they needed to remain on as guests of honor. Aside from supplying the allure of sex, they contributed the warmth of a hearty comradeship between man and man. Some of the bootleggers and cops would already have met on an under-the-table business deal, so Moe, the bootlegger, and Mac, the cop, would greet each other with a gladiatorial embrace that gave their relationship the classic vigor of a Damon and Pythias.

Since no other entertainment in the twenties might conceivably vie with a cocktail party, no one was tempted to leave it; the cocktail party of today is more a place from which to escape. Seldom is an invitation to cocktails received with anything but a groan. Almost never does one hear the statement, "I just love a cocktail party!" Most of them are attended for some ignoble reason: to insinuate one's name or photo into the newspapers or to gain publicity for some venture, however devious. Then, too, the party provides an opportunity to steal a march on a competitor or wrest an asset away from its present holder. But of the impulsive cocktail party, given for good cheer and attended out of camaraderie, there scarcely remains a trace. Perhaps such events are now being held in the Bronx, Brooklyn, or Yonkers but, as a resident of Manhattan, I have no record of this fact.

When one looks at the cocktail parties of today, it is only to realize how far Cupid has scampered from Park Avenue. Most of our social relationships are no longer very sturdy; sad to report, gentlemen have begun to prefer gentlemen. Ladies no longer dress as an incentive to romance, but only to impress fashion editors and their kind. Romance has disappeared along with vitality and the shock value of sex. Of course, a diluted form of it can be found in the East Village, where intersexual hippies exchange mates without the least twinge of jealousy. But admitting that they attain Peace, may I also hint that it could merely come from being stoned on marijuana? I always think that the gift of a flower may make a girl feel very calm but a manly clip on the jaw denotes passion.

January 1970

A Harvest Dinner in Taos

Richard Clark Cassin

I've always had difficulty in deciding which season I prefer in the high alpine valleys of northern New Mexico, but in the end October almost always prevails: fresh snow above the timberline, a blaze of gilded aspens beneath, and a luxuriant carpet of summer's green grass.

The anticipation of winter is everywhere—the chill air, the heavy odor of piñon fires warming the small mud houses, and a sense of urgency on the part of both man and beast to make sound preparations for the long snowbound months to come. Wood must be cut and stored; elk and deer must be hunted, cleaned, dried or frozen, and stocked away; preserves of all kinds must be put up in sufficient quantities to fill hungry stomachs until April or May.

There are few, if any, jobs in these tiny villages, and many of the men have just returned home from the potato and sugar beet harvests in Colorado with a few hundred dollars earmarked for midwinter emergencies. Life in the high valleys of the Sangre de Cristo Mountains is, perhaps, the last stand of true subsistence farming and hunting left in the United States. Although all of the outward trappings of rural poverty are here at their worst, there is a certain depth in the life-style of these descendants of early Spanish colonists.

The village people of northern New Mexico are far too busy surviving to spend much time reflecting upon the hardships of their life. This is particularly true in October, when winter is beginning to breathe across the sierras. The time for sober reflection comes—if at all—when the snow is deep on the ground, and there is little else to do. More often, however, even these months are spent on chores that can be done indoors in front of the fireplace. A long winter will sometimes produce some poetry, and even a few *corridos* (ballads) eulogizing the events of the previous summer.

Children are conceived, and old men die. Close families become closer, and as the village turns in upon itself, renewing old ties and friendships, it becomes protective.

For the wayfarer, October offers eating opportunities not available at other times of the year. Opportunities, perhaps, to savor tastes and whiff odors that have been rising from the hearths of mestizo women in New Mexico for at least three centuries. Life in these valleys has changed little in that time, and food perhaps least of all.

It's a plentiful month: Whatever grows is harvested, still fresh, including the many wild herbs, spices, and plants in the forests and meadows of the high country. There are fresh elk or venison steaks on many tables, along with corn, turnips, beans, chili peppers, and a host of other homegrown or gathered-in-the-wild staples. The bread is fresh, and butter is often churned outside on the porch. Capulins (chokecherries) are gathered by the men in the high alpine meadows during the summer while grazing their cattle. The bittersweet fruit is then mixed with crab apples and wild rosebuds and processed over hot wood fires into delicious jams and jellies. *Empanaditas*—slices of fruit or berries wrapped in dough and deep-fried—are a frequent dessert. *Sopaipillas*—thin, square, hollow doughnuts—are served hot, baptized with honey.

My dinner invitation in Taos was not until six o'clock, so rather than drive the direct route north from Santa Fe, I thought that I would extend the trip by detouring through Las Vegas, New Mexico, up the Mora valley, and over the pass through Tres Ritos into Taos. This region bears a resemblance to Switzerland's Bernese Alps, with its narrow green valleys and lofty mountain peaks, but low adobe houses rather than chalets dot the countryside. The fields were thick with cattle recently brought down from the high country for sale or slaughter, and the air was cold with the ever present scent of burning piñon.

After winding through the mountains for almost sixty miles, State Road #3 descends into the broad expanse of Taos valley and empties into US 85 at the village of Ranchos de Taos. Almost as a matter of habit I let myself be sidetracked into the tiny plaza of Ranchos for a look at the old mission church. Dating from the early eighteenth century, the massive adobe structure has walls that are six feet thick in places. Recently restored with foundation money, it is one of the finest examples of mission architecture of the period. Among its numerous other antiquities and treasures the church houses a painting of Christ, whose eyes mysteriously follow you around the sanctuary. There is no escape from the gaze: I've tried many times. The twelve-year-old boy whose function is to explain the history of the church humbly requests a small donation to help sustain the place and is visibly enthralled with the nickel or dime that's dropped into the tin can at the entrance. This refreshing response to a small gift renews one's faith in many things, and keeps me coming back to drop nickels in the can.

Soon after turning off the main road onto the dirt track that led into my friend's little rancho just north of Taos village, I could see the bright red *ristras,* or strings, of chili peppers hanging to dry from the ends of the *vigas* (roof beams) that protrude through the thick adobe walls of their house. I knew that Eusabio had not received an elk permit this year (in New Mexico they're drawn by lot), but the reasonably fresh deer hide drying on the wall of the woodshed was an indication of what might be in store for dinner.

My friend Eusabio Jaramillo, his wife, Amalia, and their six children live in a sprawling adobe ranch house that they built themselves, adding a new room with the coming of "every other" child. Its *vigas* had been cut in the forest and left exposed. The floors were red brick, and there was a fireplace in the corner of every room. They had a good collection of modern appliances, but central heating was a luxury they had avoided.

Not having seen them for a couple of months, I was greeted with the usual screams of the children, a stout handshake from Eusabio, and a motherly *abrazo* from Amalia. Knowing how much I really appreciate her cooking, Amalia had gone all out to make those things that she knew I especially liked.

There was still a while before we'd be ready to eat, so the children were assigned to me for removal from the kitchen and from under their mother's feet. Meanwhile, Eusabio finished some chores outside, built a roaring fire on the hearth, and finally chased the children off to wash themselves while he and I had a drink of something that came from the woodshed and tasted remarkably like bourbon whiskey.

Each time I have the opportunity of eating with Eusabio and Amalia, or at the homes of other friends in one of the other mountain villages, I am impressed with the depth and complexity of this little-known regional American cuisine. Although the names of certain traditional dishes from Mexico are applied to some northern New Mexican items as well, the similarity stops there. Ingredients, spices, modes of preparation, and presentation are quite different. Along with Louisiana's Creole cookery, northern New Mexican cuisine is one of the few clearly distinct cooking systems native to the United States. Never have I enjoyed the home cooking of my New Mexican friends without discovering some new dish, or some new variation of one that I had already sampled. In the mountains they say that there are as many recipes for green chili stew as there are women in the villages to cook them. I'm certain this applies to most other dishes as well.

This particular Saturday evening meal was very special—much of the huge dinner was new to me. I had never tasted Amalia's pea chowder before. She cooked the peas in onion and garlic until they were done, rubbed them through a colander, thickened the purée with flour and butter, added milk, and seasoned the mixture with salt, sugar, and a local variety of *cilantro,* or fresh coriander.

After we finished the deliciously creamy soup Amalia served her *temole de chile verde con venado* (green chili stew with venison), accompanied by *chauquehue* instead of rice or potatoes. *Chauquehue* is an exceptionally thick corn gruel. For vegetables we had *quelites* (wild spinach that grows along stream bottoms) and *chimajá,* or wild celery. Both are seasoned with garlic and chili pepper pulp and boiled. The roots of the *chimajá* are prepared in this way, and the leaves are dried as a spice.

Amalia's masterpiece this time, however, was the roast leg of pork—*carne de marrano con chile*—which she placed in the middle of the table. It is cooked with *cilantro,* orégano (a local variety of wild marjoram is used), and black sage, which grows in the high country.

Throughout the meal—even after starting on the roast—I detected a strange but delicious taste that I thought might be the wild venison in the *temole,* but finally inquiring, I discovered that Amalia had added just a bit of *anís* (licorice) and some yerba buena (wild mint) to the stew.

My motive for eating a great deal was twofold: I was hungry, and I could think of no better way of flattering Amalia for her labors in creating a truly different and superb dinner.

Still, I had carefully left room for the typical two-course dessert. The first and most elaborate part was something that Amalia called *capirotada.* She had taken a large bowl of bread cubes, browned them in the oven, dipped them in egg batter, and then deep-fried them until they were crisp. After draining the cubes Amalia sprinkled them with a mixture of cinnamon, sugar, citron, and finely ground piñon nuts and coated them with a syrup of sugar, cream of tartar, cinnamon, and water.

With coffee—just boiled in an earthenware pot—we had an assortment of *biscochitos* (traditional sugar cookies) and *pastelitos* (fruit-filled pastries). When it comes to sweets children are undaunted in their appetites. Soon after dinner, when I was just beginning to breathe normally again, the eight-year-old appeared with a large clear jar filled with a great variety of Amalia's homemade candies: *melcocha* (molasses candy); *dulces de calabaza* (pumpkin candy); *dulces de piloncillo* (brown sugar candy); and many others. I went to bed that evening with a full stomach and an intensely secure feeling. I could hear a quietly crackling piñon log burning in the bedroom's corner fireplace.

Before I returned to Santa Fe the next day Eusabio and I walked around his fields, discussing his desire for a heavy snowfall and a good spring runoff, the amount of beef and venison stored for the winter, and the hope that Amalia would not get pregnant again. Total preoccupation with the very nuts and bolts of human existence itself. I felt a little ashamed of my own personal concerns.

Taos is unbelievably difficult to leave. It's hard to be sidetracked—the land and the human relationship to it dominate all life. Perhaps that's why D. H. Lawrence spent several of his most creative years here. Perhaps that's why Taos still attracts a host of artists, poets, writers, and others who try to rub some of that earth into their work.

Each season has its special quality for the outsider, and its special challenge for the *Taoseños,* depending to a considerable extent on who happens to be in Taos, or on the temperature or the depth of snow, or on some other and totally unpredictable factor.

However, in spite of the bustle of summer tourists, or of the French, German, or Chicago-speaking challengers to the suicidally steep slopes of Taos Ski Valley, or of the warm-weather hippies who are trying to "make it" with nature; even in spite of the fresh green beauty of spring with heavy snow still lingering in the high country—in spite of it all, I still love Taos and the Sangre de Cristos in October.

Here are some of Amalia's northern New Mexican specialties.

SANCOCHO DE CHÍCHAROS
(*Fresh Pea Chowder*)

In a kettle cook 8 cups shelled fresh green peas, 2 onions, peeled and diced, and 2 garlic cloves, peeled and halved, in 3 cups boiling water until the peas are very soft. Strain the mixture through a sieve into a large saucepan. Make a *beurre manié* consisting of ½ stick or ¼ cup butter, softened, and ¼ cup flour, shape the mixture into small balls, and add them to the soup. Stir in 4 cups milk and slowly bring the soup just to a boil, stirring. Season the soup with 2 teaspoons each of salt and sugar, ½ teaspoon chili powder, and ¼ teaspoon *cilantro* (fresh coriander).

CARNE DE MARRANO CON CHILE COLORADO
(*Roast Leg of Pork with Red Chili Peppers*)

In a mortar grind or mash together 15 red chili peppers, seeded, 1 garlic clove, finely chopped, 1 teaspoon salt, ½ teaspoon *cilantro* (fresh coriander), and ¼ teaspoon ground sage. With a small sharp knife cut 7 or 8 small holes in the meaty part of 1 large leg of pork, reserving the cutout pieces of meat. Stuff the holes with some of the chili paste and reserve the rest. Close the openings with the reserved cutouts and roast the meat in a moderate oven (350° F.), basting every 20 minutes with the pan juices, for 25 minutes per pound. Twenty minutes before the roast is done, spread it with the reserved chili paste.

TEMOLE DE CHILE VERDE CON VENADO
(*Green Chili Stew with Venison*)

Cut 2 pounds venison, elk, or top round steak into cubes and coat them with 2 tablespoons flour. In a large heavy skillet cook the meat and 2 onions, chopped, in ¼ cup lard until the meat is browned on all sides. Add 12 fresh green chili peppers, seeded and diced, 2 garlic cloves, finely chopped, 2 teaspoons salt, and ½ teaspoon pepper. Stir in 4 cups boiling water and simmer the stew, adding water if necessary, for about 1 hour, or until the meat is tender. Fifteen minutes before the stew is done, season it with aniseed and yerba buena (wild mint) to taste.

QUELITES
(*Wild Spinach*)

In a large kettle cook 4 pounds *quelites* or well-washed spinach in boiling salted water to cover until the greens are tender and drain them well. In a saucepan sauté 2 onions, finely chopped, and 2 fresh green chili peppers, seeded and mashed, in 2 tablespoons hot lard until they are lightly browned. Add 2 garlic cloves, crushed, and cook the mixture for 1 minute more. Stir the mixture into the spinach and toss it with orégano, salt, and pepper to taste.

CHAUQUEHUE
(*Thick Corn Gruel*)

Moisten 1½ cups cornmeal with 1 cup water and stir the mixture into 5 cups boiling water seasoned with 1 teaspoon salt. Stir the mixture until it is smooth and add 1 tablespoon lard. Simmer the mixture for 30 minutes, or until it is thickened. Serve the *chauquehue* in place of potatoes.

CAPIROTADA
(*Candied Bread Cubes*)

Spread 5 cups bread cubes on a cookie sheet and heat them in a slow oven (300° F.) until they are brown. In a bowl beat 2 egg whites until they are thick, add 2 egg yolks, and beat the mixture until it is smooth. Dip the bread cubes in the mixture and fry them in hot deep oil (360° F.) until they are brown. Drain the cubes on paper towels. Combine 1½ cups pine nuts, finely ground, 1 cup finely diced citron, ½ cup sugar, and 2 teaspoons cinnamon and sprinkle the mixture over the bread cubes. Keep them warm in the oven. In a saucepan boil 4 cups sugar, 2 cups water, ¼ cup cream of tartar, and 1 teaspoon cinnamon until a candy thermometer registers 220° F., or the syrup is thickened. Pour the syrup over the bread cubes and serve them hot.

BISCOCHITOS
(*Sugar Cookies*)

In a saucepan combine ¼ cup boiling water, ⅔ cup butter, 10 table-spoons sugar, 2 tablespoons whiskey or rum, and ½ teaspoon aniseed and heat the mixture until the butter is melted. Remove the pan from the heat and mix in 2¾ cups flour sifted with ½ teaspoon baking powder and ¼ teaspoon salt. Roll the dough out ⅛ inch thick on a well-floured surface and cut it into rounds with a cookie cutter.

Brush the cookies with melted butter and sprinkle them with a mixture of ¼ cup sugar and 1½ teaspoons cinnamon. Bake the cookies in a hot oven (400° F.) for 10 minutes, or until they are golden. Makes 50 to 60 medium-size cookies.

October 1970

Down in the Low Country

James Villas

The 275-mile coastal region that extends from Wilmington, North Carolina, to Savannah, Georgia, is not only one of the nation's most remote and mysterious areas but, for me, one that evokes vivid childhood memories. The festoons of Spanish moss that cling predatorily to giant oak trees, the sounds of crickets and bullfrogs interrupting the silence of sullen marshes and black swamps, the dignified old rice plantations and vast formal gardens that recall an age of magnificence, the rich bounty of fresh seafood aboard incoming schooners, the fragrance of simmering stews, barbecued pork, and hush puppies—all typify this distinct stretch of land known locally as the Low Country.

I've driven many times down Highway 17, which connects Wilmington, Myrtle Beach, Georgetown, Charleston, and Savannah, as well as numerous small white beaches that dot the coast, but my most recent visit was for the sole purpose of learning more about the Low Country's regional cuisine, reputed to be one of the most imaginative in the South. As I traveled between the larger towns, zigzagging among villages, everything I saw brought to mind the historical importance of a territory that today appears never to have undergone any large-scale economic development. There is very little significant industry, the living pace is languid, and even in the more sophisticated towns one has the clear impression that the Low Country is one of the few remaining areas that have managed to evade the assault of time.

But there was an era when the Low Country boasted an active culture that equaled any other in the East. In early colonial days, what is now North Carolina, South Carolina, and northern Georgia comprised the single province of Carolina, a British land grant issued by Charles II. By the latter part of the seventeenth century the first colony of Charles Town (later named Charleston) had been established in the mild, fertile lowland inhabited by French Huguenots seeking religious freedom. From these early years until the American Revolution indigo was a major money crop, which helped to sustain the colony until competing dyes gradually made it unprofitable. Then Captain John Thurber brought a sack of rice back from Madagascar to the rich muddy terrain of Carolina. The grain gave rise not only to a wealthy economy but also to a lavish way of life. In the eighteenth century the great riverbanks of the Low Country were cleared for the cultivation of rice, and the crop was appropriately dubbed Carolina gold. Fortunes were made almost overnight; magnificent plantations with stately mansions sprang up along the rivers south of Wilmington; and for many years there flourished a prosperous and graceful society based exclusively on the production of rice.

Of equal importance in the history of the Low Country was the development of the cotton industry around Savannah at the end of the eighteenth century. From the time the colony of Georgia was founded by James Oglethorpe in 1733, cotton growing had proved to be at least semiprofitable to the settlement. Its early production, though, did not rival that of rice because the removal of the obstinate seeds required too much labor. With Eli Whitney's invention of the cotton gin, however, the industry was revolutionized, and during the first half of the nineteenth century Factors' Row in Savannah shipped more cotton throughout the world than almost any other port.

Unfortunately, the stable prosperity that the Low Country enjoyed for so many years was destined to decline. The cotton industry gradually moved farther and farther inland, where the dry soil was more suitable and where Southern planters could extend their valuable crop across vast plantations. Savannah's port remained active, but the town itself, ravaged by two great fires, epidemics, and war, entered a pathetic period of decay that was not entirely remedied until the middle of the 1950s.

History erroneously attributes the sudden death of the rice industry at the beginning of the twentieth century to increasing competition from Louisiana, Texas, and Arkansas. The more logical explanation is that, by a cruel stroke of fate, the rice fields of the Low Country were literally blown away by an unrelenting series of severe freshets and hurricanes. Attempts were made to revive planting, but by 1911 the mighty crop that had created such a highly civilized culture disappeared completely, leaving behind only the romantic old estates and gracious homes, many of which still stand hidden deep in the moss-draped forests.

If the history and legends of the Low Country excite the imagination, its cuisine likewise fascinates those with a keen interest in regional cookery. As I was to learn when I traveled inland, some of the coastal dishes are virtually unknown even to Southerners outside the immediate area. A friend in Charlotte, North Carolina, for example, had never so much as heard of the chicken or shrimp pilaus prepared along the North and South Carolina shores; a well-known restaurateur in Atlanta squinted his eyes questioningly when I described the popular chicken bog; and when I informed my host in Georgia's capital that the delectable Brunswick stew I'd raved about in Savannah contained hot red peppers, he flatly denounced the city and its cuisine as non-Southern.

Regardless of the impressions outsiders may have, there can be no doubt that a great deal of the food served in the Low Country is as distinctive as the strange Gullah dialect that is spoken by many of the area's inhabitants. In fact, if the cuisine in any area of the South has been strongly influenced by African traditions, it is surely that of the coastal Carolinas and Georgia. Quite naturally the daily provender of all Southerners from Wilmington to Savannah is composed at least partially of such standard Southern dishes as fried chicken with milk-enriched gravy, juicy pork roasts, baked spareribs, regional vegetables (squash, crowder and black-eyed peas, mustard and collard greens, and pole and butter beans), grits, corn bread, and mouth-watering sweet cobblers. But although tidewater inhabitants share with uplanders a mutual respect for those foods that comprise what is perhaps the nation's most original cuisine, they are more fond of the dishes that draw inspiration from the great plantation era and from the Low Country's bounteous supply of seafood.

I've always been amazed that the preparation of food along the Carolina and Georgia coasts could at once be so similar and yet so different. For example, the old-fashioned method of barbecuing pork, in which the meat is smoked over a pit of hickory and pine wood for an entire day, is adhered to as religiously in Wilmington as in Savannah. The same circumstance is true of the deep-frying of fish, which in the Low Country is a veritable art. And when it comes to an oyster roast—that most popular and festive occasion, which dates back to the earliest plantation days—there is only one way to conduct the feast properly, no matter where it takes place. Traditionally a huge pit filled with hot coals is covered with a piece of sheet metal. Bushels of freshly harvested oysters are heaped on top, covered with burlap that has been soaked in salt water, and steamed for about 15 minutes, or just until the shells begin to loosen. Opened with a special double-thumbed glove, the oysters are sprinkled with lemon juice, dunked in one of many piquant sauces, and consumed by the dozen with crackers and beer.

Appetites are hearty at these events, and usually it is not until everyone has had his fill of the delicate shellfish that the more robust items are served. These dishes would be likely to include a glazed corned beef, a *daube glacé* (jellied beef and vegetable stew), crab omelet sandwiches, red rice, hoppin' John (black-eyed peas, salt pork, and rice), a carrot or squash soufflé, a rich pecan cake, and gallons of fruit punch.

The sea and rivers furnish the ingredients for many of the area's culinary specialties, and whether one is on the shores of the Carolinas or Georgia it would be a mistake not to experiment with the seafood dishes and compare their imaginative preparations. Along the Carolina coasts (particularly in the area between Wrightsville Beach and Georgetown), some of my most rewarding discoveries have been unpretentious "fish houses" where, for incredibly low prices, one can feast on seafood platters heaped with fresh shrimps, deviled crabs, scallops, oysters, clams, and whatever fish is available. But if my palate dictates something more exotic, I enjoy flounder stuffed with crab meat, broiled bluefish or Spanish mackerel, baked sea trout covered with tiny sweet river shrimps, fresh back-fin crab meat either sautéed in butter, baked with Sherry, or blended into a soufflé pompano stuffed with shrimp paste, or delicate little spots fried quickly in oil.

No coastal dinner would be complete without the inimitable sweet-and-sour coleslaw and a large basket of hush puppies. Of course, as with so many Southern treats, there has always been an unending debate among the natives about the preparation of these legendary morsels of deep-fried corn bread that were originally tossed to hounds to quiet them. In the northern part of the Low Country a generous measure of chopped onions is added to the batter, whereas near Charleston the chefs use only a few spoonfuls, along with a little cayenne. Georgians go a bit further by including a teaspoon of chopped garlic and some red pepper; in North Carolina it is important that the hush puppy be formed in a long oval shape to reduce fat absorption; and farther down the coast "experts" insist that the crunchy little corn dodgers be rolled into balls. In any case, as long as hush puppies are light and flavorful, they are a perfect accompaniment to any seafood meal.

To my taste, the most interesting of all dishes indigenous to the Low Country are the rice pilaus. Pilau, an ancestor of the better known Creole jambalaya, is traditionally a savory combination of long-grain white rice, onions, tomatoes, bacon, various spices, and some form of shellfish. But just as the spelling and pronunciation of the word can change radically from town to town, the ingredients and preparation of the dish have numerous variations also. Generally pilau becomes more spicy as one heads farther south. In Wilmington, chicken pilau involves no more than shredded boiled chicken mixed with a cream sauce and served in a mold of dry rice. In Charleston and Beaufort, however, most recipes call for onions, whole peppercorns, thyme, and cayenne. Another favorite in North Carolina is pilau with pistachio and pine nuts, and in Savannah one of the most common vegetable casseroles is a highly spiced tomato and okra pilau. Although these and many other variations on the same theme make for interesting comparisons, I'll settle any day for the ubiquitous shrimp pilau, a hearty combination of rice, large Carolina shrimps, onions, tomatoes, bell peppers, and celery.

The remarkable cuisine of Charleston has long been famous among Southerners, and by the time I reached this historic city, with its magnificent eighteenth-century mansions, narrow cobblestone streets, formal gardens, and strange patois speech, I had all but memorized the town's gastronomic handbook, *Charleston Receipts.* To read this local cookbook is to wander mentally through the past two centuries and wonder at the origins of the plethora of ingenious dishes that have nourished generations. Insofar as culinary imagination in this nation is concerned, I am firmly convinced that Charleston cookery is equaled only by that of the Louisiana bayou country.

Following an early English custom, many Charlestonians still observe (particularly on Sundays) what is locally called the two o'clock dinner, and when my host prepared such a meal for me, I was confronted with a little more than I'd bargained for. The first course, a delicate liverwurst in aspic, was followed by a cup of she-crab soup, a euphoric blend of milk, butter, whipped cream, onion juice, seasonings, and flour, into which white back-fin crab meat with its sweet roe and a tablespoon of warmed Sherry is added. (Even today street vendors in Charleston call out "she crab" loudly and charge more for it than they do for he crab.) Virtually unknown outside the Low Country, this soup is probably the most delectable that I've tasted anywhere.

As if these two starters were not enough to whet the appetite, I was next presented with what is called *hobotee,* a mixture of minced meats (usually veal and beef) baked in a curry custard and served in individual cups. Overcoming the temptation to consume two portions, I continued to taste every item placed on the large oak table. The main course was the popular chicken bog, an old plantation preparation in which chicken is first boiled with peppercorns and bay leaves in a cast-iron pot, then baked in a casserole with stock, rice, celery, onions, mushrooms, and soy sauce. Accompanying the dish were Bull Bay oysters, sweetbreads, squash cooked with green peppers and bacon, oranges stuffed with dates, nuts, and shredded coconut, spiced grapes, Mason jars of homemade chutney and tomato chow-chow, and hominy muffins. Dessert was a Huguenot torte, a two-layer cake containing chopped apples and pecans. Normally the torte is topped with whipped cream, but this time it was covered with syllabub, a frothy sweet mixture of Sherry, brandy, lemon juice, sugar, and cream that is beaten until it is very thick. Although I recall tasting syllabub as a child in its original English beverage form (a drink similar to eggnog), I found this more modern version perfect as a cake topping.

After a day of fasting and brisk walking along the Battery that overlooks Charleston Harbor and Fort Sumter I began traveling in the direction of Savannah, stopping only long enough to admire the quiet beauty of Edisto Island and to enjoy, at Beaufort, a light lunch of sweet fresh oysters from nearby Saint Helena Sound. As I traveled south the Spanish moss became thicker and the vegetation more subtropical, and by the time I crossed the Georgia border and arrived at my destination I was instinctively aware of the leisurely life-style that is quite eminent in the Low Country's largest town.

Even if the tempo of life is still as slow in Savannah as when General Sherman magnanimously offered the beautiful city to President Lincoln as a Christmas gift, there exists a phoenix-like pride and energy that have enabled the inhabitants to recover from nearly every imaginable disaster. At the turn of the century Savannah was in a period of decline—to such a degree that as late as 1950 many of the remaining features of Oglethorpe's design for the city had deteriorated almost beyond recognition. Then the situation began to change, mostly as a result of the devoted efforts of Mrs. Anna Hunter and the newly formed Historic Savannah Foundation. The distinctive squares of Oglethorpe's original plan were relandscaped; grand-scale renovations of buildings and town houses were undertaken; and the lower wharf side of Factors' Row was transformed into shops, restaurants, and office space. Today, with active restoration still going on, Savannah is again one of the loveliest cities in the United States.

When I saw how dramatically Savannah had been transformed since my youth, I wondered if the city's culinary standards had also been altered, and whether, as in Atlanta, the great regional dishes had sadly disappeared. But I was relieved to learn, after three days of dining in both old and new restaurants and talking with residents, that Savannahians in general not only continue to cherish the elaborate menus of their ancestors but that they have established several epicurean societies in an effort to safeguard the distinctive old recipes.

Native Georgians outside Savannah are quick to comment on the city's "strange cookery," and even my aged grandmother from Monticello, Georgia, insists that the residents of the Low Country have never learned to prepare food properly. Perhaps this sort of reaction is the result of a bit of jealousy, or, more likely, of secondhand exposure. No one savors good food more than a Georgian, and when it comes to authentic, unpretentious Southern dishes, none are better than those that gladden the dinner tables of the inland towns. But as far as imagination is concerned, comparing the cuisine of Savannah with the cookery throughout the rest of Georgia is as unrealistic as comparing the gastronomic subtleties of Charleston dishes with some of the more prosaic staples that nourish other South Carolinians.

Of course, Savannah, like other areas of the Low Country, is blessed almost year-round with an abundance of fresh seafood, which accounts at least in part for many of the regional specialties. The Atlantic furnishes the local markets with a steady supply of fresh fish, gray shrimps, and the delectable crab meat that is used in numerous casseroles and in an interesting version of she-crab soup. Tiny shrimps from the Savannah River are the main ingredient for a sweet-tasting combination of shrimps and hominy. Large shad, fished in season from the Ogeechee River and broiled, provide a rare epicurean delight. And the local oysters, especially those harvested around Hilton Head Island and in Ossabaw Sound, are not only more flavorful than those from Chesapeake Bay, but they often remind me of the delicate French *marennes blanches*. Savannahians consume oysters in every conceivable way: raw in their own liquor, broiled, lightly sautéed with a dash of hot pepper sauce, simmered in savory stews, crumb-fried, scalloped, and, in popular Low Country tradition, roasted over hot coals.

Anyone familiar with Savannah cookery would agree that native ingenuity in combination with hot seasonings explains the distinctive
quality of the great dishes. Red peppers, black and white pepper, pepper Sherry, cayenne, hot pepper sauce, dry mustard, onion juice—
these are the ingredients that add the flavorful pungency to stews,
soups, vegetables, relishes, and even certain seafood preparations.
Strolling through the city I saw red bird's-eye peppers growing in pots
on the white banisters of porches, in the windows of restaurants, and
in the small gardens of elegant town houses. And certainly no restaurant worthy of its name would set a table without including a small
cruet of pepper Sherry (made by allowing scalded red peppers and
Sherry to stand for at least a full day).

I cannot recall a superlative meal that did not include at least one
item that literally brought delightful tears to my eyes. Mary Jane's
deviled crab, for example, was a spicy concoction that included specks
of red pepper, a teaspoon of onion juice, mustard, and four or five
other spices. Okra soup served Savannah style involves first crushing a
bird's-eye pepper in the bowl, scraping out the pulp, and then pouring
in the tomato-enriched soup. Throughout Georgia, Brunswick stew is
traditionally prepared with chicken, pork, and several vegetables, but
in Savannah (where squirrel is often substituted for the chicken), the
addition of a whole chili pepper and dry mustard completely trans-
forms the overall flavor of the dish. Another specialty, seafood ragout,
is a rich mélange of shrimps, oysters, chicken, and mushrooms simmered in a cream sauce with cayenne, onion juice, and a few drops of
pepper Sherry; and even a mug of Savannah grog can be (and usually
is) perked up with a dash of hot pepper sauce. Working with such seasonings is generally risky business in any kitchen, but for the cooks of
Savannah the custom comes as naturally as crushing leaves for a mint
julep.

After a hearty breakfast of eggs, fried country ham, grits, buttermilk
biscuits, and homemade peach preserves, I wistfully said farewell to
Savannah and the Low Country. Heading toward Atlanta, I tried to fix
in my memory everything new I had learned about this almost legendary region and its unique cuisine. Then I began to worry, as I do

now, hundreds of miles away. When I return, will there still be the debate over the shape of hush puppies? Will the street vendors of Charleston still be shouting "she crab"? Will the pots of red bird's-eye peppers still brighten the windows of Savannah? I surely hope so.

Below are some of the traditional Southern dishes that are specialties of the Low Country.

She-Crab Soup

Remove and pick over the meat from 12 steamed blue crabs, reserving the roe. In a saucepan melt 1 tablespoon butter, add 1 tablespoon flour, and cook the *roux* over low heat, stirring, for a few minutes. Remove the pan from the heat and pour in 4 cups scalded milk, stirring. Return the pan to the heat, stir the sauce until it is smooth, and add the crab meat, 1 teaspoon onion juice, ½ teaspoon Worcestershire sauce, ¼ teaspoon mace, and salt and white pepper to taste. Cook the soup over low heat, stirring, for 20 minutes. Divide the reserved crab roe among 4 to 6 heated soup bowls, add the soup, and lace each serving with 1 tablespoon heated dry Sherry. Garnish each bowl with minced parsley or a dash of paprika. Serves 4 to 6.

Steamed Blue Crabs

In a large kettle fitted with a bottom rack bring to a boil 2 to 3 cups water or flat beer. Add 2 teaspoons salt and ½ teaspoon pepper. Plunge in 12 live blue crabs and steam them, covered, for 15 to 20 minutes, or until they are red. Remove the kettle from the heat and let the crabs cool in the kettle.

To Remove Meat from Blue Crabs

Remove the legs from steamed blue crabs and crack them. Extract the meat. Pull the apron from the crabs and remove the shells, discarding both. Break the crabs in half along the natural ridge and with a sharp knife halve them horizontally. Discard the cartilage and dead men's fingers and pick out the meat.

OYSTER STEW

Strain the liquor from 1 quart of oysters into a saucepan. Bring the liquor to a boil, skim off the froth, and reserve the liquor, keeping it warm. In another saucepan combine the oysters, with 1 tablespoon grated onion, simmer them over very low heat for 3 minutes, or until the edges curl, and remove the pan from the heat. In another saucepan cook ½ cup each of milk and minced celery over moderate heat for 5 minutes. Stir in 1 cup heavy cream and bring the mixture to the boiling point. Remove the pan from the heat and add the oyster liquor, the oysters, 1 tablespoon dry Sherry, and salt and white pepper to taste. Ladle the stew into 4 to 6 heated soup bowls, top each serving with 2 teaspoons softened butter, and serve the stew with oyster crackers. Serves 4 to 6.

HOBOTEE
(*Baked Meat Custard*)

In a skillet sauté 1 medium onion, finely chopped, in 3 tablespoons butter until it is soft and barely colored. Stir in 1 tablespoon curry powder and cook the mixture over low heat for 2 minutes. Transfer the mixture to a bowl and combine it with 1½ cups finely chopped cooked beef, veal, or pork, 1 slice of bread soaked in milk and squeezed, 4 almonds, blanched and chopped, 2 tablespoons lemon juice, 1 small egg, ½ teaspoon sugar, and salt to taste. Butter well six ½-cup ramekins and divide the mixture among them. In a bowl combine 1 cup light cream, 2 eggs, lightly beaten, and a dash each of salt and white pepper and pour some of the mixture into each cup. Garnish each ramekin with a thin slice of lemon or a bay leaf and bake the custards in a preheated slow oven (300° F.) for 25 minutes, or until they are set. Serve the *hobotee* with rice and chutney.

Low Country Shrimp Pilau

In a skillet cook 6 slices of bacon, cut into ¼-inch dice, until they are crisp. Transfer the bacon with a slotted spoon to paper towels and reserve the bacon fat. Put 1½ cups long-grain rice in a sieve, wash it well under running cold water, and drain it. In a heavy flameproof 3-quart casserole sauté 1½ cups finely chopped onion in 3 tablespoons of the reserved bacon fat until it is soft and barely colored. Stir in the rice, combining it until it is coated with the fat. Add 2¼ cups chicken stock or chicken broth, 1½ cups peeled, seeded, and finely chopped tomatoes, 2 teaspoons lemon juice, 1½ teaspoons each of Worcestershire sauce and salt, ¾ teaspoon mace, and ¼ teaspoon cayenne and bring the liquid to a boil.

Transfer the casserole to a preheated moderate oven (350° F.) and bake the rice mixture, covered, for 20 minutes. With a fork stir in 1½ pounds medium shrimps, peeled and deveined, and the diced bacon and bake the dish, covered, for 10 to 15 minutes more, or until the shrimps and rice are tender. Remove the casserole from the oven and let it stand for 10 minutes. Fluff the pilau thoroughly with a fork, season it with salt and pepper to taste, and sprinkle it with 2 tablespoons minced parsley.

Brunswick Stew

Quarter a 3-pound chicken and sprinkle it with salt and pepper. In a skillet brown the chicken well in 3 tablespoons vegetable oil and transfer it to a dish. Sprinkle a 1-pound piece of boneless chuck with salt and pepper, brown it in the oil remaining in the skillet, and reserve it.

Chop enough celery, with the leaves, to measure 1 cup and in a large casserole sauté it with 2 medium onions, thinly sliced, in 2 tablespoons vegetable oil over moderate heat for 5 minutes, or until the vegetables are tender and barely colored. Add the chicken, the chuck, 1 medium ham hock, 1½ pounds tomatoes, peeled, seeded, and chopped, 2 sprigs of parsley, 1 small red hot pepper, seeded and minced, 1 teaspoon salt, ½ teaspoon basil, and 2½ quarts water. Bring the liquid to a boil, reduce the heat, and simmer the mixture, covered, for 45 minutes. Remove the chicken pieces with a slotted spoon and reserve them. Continue to simmer the remaining mixture for 1½ hours more, or until the meats are tender. Remove the meats with a slotted spoon and reserve them. Let the remaining mixture cool and skim off the fat. Bring the liquid to a boil, add 2 cups corn kernels, and cook the mixture over high heat for 10 minutes. Cook and mash enough potatoes to measure 1½ cups, add them to the stew with 1½ cups lima beans and ½ stick or ¼ cup butter, and cook the stew over moderately high heat, stirring constantly, for 15 minutes, or until the vegetables are tender.

Skin and bone the chicken and shred the meat. Cut the chuck into 1-inch pieces. Bone the ham hock and cut the meat into pieces. Add the meats to the stew and cook the stew for 5 minutes, or until it is heated through. Sprinkle the stew with 2 tablespoons chopped parsley and season it with salt and pepper to taste.

BARBECUED SPARERIBS

Make barbecue sauce: In a saucepan combine 1 cup each of molasses, ketchup, and chopped onion, the juice of 1 orange, 3 tablespoons minced orange rind, 2 tablespoons each of butter, vinegar, salad oil, and bottled steak sauce, 2 garlic cloves, split, 5 whole cloves, 1 teaspoon each of prepared mustard and Worcestershire sauce, and ½ teaspoon each of hot pepper sauce, salt, and pepper. Bring the mixture to a boil over moderate heat and cook it for 5 minutes.

Sprinkle 4 pounds spareribs lightly with salt. Put them on a rack in a roasting pan, cover the pan with foil, and bake the ribs in a preheated moderately slow oven (325° F.) for 1 hour. Pour off the fat. Spread the spareribs with some of the sauce and bake them in a preheated hot oven (400° F.), basting them with the remaining sauce every 15 minutes, for 45 minutes, or until they are tender and glazed. Serves 4.

DAUBE GLACÉ
(*Jellied Beef Stew*)

In a deep 3-quart ceramic or glass dish combine 1½ cups dry red wine, 3 onions, thinly sliced, 2 carrots and 1 small stalk of celery, all diced, 3 garlic cloves, split, 1 tablespoon each of chopped parsley and salt, 1 red hot pepper, seeded, and 1 teaspoon thyme. Add a 3-pound bottom round of beef and 1 veal bone to the marinade. Chill the mixture, turning the beef several times, for at least 12 hours. Transfer the mixture to a large ovenproof kettle, add 4 pig's feet, split, and 3 quarts of water, and bring the liquid to a boil. Cover the kettle with foil and the lid and bake the meats in a preheated moderately slow oven (325° F.), turning them occasionally, for 3½ hours, or until they are tender. Transfer the beef and pig's feet to a bowl, let them cool, and cover them tightly. Remove and discard the veal bone. Strain the braising liquid through a fine sieve into a saucepan and reduce it over high heat to about 5 cups. Chill the meats and braising liquid overnight.

Trim any clinging fat from the beef and cut the beef into ¼-inch-thick slices. Remove the meat from the pig's feet and dice it. Remove and discard the fat from the jellied braising liquid and heat the jelly just until it liquefies. Pour a thin layer of the liquid jelly into a 2-quart loaf pan, 9½ by 5 by 3½ inches, and chill it until it is set. Slice thinly 1 lemon and 12 pimiento-stuffed olives, alternate the slices over the jelly layer, and arrange the remaining lemon slices around the sides. Pour a thin layer of the liquid jelly over the slices and chill it. Arrange overlapping slices of beef in the pan, top the beef with a layer of the diced pig's feet and cover the dice with the remaining beef. Pour the liquid jelly over the meats and chill the *daube* for several hours, or overnight. Pour any remaining liquid jelly into a shallow small baking dish and chill it.

To unmold the *daube*, run a knife around the edge of the pan and dip the bottom of the pan into hot water for a moment. Put a serving dish over the top of the pan and invert the *daube* onto the dish. Unmold the layer of jellied braising liquid, chop it coarsely, and arrange the pieces around the *daube*. Serves 6 to 8.

SQUASH SOUFFLÉ

Peel and seed 2 pounds yellow squash and cut it into 1-inch pieces. Put the squash in a colander and steam it, covered, over a kettle containing 1 inch of boiling water for 20 minutes, or until it is very tender. Transfer the squash to a piece of cheesecloth, drain it well, and purée it with a wooden spoon.

Make béchamel sauce and stir in the purée, 2 cups grated Cheddar cheese, 2 eggs, lightly beaten, ¼ cup grated onion, and salt and white pepper to taste. Transfer the mixture to a buttered 1½-quart soufflé dish, sprinkle it with 3 tablespoons fresh bread crumbs, and dot it with 2 tablespoons butter. Bake the soufflé in a preheated moderately hot oven (375° F.) for 40 to 45 minutes, or until a knife inserted in the center comes out clean.

ONION HUSH PUPPIES

Into a bowl sift together ¼ cup flour and 1 teaspoon each of baking powder and salt and combine the mixture with 1¾ cups white cornmeal. Stir in 1½ cups boiling water and 1 egg, lightly beaten, blend the mixture until it is smooth, and stir in ⅓ cup minced onion. Drop the batter by tablespoons into hot deep oil (360° F.) and fry the hush puppies for 3 to 4 minutes, or until they are golden brown. Drain them on paper towels. Serves 4.

BUTTERMILK BISCUITS

Into a large bowl sift together 2 cups flour, ¾ teaspoon baking soda, and ½ teaspoon salt. Add 3 tablespoons shortening, cut into bits, and blend the mixture until it resembles meal. Add ¾ cup buttermilk, stirring, and blend the mixture until it forms a smooth dough. Turn the dough out onto a lightly floured surface and knead it with the palm of the hand for 1 minute. Roll out the dough ½ inch thick and with a 2-inch biscuit cutter cut out rounds. Put the rounds on a baking sheet and bake them in a preheated very hot oven (450° F.) for 15 minutes, or until they are golden. Makes about 14 biscuits.

SWEET-AND-SOUR COLESLAW

In a saucepan blend 2 eggs, ¾ cup white vinegar, 2 tablespoons each of butter and sugar, 1½ teaspoons salt, 1 teaspoon celery seed, and ½ teaspoon pepper and cook the mixture over low heat until it is thickened and coats the back of a spoon. Shred finely enough white cabbage to measure 4 cups and stir it into the mixture, combining it well. Remove the pan from the heat, let the coleslaw cool, and chill it, covered, for several hours. Makes 3 cups.

SWEET POTATO PIE

Make *pâte brisée*, substituting 1 teaspoon sugar for the salt, and roll it out into an 11-inch circle on a lightly floured surface. Fit the dough into a deep 9½-inch pie tin, crimp the edges, and chill it for 1 hour.

Remove the pulp from 5 or 6 baked sweet potatoes or yams and mash it. There should be 2 cups. In a bowl cream together 2 sticks or 1 cup butter, softened, and 1½ cups sugar until the mixture is fluffy. Beat in 4 eggs, one at a time, the mashed sweet potatoes or yams, ½ cup whiskey, the grated rind and juice of 1 lemon, and ½ teaspoon mace and pour the mixture into the prepared shell. Bake the pie in the bottom third of a preheated hot oven (425° F.) for 20 minutes. Reduce the heat to moderate (350° F.), transfer the pie to the middle shelf, and bake it for 40 to 45 minutes more, or until the crust is browned and the filling is set. Let the pie cool on a rack and sift confectioners' sugar over it.

March 1973

ALL ABOARD! CROSSING THE ROCKIES IN STYLE

Paul Theroux

I was sitting in the sunshine in the rear car of a train heading west, feeling utterly baffled and thinking: *I have never been here before.* It was not just the place (early morning in the middle of Colorado); it was also my state of mind (blissful). I was grateful for my good fortune. To think that riding a train, something I had done for pleasure all my traveling life, had been improved upon. In the past, what had mattered most in any long train journey through an interesting landscape was the motion, the privacy, the solitude, the grandeur. Food and comfort, I had discovered, are seldom available on the best trips: There is something about the most beautiful places having the most awful trains. But this was something else.

My chair was on the rear observation platform of a private railway car called *Los Angeles,* formerly belonging to the Southern Pacific Railway and today operated by Christopher Kyte's California-based company, Uncommon Journeys. My feet were braced against the brass rail, the morning sunshine was full upon my face. I had woken in Fort Morgan and, after a stroll in Denver, had reboarded to have breakfast with family and friends in the dining room of this car: home-baked blueberry coffeecake and muffins, scrambled eggs, and fresh orange juice and coffee. Then the morning paper in the lounge, and finally settling myself in the open air on this little brass porch as we started our climb through the foothills of the Rockies. An hour out of Denver it was epic grandeur, past frozen creeks and pines and rubbly hills, destination San Francisco. I was very happy.

From this position on a train, eye contact is possible, and as we passed through Pinecliffe, in Gilpin County, a woman waiting at the level crossing stuck her head out her car window and waved at me, making my day.

"Anything I can get you?" That was George, the steward, holding the rear door open. "Coffee? Cookies? More juice? Hot chocolate?"

There were four armchairs and a big sofa in the parlor just inside; and off the corridor, four bedrooms, two with double beds, and hot showers. Farther along, the dining room, the kitchen, and beyond that a big long Amtrak train, the *California Zephyr*, pulling us on its usual route from Chicago to San Francisco via Denver and Salt Lake City.

As for the rest, I was ignorant. Happiness has no questions; bliss is not a state of inquiry. Whatever squirrelly anxieties I possessed had vanished a long way back, probably soon after we boarded in Chicago, or else at Galesburg. Bliss had definitely taken hold as we crossed the Mississippi, because I remember standing right here on the rear platform and gawking at it: the chunks of ice gleaming in the lights of Burlington, Iowa, on the distant riverbank; the clattering of the wheels on the bridge; the night air; hearing and seeing the water—and smelling it too, a marshy muddiness this damp winter night—of the great river.

We had arrived in Chicago the previous afternoon in fog so thick that airline passengers had turned O'Hare into a gigantic dormitory, and departing flights were so thoroughly canceled that there was a slumber party at each gate. The fog was news, and so there was a certain sense of excitement in slipping out of it. I glanced from time to time at the Amtrak route guide, which gave helpful information. We passed Princeton, Illinois ("Pig Capital of the World"), and Galesburg (associated with Carl Sandburg and the Lincoln-Douglas debates, and where popcorn was invented by Olmstead Ferris), then through Monmouth (birthplace of Wyatt Earp). But all I saw were dark houses and dim lights and the vast Midwestern sky, and here and there a small nameless town, not noticed by the guide, and a filling station on a side road, or a bowling alley, or the local diner filled with eaters.

It is easy to understand the envy of the traveler for the settled people he or she sees, snug in their houses, at home. But I could not have been snugger here in the private railway car. Thinking of the days that stretched ahead, all of them on the rails, I was put in mind of Russia, of long journeys through forests and prairies, past little wooden houses half buried in the snow, with smoking chimneys. It was like that, the size of the landscape, and the snow, and the darkness, and the starry night over Iowa.

After hot showers, we assembled for pre-dinner drinks in the parlor and toasted our trip and talked about the train.

"This was the car that Robert Kennedy used for his campaign in 1968—he made his visit to Los Angeles on it," Christopher Kyte said.

Christopher bought the *Los Angeles* some eight years ago and restored it at great expense to its former glory. It had been built and fitted out at the height of the boom in the 1920s, and was finished just in time for the market crash in 1929.

That Robert Kennedy had used it, and made whistle-stop speeches from the rear observation platform, was a solemn thought, but it had been used by many other people—actresses, tycoons, foreign royalty. It had seen drunks and lovers and millionaires; it was not a mere conveyance, any more than a ship is—people had lived a part of their lives on it.

The *Los Angeles* is for weeks at a time Christopher Kyte's own home, one of the mobile aspects of his company. He rides it, guiding customers; he conducts business on it, using his cellular phone (on which, in Iowa, I wished my father a happy eighty-seventh birthday); he uses it for pleasure.

A humorous and self-mocking fellow whose innocence and innate goodwill make his humor all the more appealing, Christopher Kyte reminded me of Bertie Wooster, and he was all the more Woosterish when he was in his double-breasted dark suit, recalling a scandalous episode, with George the steward at his elbow, helping with a name or date. Eighteen years on Southern Pacific, George was Jeeves to his fingertips—efficient, helpful, silent. It is a wonder, given their generous dispositions, that Uncommon Journeys makes any money at all, although, at about $800 per person per day for a small group, the company has more than prospered.

Nostalgia is not the point, nor is it the glamour of the antique railway car. The idea is comfort, and privacy, and forward motion. It is a grand hotel suite on wheels, with fine food, views of the Great Plains, and any stopovers you like.

"I'd like to spend a day skiing," I had told Christopher, a few weeks before we left on the trip. I knew we were passing through Colorado and Utah and snowy parts of California. "What if we stopped for a night somewhere in Utah?"

We decided on Provo, just about sixteen miles from the narrow canyon in the Wasatch Range, where Sundance is located. That would be our second night.

"We'll drop you in Provo," Christopher had said. "A car will pick you up at the station. Then you can meet us the next day at the station in Salt Lake City and plan to have dinner on board. The chef will have something special."

Meanwhile the Iowa plains were passing, and we filed into the dining room for our first night's dinner, six of us around the table, feasting on pot roast. The conversation was enlivened by a mealtime quiz show of guessing celebrities' real names (significant answers: Reg Dwight, Gordon Sumner, Malcolm Little, Bill Blythe, Newton McPherson).

That night the *Zephyr* pulled the *Los Angeles* through Nebraska, from Omaha to Benkelman, near the Colorado border. But I was still asleep as we entered Colorado. I roused myself around Fort Morgan, in the high plains, and a little later watched people gathering for the Annual Stock Show and Rodeo outside Denver, next to the tracks. I got off to buy a newspaper in Denver, and later, in the clear bright day, was sitting on the rear observation platform.

Snow and cold drove me inside around lunchtime, and soon we came to the small town of Winter Park, not far from Fraser (which proudly calls itself "the icebox of America"). That afternoon we had a long snowy ride under the steep shale pinnacles of Glenwood Canyon to Glenwood Springs. Where the rock was uncovered, it was the color of honey in the fading daylight. Skiers got off the train to make their way to Aspen and Vail. We followed the course of Spanish Creek, which flows toward the Colorado River.

"Who has been your oddest passenger?" I asked Christopher over dinner, as we clattered down the canyon.

"Most of our people are wonderful," he said. But he was smiling, remembering.

There was, for example, the man who showed up in the dining room one morning, stark naked.

"You have no clothes on," Christopher had said to him.

"But I always eat breakfast like this," the man replied.

Ever the diplomat, Christopher suggested that he might be more comfortable having breakfast in the privacy of his room.

Oh, yes—Christopher was still smiling gently—and there was the fellow who was rather sedate during the day, and at night put on a wig and a dress, drank far too much Drambuie, and turned cartwheels on the rear platform.

We were by now on dessert, and also near the top of the Wasatch Range, at Soldier Summit, almost 7,500 feet high, snow everywhere. From here we traveled in loops and through tunnels to Provo, where the prearranged van was waiting. It was round about midnight.

"Dinner will be served at eight tomorrow," George said. "We'll be waiting for you."

The mist at the station gave way to sleet outside town, and before we had reached Sundance it was snow, drifting down the canyon. We could see the slopes and the lifts and the stands of snow-clad pines gleaming in the lights of the resort. All night the snow fell, and it was still falling the next morning. Two of us set off to the downhill slopes, and two to the wooded cross-country trails. We rented skis, poles, and boots; we had all the rest of our gear. After the eating and drinking on the train, this was perfect—kicking and gliding cross-country through the meadows and woods of Sundance. A break for lunch in The Tree

Room, and then a whole afternoon of skiing. The snow still fell, the air was mild—hardly freezing. Except for a flock of crows and one invisible woodpecker, the woods were silent.

At dark we handed back our ski gear and were taken to the Salt Lake City train station, about an hour away. And there, solitary, detached, at a platform in the middle of the train yard, its lights blazing, was the *Los Angeles.*

A movable feast, I was thinking, as a woman in a white smock greeted us. This was the *Los Angeles*'s executive chef, Regina Charboneau, joining the train as she occasionally does from San Francisco, where she owns Regina's Chichi Beignet restaurant and also the Biscuits and Blues bar.

The Southern cuisine was Regina's inspiration, but it was Southern cooking with a difference: traditional dishes—crab cakes and buttermilk biscuits—served with a flourish. Tonight we were being served pheasant and okra gumbo, salmon with potato crust over creamed hominy grits, and warm chocolate bread pudding. The gumbo, hearty and flavorful, was to fortify us after our day of skiing. The grits had come from Regina's childhood. She had gotten to San Francisco by way of Natchez (where she was one of nine children, her father a chef and restaurateur); Missoula, Montana (where she gained a sense of reality); Chignik Lake, Alaska (where at the age of twenty-three she was camp cook); Paris (La Varenne cooking school), and Anchorage (several successful restaurants). Her stories could not top Christopher's, but they were very good and included a plane crash and strange times at the work camp in Alaska, with at least one marriage proposal from a young Aleut.

Later, in my room, full of food and warmth and a pleasant fatigue, I thought, *I don't want this trip to end,* and I began to understand the meaning of "gravy train"—not the sinister implication of excessive self-indulgence, but as a friendly journey, where everything is rosy.

Sometime during the night the *Zephyr* snatched our car up and whisked us westward across the Great Salt Lake Desert at ninety-five miles an hour. We were still in high desert in the morning, a landscape like Tibet's: arid, stony ground with the peaks and ridges of snowy mountains showing in the distance on almost every side.

"Those are the Ruby Mountains," Christopher said, indicating a great white wall to the east. And a bit later, about eighteen miles out of Reno, "That's Mustang Ranch." It was, pinkish and sprawling, three or four one-storey buildings by the side of the tracks; not very glamorous, it had the look of a boys' camp, which in a sense it was. Reno itself, part circus, part residential, seemed a complete blight on the landscape, "kitsch in sync," in the words of one wag.

Some friends of ours from Colfax, farther down the line, joined us here. They got on board, and we continued on our way, following the route of the Donner party. One of them brought me a copy of *Ordeal by Hunger*, the story of those ill-fated pioneers by George Stewart, and there I sat, completely absorbed, as we clunked past Truckee—deep in snow—and Donner Peak and Donner Lake, where the tragic events of death and cannibalism unfolded.

It was downhill after that in every sense, through the foggy forests of ponderosa pines to Colfax and farewells; to Sacramento at dusk; and the moonrise at Martinez, where Howard Hughes's top-secret spy vessel, the *Glomar Explorer*, was riding at anchor.

"Joe DiMaggio was born here," Christopher said. "And so was the Martini. Maybe."

Then we were rolling through the Bay Area's backyard.

"May I suggest we put the lights out?" Christopher said. The darkness inside the *Los Angeles* revealed everything outside—the lights of the bay, the bridge we had just crossed, the muddy little docks in the foreground, Oakland just by the tracks, the skyline of San Francisco, Emeryville up ahead, where we glided to a stop.

I hated separating myself from the snug comfort of the *Los Angeles*. Taking nothing for granted, I travel hopefully; but I am not surprised when everything goes wrong. I am very grateful when things turn out well. If bliss can be described as an exalted state of not wishing to be anywhere else, then this had been bliss.

May 1995

Two for the Road: Havana, North Dakota

Jane and Michael Stern

As dawn's mist lifts away from the black earth west of the Bois de Sioux River and rows of sunflowers coil up to face the daybreak like soldiers coming to attention, a pot of coffee is put on to brew at the Farmers' Inn. It is the first of many pots to be made and poured that day in the town café, which is frequented by farmers and farmwives who live in and around the North Dakota village called Havana.

A most unusual enterprise, the Farmers' Inn is the only restaurant for miles around—a valued gathering place for locals and a farm-food oasis for hungry travelers. Its heartland menu and small-town character are inextricably bound up with the life of the little enclave, for it is owned and operated communally by the townspeople. This is a place neighbors can come to break bread together, where retired farmers hold court, young men eat five-thousand-calorie breakfasts, and toddlers play with toys (a box of them is always on hand). Last Fourth of July, when the Inn was open only until 11 A.M., ninety-four meals were served—an amazing tally for a café in a dot-on-the-map town in the middle of nowhere with a population of one hundred, not including dogs, cats, and livestock.

Havana used to be bigger. When Slim Miller opened the Havana

Café in 1913, there were 450 residents of the thriving grain-producing stop on the Great Northern rail line just one mile north of the Dakotas' border. For decades his restaurant served as an ad hoc community club where people could come not only to eat breakfast and the midday meal (known as dinner) but to exchange tidings over coffee. Slim sold the place in 1948, after which several owners came and went. In the postwar years many farms switched from grain to row crops; agriculture modernized and small family farms grew more scarce. As time passed, Havana's population thinned, business at the restaurant dwindled, and the old building began to crumble. Finally, in 1984, the Havana Café closed, leaving the town without a restaurant.

It was only then that citizens realized how much the place had meant to them. Jay Saunders, who runs the gas station, put a pot of coffee in his office for visitors to share. American Legionnaires opened up their hall as an informal gathering place. But neither of those well-meaning expressions of welcome provided the kind of easy, come-and-go atmosphere of a small-town café that is so conducive to a relaxed exchange of news and opinions.

Understanding that a restaurant in so remote a location had no chance of success if someone tried to operate it as a profit-making business, the members of the Havana Community Club decided to reopen the café on their own. Men pitched in and fixed up the old building; women volunteered to run the kitchen, agreeing to cook their specialties for neighbors and friends one day a month. The Havana school had just closed (children now travel to the bigger town of Forman for their education), so the refurbished eatery was able to get good equipment from the old school lunch room. When the Farmers' Inn opened a few days before Christmas in 1984, a comical sign on the bulletin board reflected the true soul of a meeting place in the midst of a sparsely peopled landscape: "Therapy Session 9–12 and 1–4. No Charge."

Some days, more than forty people came for dinner. In the bitter North Dakota winter, when temperatures drop far below zero and farmers often finish chores early, tables were occupied for hours with pinochle players. And from 6 A.M. on, the coffee never stopped flowing. "If we charged fifty cents a cup, we'd be rich!" declared one volunteer cook last summer as she watched a gentleman in overalls help himself to what she estimated was his twelfth free refill of the day.

Once the citizens of Havana realized their cooperative effort was going to work, they determined that the old café building was hopelessly dilapidated. So they pooled their resources and built a new one, which opened in the winter of 1986. Farmers' Inn II is a utilitarian steel structure with a spanking-clean, carpeted dining room where wood-grain Formica tables are outfitted with hand-hewn wooden napkin holders in the shape of cows, pigs, tractors, and horses—all cut and painted by a local retired elevator operator (that's a *grain* elevator, by the way—the only structure around here more than two stories tall). A bulletin board includes a flyer for a polka band, and a manila folder tacked up with a note on it saying "Please Put Your Havana News in Folder." Items deposited find their way into the "Havana News" column of the *Sargent County Teller,* which includes such stories as: "Joe Barbknecht arrived and joined his family at the Walt Barbknecht farm."

Passersby are welcome at the Farmers' Inn, but not many strangers find their way through the door. If you happen to be motoring along Route 32, which is straight as an arrow through land that is flat as a floor, it is actually quite shocking to encounter any kind of enterprise other than a farm. But here it is, a beguiling sight: a roadside house with a primitive sign that reads "FARMERS INN ... HOME COOKED MEALS" and features an idyllic painted mural of the landscape. Turn off the highway at the house and soon you find the main street of Havana, two short blocks of buildings that face the train tracks and a dozen grain elevators. Other than the restaurant, the only businesses are a self-service gas station (residents have their own keys) and the combination general store and post office. Newcomers who drop in will likely be asked to sign the guest register—a visitor in these parts is cause for celebration.

Usually, there are waitresses: high-school girls in the summer, who get paid an honorarium of $10 per day, plus tips. Still, it is common for regulars to help themselves to coffee from the pot and to walk up to the kitchen window and tell the cook on duty what they want.

"Two eggs, over," announces one gentleman, clearly a regular. "Over hard ..."

"I know, I know," says Murdean Gulsvig, who shares kitchen duties this day with Doris, his wife of more than fifty years. " 'Throw 'em up against the wall, and if they bounce they're hard enough,' right?"

Murdean is a playful character who manages to tend the griddle with experienced savoir faire and keep up several conversations all at the same time. A septuagenarian retired farmer with a few tufts of red hair combed across his scalp and a Farmers' Inn apron tied around his corn-fed girth, he is something more than just this day's cook; he also serves as operations director for the café, ordering supplies and overseeing the planning of each month's menu and daily cooking assignments. When he and Doris do draw kitchen duty, Murdean is known for the delicious coarse-ground breakfast sausage he makes, as well as for pancakes that are plate-wide and fluffy inside, with an ethereal lace-textured surface.

At 6:30 in the morning, when the dining room is getting crowded and the air swirls with the wake-up smells of brewing coffee and sizzling breakfast meats, Doris Gulsvig totes a pan of oven-hot caramel rolls out of the kitchen and sets them down to cool near the coffee station, then stops to write the dinner special on a blackboard. As is always the case, there is one *prix-fixe* hot meal—today's is pork roast with dressing, gravy, mashed potatoes, corn, cole slaw, and lemon pie (for $4.50)—as well as a small assortment of soups, sandwiches, and hamburgers just in case the kitchen runs out of its main course.

Once the breakfast crowd clears out, Murdean and Doris spend the morning stirring the lemon filling for the pie, boiling potatoes, tasting the stuffing to see if it's seasoned right, and watching the roast cook. "You better mash those potatoes now, or they'll get too soft," Doris calls to Murdean, who has managed to escape the kitchen to a dining-room table where he visits with friends.

Murdean shrugs with good-natured resignation. "See how hard she makes me work?" he says, pretending to seek sympathy as he heads back through the swinging door. Doris holds the pot and pours in the hot milk while Murdean does the mashing. As he works, he boasts, "We got a ninety-nine when the health inspector came around. It would have been one hundred, but we won't wear hairnets. Jiminy Christmas, I don't have enough hair to put a net over!"

You can count on Doris and Murdean in the kitchen at least a couple days every week. Nowadays, instead of a different cook every day of the month, the rotation has been trimmed down to about half a dozen cooks taking turns. The cooks we met made a point of distinguishing their cooking—"farm cooking"—from restaurant cooking. The latter, they said, is more deluxe and uses ingredients they don't find in the grocery store and, worse, that their husbands wouldn't recognize. While not at all embarrassed to use canned soup for a casserole or cake mix for pineapple upside-down cake, they also know how to make slow-risen butter horn rolls and old-fashioned "knefla" soup with hand-rolled dumplings.

In the summer, they make use of garden tomatoes and cucumbers and, when Harlan Klefstad returns from his winter home in Arizona, there will be pies prepared from the lemons he brings back from his tree there. Mary Ann Fliehs is especially talented when it comes to pies—rhubarb, sour cream, lemon meringue, and coconut cream. Marie Underberg is delighted when the menu calls for roast turkey, because then she can bake her big pumpkin cake for dessert.

"This is what I call a gravy-and-potato café," declares Harvey Peterson, whose wife, Gloria, is known for the raisin sauce she makes for ham. Mr. Peterson, who has farmed the land for more than fifty years, is a regular who, amazingly, drinks no coffee. One summer morning, at a table with his wife and some other cooks and his grandson, he spoke of the days long, long ago, when Havana had four flourishing grocery stores, two department stores, and a twenty-piece band for promenade concerts in the warmer months. He recalled how empty the town seemed when the Havana Café closed. "Now look at what we have," he said with a measure of pride, gesturing to a dining room crowded with Havanans, including oldsters bragging to each other about grandkids' school scholarships and baseball hitting averages; young families marshaling their members for a nearby tee-ball tournament; and working farmers engaged in an incredibly precise discussion about the spring wheat they raise versus white wheat, winter wheat, and soft red wheat.

"The Farmers' Inn holds our community together," Mr. Peterson concluded.

"It's like going to church on Sunday," one of the cooks added. "Except you don't have to be Lutheran to have your coffee here."

"Maybe we did save this café," another added thoughtfully. "But the way I see it, this café saved us."

The following recipes were taken from the *Farmers' Inn* cookbook, a collection published by the town in 1994 to celebrate the café's tenth anniversary.

DORIS GULSVIG'S RHUBARB CRUNCH
Farmers' Inn

1½ pounds rhubarb (about 12 stalks)
1 stick (½ cup) unsalted butter
¾ cup granulated sugar
2 tablespoons cornstarch
1 cup water
½ teaspoon salt
½ teaspoon vanilla
1 cup all-purpose flour
¾ cup old-fashioned rolled oats
1 cup packed light brown sugar
1 teaspoon cinnamon
Accompaniment: vanilla ice cream

1. Preheat oven to 350°F. and grease a 13- by 9-inch baking pan.

2. Trim rhubarb and cut into ½-inch pieces (you should have about 5 cups).

3. Arrange rhubarb evenly in baking pan. In a small saucepan melt butter.

4. In another small saucepan stir together granulated sugar, cornstarch, water, and ¼ teaspoon salt. Bring mixture to a boil and simmer, stirring, until thickened and clear, about 3 minutes. Stir in vanilla and pour mixture over rhubarb.

5. In a bowl stir together flour, oats, brown sugar, cinnamon, butter, and remaining ¼ teaspoon salt until mixture resembles coarse meal. Sprinkle mixture evenly over rhubarb.

6. Bake crunch in middle of oven 1 hour, or until rhubarb is tender and top is crisp and golden.

7. Cool crunch in pan on a rack 15 minutes.

8. Serve crunch warm with ice cream.

MILDRED BRUMMOND'S CHOCOLATE BEET CAKE
Farmers' Inn

3 medium beets (about 1¼ pounds)
1¾ cups all-purpose flour
1½ teaspoons baking soda
¼ teaspoon salt
1½ cups sugar
3 large eggs
¼ teaspoon vanilla
1 cup vegetable oil
½ cup unsweetened cocoa powder (not Dutch-process)
½ cup water

1. In a saucepan cover beets with salted water by 1 inch. Bring water to a boil and simmer beets, covered, until tender, 35 to 45 minutes. Drain beets in a colander and rinse under cold water until cool. Slip off skins and with a hand-held grater coarsely shred enough beets to measure 1½ cups.

2. Preheat oven to 350°F. and grease a 13- by 9-inch baking pan.

3. Sift flour, baking soda, and salt into a bowl and whisk together.

4. In a large bowl with an electric mixer beat together sugar, eggs, vanilla, and oil until smooth.

5. Add beets and cocoa powder to sugar mixture and beat until combined well.

6. Add flour mixture and water to beet mixture and beat just until combined.

7. Pour batter into pan, smoothing top, and bake in middle of oven 35 minutes, or until a tester comes out with crumbs adhering.

8. Cool cake in pan on a rack and cut into serving pieces.

DORIS GULSVIG'S "KNEFLA" SOUP
Creamy Chicken Soup with Dumplings
Farmers' Inn

FOR SOUP
2 pounds boiling potatoes

1 medium onion
1 carrot
1 celery rib
2 chicken boullion cubes
5 cups water
⅓ cup unsalted butter

FOR "KNEFLA"

3 cups all-purpose flour
1 large egg, beaten lightly
1 teaspoon salt
1 cup whole milk

a 12-ounce can evaporated milk

1. Peel potatoes and cut into ½-inch cubes. Chop onion and cut carrot and celery into ¼-inch dice.

2. In a large heavy kettle combine potatoes with rest of soup ingredients and simmer, uncovered, until vegetables are tender, about 15 minutes.

3. With a wooden spoon, in a bowl stir together all knefla ingredients until mixture forms a dough and with floured hands on a floured surface pat into a 6-inch square about ½ inch thick.

4. With a sharp knife cut dough into ¾-inch-wide strips. With floured hands on a lightly floured surface roll a strip of dough with palms of hands to form a narrow rope 8 to 10 inches long and ½ inch wide. Cut rope crosswise into ½-inch pieces and lightly coat with flour. Transfer knefla to a tray and arrange in one layer. Make more knefla with remaining dough strips in same manner.

5. In a 6-quart kettle bring 4 quarts salted water to a boil for knefla.

6. Working in batches, put knefla in a sieve and shake off any excess flour. Drop all knefla into boiling water and cook, stirring once, just until tender, about 20 minutes.

7. Drain knefla and stir into soup. Just before serving, stir evaporated milk into soup and season with salt and pepper. Makes about 12 cups.

July 1997

PERSONALITIES OF *GOURMET*

Edouard de Pomiane

Elizabeth David

"Art demands an impeccable technique; science a little understanding."
Today the mention of art in connection with cookery is taken for pretension. Science and cookery make a combination even more suspect.
Because he was a scientist by profession, making no claims to being an
artist, Docteur Édouard de Pomiane's observation was a statement of
belief, made in all humility. Vainglory is totally missing from de Pomiane's work. He knew that the attainment of impeccable technique
meant a lifetime—in de Pomiane's case an exceptionally long one—of
experience and discipline. Out of it all he appears to have extracted,
and given, an uncommon amount of pleasure.

Docteur Édouard de Pomiane's real name was Édouard Pozerski.
He was of purely Polish origin, the son of emigrés who had fled Poland
and settled in Paris after the revolution of 1863. Born and brought up
in Montmartre, he was educated at the École Polonaise and subsequently at the Lycée Condorcet. (The École Polonaise was described
by Henri Babinski, another celebrated Franco-Polish cookery writer,
as an establishment of ferocious austerity. Babinski was the real name
of Ali-Bab, author of that immense and remarkable volume *Gas-*

tronomie Pratique.) De Pomiane chose for his career the study of biology, specializing in food chemistry and dietetics. Before long he had invented a new science called gastrotechnology, which he defined simply as the scientific explanation of accepted principles of cookery. For a half-century—interrupted only by his war service from 1914 to 1918—de Pomiane also made cookery and cookery writing his hobby and second profession. After his retirement from the Institut Pasteur, where he lectured for some fifty years, he devoted himself entirely to his cookery studies. He was eighty-nine when he died, in January, 1964.

De Pomiane's output was immense—some dozen cookery books, countless scores of articles, broadcasts, lectures. In France his books were best sellers; among French cookery writers his place is one very much apart.

Many before him had attempted to explain cookery in scientific terms and had succeeded only in turning both science and cookery into the deadliest of bores. De Pomiane was the first writer to propound such happenings as the fusion of egg yolks and olive oil in a mayonnaise, the sizzling of a potato chip when plunged into fat for deep-frying, in language so straightforward, so graphic, that even the least scientifically minded could grasp the principles instead of simply learning the rules. In cooking, the possibility of muffing a dish is always with us. Nobody can eliminate that. What de Pomiane did by explaining the cause was to banish the *fear* of failure.

Adored by his public and his pupils, feared by the phony, derided by the reactionary, de Pomiane's irreverent attitude to established tradition, his independence of mind backed up by scientific training, earned him the reputation of being something of a Candide, a provocative rebel disturbing the grave conclaves of French gastronomes, questioning the holy rites of the "white-vestured officiating priests" of classical French cookery. It was understandable that not all his colleagues appreciated de Pomiane's particular brand of irony:

"As to fish, everyone agrees that it must be served between the soup and the meat. The sacred position of the fish before the meat course implies that one must eat fish *and* meat. Now such a meal, as any dietician will tell you, is far too rich in nitrogenous substances, since fish has just as much assimilable albumen as meat, and contains a great deal more phosphorus."

Good for Dr. de Pomiane. Too bad for us that so few of his readers—or listeners—paid attention to his liberating words.

It does, on any count, seem extraordinary that thirty years after de Pomiane's heyday, the dispiriting progress from soup to fish, from fish to meat, and on, remorselessly on, to salad, cheese, a piece of pastry, a *crème caramel* or an ice cream, still constitutes the standard menu throughout the entire French-influenced world of hotels and catering establishments.

Reading some of de Pomiane's neat little menus (from *365 Menus, 365 Recettes,* Albin Michel 1938), it is so easy to see how little effort is required to transform the dull, overcharged, stereotyped meal into one with a fresh emphasis and a better balance:

> *Tomates à la crème*
> *Côtelettes de porc*
> *Purée de farine de marrons*
> *Salade de mâche à la betterave*
> *Poires*

An unambitious enough menu—and what a delicious surprise it would be to encounter such a meal at any one of those country town Hôtels des Voyageurs, du Commerce, du Lion d'Or, to which my own business affairs in France now take me. In these establishments, where one stays because there is no choice, the food is of a mediocrity, a predictability redeemed for me only by the good bread, the fresh eggs in the omelets, the still relatively civilized presentation, which in Paris is becoming rare—the soup brought to table in a tureen, the hors d'oeuvre on the familiar, plain little white dishes, the salad in a simple glass bowl. If it all tasted as beguiling as it looks, every dish would be a feast. Two courses out of the whole menu would be more than enough.

Now that little meal of de Pomiane's *is* a feast, as a whole entity. It is also a real lesson in how to avoid the obvious without being freakish, how to start with the stimulus of a hot vegetable dish, how to vary the eternal purée of potatoes with your meat (lacking chestnut flour we could try instead a purée of lentils or split peas), how to follow it with a fresh, bright, unexpected salad (that excellent mixture of corn salad and beets—how often does one meet with it nowadays?), and since by that time most people would have had enough without embarking on cheese, de Pomiane is brave enough to leave it out. How much harm has that tyrannical maxim of Brillat-Savarin's about a meal without cheese done to all our waistlines and our digestions?

For a hot first dish, de Pomiane's recipe for *tomates à la crème* is worth knowing. His method makes tomatoes taste so startlingly unlike any other dish of cooked tomatoes that any restaurateur who put it on his menu would, in all probability, soon find it listed in the guidebooks as a regional specialty. De Pomiane himself said the recipe came from his Polish mother. That would not prevent anyone from calling it what he pleases:

Tomates à la Crème

Take six tomatoes. Cut them in halves. In your frying pan melt a lump of butter. Put in the tomatoes, cut side downwards, with a sharply-pointed knife puncturing here and there the rounded sides of the tomatoes. Let them heat for five minutes. Turn them over. Sprinkle them with salt. Cook them for another ten minutes. Turn them again. The juices run out and spread into the pan. Once more turn the tomatoes cut side upwards. Around them put 80 grammes (3 oz. near enough) of thick cream. Mix it with the juices. As soon as it bubbles, slip the tomatoes and all their sauces onto a hot dish. Serve instantly, very hot.

The faults of the orthodox menu were by no means the only facet of so-called classic French cooking upon which de Pomiane turned his analytical intelligence. Recipes accepted as great and sacrosanct are not always compatible with sense. Dr. de Pomiane's radar eye saw through them. "*Homard à l'américaine* is a cacophony ... it offends a basic principle of taste." I rather wish he had gone to work on some of the astonishing things Escoffier and his contemporaries did to fruit: choice pears masked with chocolate sauce and cream, beautiful fresh peaches smothered in raspberry purée and set around with vanilla ice seem to me offenses to nature, let alone to art or basic principles. How very odd that people still write of these inventions with breathless awe.

De Pomiane, however, was a man too civilized, too subtle, to labor his points. He passes speedily from the absurdities of *haute cuisine* to the shortcomings of folk cookery, and deals a swift right and left to those writers whose reverent genuflections before the glory and wonder of every least piece of peasant cookery lore make much journalistic cookery writing so tedious. By the simple device of warning his readers to expect the worst, de Pomiane gets his message across. From a village baker-woman of venerable age, he obtains an ancestral recipe for a cherry tart made on a basis of butter-enriched bread dough. He passes on the recipe, modified to suit himself, and carrying with it the characteristically deflating note: "When you open the oven door you will have a shock. It is not a pretty sight. The edges of the tart are slightly burnt and the top layer of cherries blackened in places.... It will be received without much enthusiasm for, frankly, it is not too prepossessing!

"Don't be discouraged. Cut the first slice and the juice will run out. Now try it. What a surprise! The pastry is neither crisp nor soggy, and just tinged with cherry juice. The cherries have kept all their *flavour* and the juice is not sticky—just pure cherry juice. They had some good ideas in 1865!"

Of a dish from the Swiss mountains, Dr. de Pomiane observes that it is "a peasant dish, rustic and vigorous. It is not everybody's taste. But one can improve upon it. Let us get to work." This same recipe provides an instructive example of the way in which Dr. de Pomiane thinks we should go to work improving a primitive dish to our own taste while preserving its character intact. Enthusiastic beginners might add olives, parsley, red peppers. Dr. de Pomiane is scarcely that simple. The school-trained professional might be tempted to superimpose cream, wine, mushrooms, upon his rough and rustic dish. That is not de Pomiane's way. His way is the way of the artist, of the man who can add one sure touch, one only, and thereby create an effect of the preordained, the inevitable, the entirely right and proper:

Tranches au Fromage

Black bread—a huge slice weighing 5 to 7 oz., French mustard, 8 oz. Gruyère.

The slice of bread should be as big as a dessert plate and nearly 1 inch thick. Spread it with a thick layer of French mustard, then cover the whole surface of the bread with strips of cheese about ½ inch thick. Put the slice of bread on a fireproof dish and under the grill. The cheese softens and turns golden-brown. Just before it begins to run, remove the dish and carry it to the table. Sprinkle it with salt and pepper. Cut the slice in four and put it onto four hot plates. Pour out the white wine and taste your cheese slice. In the mountains this would seem delicious, but here it is all wrong. But you can put it right. Over each slice pour some melted butter. A mountaineer from the Valais would be shocked, but my friends are enthusiastic, and that is good enough for me.

This is the best kind of cookery writing. It is courageous, courteous, adult. It is creative in the true sense of that ill-used word, creative because it invites the reader to use his own critical and inventive faculties, sends him out to make discoveries, form his own opinions, observe things for himself, instead of slavishly accepting what the books tell him. That little trick, for example, of spreading the mustard on the bread *underneath* the cheese in de Pomiane's Swiss mountain dish is, for those who notice such things, worth a volume of admonition. So is the little tomato recipe quoted on page 204. You may not realize it the first time you cook the dish. What you discover after trying it twice is that you have learned an uncommon little piece of cookery skill. How many people can fry tomatoes—*and* without peeling them—so that they do not stick to the pan? You have learned also how to make the simplest, freshest little cream sauce merely by pouring cream into a frying pan. And, I should add, this is a method of making something worthwhile even with such second-rate tomatoes as normally come our way.

All de Pomiane's vegetable dishes are interesting, freshly observed. He is particularly fond of hot beets, recommending them as an accompaniment to roast saddle of hare—a delicious combination. It was especially in his original approach to vegetables and sauces that de Pomiane provoked the criticism of hidebound French professional chefs. Perhaps they were not aware that in this respect de Pomiane was often simply harking back to his Polish origins, thereby refreshing French cookery in the perfectly traditional way. De Pomiane gives, incidentally, the only way (the nonorthodox way) to braise Belgian endive with success—no water, no blanching, just butter and slow cooking.

The public knows little of de Pomiane's work and it is missing something of great value. Although his *Cooking in Ten Minutes* (Bruno Cassirer, distributed by Faber), a lighthearted treatise on how to make the most of *charcuterie* or delicatessen food—first published in England in 1948—has proved a great favorite, there exists a much more representative book—a collection of lectures, radio talks, recipes, and articles—called *Cooking with Pomiane* (Bruno Cassirer, distributed by Faber. Published in the United States by Roy Publishers, Inc., 1962). It is most adroitly put together and translated into English cookery usage by Mrs. Peggie Benton. Published eight years ago and still relatively unknown, the book is modest in appearance and in size, its jacket is the reverse of eye-catching, there are no color photographs, no packaging. It is just a very good and immensely sane book.

March 1970

M.F.K. FISHER: A PROFILE

Elizabeth Hawes

When Mary Frances Kennedy Fisher heard a critic suggest that if Americans followed the Japanese custom she would be designated a "living national treasure," she responded with an airy chortle. "Ridiculous," she said. "I'm becoming marbleized. And my bones are so creaky, I shall soon turn to stone."

M.F.K. Fisher has a peculiar eminence. Proclaimed America's greatest food writer, she has been quietly turning out fine, precise, and evocative prose, full of sensuality and touched with wit and humanity, for nearly half a century. She has written seventeen books and been published in a wide spectrum of magazines: *The New Yorker, The Atlantic Monthly, Vogue, Gourmet, House & Garden,* and *Family Circle.* Over the years she has acquired a very special and ardent group of fans, and more often than not they refer to her as M.F.K., for her prose has a pungent intimacy that tempts many into an unusually close reader-relationship with her. And yet, until the 1982 publication of her collection of essays, *As They Were,* which was deemed autobiographical, she was something of a literary secret.

Mrs. Fisher is very modest about her work. She laughs away com-

pliments and is neither surprised nor impressed by the recent attention focused on her. "Things just happen, that's all," she might say, with
a rather mystical far-off gaze. Or "I don't know, I don't care, I don't
read reviews," with a set of her mouth, and "I just cook and talk and
have fun" about the number of interviewers she has indulged for the
past six months, having relaxed only briefly her stern dictum about
privacy. Moreover, she would point out, it is both odd and ironic that
As They Were is responsible for all the fuss because the book was meant
to be simply about places.

Mrs. Fisher is settled deep in the lap of a Victorian chair before a
wood-burning stove in the living room of her house in northern California. Her cat Charlie paces. A luncheon guest is arriving. A new
poster, designed by a friend for the San Francisco Culinary Fair, is
tacked to the door. Entitled "UFO," it shows a dark purple and blue
landscape above which floats a lustrous pearl-white pattypan squash.

That Mrs. Fisher is the food writer extraordinaire of the twentieth
century is indisputable. But her title is too narrow a fit, for when she is
writing about a solitary meal in the Gare de Lyon or a ritual tasting
of fresh peas in Switzerland, her kitchens in Provence or the last
virgin truffle hunter, she is writing about far more than food. Accord-
ingly, her admirers insist she *is* more, and reach for other labels—
philosopher, social critic, poet—often settling for the adjective "unique."
Familiarity with her work breeds complexities. She is both feminine
and a feminist; she loves men but celebrates independence. While
writing intimately, she doggedly eclipses the facts of her personal life.
She is consummately "truthful," yet a puzzling mysticism pervades her
work.

As if to jostle the categorical reader, Mrs. Fisher's solitary novel,
originally published in 1947, has been recently reprinted. Called *Not
Now But Now,* it follows a beautiful hedonist through a time warp. *A Cordial Water,* a small gem of a book about elixirs, nostrums, restoratives,
and fortifiers—a work Mrs. Fisher considers "the pick of the litter"—
has reappeared. And in April of this year Alfred A. Knopf published
Sister Age, a volume of short stories about aging in which food is the
most minor of characters.

James Beard's first brush with M.F.K. Fisher was his reading of *How to Cook a Wolf,* which was brought out during World War II in a time of shortages and rationing. It might pass for a cookbook because ever so casually recipes are adjoined to the text: "like birds in a tree—if there is a comfortable branch." But as the title promises and the chapter heads tease (How to Be Sage Without Hemlock, How to Distribute Your Virtue, How to Boil Water, How to Be Cheerful Though Starving, How to Carve the Wolf), it is also a witty and sympathetic dissertation on both the wartime table and the wartime mentality.

"I was hooked," Mr. Beard says in his "Appreciation" in a late edition of *The Art of Eating.* "Oddly enough, though we eventually moved in the same professional sphere, corresponded, talked by telephone long distance, and shared a number of friends, it took twenty-five years more for us to meet. By then I had long been a captive to her prose, her charm, and her taste for the better things of this planet."

"There have been so many changes in the food world and our sensibilities in the last twenty years," Mr. Beard says. He is sitting in the lofty greenhouse attached to the kitchen of his Greenwich Village town house. "In 1961 I don't think the general public was ready for *Delights and Prejudices* [his volume of memoirs]. I don't think it was ready for M.F.K. either.

"Mary Frances has had a secure place in the food establishment," he ventures, "but now I think she rests on her laurels as a critic and as someone who uses the English language the way it was meant to be used. It's as if she had her portrait done; food frames it, yet is not a vital part of the composition. I think of her as a goddess, Juno maybe, who descends to earth now and then. She doesn't write about food the way I write about it, or Julia [Child] does, or Marcella [Hazen] does. It's a means to an end with her."

North Beach is a part of San Francisco that M.F.K. Fisher has haunted for most of her life and might choose to live in if she were twenty years younger. It is a neighborhood of abundant warmth and a sweetly perverse nature, the bookstores and food vendors now mixed with pornography shops and transistor palaces. Though the area is frayed and fragmented, its Italian character still holds on, most conspicuously in great old restaurants like Vanessi's, on Broadway. At Saturday lunch the place is a haven for regulars of thirty years' standing, an unpredictable array of types united in the obvious pleasure they take at the table. Seated at the counter a big man, neither florid nor beefy but whose face brings both adjectives to mind, has polished off an order of antipasto, *linguine* with clam sauce, steak *pizzaiola* with vegetables, and plenty of the bread, radishes, olives, and tiny hot peppers that are lined up next to the salt, pepper, and sugar shakers. His chin glistens with olive oil as he offers a taste of his remaining pasta—and conversation—to a newcomer on the next stool. He is in the advertising business, he says, travels a lot, plays the horses, and has sumptuous gardens in Marin County. Has he ever heard of M.F.K. Fisher? "Sure. I have three of her books. I open them anywhere and read at night. She's an angel," he says, "a real gutsy angel."

Not too long ago in America food was food—not quite a hand-to-mouth matter, but hardly sensual. To be sure, in the inner sanctums of mahogany-paneled clubs and quaint old inns there existed a special breed of eater who discussed with authority Bordeaux versus Burgundies and perhaps the appealing qualities and even cultural significance of an extraordinary *plat.* Elsewhere, though, the word "gourmet" was tinged with pomposity, and the straight thinking of Fanny Farmer and *The Joy of Cooking* held sway. The aphorism "You are what you eat" was not in the national idiom.

It is evident that M.F.K. Fisher has led the way to the current sophistication about food, or at least greased the wheels of the culinary revolution that has swept America in the last twenty-five years. In the beginning, Mrs. Fisher was a rarity in a gastronomic field that produced hundreds and thousands of cookbooks but few expressive writers in the European tradition of Jean Anthelme Brillat-Savarin. Now the country stirs everywhere with people who have turned to the preparation, presentation, and even contemplation of food as an expression of personality, aesthetics, and culture. Northern California, where Mrs. Fisher now lives, is a hotbed of original and passionate culinary enterprise. More profoundly than fashion, food, it is said, can turn the soul inside out.

There was no precedent for Mrs. Fisher's first volume, *Serve It Forth*

(1937), which even Lucius Beebe (a sophisticated but sometimes waspish reviewer who in his day was America's best-known gastronome) described as elegant and original, although he was disgruntled to find out that M.F.K. was a woman. Her subject is "eating and what to eat and people who eat," and she is erudite and writes easily as a person with passions, prejudices, and vulnerabilities, drawing upon her memory with amazing clarity. Some stories are historical reflections, others, musings on secret eatings or recollections of a snail hunt or dirty kitchens. Occasionally, recipes appear.

Mrs. Fisher's focus is wide and unpredictable and that is confirmed in *Serve It Forth, Consider the Oyster* (1941), *How to Cook a Wolf* (1942), *The Gastronomical Me* (1943), and *An Alphabet for Gourmets* (1949), all of which were later included in *The Art of Eating* (1954). The concentration on food is constant, and details of fleeting tastes and feasts are as vivid and rich as if they had just happened. Sometimes they linger indelibly: a fried egg sandwich tucked into a child's pocket "tough, soggy, indigestible and luscious"; a tangerine drying delectably on a radiator with skin as "thin as one layer of enamel on a Chinese bowl, that crackles so tinily, so ultimately under your teeth."

In the foreword to *The Gastronomical Me* Mrs. Fisher explains her purpose: "It seems to me," she says, "that our three basic needs, for food and security and love, are so mixed and mingled and entwined that we cannot straightly think of one without the others.... There is a communion of more than our bodies when bread is broken and wine drunk. And that is my answer, when people ask me: Why do you write about hunger, and not wars or love?"

On July 3 of this year, M.F.K. Fisher turned seventy-five. (Had she been born a day later, her father had threatened to name her Independencia.) She grew up in small-town Whittier, California, the oldest of four children, happy and secure, well-fed and well-bred. She was influenced by her family's genteel exuberance and the social ostracism of being the only Episcopal family in a snug town of Quakers. She was affected by her father's devotion to his post as editor of the nonpartisan newspaper in a partisan town and her Grandmother Holbrook's nervous stomach. ("Even when I was a little kid," she says, "I noticed the difference food made to people's spirits. When grandmother left, we had such a different time.") A gallery of memorable characters— dowagers, politicians, cooks, and carpetmen—drifted in and out of the household. "Father's Lame Ducks" is how Mrs. Fisher traces her tolerance for and attraction to the odd and the down-and-out, in fact and in print. Other youthful experiences took hold too: Cooking made her feel important, and newspaper training made her orderly with words. Eagerly she swept through her father's bookshelves and the countless periodicals that filtered in to his attention, from *Photoplay* to *The New Masses* and Bernard McFadden's *Physical Culture*. At twenty, after several idling years at college, she married Albert Young Fisher, the son of a Presbyterian minister, and left behind a comfortable but complex conventionality for France.

Of all the influences in M.F.K. Fisher's life perhaps the most important is France. "I am more of me in France," she tries to explain, "more of the way I *think* I am. I'm more awake, more aware, and as far as senses and personality, stronger. Every minute is more of a minute there. Here, I'm really passing through." All told, perhaps two decades, and many lifetimes, have been spent there. In the late 1920s as a student at the University of Dijon with her husband Al, a scholar (who later chaired the English department at Smith), she responded to a new culture with all the spirit of adventure inspired by first love, a lean pocketbook, and a relentlessly curious nature.

The post-Depression years brought the Fishers back to America, to WPA jobs, and to emotional changes. By the time of her next stint in Europe—Switzerland, in the shadow of the French Alps—which came as World War II was brewing, Mrs. Fisher had divorced Al and married their friend Dillwyn Parrish, a painter and a novelist with whom she had an intense idyll of five years before he died in 1941. During these years, she tells us in *The Gastronomical Me,* "I seemed beautiful, witty, truly loved, the most fortunate of women ... with her hungers fed."

After Parrish's death Mrs. Fisher recuperated in Helmet, California, cultivating a vineyard and doing a stint as a Hollywood screenwriter. She also "took a gamble" on a third marriage to the publisher Donald Friede, with whom she had two children, and then divorced. In

1954 Mrs. Fisher returned to France, and with her daughters, Anne and Kennedy, in tow she took up residence in Aix-en-Provence, a place, she writes in *Map of Another Town,* that "is intimate to my being." There were good times, and bad. "I am somewhat like a cobweb there. I do not bother anyone ... I can walk the same streets and make my own history," she muses, "my growing ability to be alone would protect and help me from being arrogant." When she left France to resettle in Saint Helena, an old wine town in northern California, in a big Victorian structure that bustled like a boarding house, she told herself, "I need not worry about coming back, for I [am] there anyway."

Once more, in 1961, Mrs. Fisher managed to live at length in France, this time on assignment to write Time-Life's *The Cooking of Provincial France* in collaboration with Julia Child, who became a lasting friend, and Michael Field. In other years, as "her demons called," she returned to Aix-en-Provence, Arles, and Marseilles, as if to check up on them and on herself. At times her company was her sister Norah—her best friend—or Donald Friede, his new wife, Eleanor, and the children (they called themselves "The Five Flying Friedes"— an unconventional but very merry band); or Julia and Paul Child, Dame Sybil Bedford, or simply her five senses. In 1978, when New York City's Les Dames d'Escoffier honored her with a title, she seized upon her proximity to France for a "final" visit.

M.F.K. Fisher has an impressive fortitude. Like other strong women of the twentieth century she is self-contained. "Over the years, I have taught myself, and have been taught, to be a stranger. A stranger usually has the normal five senses, perhaps especially so, ready to protect and nourish him." She is well nourished by small moments. In *As They Were* she writes of a world contained in the sounds of the Rue Brueys in Aix-en-Provence: "there was the feeling that I listened to a whole carnival, blurred, just off a cosmic Midway.... a huge sponge dripping with sound...."

Seen through her senses, M.F.K. Fisher's world has the romantic impact of a wonderful earthy stew—gypsies, transvestites, California, France, Mexico, freighters, wharfs, vineyards, friends who are food people, revolutionaries, countesses, calligraphers, painters, ranchers.

Yet there is a chill in her stories as well as her life. Her puzzling mystical dimension is tied to sensual awareness: Lushness contains a touch of evil, love cools, "sulky" peaches will go rotten.

To a certain extent the coincidental has shaped Mrs. Fisher's life. She began writing gastronomic pieces for her husband Al when someone in the library where she worked left behind a tempting volume on the culinary arts. Her research into that field led to the discovery of Brillat-Savarin's *La Physiologie du goût*, which she translated in 1949 and which stands as one of her noblest accomplishments. (In the 1940s she might have devoted her life to translating Colette, with whom she is often compared, had not the publisher insisted upon emphasizing the sensational in the subject's life.) The purchase, in Zurich in 1937, of an odd nineteenth-century painting of an ugly old woman is responsible for *Sister Age*.

The way in which Mrs. Fisher approaches her work is revealing. She is determined to be frank and unsentimental and insists upon calling her stories or memoirs "reports." "They are meant as the truth. I love to tell stories, but I can't fabricate," she says. "Everything happens for a reason, with a real beginning and an end. It may have started two hundred years ago and we don't know the end yet, but it has happened. Even the stories in *Sister Age*, which are told in the third person, were dreams of mine."

In the face of curiosity about her life and the resulting accusations of coyness leveled at her, Mrs. Fisher is adamantly private. "Cézanne felt that the light in his pictures was more important than the color. And Henry Moore certainly proved that space is more important than the outline of space. If I were writing the story of my life, I would put in names and dates, times and places, as I did in *Among Friends*. But, Good Hell, whether I am with my second husband or my third lover—who might be Artemis J. Swooney, who was born in Philadelphia, and whom I met in a café in Munich—has nothing whatsoever to do with the reason I am walking down a street in Zurich."

Mrs. Fisher is in fact evasive if not vague about what she has written because it is in the past. She doesn't read reviews, she rarely rewrites, and she does not reread finished work. When a psychoanalyst friend suggested that she look at her past work, she felt sick. Why? Judith Jones, Mrs. Fisher's editor at Knopf, who copes with her idiosyncrasies, says, "she simply sets very high standards. She is a perfectionist, with great modesty and an old-fashioned sense of propriety." Mrs. Fisher says, "Well, I get so self-critical, I get sick. I think, 'I have to pull this thing back,' but I can't; it is over. Writing is the only thing I know how to do, the only thing that makes me very happy. I write all the time—my house is bulging with things that will never be printed. If we survive another fifty years, these pieces might have some value—they might not. I don't care. *I really don't care.*"

"The Last House" is what M.F.K. Fisher calls her stucco cottage nestled in the front corner of a large ranch in the Valley of the Moon, fifty-two miles north of San Francisco. She is not being dramatic, merely honest about the fact that with troublesome eyesight and creaky bones, she can no longer travel. (She has already envisioned "the queer old-lady authoress, found quietly dead between the stove and the icebox, with a glass of vermouth in one hand and an overripe pear in the other.") To lure her out of her oversized house in nearby Saint Helena, this house was built to her specifications a decade ago by David Pleydell-Bouverie, an English architect-friend who owns the five hundred acres of vineyards and wild country outside her high arched windows. Essentially two rooms and a bath, it is described by Mrs. Fisher as a *palazzina.* California light rushes in; the Sonoma mountains intrude to the west and the Mayacamas to the east. Cobwebs hang here and there. The ceilings of the bedroom-workroom and the living room–kitchen rise up to unfinished redwood domes. The bathroom is practical but voluptuous and is outfitted with the largest tub in the region, a rocking chair, Oriental rugs, and on one wall, painted the same Pompeian red as the ceiling, an art gallery that includes several large oils by Dillwyn Parrish, a Rouault, and a tiny valentine. In every room are books, artwork, and mementos. There are no photographs or gadgets. And although Mrs. Fisher's kitchen is streamlined and compressed into one long counter, it quietly dominates.

"When I can't work, I read; when I can't read, I cook," is how Mrs. Fisher explains her days. Apart from a weekly marketing excursion with a helpful young friend, she remains at home, supplied with a bounty of fresh produce by local farmers and with social intercourse by a steady stream of friends and admirers. Although she lives alone, she is not afraid of isolation and is unwilling to depend on others. Invariably Mrs. Fisher prepares meals for her visitors—soup, salad, and cookies, perhaps, or a ragout and a fruit *clafouti*. She is a practical and inventive cook who shuns pretension. Though there are three thousand cookbooks carefully ordered about the room, she would prefer to draw inspiration from the season or her own stash of recipes, many of which appeared in her early books, in particular *With Bold Knife and Fork*. (She is well known for her vegetable soups.) The contents of her refrigerator are telling: small packets and bowls of leftovers, a pitcher of a fruit juice brew, a bag of tiny potatoes scavenged by a friend from the fields of Long Island, a tin of caviar, and open bottles of wine.

Mrs. Fisher has readied a supper for two friends who own a kitchen shop in Sonoma: sliced tomatoes sandwiched with *pesto,* scalloped oysters sprinkled with nutmeg at James Beard's suggestion, a salad of baby lettuces, and fresh fig ice cream. Dressed in a purple velour outfit and her long silver hair arranged in a neat twist, she sips a glass of vermouth. With prominent cheekbones, high arched eyebrows, and bright, rather imperious eyes, she is still beautiful. In her youth a food critic once described her as "a blond gorgeous enough to eat." Clifton Fadiman, who wrote the introduction to *The Art of Eating,* tells of falling in love with both her picture and her prose.

Nonetheless, Mrs. Fisher says she has aged faster than she anticipated and feels that most Americans are unprepared for old age. "We are helped by wise parents and teachers to live through our first couple of decades, to behave more or less like creative, productive social creatures, and to withdraw from the fray, if possible on various kinds of laurels. And then what?" For forty years Mrs. Fisher accumulated notes and clippings to write a book on the art of aging, and recently she shipped the material off to Radcliffe's Schlesinger Library, where her other papers and manuscripts are stored. What came out of this research are the stories contained in *Sister Age.*

M.F.K. Fisher has a very special place in the California food establishment and in the wine community, for which she has written two books. She is a wine connoisseur. France aside for practical reasons, northern California is the right place for Mrs. Fisher to be. The fields smell of eucalyptus, rosemary, and fennel. It is surprising that Mrs. Fisher hasn't written more about California, because the state's lore and history are the ingredients of her casual conversation and her wide circle of local friends could be characters in her stories.

Alice Waters, owner/chef of the celebrated Chez Panisse in Berkeley, whom Mrs. Fisher calls a phenomenon, shows deep affection for M.F.K. On visits to Mrs. Fisher's ranch she brings rare mushrooms, evocative flowers, handfuls of the young bitter lettuce known as *mesclun,* and old Marcel Pagnol movies and a projector. "Few people have stirred my culinary feelings deep down and provoked me the way M.F.K. Fisher has," she says.

In 1978, to commemorate Mrs. Fisher's seventieth birthday, Alice Waters, with James Beard, planned a surprise party for her in San Francisco. Mrs. Fisher's close friends were present as well as a number of admiring restaurant patrons, one of whom recited spontaneously from her works. The menu was contrived by Alice Waters to celebrate M.F.K. Fisher's books. The first course, called *Consider the Oyster,* consisted of eight varieties of the shellfish on the half shell. Next, *A Considerable Town,* featuring Marseilles, presented California *escargots* with Pernod, tomatoes with garlic, whole Pacific rockfish charcoal-grilled with herbs and anchovies, spit-roasted pheasants with new potatoes, a bitter lettuce salad with goat cheese croutons, and three plum sherbets in orange rind boats. *A Cordial Water* suggested the last course, a Muscat de Beaumes-de-Venise, coffee, and cordials.

M.F.K. Fisher, for once, accepted the deeply felt tribute. Mr. Beard commented, "It was one of those exciting times that you never expect to happen, but when they do you feel as if a magical moment has been created."

November 1983

James Beard, an American Icon:
The Early Years

Jay Jacobs

> The Proust *madeleine* phenomenon is now as firmly estab-
> lished in folklore as Newton's apple or Watt's steam engine. The
> man ate a tea biscuit, the taste evoked memories, he wrote a
> book.... In the light of what Proust wrote with so mild a stimu-
> lus, it is the world's loss that he did not have a heartier appetite.
> On a dozen Gardiner's Island oysters, a bowl of clam chowder, a
> peck of steamers, some bay scallops, three sautéed soft-shelled
> crabs, a few ears of fresh-picked corn, a thick swordfish steak of
> generous area, a pair of lobsters, and a Long Island duck, he
> might have written a masterpiece.
> —A. J. Liebling, "Memoirs of a Feeder in France"

The Proust *madeleine* phenomenon is not an uncommon experience;
with one stimulus or another we all undergo it from time to time, but
the memories evoked usually are fragmentary in the extreme, usually
confined to a particular moment in time, usually savored discretely,
and seldom provide inspiration for novels of stupefying prolixity. In
the case of Marcel Proust the Proust *madeleine* phenomenon was set off

by involuntary sensory response to the casual ingestion of a bit of tea-moistened cake. The response duplicated an earlier sensory experience that the author of *Remembrance of Things Past* could not have summoned up merely by a conscious mental effort.

What Proust lacked (and the majority of us lack) was what its relatively few possessors call "taste memory"—the ability to recall precise palatal sensations at will, often long after the fact and without benefit of physical stimuli. As Proust himself put it, "The sight of the little madeleine had recalled nothing to my mind before I tasted it; perhaps because I had so often seen such things in the interval, without tasting them, on the trays in pastry-cook's windows...."

To some extent, of course, taste memory is common to us all. If nothing more, it is a rudimentary device whereby we are enabled to choose the particular foods we feel like eating at a given moment, a choice made by drawing on generalized memories of past eating experience. We know, for example, how bacon and eggs taste en masse, so to speak, even though we may not recall the specific differentiating flavor, texture, or aroma of any single egg or rasher of bacon we may have eaten in the past. We also may recall how liver and onions taste in the same generalized sort of way and choose between the two dishes according to which roughly remembered aggregate experience we prefer to duplicate at the moment. The taste memory of the professional eater (or the gifted amateur), on the other hand, is distinguished by degrees of specificity, accuracy, and intensity denied most of us. Recall is precise and detailed, with stored data instantaneously retrievable at will.

The impression made by James Andrews Beard on anyone who meets or reads him is that the man remembers in minute detail each and every one of the eighty-seven-thousand-odd meals and the hundreds of thousands of individual dishes he has eaten since his birth, in Portland, Oregon, on May 5, 1903. In his largely autobiographical book, *Delights and Prejudices,* published in 1964, Beard described the meals and dishes of his earliest childhood onward with an immediacy that would have been astonishing coming from an inveterate—and incredibly precocious—diarist. Coming from a man who flatly states that he never has taken a note in his life, it seems altogether incomprehensible. Today, two decades and some twenty-two thousand meals after publication of the book, the impression one gets is that the data bank remains in perfect working order in its eighty-first year of operation and that Beard can savor any of the gustatory experiences of a long lifetime more vividly in retrospect than most mortals savor their food while it is still hot on the plate. It goes without saying that taste memory of this extraordinary sort is dependent not only on a highly sensitized palate, but also on something very close to total recall of experience in general. James Beard's earliest memory, which he maintains is quite fresh, is of the Lewis and Clark Exposition of 1905.

To a great many Americans Beard is the physical personification of gourmandise: a large-framed, rubicund, corpulent eating machine who beams with gustatory satisfaction from the dust jackets of cookbooks and the advertising pages of magazines ("James Beard, noted food authority, says ..."). Usually depicted looming over a tableful of edibles, knife and fork poised for action, eyes twinkling with anticipatory glee, capacious jowls waiting to be filled, he is an instantly recognizable icon, the most serviceable emblem we have of the good gastronomic life. Although the faces and figures of such eminent coreligionists as Julia Child and Craig Claiborne (both Beard protégés) probably have received more public exposure than has Beard during the past twenty years or so, it is Beard's magisterial image that the public at large identifies more readily with the preparation and consumption of good food. To anyone unfamiliar with their names and reputations, there is little about the physical appearance of either Child or Claiborne to suggest more than routine involvement with gastronomy. Put Beard in the center of a crowd in Peking or Calcutta, though, and, although nobody may know *who* he is, everyone will know *what* he is: a man passionately and single-mindedly devoted to the pleasures of the table, a man of such manifestly vast experience that his opinions on food and eating seem unassailable.

When James Beard puts his facial seal of approval on any of the several products, services, and restaurants he publicly endorses, his judgment seems infallible. Even on one occasion where his quoted testimonials appeared to be wildly contradictory as published in *The New*

York Times ("My one and only choice for Chinese food would be David K's" and "The heady, piquant and stimulating dishes are what attract me to Uncle Tai's Hunan Yuan"), the man's authority is such that both assertions seem gospel. Similarly, even when his historical pronouncements flout scholarly consensus, Beard's occasional mispremised fictions can seem more plausible than fact. For example, he ascribes the term "barbecue" to early Louisiana Creole cooks who spitted whole animals "from barbe à la queue—literally, from whiskers to tail." According to etymologists, however, the term ultimately derives from the aboriginal Taino language of the West Indies and originally denoted a broiling grill of green saplings set on posts. To most laymen Beard's errant conclusion has the ring of unassailable authority about it, but accepted scholarship, tortuously backtracking from English through Spanish and Haitian Creole to an obscure source in an extinct tongue, seems insupportably attenuated.

In part, Beard's effectiveness as a proselytizer of good cooking and good eating is attributable to his early training as an actor. To act any part with conviction, however, one must in some sense have lived it, and Beard has lived his role to the hilt. Whereas the externalities of that role have been enormously enhanced by his actor's gift for artifice, his ability to depict zestful enjoyment on a larger-than-life scale, the man comes by his iconic stature honestly. His enthusiasm for just about any food prepared with logic and integrity—whatever its ethnic or historical derivation, its degree of elaboration or simplicity—is unfeigned, boundless, utterly infectious. To those familiar with his career and attainments he is quite simply the bellwether of an American culinary coming of age. A generation removed from pioneer forebears on his father's side, he is the indisputable pioneer of a gustatory revolution that, after tentative postwar beginnings, has steamrollered its way into the forefront of contemporary American social life.

James Beard was exposed early and intensively to what would become the two enduring passions of his life: food and theater. Both interests were inherited from his English-born mother, Elizabeth Jones Brennan Beard, a woman of remarkable independence for her era, a devoted theatergoer, and, apparently, a superb cook. As Beard describes her in *Delights and Prejudices*, "She swept through a room or down the street with an air of determination and authority, and she met men on their own terms. In any social gathering, men surrounded her, and on outings she was among them, clamming, fishing, berrying. She could talk their language and used profanity on occasion, though without vulgarity. Women, as could be expected, were less drawn to her, except for those who gave her the boundless devotion often felt by the weak for the strong."

Offered a position as governess with a Canadian family then about to embark on a prolonged tour of the United States, Elizabeth Jones left London at sixteen in the late 1870s. Finding herself in Portland when her employers were summoned home to Toronto, she opted to remain there on her own, found work, and, after accumulating a nest egg, relocated in New York, where, as Beard has written, "she met many people in the theater and made lifelong friends." Then, after a brief return to England (where she reviewed and summarily dismissed the marital candidacy of a former beau), she returned to Portland, where she worked on and off for a Mrs. Curtis, the owner of several small residential hotels, and whence she departed on several leaves of absence for travels in the United States, Europe, and Central America. Between journeys she married a man named Brennan but found herself widowed a year later. In 1891, offering her by then extensive exposure to the gastronomic capitals of the world as credentials, she was appointed manager of the Curtis Hotel in Portland. Five years later she was the owner of a small hotel of her own, the Gladstone, which was housed in a four-storey building a couple of blocks from the Curtis.

Even in a city that knew and loved good food the dining rooms of Elizabeth Brennan's Gladstone Hotel appear to have been something quite out of the ordinary. Weary of the comings and goings of imported European chefs who tended to vanish without notice once the more cosmopolitan pleasures of life in San Francisco were called to their attention, Elizabeth took on and trained three local Chinese, as chef, *sous-chef*, and pastry chef. Under her tutelage the trio turned out such offerings as terrapin stew, *vol-au-vent* with creamed Olympia oysters, an asparagus-garnished sauté of chicken and wild mushrooms served with a Cognac-laced blend of cream and egg yolks, and, in spring, poached fresh salmon napped with what Beard terms a "sensational Russian dressing, made with caviar, herbs and seasonings, and mayonnaise."

These and many other Gladstone specialties would have been considered quite sophisticated by New Yorkers, or even Parisians, of that era. In Portland, a city that wasn't settled until around 1842—a time when the first serious restaurant in this country, Delmonico, was only eleven years old and still educating the first generation of New York epicures—and a city still somewhat rough around the edges, the menu at the Gladstone must have come as a revelation, notwithstanding that continuous interchange with the East Coast and Europe.

As James Beard describes his earliest memories of his mother, she was "a lovely woman with a good figure for those days [the halcyon days of Lillian Russell], and she carried her pounds with grace and aplomb. Her complexion was the pink-and-white of the English, and her black hair was extremely fine, worn in a French roll from the top of her head to the neck, where curly wisps called 'scolders' were arranged." Aside from her strawberries-and-cream epidermis and gracefully carried embonpoint, Elizabeth was intelligent, cultured, witty, and by the time mutual friends introduced her to a handsome widower named John Beard, financially secure.

To those who knew them, John Beard and Elizabeth Brennan seemed an ideal prospective couple. Both had entered their forties in fine fettle; both were attractive, charming, apparently successful in their respective careers (he was assistant appraiser for the Port of Portland), and citizens of reasonable substance. Moreover, Beard shared Elizabeth's love of good food, if on a somewhat less cultivated level.

In retrospect James Beard has concluded that his mother's feelings toward her suitor were rather less than wholehearted from the outset. Whether John Beard was equally dispassionate about Elizabeth is conjectural. In any event neither party was altogether unmotivated by practical considerations. Elizabeth was childless, with time running out; Beard had a motherless teen-age daughter on his hands; both craved the stability and respectability of a domestic alliance. They married in 1899.

As it soon developed, the groom was not the pillar of fiscal reliability Elizabeth had taken him to be. Indeed, he was up to his cravat in debt, and, to exacerbate the strain produced by this condition, his freeloading kinfolk descended on the hotel in numbers, while his daughter in no way alleviated matters by resorting to infantile acts of kitchen sabotage when her stepmother refused to become her maidservant. Elizabeth Beard quietly paid off her husband's debts, arranged to sell the hotel, and then made an announcement to her spouse, which James Beard quotes (presumably from the original source) without comment in *Delights and Prejudices:* "I'm selling. I've built and furnished a house in Hawthorne Park near the Summerses [the couple who had introduced them]. I want a child. After that's achieved you have a home in my house but it's not your house. Live your life and I'll look after mine. Lucille [her stepdaughter] will be under my supervision."

Whatever John Beard's reaction to his wife's fiat may have been, he acceded in full to her terms. A son, James, was born in Elizabeth's forty-third year, and, although James Beard's infrequent references to his father seem tinged with a sort of wistful affection, Beard *père* plays little more than a shadowy spear carrier's role in memoirs dominated by the force of Elizabeth's personality:

I grew up in the helter-skelter of her life. For periods I saw her constantly, and at other times she disappeared for a long stretch into one of her projects. I was alone frequently but I was enterprising, and I read a good deal, far beyond my years. And perhaps I spent too much time in the company of Elizabeth Beard's guests, for I listened to a lot of adult talk, adopted snobbish ideas and expressed myself freely on almost any subject. I could toss a remark into mixed company that unnerved the entire gathering, which, I have always imagined, secretly delighted my mother. I soon became as precocious and nasty a child as ever inhabited Portland. Even my mother's closest friends ran and locked their children away when I appeared. At home everyone spoiled me, and I was a special favorite of Let's [the erstwhile chef of the Gladstone, who often cooked for and with Elizabeth for years after the hotel was sold].

For whatever it may connote, John Beard is usually referred to as "my father" when he is mentioned at all in *Delights and Prejudices*, whereas Elizabeth almost invariably is "Mother." The New York wine dealer Sam Aaron has been one of the closest of Beard's many close friends for the past forty years. When the subject of John Beard was broached in conversation with him not long ago, Aaron reflected for a moment and said, "In all the years my wife and I have known Jim, during all the trips we've taken together, as often as he's stayed at our house, I've never heard him mention his father." James Beard's circle of friends of long-standing includes a good many dynamic, brilliantly successful women in various fields of endeavor. He has been a lifelong bachelor.

From a purely gastronomic standpoint Beard's early years were idyllic. Because its basic thesis is concerned with one man's response to good cooking and eating, *Delights and Prejudices*, the most autobiographical of his books, may appear to slight other facets of Beard's childhood. The impression one gets in conversation with the man today, however, is of a childhood in which all activity, save reading and theatergoing, was directly food-related, in which the edible bounty of each day both defined and justified one's uses of the day itself.

As is no longer the case in much of the industrialized world, the nature of eating in the first decade of the twentieth century—and for some decades thereafter—was determined in large part by the calendar. For better or worse most foods could be consumed fresh only during short local growing seasons, and enjoyment of them could be prolonged or deferred only by various means of preservation. As a consequence the home kitchen of those days was a much busier place than it is today. It was not only the nerve center and command post of quotidian domestic life, but it was the agency whereby good living was perpetuated throughout the year. This was particularly so in a rural America isolated from ready sources of store-bought supply and hardly less so in the major cities of the American West, which had been settled not long earlier by a self-reliant yeomanry steeped in centuries-old traditions of seasonal provision for the future. In such circumstances the small boy who craved the company of his mother perforce spent a good deal of his waking day in the kitchen.

There were other enticements besides pure, unalloyed filial love to lure Elizabeth Beard's pampered child kitchenward. For the fair-skinned, golden-haired, overweight toddler who years later would re-mark that "there has always been enough meat on the bones for two," the first conscious sensations of each day were the yeasty redolence of baking bread and the salivary anticipation of hard-wheat loaves to be taken hot from the oven, sliced, and slathered with fresh farm butter. Although Elizabeth had sold her hotel, she continued her culinary ac-tivities as if still operating a public restaurant. And, although her son prides himself still on never having taken a formal cooking lesson, to all intents and purposes he grew up in a professional kitchen and was exposed to professional cooking procedures from early childhood on-ward. For Americans of even moderate means eating was no casual ac-tivity in the early 1900s. The day's meals—breakfast, high tea, and, often, late supper included—were serious, often interminable pro-gressions through course after substantial course, and the American appetite of Beard's formative years was personified by the spectacu-larly edacious William Howard Taft, who crowded his mountainous bulk into the White House when Beard was five years old, by the leg-endarily voracious Diamond Jim Brady, and by Brady's favorite con-sort, the splendorously upholstered soprano, Lillian Russell. (It was La Russell who seriously dented the customary aplomb of Oscar Tschirky, better known to the world as "Oscar of the Waldorf," by out-eating Brady himself with no apparent strain. As Tschirky later ob-served, the spectacle of "the loveliest woman I had ever seen" pigging out in such epic fashion was "the surprise and disillusionment of [a] lifetime.")

Despite the widespread current belief that this country historically has been a gastronomic wasteland redeemed only by a very recent revolution in the culinary arts (a revolution James Beard was instru-mental in fomenting), the fact is that a great many Americans dined in high epicurean style from pre–Civil War days until around the onset of World War I. Moreover, the so-called new American cuisine (an imaginary phenomenon of the late 1970s and early 1980s for which Beard reserves his utmost contempt) is little more, and perhaps some-thing less, than a reprise of what less portentously was considered good, honest, logical cooking in Elizabeth Beard's day. (All the Gladstone Hotel dishes mentioned earlier, for example, anticipated the current "American nouvelle" style, sans foofaraw, by a mere three quarters of a century.)

The cooking to which the young James Beard was exposed during the first decade of the century began with ingredients of an integrity and quality virtually unknown today, even in the midst of a sudden burgeoning revival of interest in native American foodstuffs. Although the states of Oregon and California were contiguous then, as they are now, Beard tells us in *Delights and Prejudices* that his mother "maintained that little fruit which traveled from California had the quality of well-matured local fruit in season, but she kept trying the imports anyway. She generally rejected them in disgust." One wonders what she would have made of today's California tomatoes, those eerie, etiolated, unripenable fruits bred to survive transcontinental shipment unblemished.

Just as today's "new American" chefs depend for their provisions on highly specialized growers, gatherers, and other suppliers, often building up a cadre of regional, seasonal particularists, Elizabeth Beard cultivated an extensive network of small provisioners. Many of these were brought to her attention by a second network of "scouts," friends and acquaintances who kept their eyes peeled for the dairy farmer, truck gardener, pig keeper, or apiarist who might meet Mrs. Beard's exacting standards. Apparently those standards were known and respected throughout the Portland public market, which lined a five-block stretch of Yamhill Street. In *Delights and Prejudices* Beard describes an early visit to the market in the company of his nursemaid: "We had just been to the doctor's and on the way back stopped to buy a few things for my mother. When they were wrapped and handed to the maid, she said quietly, 'Please charge them to Mrs. Beard.' The clerk blanched and said, 'For God's sake, give me that package. If I sent that to *her*, she'd kill me.'"

The market vendors, like the rest of Elizabeth's network of purveyors, had good reason to dread any breakdown of confidence on her part, for she shopped on a restaurateur's scale and loss of her patronage would have amounted to a significant loss of income. As Beard puts it, "Mother had really never left the hotel in her own mind, and . . .

all. We feasted on them sautéed in butter or occasionally grilled over the fire."

Crabs were boiled, cracked, and dipped in mayonnaise; crab meat was deviled, sautéed in the West Indian style, and used in salads and soufflés. Young James caught crayfish with liver-baited string; others caught and contributed trout, cod, catfish, and, according to Beard, "pogy"—not to be confused with porgy. "It was a local name for a small flatfish that lived in a nearby river," Beard explained. "Its distinguishing characteristic was that it spawned live young; it didn't lay eggs. I don't know whether pogies even exist today. They didn't really amount to much, but catching them was fun."

As recently as twenty-five years ago mussels sold—or, rather, didn't sell—for as little as a dime a pound in this country. They were eaten mostly by Italian-Americans and were generally ignored by the rest of the population, especially (and ironically) where they grew in abundance. Their popularity and price since have taken a quantum leap, but until around the early 1960s generations of Americans steadfastly disdained a mollusk esteemed for centuries in other parts of the world. Elizabeth Beard was one of a relative handful of Americans who appreciated the gastronomic value of mussels in the early years of the century. Unfortunately, Pacific Coast mussels often carry a lethal toxin during the summer months. "This," Beard writes, "greatly upset Mother, who had a passion for mussels and who looked longingly whenever we saw them clinging to the rocks." Elizabeth indulged her passion for mussels later in the year, when the Beards customarily returned to Gearhart for a few days after Christmas. (Her taste for generally scorned marine esoterica was not restricted to mussels; as Beard puts it, she was one of two people in the district who would eat skate, the other being a transplanted Breton fisherman who occasionally caught and shared a *raie* with her.)

Elizabeth Beard's omnivorous tastes were not lost on her only child; aside from a lifelong aversion to chicken livers and wild rice and a very recent distaste for broccoli, Beard finds intrinsic goodness in just about every known foodstuff provided its integrity is not compromised at any point in its journey to the table. Two in particular among the major continuing culinary interests of his life derive directly from those early summers at Gearhart. One, of course, is his already mentioned reverence for fresh regional foods consumed in season and *in situ*. The other is his love of outdoor cooking and eating, a genre of which he is the trailblazer among American food authorities and which he has espoused fervently in several books, numerous articles, and innumerable demonstrations.

Much of the cooking at Gearhart was done outdoors, over bark-and-driftwood fires (Elizabeth disdained the use of charcoal), and it is easy to imagine the effects produced on a young boy by the aroma of fresh foods slowly broiling in the salt air of a region hardly changed since the Tillamook Indians tended their own cooking fires there not long earlier. In the seven-plus decades since those early summers at the beach, James Beard has eaten, relished, and sung the praises of virtually every known dish and edible substance. He can wax as rhapsodic as the next *bec fin* over *foie gras*, caviar, and the like, but he is never more contagiously enthusiastic, in print or in person, than when extolling the simple, solid satisfactions afforded by no-frills American cookery. When he hymns the virtues of home-baked bread and sweet country butter he is as eloquent as a Brillat-Savarin meditating on the mysteries of the Périgord truffle. He can find nobility in a well-made sandwich, gastronomic glory in an honest batch of popcorn.

As Beard recalls the annual end-of-summer return from Gearhart to Portland, it was a time when "work began in earnest." This is how he describes the final, frenzied effort to provide what Elizabeth deemed adequate sustenance for the long winter ahead:

> Our farmer in the country was visited and asked to slaughter two hogs for us, always two. He made sausage and bacon and smoked the hams, while we made head cheese, chitterlings, scrapple, and all the other delicacies one makes from the pig. We ate copious quantities of spareribs and knuckles, as well as some smoked loin. Our farmer also made us a barrel of sauerkraut and a barrel of pickles. Sacks and sacks of potatoes were ordered—several different varieties.
>
> And the canning went on: early apples from our trees—magnificent Gravensteins—for jelly and applesauce; corn on and

off the cob; prunes, petite prunes and red plums, whole and in conserve; damsons for jam and damson cheese [a thick plum purée, sweetened pound for pound with sugar and flavored with orange rind and cinnamon]; oil pickles, sweet pickles, tomato pickles, hot apple chutney, piccalilli....

Another farmer supplied Hubbard squash, banana squash and pumpkins, winter apples were ordered from Hood River—many varieties—and pears began to arrive. Bartletts were canned in halves and made into pear butter. The harder pears were used in a sliced pear preserves which was stringy, syrupy and utterly wonderful. Then came the peaches. We usually waited for the late varieties, the Muirs and the Crawfords, and these were also canned whole and in halves, and made into peach butter. Some were brandied as well. Grapes followed and were used for juice, jelly and conserve. Then finally tomatoes were canned and chili sauce made.

With the larder at last stocked to capacity ("a beautiful sight and a challenge for anyone to equal"), the game season got under way. John Beard was not a hunter, but numbers of Elizabeth's friends were, and as Beard *fils* recalls, "it was unusual to go to our cellar and not find several ducks, both large and squab-sized, and pheasants hanging in feather." Unruffled feather, presumably, but in the case of members of the Beard household: "There was always a tremendous show of tempers in the house when we had duck. I liked mine cooked rare with a little onion and parsley inside. Mother liked hers not so rare with the simplest seasoning of parsley, salt and pepper. My father said that rare duck was for savages and insisted on having his stuffed and braised till it was thoroughly cooked. Naturally, out of sheer spite, Mother always gave him the oldest birds and refused to taste one of them."

Elizabeth's spite was not motivated by a mere disagreement over the proper preparation of duck. She had never forgiven her husband's lack of premarital candor regarding his financial situation or forgotten the terms she had prescribed for their future life together. Reticent as their son habitually has been about his parents' relationship, he allowed himself to be drawn out on the subject not long ago. Alluding frequently to "domestic unhappiness" and "a family that was bitter, one against the other," he portrayed himself as something of a pawn in a continual, petty struggle for dominance. "There was a constant battle over me," he recalled, "and as a result I grew up without the appurtenances of an average childhood. They made me the subject of all sorts of arbitrary, rather silly rules. If one decided I couldn't ride horseback, the other decided I couldn't ride a bike. If one refused to permit me to roller-skate, the other would respond with something equally silly. The great tragedy of Mother's life was that she was afraid to divorce my father, afraid to acknowledge to her friends that she had made a mistake in marrying him. I think she died a very unhappy woman."

The Beards' duck dinners usually began with turtle soup (then one of the splendors of the American table but destined to sink into irredeemable obscurity when the sale of all alcoholic beverages, including the fortified wines without which turtle soup is unthinkable, was first drastically reduced upon this country's entry into World War I and subsequently obliterated by the Volstead Act). Fried polenta (to this day relatively unknown in the United States, the recent popularity of the northern Italian cuisines notwithstanding) usually accompanied the bird, along with apple compote or currant jelly. (On the subject of currant jelly Beard reveals an awareness, seldom expressed elsewhere, of Elizabeth's fallibility: "Mother never realized how the flavor of currant ruined the palate for the accompanying wine. She was not, I'm afraid, as sensitive to wines as she was to food.") Dessert was either orange soufflé or Spanish cream, except when the Chinese chef, Let, cooked for guests, in which case it might be Bavarian cream, Let's "fabulous" charlotte mousse, or various fruit tarts or pies.

To read *Delights and Prejudices* today, twenty years after it was written and as long as seventy-odd years after many of the meals described therein were prepared, is to marvel at the immediacy of Beard's taste memory and vicariously to experience a way of eating and a way of life few of whose participants survive to remember firsthand:

When there was good pheasant, special friends were invited to a rather informal gathering. We had a way with pheasant—sautéed in butter, *flambé* with cognac, and served with a sauce made with cream, the pan juices and the giblets chopped fine. This was the most delicious pheasant I have ever eaten. It was moist, tender and sensationally good. Pheasant always called for perfectly mashed potatoes, a garnish of watercress, if possible, and braised celery and some of Mother's special asparagus, served separately. To start the menu there was usually a clear soup, and to finish, for some reason, we invariably had pears baked in brown sugar with cloves and a little rum added to them. They were winter pears, full-flavored and exquisitely rich with syrup. Sometimes this dessert was varied with a little ginger or ginger syrup for the large crocks of preserved ginger we kept on hand. With the pears went small sugar cookies or shortbread cookies, which Let made and which later on became a specialty of my mother's....

Older pheasants were done for the family alone, and perhaps one close friend. These were braised with our farmer's homemade sauerkraut and either apple cider or white wine and with bits of garlic sausage scattered through the sauerkraut, all somewhat in the Alsatian fashion. This was a superlative dish when eaten with boiled potatoes and pickled prunes, canned during the harvest season.

As the year wore on and the holidays approached, Elizabeth Beard would embark on the last of her great annual culinary enterprises: the preparation, a twelvemonth in advance, of the traditional yuletide fruitcakes ("a black one, a white one and an English currant cake"), mincemeat, and plum puddings. As Beard describes the embalming process that endowed these goodies with their keeping properties, they were subjected to periodic dosages of booze on a scale that might have given pause to a W. C. Fields. (He remarks parenthetically that Elizabeth managed to preserve some of her wedding cake for twenty-five years by swaddling it in brandy-soaked cloths and storing it in a tightly sealed container—a surprisingly sentimental gesture on the part of a woman whose disillusionment with her marriage was total and immediate.)

As was the case with all her other culinary enterprises Elizabeth's holiday output was prodigious. "The making of these holiday specialties seemed to go on and on," Beard recounts in *Delight and Prejudices,* "and assembling the ingredients was a colossal undertaking in itself. Mother went to all the best stores ... to compare prices and order. Currants, seeded raisins, sultana raisins, citron, lemon peel, candied pineapple and cherries, angelica, almonds, walnuts, hazelnuts, spices—all were bought in tremendous amounts, together with a store of the proper apples for the pudding and mincemeat. Orange and grapefruit peel were candied at home, cider was boiled, and frequent visits were made to Mr. Waddle and other wine and spirit dealers to obtain cognac, rum and sherry." It may have required uncommon forbearance for the English-born Elizabeth, who read Dickens to her son almost from his infancy onward, to resist bestowing her custom exclusively on a purveyor with the marvelously Dickensian name of Mr. Waddle, especially during the most Dickensian of seasons, but, as Beard remarks elsewhere, "Mother was not one who felt that she should limit her patronage to one shop."

If James Beard grew up without the appurtenances of an average childhood, he doesn't seem to have been particularly unhappy about the deprivation. "I really don't know whether I missed them or not," he observed recently, while chatting with a visitor in the study of his Greenwich Village town house. In any event there were compensations, during young James' long summers at the beach, for the arbitrary restrictions imposed by his squabbling parents of his boyhood activities in Portland. John Beard's excursions to Gearhart were limited to infrequent weekends, and, as his son recalls today, "The beach was my world of freedom. I had an enormous circle of friends there, a very different circle from my friends in town. [Beard's circle of friends in town was a tight group of some twenty "neighborhood children who all knew one another, all started elementary school on the same day, all but about three of whom went straight through high school together, and fifteen of whom started college together. One child's father was principal of the elementary school and moved us along together as a unit, which was marvelous. We made it through nine grades in six years. It was a very interesting experience, and I still see two or three of the people who started out in public school with me."]

"I was happiest at the beach—much happier there. I loved the sea and clamming and crabbing, swimming and hiking. Also the summers at the beach afforded me a wonderful opportunity to read. The library in town would allow up to twenty books to be taken along on vacation. I was always pretty well ahead of my contemporaries as far as reading was concerned. I had Dickens read to me before I could read him myself, and whenever I had measles I'd insist on having *The Swiss Family Robinson* read to me. I started reading the Russians very young and had gone through Turgenev and Tolstoy before I was fifteen.

"By the time I entered high school I had completed the entire high school book list. I remember a teacher asking what I was reading the first day of high school. *'Anna Karenina,'* I said. He asked whether I was making sense of it and I said, 'Of course. I wouldn't be reading it if I weren't.' After the Russians I read the Scandinavians—Hamsun, Lagerlöf, and so on. Then I read every theatrical biography I could find. Some were pretty tiresome, but I got through 'em all."

In both his writings and in conversation Beard is somewhat vague on the subject of his mother's theatrical connections, most of which appear to have been formed before his birth. Although devoted to the theater and opera, Elizabeth never was professionally involved with the performing arts but seems to have met most, and befriended many, of the leading actors and singers of her day (a day, it might be noted, when "theatricals" weren't assiduously cultivated by polite society). "Mother had a close friend, an Englishwoman, who was quite a well-known actress in New York," Beard recalls. "I don't know how they met—it was before I was born—but they were inseparable companions and Mother met a great many theatrical personalities through her. Mother's autograph book of that era is quite fascinating. It amounts to a Who's Who of the theatrical world of the time."

At this remove one can only indulge in idle speculation about the origins, nature, and depth of commitment of Elizabeth's apparent passion for the theater. Was she a mere forerunner of today's rock music groupies? Was the theater a narcotic dependency generated by her entrapment in a joyless marriage, a marriage to a humdrum civil servant with whom the nearest approximations of high drama were petty squabbles over the proper preparation of the Sunday dinner and whether or not a cosseted only child was to be permitted to ride a bicycle? Whatever the reasons, theatergoing and opera-going were Elizabeth's major nonculinary activities, activities to which her son was exposed early and often. "I went to the opera from the earliest time I can remember," Beard recalls. According to an interview published last year in *Opera News*, young James' first exposure to opera—a performance of *Madama Butterfly*—moved him to tears ("I suppose that was the correct reaction"). As a small child he was taken to hear Tetrazzini (now more an eponym for certain culinary preparations than a diva within the scope of living memory) sing *Lucia* and Mary Garden "in practically everything she ever did." He saw Pavlova dance in her prime and he saw many of the leading dramatic actors of the day, either on tour in Portland or in San Francisco. Later, when he developed into a "pretty good" natural baritone, the well-upholstered young man who eventually would come to epitomize good cooking and eating would embark on his career—as a singer.

January 1984

James Beard, an American Icon:
The Later Years

Jay Jacobs

Upon graduation from high school in his native Portland, Oregon, James Andrews Beard, by general consent this country's preeminent living authority on cooking and eating and the dominant force in American gastronomy for the past four decades, entered Reed College, also in Portland. Of his abbreviated sojourn in the groves of academe, Beard told a recent interlocutor that, "Being something of a rebel, I was asked to leave the then most progressive college in the United States." Many years later he was awarded an honorary degree by his abortifacient alma mater "because they thought it would make good fodder for the collectors of money." The mildly ironic tone of the observation hardly typifies Beard's utterances; as Judith Jones, his long-time editor at the publishing house of Alfred A. Knopf, remarked not long ago, "I've never heard him put anyone down in his life."

Now in his eighty-first year, Beard, who for a couple of generations of Americans has personified larger-than-life gourmandise, remains a singularly bighearted member of an insular profession otherwise characterized by a widespread bitchiness and rife with petty rivalries. As Sam Aaron, a prominent New York wine merchant, friend, and business colleague of forty years' standing, puts it, "The man is incapable of saying 'no' to a request for a favor. A few years ago he went into intensive care at New York Hospital with a heart condition. I visited him the next day and found him doing a radio show for Patricia McCann from his hospital room. Julia Child called him a few weeks ago to ask if he'd help her do a show on the West Coast, so he schlepps all the way to Santa Barbara for no money."

In Aaron's view Beard is nothing less than one of the cultural giants of the twentieth century. "In art," he says, "there was Picasso; in science, Einstein; in wine, [Frank] Schoonmaker; in food, Jim. Jim was the great pioneer, the trailblazer of American cooking as we know it today. You have to remember that there was *nothing* on the American scene until he came along. We were just coming out of Prohibition, and there was no motivation to produce good food. Jim was the father of the whole movement. First there was Beard, and everyone else followed. Jim played a very important part in Craig Claiborne's life, and Julia Child couldn't have existed without him. Sure, he's made mistakes, but he had no one to learn from. He had to practically re-invent American cooking, and everyone who came along afterward had Jim to show them the way."

Joseph Baum is no less fervent on the subject. Baum, who headed up Restaurant Associates during that corporation's palmy days, has known and worked with Beard for thirty years and describes Beard's influence on contemporary American cooking and eating as "incalculable." According to Baum, "There are very few Americans as respected on both sides of the Atlantic." There is, Baum goes on to say, "a grandness about Jim that derives from the great days of Lucius Beebe, Jeanne Owen [secretary of the Wine and Food Society two generations ago], and others of that caliber—the great days of generations bridging styles. Food and wine are at their best in good company, and Jim is *great* company. The way you work with him is by allowing him to bring into play qualities that almost nobody else has: his prodigious memory, together with his evocative touchstones—who else can say 'a lamb stew you can hold in your arms'—his appetite, excitement, and style. He has such enviable style, a mixture of high and low, formal and informal. At one point, early in the history of Restaurant Associates, when a lot of time was being wasted in debates over the definition and underlying nature of American cooking, Jim summed it all up in one sentence: 'American food is what your mother cooked for you.' All his other characterizations are just as pithy and just as valid.

"The main thing, though, is that Jim's palate and taste memory are infallible. In the thirty years we've known each other, there have been some pretty stiff challenges, but I've never known him to miss when he had to rely solely on his palatal judgment and taste memory, as in his work with Albert Stockli, for example. [Stockli, one of the great *gros bonnets* of his era, was executive chef for the entire Restaurant Associates operation during Baum's tenure at its helm.] Jim would taste Stockli's dishes and make suggestions. Stockli would say, 'F— him,' and do the dish the same way. Jim would taste it again, sometimes days or weeks later, and say, 'Well, it tastes exactly the same.' Stockli would say, 'The son of a bitch knows what he's talking about,' and make adjustments and ask Jim's opinion. Finally, when they'd strike a compromise they could both live with, they'd laugh their heads off."

The big man with the infallible palate put his mouth to other uses at the outset of his professional career. After intensive exposure to both grand opera and the theater from early childhood onward (and after some juvenile theatrical work in the Pacific Northwest with a touring company called the Red Lantern Players, of which Clark Gable was a youthful member), Beard set off for London in 1922 to study with the voice coach Gaetano Loria, who had been Caruso's secretary-factotum until the great tenor's death the previous year.

Loria, who "had coached practically every great singer of the age," failed to make a great singer of Beard. After learning an extensive repertory of baritone roles, Beard decided opera was not his true calling. "I was enough of a realist to know I didn't have the voice I wanted," he told a recent visitor to his Greenwich Village town house, "and didn't have the musical background either." What he *did* absorb from Loria was something of an education in Italian gastronomy; the voice coach was an enthusiastic diner out and introduced his American pupil to many of his favorite Italian restaurants in London. Writing in *Delights and Prejudices* some forty years later, Beard evoked the experiences with startling immediacy in detailed descriptions of his first exposure to raw artichokes, dandelion greens sautéed with cubed salt pork, fresh mint, and wine vinegar, and other dishes that had eluded even the notice of his mother, Elizabeth Jones Brennan Beard, one of the most sophisticated and encyclopedic American cooks of her day.

As Elizabeth had before him, the young James Beard enthusiastically availed himself of the pleasures of the table while away from home, first in London, then in Paris. Although he had no intimation, at age twenty, that cooking and gastronomy ultimately would turn out to be his lifework, it is apparent from his later writings and conversations that each of his dining experiences was not merely an exercise in sensual gratification to be enjoyed passively like a hot bath or a massage but also an intellectual experience to be appraised analytically and mentally catalogued for future reference. At an age when his critical faculties might have been expected to be skewed by the excitement of long-anticipated visits to legendary institutions, his responses were surprisingly discerning:

> My first visit to Paris in 1923 was a tremendously exciting event, and one dream I had preserved for a number of years was to dine at Maxim's—no doubt because of the song from *The Merry Widow* and other alluring associations. This was to me the most glamorous place of all time, and I was prepared to spend my pittance for a good meal there. So one evening I reserved a table, put on my best suit, and went with a friend to the famed Maxim's. A couple of hours later I left, disillusioned and miserable.

Barely out of his teens, this hulking American innocent abroad had perceived what has eluded legions of experienced travelers and mature Parisian boulevardiers alike: that the food at Maxim's was "mediocre and the service indifferent." (Beard's disappointment, it might be noted, doesn't seem to have been backlash to an overdose of hype, for he later described his first visit to the equally vaunted Tour d'Argent as "a supreme pleasure.")

The Paris of Beard's first sojourn was the Paris of Hemingway,

Fitzgerald, Gertrude Stein, Henry Miller, Gerald and Sarah Murphy, and like conspicuous consumers of one thing or another. Beard appears to have consumed nothing but food. An occasional splurge aside, most of the food he consumed was not *haute cuisine* but the solid bourgeois fare served in cheap bistros and students' pensions. He was living on a limited budget and mostly on such good humble dishes as calf's feet *poulette, daubes,* and various other stews, at least when not engaged in pastry orgies at Rumpelmayer's, Louis Sherry, and similar establishments—establishments whose loss Beard would mourn forty years later in *Delights and Prejudices* ("gone forever and with them the charm of small teashops and the art of producing great pastry").

In the light of the decisive turn Beard's career was destined to take some years later it's regrettable that both his means and knowledge were limited during his first stay in Paris. "I only wish I had known in 1923 what I know now about Paris restaurants," he would write at age sixty. "I might have found many more interesting places, in vogue at the time, which have disappeared into history. I am unhappy every time I think that the great Montagné was cooking in Paris in that era and I didn't know it. But I am grateful that I was enterprising enough to explore among the smaller restaurants and learn the basic dishes of French cuisine, when I might have been spending my money in the fleshpots."

If the singer *manqué* was spending no money in the fleshpots of Gay Paree, he was earning no money either. Toward the end of 1923 Elizabeth Beard arrived in Paris to fetch her son home to Portland and, presumably, the realities of winning his own bread instead of gorging on subsidized pastries. (Beard today seems somewhat unsure about his parents' financial condition, to which it appears he never was made privy. "As far as I know," he says, "my father made a good salary for the times and Mother held on to her own money. We lived well and apparently could afford it. Mother had several offers to go back into business but didn't seem to see any need." He volunteers no speculation on the possibility that a return to business might have meant a loss of face to Elizabeth, who continued to manage her home life as though still managing the hotel she had sold just after marrying.)

With his operatic ambitions at an end, Beard turned once again to the theater. In 1924 he went on tour in *Cyrano de Bergerac* with Walter Hampden, a leading actor of the day, and later appeared in *Othello*. Photographs of Beard taken during the early years of his resumed theatrical career show him to have been somewhat too fleshy either to play romantic leads or to convince any casting director that he was precisely what Shakespeare had in mind for the role of Cassius. In the starring role of the light comedy *The Bishop Misbehaves,* he bore a vague resemblance to both Charles Laughton and Fatty Arbuckle as they looked at the time; and in a close-up taken in 1933, when, at thirty, he was a mainstay of a Portland repertory group called the Taylor Street Players, he might have been a rather soulful football lineman.

Although Beard never achieved national renown as a stage actor, he became fairly well known on the West Coast, where he spent most of his theatrical career. "I spent years in San Francisco, Los Angeles, and Portland," he recalled during a recent conversation. "I did a great variety of things, including some directing. There was lots of theater out there just before the advent of the talkies, and I did a good deal of work. I did a great deal of work in radio, too, and then made some attempts at breaking into the movies. I'm afraid I wasn't very successful. I got some bit parts but nothing much more. I knew everyone in Hollywood, but it seems I wasn't the right type. My movie career didn't amount to much, but it was fun."

Later in the day, when the conversation turned to the foods of his early childhood, Beard would unconsciously paraphrase his summation of his film career, when questioned about the freshwater fish he calls "pogy": "They didn't really amount to much but catching them was fun." One gets the impression that throughout his long life Beard has managed to derive a full measure of enjoyment, winning or losing, from whatever he has undertaken.

Beard abandoned Hollywood in 1929 and returned to his hometown, where he acted with the Portland Civic Theater, doubled as a scenery and costume designer, and moonlighted as an acting coach. Two years later, after a sojourn in Seattle during which he studied with the Shakespearean actor Iden Payne, he made the third and penultimate major career decision of his life. Deeply affected by his studies with Payne, he decided to concentrate thenceforth on directing and teaching. To that end he enrolled at Carnegie Tech, earned a degree in drama, and, after spending some further time on the West Coast, settled in New York in 1937. He was then thirty-four years old and ready for more stability than his life in the theater had thitherto provided. With the country in the midst of the Great Depression, however, few would-be thespians were beating paths to the doors of fledgling drama coaches and few theatrical backers saw any reason to entrust their investments to marginally experienced directors. In order to eat at least roughly in the style to which he had been accustomed since birth, Beard taught French, English, and social studies at a friend's day school in New Jersey.

At this juncture James Beard once again surveyed his situation and found it wanting. As he described the moment in conversation not long ago, "I put myself on a large meat hook and took stock of what I found hanging there. If I had had money, I'd have stayed in the theater, but I had no money and so I began to consider the alternatives. In that sort of situation you think of all the possibilities. You think, I've always known and been interested in food. You think, wouldn't it be fun to have your own restaurant? Well, then you analyze the thought and you decide, no, it wouldn't be fun.

"At about that time," Beard went on to say, "I was fortunate enough to meet a German-born brother and sister who shared my interest in fine food and my feelings about somehow getting involved professionally in the food business. We discussed the possibilities endlessly and finally talked ourselves into starting Hors d'Oeuvre, Inc." The two men met at a cocktail party, thereby putting a large dent in the suit of armor Beard habitually wore on such occasions. In recounting the meeting in *Delights and Prejudices* he would write:

> I have never really enjoyed large cocktail parties. I find them a bastard form of entertaining. One gets a drink, tries all the little dabs of food (I have coined a word for them: doots), spends some time chatting with one group, then says to himself mechanically, it's time to move on and circulate....
>
> Well, the party on this occasion was quite pleasant. I had been

there for a while when I was introduced to Bill Rhode, a handsome, witty, thoroughly disarming man. His background, I was to learn, was Berlin, good schools, and a full social life on two continents.

Rhode not only shared Beard's interest in food but shared his aversion to doots. He introduced his new acquaintance to his sister, who "had attended the famous school of the Grand Duchess of Baden and had learned, as did all young ladies of her social position, the ground rules of good housekeeping, including truly elaborate cooking.... We three talked far into the night. I soon learned that both Bill and Irma had also dreamed of getting into the food business, and we developed plans that would astonish the bellies of New York. Something, we agreed, should be done about cocktail party food. We had eaten too many pieces of cottony bread soggy with processed cheese, anchovy fillets by the yard, and dried-up bits of ham with smoked salmon."

Having calculated that "at least 250 cocktail parties [were held] every afternoon in Manhattan in the area bordered by 96th Street, 51st Street, Fifth Avenue, and the East River" (a calculation presumably facilitated by Bill Rhode's "full social life"), the trio decided there was room in town for a more imaginative catering service than any then in existence. They opened for business—on a shoestring—in minuscule, ground-floor-and-basement premises, opposite the Seventh Regiment Armory on East Sixty-sixth Street, with Bill Rhode in charge of sales and promotion at the front of the store and with Beard and Irma Rhode preparing the food backstage. Thanks in large part to Rhode's extensive connections, the enterprise was launched with considerable press fanfare. "The media people helped enormously," Beard recalls. "Clementine Paddleford, Lucius Beebe, Danton Walker, and many others generated lots of publicity. The Upper East Side Cocktail Belt quickly was made aware of our existence, and we soon were doing a very brisk business in tea sandwiches. We shied away from the little ditsy things that had become such awful clichés, and we had a modest but going business until the advent of the war made so many foods unavailable."

Today, four and a half decades later, the sandwiches and appetizers devised by Hors d'Oeuvre, Inc. have themselves long since become the awful clichés of the cocktail circuit. In the late 1930s, however, variously filled cornets fashioned from salami, smoked salmon, and the like, although familiar enough in Europe, seemed stunning in their originality in this country. So, for that matter, did vichyssoise, which now elicits canyonlike yawns from experienced restaurant-goers but which, Beard recalls, "sold by the gallon at a good price" when he and his associates pried the recipe away from its originator, Louis Diat, who himself merely had gussied up a venerable staple of the French peasant table and given it a new name.

The fact is that American cooking had reached its lowest ebb in more than a century by the time of Beard's professional debut on the culinary scene. Roughly a hundred years earlier, James Fenimore Cooper, having refined his palate during an extended sojourn in Europe, returned to his homeland to castigate his countrymen as "the grossest feeders of any civilized nation known" and their cuisine as "heavy, coarse, and indigestible." Until the Swiss-born Delmonico brothers opened their first full-service establishment in lower Manhattan in 1831, there wasn't a single restaurant worth the name in the nation, and with few exceptions (notably Thomas Jefferson's) home kitchens turned out much the same stodgy, unimaginative fare that was to be found in the public eating houses.

The impact of Delmonico's on American gastronomy was such that the nineteenth-century historian James Ford Rhodes, surveying what he took to be the pivotal events of the period 1850–77, wrote that anyone "who considers the difference between the cooking and service of a dinner at a hotel or restaurant before the Civil War and now will appreciate what a practical apostle of health and decent living has been Delmonico, who deserves canonization in the American calendar." As a contemporary of Rhodes' put it, for Americans "who had been in the habit of regarding their dinners as a mere means of sustaining nature and a scrupulous attention to dinner as unworthy of an earnest mind," Delmonico's was nothing less than "an agency of civilization."

Following the Delmonican lead, American gastronomy underwent a significant upturn. Throughout the late Victorian and the Edwardian eras (during which latter, of course, James Beard was born and cut his teeth on such delicacies as the Olympia oyster, Dungeness crab, and

Columbian River salmon) American gourmandise compared favorably with any in the world, in the somewhat overblown fashion of the day. With this country's entry into World War I, however, there began an abrupt decline, a decline that already had been foreshadowed by the imposition of increasingly restrictive game laws, that accelerated when sales of alcoholic beverages drastically were curtailed throughout the nation, and that was further exacerbated by the establishment of the Aberdeen Proving Ground on thirty-five thousand acres of Chesapeake Bay wetlands: wetlands where the canvasback duck, until then one of the singular glories of the American table, immemorially had dined on the wild celery that imbued the bird with its distinctive flavor. The Volstead Act of 1919 in no way ameliorated matters. Nor did the onset of the Great Depression an arid decade later. As a result of these and other factors too numerous to mention, America had to all intents and purposes reverted to gastronomic barbarism by the time Hors d'Oeuvre, Inc. was formed. The nation would remain a gastronomic wasteland until well after World War II and ultimately would be redeemed largely through the intervention of James Andrews Beard.

Beard himself tends to discount whatever impact Hors d'Oeuvre, Inc. may have had on the nation's eating habits, and, indeed, that impact appears to have been minimal. The venture lasted only a couple of years, played to a limited, rather parochial neighborhood audience, and seems significant in retrospect only because it was the agency whereby Beard at last got himself into his proper line of work. The enterprise folded in 1940 with the onset of food rationing, but it had established Beard as an authority on finger foods—recognition that led to publication that year of his first cookbook, *Hors D'Oeuvre and Canapés.*

Nineteen forty also was the year of Elizabeth Beard's death. After returning to Portland to see his mother through her last days, Beard came back to New York, went to work part-time at Sherry Wine and Spirits (now Sherry-Lehmann), and did some free-lance food writing. During the same period his erstwhile partner Bill Rhode became an editor at *Gourmet,* which began publication in 1941 in what then must have seemed one of the most foolhardy ventures ever undertaken;

with the nation on the brink of war and shortages rife, conditions hardly were propitious for "The Magazine of Good Living."

Reminiscing recently about the period, Beard shook his head in wonderment over the changes that have taken place since—changes in which he had been as instrumental a force as anyone now alive. "People today," he said, "are one hundred percent more knowledgeable about food than they were then. Everyone has traveled, gone through the three-star restaurant experience, seen the dancing chefs—the whole schmeer."

In 1942 Beard was inducted into the Army Air Corps. He characterizes the experience as "one of those crazy war stories that happen only in the army and navy. I was supposed to go to school for hotel and catering services, but didn't. Instead I became a cryptographer. I had all this training and knowledge, but when I talked to my colonel about where I was to put it to use, he said, 'You can go to Presque Isle, Maine, or Washington, D.C.' I said, 'No, I want to go overseas,' and he told me the only way I could do that would be to get myself allied to someone who could give me civilian war work, and get out of the service."

Farming was civilian war work by government definition. Through the intercession of a friend whose family operated a dairy farm near Reading, Pennsylvania, Beard was taken on as a farmhand and left military service. The heart of Pennsylvania Dutch country wasn't precisely the overseas assignment that Beard coveted, but the man always has had an eerie talent for running into the right people at the right time. "I would come to New York on weekends," he recalls, "and one Saturday I had come in from the farm to see the second performance of *Oklahoma!*, which had opened the night before. While in the city I met an old friend who said, 'We've been looking all over for you. How would you like to go overseas with the United Seamen's Service?'

"The United Seamen's Service did for the merchant marine what the Red Cross and USO did for the military services. It had started as a national, but had become an international, organization, following the fleet as it were. I joined up and trained here in New York. There were some interesting people in the organization. There was a Hopkins who had been the Hopkins of Peggy Hopkins Joyce's life and other interesting characters. I was slated to manage a domestic club, but about a week before I was scheduled to start there I was sent to Puerto Rico. They were having a great many torpedoings off the island at that time, and sometimes we literally had to pull the survivors out of the water. We'd take care of them while they were on the beach, awaiting transshipment. At that time Puerto Rico was the venereal capital of the world. We functioned as a social service."

Beard's travel horizons widened when the Hopkins who had been the Hopkins of Peggy Hopkins Joyce's life "reverted to the bottle," was relieved of his post in Rio de Janeiro, and was replaced by Beard. What the replacement found on his arrival in Rio was "a beautiful house in a nice section of the city, within two hundred feet of a bathing beach and with about one fifth of all the cockroaches in Brazil." The Seamen's Service club, as he describes it, was "a messy situation all round. The place was in terrible shape, and the food was worse. My first dinner there was a chop and a boiled potato filled with a pastry-bag mashed potato rosette. Well, we got Mr. Hopkins off to New York, we got rid of the roaches, we got rid of the chef, and we acquired a remarkable woman, a sort of Mrs. Five-by-five, who'd cooked for the Italian and Argentine ambassadors. I had a Brazilian majordomo who was a delight—I've always wanted to do a book on him—and an extremely good marketer. I was the sole American representative of the service whose club served fresh native stuff. We had a flock of turkeys, which we fattened, and the streetcar lines had flatcars for delivering market stuff to us."

Ironically, Beard hardly had completed his revitalization of the club when "traffic lessened as the overall picture of the war changed, and we finally had to close it." With the demise of the Rio operation, Beard confidently expected reassignment to Europe. "I was all ready to go," he recalled not long ago. "Then came a call [at this point in his narrative, Beard was convulsed with laughter] ... a call, and I heard a voice saying, 'Will you go to [more laughter] Panama and see what's wrong in Cristobal and Panama City? It will only take you a few days, then you can go to Europe.'"

The trip from Puerto Rico to Panama was curiously circuitous and nearly disastrous for both Beard and the future of American gastronomy. "We were to fly to Panama via La Paz, on a DC-3," he recalls. "Along the way we lost an engine, and the pilot was faced with the choice of trying an emergency landing in the Andes or on sand flats in northern Chile." Fortunately reason prevailed ("Otherwise, I'd never have seen Arica, Chile.").

Having seen Arica, Chile, Beard resumed his journey to Panama, where he found the Seamen's Service club of Cristobal to be housed in "a handsome building, but run by the wrong people for that sort of operation." The operators appear to have been religious missionaries whose goals weren't entirely compatible with those of sailors ashore. To create a somewhat less inhibiting atmosphere for the club's guests Beard hired a jailhouse cook ("my marvelous Margaret Tingling"), about whom he later would relate some choice anecdotes in his largely autobiographical book, *Delights and Prejudices.* Enthroned in his favorite armchair, his eyes twinkling impishly four decades after the fact, Beard regaled a recent visitor to his Greenwich Village digs with a retrospective account of a monthly soirée he instituted at the club. "In Panama, where the girls worked in cribs, I took it upon myself, much to the horror of the ladies on my board, to entertain ladies of the evening once a month. The cook loved that. She didn't mind cooking for all those whores, but she'd have nothing to do with other women."

His Panama mission completed, Beard "took a little holiday in New York," then "finally headed for the other side." He landed in Casablanca, traveled thence to Tunis, and "took a plane, a 'bucket job,' to Naples, with a Brazilian general and two Brazilian nurses. By then I knew enough Portuguese to get by. It got very cold on the plane, so we all stretched under a gaucho cape I'd bought in Brazil. We landed in Naples, only to find that it was V-E Day." With the war in Europe at an end, Beard knocked around Italy on various assignments that took him from Naples to Bari, Ancona, Venice, Bologna, Florence, Rome, and back to Naples. "Finally," he says, "I took off for Marseilles, where I was headed in the first place."

Three of Beard's books had been published by the time he returned from overseas in late 1945: *Hors d'Oeuvre and Canapés* ("It's still in print after forty-three years but not in its virginal beauty—we've made some deletions and some additions"); *Cook It Outdoors* ("It was probably the first book on the subject, and I'm not too proud of it now, but it did establish *something,* I suppose"), and *Fowl and Game Cookery.* Their author arrived in New York to discover he had become a food authority of some repute during his absence. Then, by one of those happy coincidences in which his life seems to have abounded, he "bumped into" a friend who informed him that "NBC has been looking for you."

In those early days of network television NBC broadcast a weekly magazine-format show called *Elsie Presents,* the Elsie in question being the bovine personification of Borden's dairy products. Beard was hired to do cooking demonstrations and merrily falsified his ingredients, substituting more photogenic or more durable substances, such as ink for the natural veining of Roquefort cheese and mashed potatoes for ice cream, as the exigencies of the then-primitive new medium dictated. The show (produced, incidentally, by then-Senator John F. Kennedy's sister Pat) followed the Friday night fights, and Beard, by then the heavyweight champion (in all senses of the term) of American gastronomy, loomed as an emblematic figure on the flickering screens of the nation's saloons. As he remarked to one interviewer about a year ago, "most of the television sets at the time were in bars."

Beard appeared regularly on the show for about two years, during which time his image crystallized as *the* American icon of gourmandise. He was the first professional cook in the country to receive nationwide visual exposure, and he played his role to the hilt. At long last his theatrical and gastronomic talents had come into play simultaneously. He had blazed the trail for a broth-spoiling overabundance of television cooks, including such disparate personalities as Dione Lucas, Julia Child, and Graham Kerr, the self-styled "Galloping Gourmet." In the nearly four decades since his video debut, however, no one else even remotely has personified the pleasures of the kitchen and table as convincingly as he.

Beard's prodigious memory and cooperative nature notwithstanding, it's next to impossible to sort out the details of his middle years with chronological accuracy. For one thing, many of his manifold activities overlapped (as he has put it, "I would wake up in the morning and not have the faintest idea who would be paying me for the day");

for another, any Beardian attempts at linear narrative invariably sheer off into often hilarious anecdotal digressions that lead successively one to another, like strings of exploding firecrackers, and occasionally are abandoned in mid-sentence as the raconteur is reminded of a better story and interrupts himself to tell it. Simultaneously or in rapid succession during the two years or so following his television stint he held down various restaurant and food product consultancies, produced his fourth book, *The Fireside Cookbook,* wrote free-lance articles for various magazines, and joined the editorial staff of *Gourmet,* on whose masthead his name appeared for the first time, as associate editor, in May 1949.

Salient among Beard's multifarious activities of the period was publication of *The Fireside Cookbook,* a handsome volume with engaging illustrations by Alice and Martin Provensen and an immediate popular success. "The thing that made Jim famous," according to his longtime friend and associate, Sam Aaron, "was that he was fortunate enough not to have a very good agent and was hired for a fixed fee by Simon and Schuster to write the *Fireside* book." Aaron's clear implication is that an agent more concerned with his client's welfare and his own commission might have scuttled Beard's chances of getting the assignment by demanding the customary royalty arrangement with the publisher. If the book produced no great financial reward for its author, its impact on his career was seismic. It established the public's perception of him as the foremost living American authority on cookery. It remains an American classic today, and its influence on the course of American gastronomy has been incalculable; one has only to talk with almost any American chef still on the sunny side of middle age to be told that he or she was "one of Beard's children" and that the agency of parturition was *The Fireside Cookbook.*

While Beard was with *Gourmet,* "the French commercial counselor in San Francisco bethought himself a most pregnant idea which later in 1949 became a successful reality." The quotation is from the opening sentence of "Vintage Tour—1949," an article Beard wrote for the magazine late that year. (Both his prose style and that of the magazine have improved considerably since.) The most pregnant idea was to stage a twenty-two-day wine tour of France—a junket for ten members of the Wine and Food Society, Beard included, underwritten by various French promotional and governmental agencies. As Beard described the tour, a very good time indeed was had by all; so good a time, apparently, that it provided inspiration not only for the *Gourmet* article but for a second piece, which cannibalized the first to some degree and was published in Sherry's wine catalogue, much to the consternation of the magazine's founder and publisher, Earle R. MacAusland. As Beard recounts the incident today, "I found myself out on my can, but I know for a fact that he wept after he fired me.

"The funny part is that the day I was fired I called Jack Aaron [Sam's brother] at Sherry. He said, 'Meet me at "21" and take your job back.' I went to lunch and met Jerry Mason of *Argosy* magazine and found myself writing for *Argosy*. It was a very different kind of food reporting, and I wrote a regular column for several years."

In the spring of 1950 the *Argosy* columnist was dispatched to France by Sherry Wines, which was then planning to open a Paris branch. As he had in his youth, James Andrews Beard once again was living one of the civilized world's fondest fantasies. He was being paid to enjoy the epicurean delights of the French capital. "I stayed in Paris nine or ten months," he recalls. "Those were still the days of black market money. When I got my checks I'd take them to a little camera store and get good money for them. Strangely enough, it was in Paris that I first ate haggis. I had met Sandy Watt on the wine tour the year before. He had an apartment on the Ile de la Cité, and it was there that I had haggis for the first time. His mother sent it to him every year, and he'd serve it to his French friends.

"I have a theory about haggis: I feel it's an outgrowth of *boudin*. The French influence in Scotland was more than small. Where does the expression 'bonny' come from but France? And then there was Mary Stuart's French background. Besides, Scottish women excel at *feuilletage*." (Beard's middle name and keen interest in Scotland and things Scottish are inheritances from his paternal forebears. "The family on my father's Scottish side," he says, "were gluttons and horse thieves. They had a very pretty tartan.")

Alexander Watt worked as a journalist when not regaling French friends with his mother's haggis or himself with the gastronomic largesse of Paris. During Beard's sojourn in the city the two men decided to put their gustatory proclivities to practical use by collaborating on a guide-*cum*-cookbook, *Paris Cuisine.* In a recent, preposterously fulsome magazine article on Beard ("James Beard stands with Lincoln and Franklin in the pantheon of best-loved Americans"), the book, published upward of two decades after Julian Street's *Where Paris Dines,* erroneously was termed "the first pre-Michelin guide to Paris restaurants" and "the first efforts by an American to unravel the mysteries of French haute cuisine for the American or English traveler." That Watt and Beard made no such claims on their own behalf was evident in their introduction, which explicitly stated that theirs was "not just another French cookbook...."

If *Paris Cuisine* was not the first attempt in English either to provide a vade mecum to the restaurants of Paris or a collection of French recipes, it may well have been the very first, on both counts, of its degree of sophistication. Its stated objective was to "set down ... in black and white the best of the best." In its time it was itself the best by far of an otherwise indifferent body of existing work on its subject, and it sold well, in both Paris and North America, although it made few concessions to the presumable naïveté of English-speaking readers. Among the two-hundred-odd recipes the authors managed to pry away from what they deemed the best chefs then working in Paris were numerous dishes that still don't enjoy widespread popularity outside France, even in the present era of relative gastronomic enlightenment. *Pied de pork St. Menehould* was included, for example, along with such all-time American non-favorites as *brandade de morue,* stuffed oxtail, *tripes à la mode de Caen,* hot carp pâté, *pieds et paquets* (a Provençal specialty made with sheep's trotters and mutton tripe), and *matelote d'anguille.* Moreover, no effort was made to spare the sensibilities of novice epicures ("Do not draw [woodcock] for they are traditionally eaten with their intestines") or the labor of neophyte cooks: "This [*poularde de Bresse*] is a long process, but well worth the trouble...." The book is prized as a collectors' item by food mavens today.

Beard spent the summer of 1953 in Nantucket, where he managed—and rather famously upgraded—a restaurant called Lucky Pierre's.

While there, he met André Surmain, who years later would open the vaunted New York temple of *haute cuisine*, Lutèce, and who would play a pivotal role in Beard's career. The following year was a particularly significant one for Beard: First, he met Joseph Baum, with whom he would be professionally associated for the next couple of decades, and, second, with the publication of *Jim Beard's New Barbecue Cookbook*, it was clearly established that he was by then not only *the* generally accepted American food authority but that his name had become a household word and a salable commodity in itself. Thenceforth, it would be incorporated into the titles of many of his books.

Unlike Beard, Joseph Baum is a formally trained food service professional. He grew up in an upstate New York hotel operated by his family, was schooled at Cornell, and had made enough of a name for himself as director of food and beverages for a Florida hotel chain to attract the notice of Restaurant Associates while still in his early thirties. At that juncture Restaurant Associates operated nothing grander than a chain of fast-turnover beaneries in New York City and a snack bar at Newark Airport. Baum was hired to convert the Newark venture to a luxury restaurant when the airport was refurbished in 1952. He promptly demonstrated a genius for showmanship that was to become his hallmark. As Michael and Ariane Batterberry described his debut with Restaurant Associates in their book *On the Town in New York*, "He turned the Newarker into something like the proverbial three-ringed circus. Oysters were served by the sevens, lobsters came with three claws, and everything was flambé.... According to Gael Greene, Baum's explanation was: 'The customers like to see things on fire ... it doesn't really hurt the food much.' "

His penchant for facile razzle-dazzle notwithstanding, Baum was and remains a consummate restaurateur, probably the ablest and most innovative ever born in this country. He and Beard met at the Newarker through the intercession of a mutual friend. They hit it off at once (years later, Beard would characterize Baum as "the one true genius of the restaurant industry"), and Beard was appointed consultant to Restaurant Associates. The organization was then on the threshold of its great expansionist phase. During the next few years it would open or take over the management of a baker's dozen establishments in rapid succession, each with its own distinctive character, each tailored to the taste, needs, and means of a specific prospective clientele, most built around a particular historical or geographic theme.

Baum, the mastermind of the whole operation, supplied the themes. Beard largely orchestrated the menus and vetted the creations of the Swiss-born executive chef, Albert Stockli, who wasn't altogether delighted with having to perfect Mexican dishes for Fonda del Sol, Polynesian specialties for the Hawaiian Room, and Colonial American fare for Paul Revere's Tavern and Chop House. As Beard summed it up in a recent magazine interview, "Poor Albert really hated doing all that Hawaiian stuff, but he did a good job of it."

The grandiloquent menu devised for the Forum of the Twelve Caesars doubtless was another source of unhappiness for poor Albert, who was compelled to test and perfect recipes for such fanciful productions as flamed Fiddler Crab Lump à la Nero, Tart Messalina, and The Wild Fowl of Samos, which last, according to the menu gloss, was "cooked in sherried tomatoes under a mantle of crusty corn." According to some observers it was not only the Wild Fowl of Samos that was mantled with corn but the Forum itself, with its pun-studded menu and its resident pyromaniacs, who set just about everything but the house afire in accordance with Baum's penchant for showy effects.

Spectacular as Baum's various brainstorms may have been, none of his ventures achieved true greatness until he devised his first indubitable masterpiece, The Four Seasons, which opened in 1959. The restaurant, housed in the Seagram Building in premises designed by Philip Johnson, had (and has) a physical grandeur about it that demanded nothing less than a total restructuring of existing concepts of dining out in the United States in the second half of the twentieth century.

As Baum envisioned The Four Seasons, the restaurant's theme would be set forth by its name and its style characterized by simplicity, quality, integrity, and an absence of Old World—particularly French—pretension and menu terminology. The menu (and décor) would change quarterly in accordance with what was optimally desirable in native American foods in season. In James Beard, a passionate advocate of everything the restaurant was to stand for, he had the best-qualified man alive for the job at hand. "I did the wine list," Beard was to recount a quarter of a century later. "I didn't want a sommelier, so I trained the waiters to know every wine.... They had to come to classes."

Beard did more than just the wine list. His personal credo is abundantly manifest in the restaurant's early menus. In *The Fireside Cookbook* he had unequivocally stated: "There is absolutely no substitute for the best. Good food cannot be made of inferior ingredients masked with high flavor." Throughout his life he has espoused the use of native regional foodstuffs harvested at the peak of their goodness and prepared with the utmost simplicity. In essence, the food served at The Four Seasons was the food he was weaned on. It was distinctly American food, which, as he remarked recently, "is the food I grew up on—good food."

What Beard, Baum, and Stockli accomplished at The Four Seasons was nothing less than the origination of what is now termed the "New American Cuisine" a generation before the genre was a gleam in the eyes of its current, self-congratulatory practitioners. That they also more or less anticipated French *nouvelle cuisine* by a decade and a half or more is almost incidental. The earmarks of both styles—with their mix-and-match combinations of previously uncombined ingredients and lean, unambiguous presentations—clearly were anticipated in starters listed in plain English as Small Clams with Green Onions and Truffles, Lobster Chunks on Dill, Oysters with Horseradish Ginger, and Crisped Shrimp with Mustard Fruit; in such soups as Beet and Lobster Madrilène and Vermont Cheese Soup; in entrées like Marinated Lamb with Cracked Wheat, Larded Pigeon with Candied Figs, and Bouillabaisse Salad; and in accompaniments such as Belgian Endive with Grapefruit; Nasturtium Leaves; Zucchini and Hearts of Palm with Lemon Dressing; and all manner of seasonal American field greens.

As mentioned earlier, Beard is nothing if not charitable in his reference to other food professionals. He is decidedly less so, however, when the subject of the "new" cuisines arises. As he remarked not long ago, "[French] *nouvelle* and American *nouvelle* disgust me with their often outrageously illogical combinations of ingredients and their preciosity. They make me want to throw up. And the idea of an international school of cooking is awful—a mess. Nobody seems to know what they're talking about when the subjects come up. That issue [of a well-known culinary magazine] on American food was incredibly stupid. You know, I once was asked what I saw as my role in the whole picture. I said, 'Loyal opposition.' "

Beard's involvement with Baum and Restaurant Associates was to continue for twenty years, during which time he remained astonishingly productive on other fronts. In addition to numerous magazine articles and the barbecue cookbook already mentioned, *James Beard's Fish Cookery* was published in 1954 and *The Complete Book of Outdoor Cookery* (written in collaboration with Helen Evans Brown) the following year. At about the same time he added still another string to his bow by yielding to an urge he had harbored for years.

As mentioned earlier, Beard had taught off and on, both in and out of the theater. He had enjoyed teaching as an extension of acting, and he finally put all his talents together in one package by launching a cooking school in 1955, at the urging of André Surmain, who was then an airline caterer. Classes were held in Surmain's kitchen, and the first semester nearly put an end to Beard's pedagogical career. "We had successes and failures," he later would recall in *Delights and Prejudices,* "but I'm afraid I was largely discouraged at the end of the year. We lacked a cohesive plan. In black moments I thought perhaps the whole idea of a school had no merit."

"After reflecting for some weeks on the shortcomings of the previous year," Beard decided to give teaching another whirl. With Ruth Norman (whom he had befriended back in the days of Hors d'Oeuvre, Inc.) as manager of the school and Albert Stockli as guest chef, Beard conducted classes in the test kitchen of Restaurant Associates in the Lexington Hotel. The second venture apparently was a good deal more encouraging than the first: By the following year enrollment had increased to the point where larger quarters were needed, and, at the invitation of Helen McCully, then food editor at *McCall's,* night classes were held in the magazine's "beautifully equipped" test kitchens. "We had only to pay part of the gas and electric bill and leave the place clean. It was a magnificent break, and without it I doubt if we could have survived for the next two or three years."

The school not only survived but prospered for three years. When a change of management at *McCall's* ousted the nocturnal squatters at the end of that time Beard was prepared to buy his own premises. He did so when a town house on West Tenth Street became available. Later he would write, "I moved in during the fall of 1959, and the kitchen was ready just in time for the first class. It is an ingeniously designed room, dominated by a U-shaped counter containing six electric stove units; a double oven and broilers are built into the wall. The space comfortably holds twelve students, Ruth, me, and a helper. I can stand behind the counter and use the stoves while the students surround me. When there is a single student, it provides the luxury of working with several burners, with the teacher on one side of the counter and the student on the other."

In his nearly thirty years as a teacher Beard has never tolerated vanity cooking. Although he often has expressed admiration for elaborately presented dishes, he insists that presentation function as an adumbration of the underlying nature of the food and not as an attention-getting end in itself. During the school's early years he occasionally drew potshots from his inferiors for his alleged indifference to culinary "classics," i.e., the showy, dated products of a Carême-derived French *haute cuisine,* many of them oversauced in a style that ceased to make sense with the development of refrigeration. His response was to quote one of the leading French chefs of the day, Raymond Thuilier, who could cook as elaborately as anyone of his generation but who, in a *cri de coeur,* wrote, "The triumph of cooking is to be able to produce the simple things so that they taste as they were meant to." (Someone else once defined *haute cuisine* as food produced by madmen for the delectation of foods. Beard—certainly no madman—does not suffer fools gladly. In conversation not long ago he posed a rhetorical question: "What is it that compels these—these *Feinschmeckers* to gussy up everything they eat? Why can't they appreciate a good piece of meat or fish for what it is instead of piling all kinds of crap on it?")

Ironically, Beard's success as a teacher spawned countless imitators, many of whom were ill equipped to follow his lead. "We've been overrun with cooking classes," he remarked not long ago. "People have made fortunes just *demonstrating*. How can you learn without participation? You've got to get your hands into the work. You've got to knead dough, bone meat—the whole schmeer. I had a group of women a few months ago, contest winners. They said, 'You don't mean *we're* going to cook, do you?' I said, 'Of course, how else can you learn?'

"Julia [Child] came back here with Simca after they finished the first volume of *Mastering the Art of French Cooking.* Judith [Jones] asked who they'd like to meet in the city, and Julia said, 'Beard.' Well, Julia and Simca arrived in the middle of a class one night. It was a soufflé class that evening, and I had decided that if people were to learn to fold egg whites they had to do it with their hands first. Simca walked in and was astonished to find all those people working the food with their hands. It was the perfect scene for our first meeting."

Many of Beard's students have become distinguished teachers, cooks, and cookbook authors in their own right, and he conveys the distinct impression in conversation that he has derived more satisfaction from teaching than from any other of his manifold activities. "I'm very happy when I teach," he says, "especially if I have the right students. I think I'm a very effective teacher with some people and absolutely no good for others. The loyalty and friendship of my students down through the years has been a heartwarming thing."

Beard's various other activities continued unabated—indeed, increased—while he was simultaneously involved with the school and with Restaurant Associates. By 1968 he and Earle MacAusland had patched up their differences, and a monthly column, "Cooking with James Beard," appeared in *Gourmet* during the next four years. He then put in a five-year radio stint with a daily program called "Dollars and Sense Cookery"—a title whose precise implications may have been lost on listeners who didn't see it spelled out.

Meanwhile, his book production continued apace. *How to Eat Better for Less Money,* on which he collaborated with Sam Aaron, was published in 1954; *The James Beard Cookbook,* in '59; *James Beard's Treasury of Outdoor Cooking*—his third book-length essay in a genre that has fascinated him since his childhood summers on the beach at Gearhart, Oregon—in '60; *Delights and Prejudices,* in '64; *James Beard's Menus for*

Entertaining, in '65; *James Beard's American Cookery,* in '72; *Beard on Food,* in '74; and so on.

All this output was interspersed with frequent trips abroad and to the West Coast, where until last year Beard conducted cooking schools each summer in Oregon and at San Francisco's Stanford Court hotel. Finally forced to husband his energies somewhat, Beard expressed intense regret not long ago over having had to curtail his West Coast activities: "I hated to give up the Oregon classes. They were very special to me. People would bring their families at vacation time and it was more a colony than a school. There was a very pleasant camaraderie. They'd work all day in class and entertain one another at night."

In 1975, some years after both Joseph Baum and Beard had dissolved their association with Restaurant Associates, the two men resumed their professional relationship when Baum embarked on his magnum opus to date, the extraterrestrial restaurant Windows on the World, atop the 107-storey north tower of the World Trade Center in lower Manhattan. Once again Beard came aboard as food consultant.

What Baum envisioned was the Compleat Restaurant and a good deal more. According to his original plan, "Windows" was to be a private club whose "particular purpose ... is to enable business and professional men and women to meet and confer and through their business and social relations to promote and foster the expansion of world trade." Annual dues were to run as high as $420 ("for a member whose principal place of business is south of Canal Street") and would entitle the dues payer to member privileges in all other world trade center clubs from Moscow to Wellington, New Zealand. (Wellington, of course, is somewhat south of Canal Street. Because it also lies outside the immediate environs of the Port of New York, Wellingtonians were expected to pony up a mere fifty dollars, as were Muscovites.) Baum's grand design was skewed somewhat when it was pointed out that the World Trade Center was a function of an interstate administrative agency, the Port Authority of New York and New Jersey, and that taxpayers understandably might bridle at their exclusion from a facility they had helped to finance. The restaurant opened in 1976, as a rather more democratic amenity than its creator had envisioned.

The prevailing opinion among professional observers is that Windows on the World unquestionably achieved true grandeur (the view alone guaranteed *that*) but narrowly missed true greatness (not surprising in view of the volume of business it has transacted since its opening). In this instance Baum's reach simply had exceeded the grasp of any restaurateur in the known universe. But, if execution has been mildly flawed over the years, the underlying culinary concepts were perfectly sound. To what extent those concepts were Baum's and to what extent Beard's is impossible to determine. The two men were by then so thoroughly of one mind that each reacted to the other's ideas as though he had formulated them himself. Today, about a decade after those ideas first were broached, Baum still marvels at the boyish enthusiasm with which Beard, then a septuagenarian, threw himself into the project and still treasures the following letter, which he received from Beard:

I've been thinking since we talked about the Grill and it seems to me that I've enjoyed things like dressed crab, a half lobster with mayonnaise. Then I think the Grill is the place to do a superb devilled crab. And crab cakes! Tiny ones for people who want a small portion, and big ones for those who like the big ones—luscious and hot and wonderful. And lobster cakes! One of the greatest things I've ever had in my life was a great, bulging lobster roll in a little place on Long Island out near Montauk. It was a hot, beautifully baked roll, just bulging with good lobster and a buttery sauce. Superb!

I think we should do some interesting chicken hashes that are crispy and brown and have potatoes in them, very much the way a roast beef hash is done but with variations—like putting black olives into it and pine nuts and things like that, and maybe turning it into a little frittata.

And that open hearth charcoal grill we have will do marvelously for all the broilings, which after all is what a real grill is all about. I think we've got to have all manner of steaks and chops, especially some good, thick, lamb chops.... And honest grilled fish. We're so lucky to have the best of all American fish, the great Striped Bass, and perhaps salmon steaks grilled in Japanese fashion. Of course, we must also have a fine, simple hamburger served with a charcoal grilled onion slice, or with a sharp Sauce Poivre for a special lift. That smoked chicken and Vermont ham sandwich you've been talking about on Russian rye with mustard pickles sounds sensationally good.

I think your idea of an International Cooks' Table is terrific. A kitchen stage. People will get a kick out of watching the ever-changing culinary scene.... A big round table where you can sit when you're alone and don't feel like being alone, gets a definite yes from me. Well, look, this could go on forever.

By the mid-1970s the state of Beard's health had become a matter of serious concern. In the introduction to his book *Theory and Practice of Good Cooking,* published in 1977, he conceded that "Within the last year I have been put on a no-salt, low-calorie diet and I'm discovering all kinds of things about flavoring I never knew before." According to Sam Aaron, "When Jim was fifty-five his doctor said, 'You'll never reach sixty,' but if you have the right ancestors you can withstand all onslaughts. Jim has a circulatory problem today that affects everything else. It's medically impossible, but he may live to be a hundred." Beard himself takes a wry view of "how it gets when you grow old." Confessing to a recent visitor that he'd been somewhat under the weather the previous week, he evoked images of a deteriorating New York City subway system. Patting his still-monumental corporation, he said, "There was trouble on both the IRT and BMT lines."

Beard may have grown old but he also has grown new. In 1981, well past the biblical three score and ten, he informed his readers of a second coming of sorts in his introduction to *The New James Beard.* By that time his public long since had acquired the habit of referring to each of the master's successive volumes as "the new Beard," but in this case the subject of the title was the author, not the book: "At my ripe age, I acknowledge with some pleasure that my lifelong liaison with good food has gradually been creating a new me." The book was intended to be a companion volume to *Theory and Practice* and as a second updating of *The James Beard Cookbook.* Beard, who doesn't boggle at indulging his penchant for ironic iconoclasm even when he himself happens to be the icon in question, originally had intended to call the book *The Revised Standard Beard*, "but something had been quietly happening, I came to realize: a shift straight across the whole spectrum of my cookery, all the way from menu making right down to how I now wrote recipes."

In much the same way that the painter Titian had four centuries earlier, Beard had undergone a stylistic metamorphosis on the threshold of his eighth decade: As *The Oxford Companion to Art* puts it in the case of Titian, "an increasing looseness in the handling and a sensitive merging of colours which makes them more and more immaterial." As Beard himself describes the changes in his style, "What I want to stress is the new, flexible approach to ingredients, the way we put them together, and the way we plan a meal." He goes on to say:

> The chapters are arranged in an unorthodox order, a change in structure which corresponds to my new thinking about menus. Almost any dish in the first six chapters can be served either as an appetizer or as a main course, including most of the soups, the salads, and the vegetables. Put the emphasis where you please. Feel free.
>
> In a number of chapters, I explore different flavor affinities, in the hope that you will adapt these suggestions in creating a dish of your own. The recipes themselves have other suggestions. Take a fresh look. My emphasis is on options, my motto is "Why not?" and my hope is to provide you with inspiration as well as practical guidance.
>
> Old-fashioned cookbooks, including my early ones, used to treat recipes as formulas. But in cooking along with my friends, colleagues, and students, I came to find the formula style boring and rigid. Listening is much more useful than prescribing *what*, and everybody learns best through thinking, not just performing....

In the fullness of his years the new Beard was calling into question the techniques, traditions, and conventional wisdom on which he had been nurtured and which he had taken for granted all his life. Moreover, he was reexamining and revising his habitual palatal responses and tasting foods more keenly than he ever had before. "Since doing time on a salt-free diet," he wrote, "I approach a plain baked potato reverently. Maybe I've been missing the truth—the nutty, delicate earthiness of a perfect baked potato."

He questioned conventional notions of the progression of a meal, too: "In my youth, a 'proper' dinner had to have something light at each end, like consommé to begin and fruit to finish—you could call the menu diamond-shaped, with a big bulge at the main course.... By the middle of the century ... the number of courses had shrunk, but the big bulge ... remained." Now, he saw no particular merit in the diamond-shaped menu: "This year for my annual celebration of the first shad roe, we had a luscious pair of sautéed roe apiece ... then very small paillards of veal with a little cucumber salad—together on the plate, so the juices could mingle, which used to be heresy—and wound up with just a taste of fresh strawberry sorbet. A wedge-shaped dinner, then. And why not? It tasted wonderful, and taste is the only rule a cook need acknowledge, in this happy time of freshness and freedom."

Edward Giobbi is a noted painter, sculptor, and printmaker and, according to Craig Claiborne, "without question the finest and most enthusiastic nonprofessional cook I've ever met." Giobbi and Beard met for the first time in 1971, soon after Beard had warmly reviewed Giobbi's first book, *Italian Family Cooking*. As Giobbi describes the meeting, "I had invited Jim up to the house for lunch, and he arrived in this big black limousine provided by Random House. He was the nicest, most natural person in the world. He seemed to embrace us— the whole family—the moment he stepped out of the car. I served him *verdura trovata* [greens found growing wild on the Giobbi property near Katonah, New York] and stuffed breast of veal, two recipes from the book. He never made us feel like we were feeding an authority— *the* authority—on food. He was just a big friendly guy who liked to eat simple, honest cooking. We've been friends ever since, and there's no gentler, more wonderful human being in the world. There's absolutely nothing competitive about him. He goes out of his way to help people. One way or another, he's touched everyone in the food world, and a lot of them don't even know it. I don't think it's possible to find anyone who will say a bad word about him."

Giobbi appears to be eminently correct in his assessment of the futility of seeking anyone inclined to badmouth Beard. To talk about the man with members of the food establishment is to participate in something like a giant love-in: a spontaneous outpouring of affection and esteem unclouded by the backbiting usually to be found in any professional circle, and in the food world in particular. Both Joseph Baum and his longtime associate Alan Lewis, the present director of Windows on the World, treasure Beard in equal parts for his gastronomic infallibility, the Belle Epoque grandeur of his presence, his unstinting generosity, and his Rabelaisian zest for the outrageous:

BAUM: Jim is the only man alive today whom you can invite to the country and find walking around the grounds in a flowing silk robe and sleeping cap. He ...
LEWIS (breaking in): We once had just one day to spend together in Paris and narrowed our dining choices down to four restaurants, but couldn't decide among them. Jim's solution was to have two complete lunches and two complete dinners. After the fourth meal, we took a carriage ride. I said, "Jim, you were born to ride in a fiacre."
BAUM: Jim and I were touring France one year and facetiously talking of doing a *pissoir* guide—which trees and bushes were endorsed by James Beard. He was so enthusiastic that ...
LEWIS (again interrupting): To this day I can dial "Oregano 5" [Beard's telephone exchange is Oregon 5] and say, "Jim, give me the name of that oyster dish we had at such-and-such a place twenty years ago," and he'll supply it instantly. Jim's a walking memory bank. He never has to consult files or notes. I've been calling him for years and saying, "Hey, Jim, I want to do this or that esoteric dish," and he'll supply the recipe one-two-three off the top of his head right over the phone.

To Craig Claiborne, Beard is "simply the founding father of the national interest in good eating, the bedrock. He's been a real missionary throughout his career and has been *the* great force in developing the national palate. He's the most imposing figure in the food field in America." To Leon Lianides, owner of the vaunted New York restau-

rant The Coach House, who has known Beard for some thirty years, he
is "a rare human being, a wonderful man with a tremendous sense of
humor—a joy. Jim never has a bad word to say about anyone. He's a
walking encyclopedia of every aspect of the preparation, history, and
enjoyment of food. All these young people in the food world today
who pretend to know so much—it will take them a long, long time
before they catch up with Jim Beard."

About ten years ago Beard moved to his present Greenwich Village location, where he lives and works in the two lower storeys of a four-
storey town house. He is assisted by a general factotum, Richard
Nimmo, a houseman, Clay Triplette, and occasionally hampered by
an exuberant pug, Percy, a four-legged projectile with a propensity for
launching itself, with alarming velocity, in the general direction of its
master's lap. A second-floor study, which opens on a lofty, glass-
enclosed duplex area at the rear of the house ("It's a working room—
I don't know whether you call it a conservatory or a greenhouse, or
what the hell you call it"), is eclectically furnished and decorated, in
large part with Chinese heirlooms: "Things I grew up with. We had
so much Chinese stuff, a good collection, but I got rid of a lot of it
when I broke up the house in Portland. We had many, many Chinese
friends in Portland, and I've always been very much at home with the
Chinese. If you look, you'll see that my eyes are almond-shaped." (At
certain moments, indeed, Beard bears eerie resemblance to traditional
Chinese porcelain and carved depictions of such subjects as the Bud-
dha, the eighth-century poet Li Po, and Shou Lou, the patron of
longevity—resemblances he heightens at times by affecting Chinese
dress.) Downstairs, a kitchen large enough to accommodate classes of
ten also opens on the conservatory (or whatever), which in turn opens
on a lush backyard garden.

"Let's talk downstairs, where we can get some sun," Beard suggested one morning last fall. "You go ahead, I'll join you in a moment."
His guest paused on the way to a spiral staircase to examine a framed
photograph of Escoffier. "It's signed," Beard said, "but not to me. I did
a magazine article some years ago in which I described a certain dish,
and a woman who read it offered to trade the photograph for the
recipe. You know, I think Escoffier was the most misunderstood of the

great chefs—he valued simplicity more than anyone else. But I'm not sure I don't think Montagné was the greatest cook of the century. All the chefs of Paris ate at his little restaurant." The visitor negotiated the narrow spiral staircase, leaving two James Beards—the master in the flesh and a stuffed-cloth caricature—behind him.

Beard appeared downstairs a minute or two later and seated himself at a sunwashed tiled table. As might be expected, Beard at eighty isn't quite the physical colossus that mention of his name still conjures up for most Americans. But his circumference at the equator remains awesome, as befits a man once given to describing beefsteaks and barons of lamb as "snacks" ("Try eating with Jim," Judith Jones remarked recently, "and you have to be mighty quick to get your share"), but his shoulders seem narrower than in the past. He remains a commanding presence in a roomful of people, even standing beside the strapping, Watusi-tall Julia Child at a gathering in her honor last fall. He still puts in a day's work that his juniors by half might find grueling, and, if a proper noun occasionally eludes him for a moment or two, his taste memory remains unimpaired.

An inveterate early riser, Beard has "showered, shaved, and had tea by seven o'clock." As he describes his normal working day, "I *have* to read the papers, two in the morning, one in the afternoon. I'm not a radio listener or a television watcher. I do my best work in the morning, which sometimes is interspersed with endless telephone calls. The art of letter writing is gone, I'm afraid, forever. I go over my mail just before lunch. If I'm staying home, I have a simple lunch. If I have business to conduct, it's better to go out, but I don't go to restaurants as often as I once did, except when I'm on the road. Usually, I frequent a circle of nearby places because it's easier for me—Sally Darr's place [La Tulipe], The Coach House, La Gauloise, Frank's over in the meat market, Alfredo Viazzi's Trattoria da Alfredo, and, uptown, The Four Seasons. In the afternoon I may do some experimenting or research various things I'm working on [among other things, Beard's current activities include work on still another, reputedly autobiographical book, a syndicated weekly newspaper column, a somewhat diminished teaching schedule, several consultancies, and a great many personal appearances].

"Then, there are so many books you have to skim through, at the very least. I may go out one or two nights a week, but sometimes I stay home for two or three weeks at a stretch. I still love the theater and opera but don't go as much as I used to. I used to be much more social than I am now. Mind you, that doesn't mean I'm any less interested in people. New people and new ideas are a never-ending source of pleasure, but when you get old, well...." Prodded by an occasional question, Beard basked in the sunshine for the next hour or so, free-associating about his life in food and the foods in his life. Telescoped somewhat, the following were his observations.

"Well, I still can't stand chicken livers, but there are very few other things I dislike, provided they're properly cooked. I've come to dislike broccoli lately, and I've never liked wild rice much, but I do love sugar snap peas. I find myself turning against fish in most restaurants because it's usually overcooked and oversauced. I love poached salmon cooked à point, with maybe just a little lemon butter—little enough so that you can taste the fish. There are very few restaurants that can do a sauté meunière well, and my insides revolt against poor examples. I find myself losing interest in pâté. I remember [chuckling] doing this party in South Carolina. Someone said, 'Oh, Mr. Beard, there's nothing for a party like a little pate.' That was a party put on by some gurmay society or other; that's pronounced gurmay when it's a gourmet society.

"I worked for the Cognac Association for about five years at one point and went over there [the Cognac district] fairly often. I took a group of newspaper people over one year. They were a pretty rough-and-tumble bunch, not food critics. We were given a formal luncheon at Hennessy at which the wines were presented and identified one by one. One comic stood up in the middle of the litany and said, 'Stanford 1928.' Then we went to Hine. They presented each newspaperman with a beautiful Baccarat decanter as we were leaving. Three of them drank off the contents before we were barely out of sight of the grounds, opened the windows, and tossed the decanters onto the road.

"The owner of Rémy Martin had a farm practically in Cognac. At dinner he sat between the two prettiest girls and pinched their bottoms all evening. He served me meat and said, 'You'll never guess what this is.' Well, it was quite delicious, but I had to confess I couldn't identify it. Turned out it was mule.

"It's funny how old things spring up in your taste memory: marvelous grilled sardines at the Ritz in Barcelona and a beautiful *brandade de morue* made in a little *charcuterie* in Saint-Rémy. In the old days on the *Independence*, there was a barman from Trieste who, if he liked you, would say, 'Have lunch in the bar.' He made a codfish salad that was one of the best things I've ever eaten.

"When I lived in Saint-Rémy years ago there was a little bistro opposite—what was his name, the great Provençal poet? Yes, Mistral—opposite Mistral's house. It was owned by Madame Fraise, who served enormous bowls of the most delicious little *tellines* [thumbnail-size Mediterranean bivalves] and huge savory pâtés with knives stuck in their tops. I can still taste those things as well as I can last night's dinner. At my first lunch in Portugal I had an absolutely dreamy dish of *bacalau*, a cross between a soufflé and a *brandade*. Beautiful. Richard Olney, Simca, Julia, and I used to knock around the south of France together. We found this great place for Moroccan *brik* and told Roland and Lee Penrose about. Picasso sneaked in and had two helpings. Then he turned his plate over and did a sketch on it 'in lieu of *pourboire*.'

"Another absolutely amazing meal was in a monastery in Japan. The entire meal was made up of flowers. Fascinating things. There was a jasmine, dipped in batter and deep-fried. It came to the table redolent of that perfume peculiar to jasmine. And there was a salad of various raw blossoms. It was a terrifically exciting meal. Some of my most definite early taste memories are of freshly gathered wild mushrooms and razor clams. And the Dungeness crabs of my childhood, of course, and another thing I loved were those tiny, tiny shrimp that used to be sent down the coast from Alaska."

For some reason or another the Alaskan shrimp reminded Beard of a gurmay dinner held decades ago. "There were to be two speakers, Richardson Wright, the editor of *House and Garden*, and Lucius Beebe. I was to introduce Lucius. I watched him have several bourbons in teacups during dinner, along with the usual complement of wines. Well, after my introductory remarks, Lucius stood up in all his sartorial splendor and slid right under the table and was heard of no more.

"While I was with Sherry's—it would be awfully hard to analyze my position there because I was doing everything—I had the opportunity to taste a great many wines I wouldn't otherwise have tasted at that stage of the game, and I befriended Frank Schoonmaker and Alexis Lichine, who were to have a great influence on my life. I think Schoonmaker had the greatest palate I've ever known. We had a long friendship and traveled together a great deal. We had adjoining houses on the Costa Brava one summer and I found him to be a very impressive person, as good a judge of food as of wine. You know people pretty well when you swim with them in the morning and eat three meals together every day. Frank's wife had fired their cook, so they ate all their meals at my place.

"After the war I became very close to Jeanne Owen, secretary of the Wine and Food Society. Alfred Knopf was on the board, along with people like Crosby Gaige and Sophie Kerr—all pretty intelligent eaters and drinkers and all ruled with a very firm hand by Mrs. Owen. My association with her began when we had the shop [Hors d'Oeuvre, Inc.] and she decided to hold tastings of apéritifs and our hors d'oeuvres. Billy Rhode said, 'I don't want anything to do with her. You go.' That began a friendship that lasted fifteen years. Jeanne had a theater and radio background, and we went to theaters and restaurants together almost constantly. She was an extraordinarily good cook and I learned a great deal about food and drink from her. She was close to Earle MacAusland and the restaurant and wine people, and I grew into that milieu with her encouragement."

Beard fielded a question he doubtless has been asked thousands of times by lowering his voice to a deep, portentous rumble and syllabizing extravagantly. "My phi-los-o-phy? Well, my philosophy, if you want to call it that, is: Be simple. Be honest. Don't overcook and don't undercook, but it's better to undercook than overcook. The worst meals I ever had in my life were cooked by one aunt in Oregon. She never learned that timing is an interesting kitchen procedure. She'd serve these great huge roasts that had been cooked till they fell off the bones, watery mashed potatoes, and pies in impenetrable crusts. We all dreaded visiting her, and I've always associated her with a song most people today are too young to remember: 'We never speak of Aunt Clara; her picture's turned to the wall.' Shop for the very best of everything—not necessarily the most expensive things but the freshest and best of their kind—and don't be afraid to try new things. Something I habitually say in my classes is 'Think. Taste. If you don't like what you taste, change it to your taste.' What is cooking? A series of variations on a theme, nothing else.

"My ideal meal? It would depend on the season. In the spring an exemplary menu would begin with a hearty serving of asparagus. I loathe hollandaise on asparagus, and I'd just serve them as is, with just a little freshly ground pepper. I'd follow that with a plain roast *poussin* and probably some little tiny new potatoes [making a chick-pea-size circle with his thumb and forefinger]. I think I'd have a salad of either watercress or *mâche* and probably some cheese. If I had a dessert, I think I'd have strawberries if it were late enough for them. If not, *crème caramel*, which I just happen to love.

"If it were late summer or early fall, I think we'd have fresh corn, but it'd have to be pulled and cooked in minutes. I'd serve it as a first course—the only place in a meal where it belongs. After that, I'd be very tempted to have a *gigot*, and with that I'd have good beans—*haricots verts*, so as not to repeat the starch. And I also might have a good broiled tomato, or else superb tomatoes with a Cognac dressing. And if it's fall a *tarte au pruneaux*. I love Italian prunes better than any others.

"For a winter meal, let's start with oysters. Oysters with lemon juice, period. Well, possibly a *mignonnette* sauce, but I don't think so. Olympia oysters? Hm-m-m, well, maybe, but I'm very fond of English and French oysters. I once went to an English oyster center near Cambridge and went out in an oyster boat. We were out on the water about an hour and a half and I was practically frozen, and we got back without one goddamn oyster. I guess I'll be a traditionalist and have some brown bread and butter with the oysters.

"Then, I think we'll have wild duck, teal if possible. I think teal are the greatest of all ducks. For years they were raised on a farm in British Columbia and sent to market tagged. I was in the Yucatán once and was served two 'wild' teal with the Canadian tags still on them. I've always marveled that they knew where to fly. Canvasbacks? Oh yes, I can remember the way they tasted before the first World War, but I've always thought teal were better. Of course, canvasback was eastern and that may have colored my perception of it as a child.

"With the duck, let's have some glazed turnips and—though it's corny and I've said I don't much like it—wild rice. In the right context it *can* be good. I think just some watercress with the duck. No salad and no cheese. Maybe an apple charlotte to finish but *no* hard sauce.

"I like a well-tailored plate of food, and I want things to look and taste like what they are. I detest cooking that masks one flavor with another, and I dislike fussy presentations that don't respect the identity of the ingredients. A tomato is a tomato, not a rose. Noodles are noodles, not birds' nests or baskets."

"Our life," wrote Thoreau, "is frittered away by detail.... Simplify, simplify." And Willa Cather wrote, "Art, it seems to me, should simplify. That, indeed, is very nearly the whole of the higher artistic process; finding what conventions of form and what detail one can do without and yet preserve the spirit of the whole...."

As has been the case with all great artists of appreciable longevity, James Beard's style gets simpler and better as he gets older. His long gastronomic life has been spent in "finding what conventions of form and what detail one can do without." He was the icon of American gastronomy during the first stirrings of a renascence he almost single-handedly set in motion; he remains emblematic of American cooking and eating at their best today. His guiding principle—more honored in the breach than the observance by food snobs and food couturiers—is that the culinary arts are not legitimately concerned with displays of virtuosity or originality but with the fullest possible enjoyment of the intrinsic goodness of honest food.

February 1984

ESCOFFIER

Naomi Barry

The portrait of Auguste Escoffier at the age of eighty shows a distinguished gentleman with white mustache wearing a Louis-Philippe–style frock coat. Quiet command emanates from the seated figure. No one would guess that Escoffier wore high-heeled shoes: The giant of modern restauration was so small he needed the lift to give himself a few more inches of breathing space above the hot stoves.

The man whom César Ritz, founder of the world-famous Ritz hotels, proclaimed the finest cook he had ever met was a pint-sized thirteen-year-old when apprenticed to his uncle, who owned Le Restaurant Français in Nice. The year was 1859, a time when a restaurant cook was at the bottom of the social pile.

The boy yearned to become a sculptor, but his blacksmith/tobacco planter father and his grandfather decided he should learn a trade that promised at least a modest living. The grandfather, a man of innate courtesy, taught Auguste and his brother to be polite in all circumstances, to behave at table, to remember always to remove their caps when addressing a lady. "He told us savoir-vivre was of utmost importance," recalled Escoffier, "and in later life I profited from his valuable advice."

No leniency was shown to the nephew who had been pushed into a profession he would never have chosen on his own. Nonetheless the sensitive youngster determined that "as long as I was in it [the cooking profession], I would climb out of my rut and do everything in my power to restore the prestige of a *chef de cuisine*." During off-hours he frequented the kitchen of a neighboring *pâtissier* (pastry cook) to learn another branch of his craft. Having made back-door friends with the cooks of the Russian aristocrats who spent the winter season on the Côte d'Azur, he took copious notes on Russian cuisine, which was then enjoying great favor in Nice.

Despite the lowliness of his position, young Escoffier knew that under the former monarchy a *chef de cuisine* had ranked as an officer of the crown, a sure indication that there was nothing demeaning about a man in the kitchen. Indeed, Louis XIV's nephew Philippe d'Orléans often slipped away from the Palais-Royal for an evening at the Comtesse de Farabère's farm in Asnières, on the outskirts of Paris. Upon arrival the regent of France would wrap an unbleached linen apron about his silk breeches and prepare a sophisticated supper for the countess and a few of the farmhands. By the end of Escoffier's long career, and largely thanks to his efforts, a cook was once again a respected personage. By 1928 Escoffier had become the first chef to be named an officer of the French Légion d'Honneur. He dined with dukes and princes, actresses and divas. Through hard work and meticulous application he spread the fame of French cooking and the products of the French soil far beyond the national boundaries.

"The art of cuisine is perhaps one of the most useful forms of diplomacy," he once wrote, and he proved it in the most sumptuous palace hotels of the world by employing French techniques, French produce, and "above all, French personnel." The two thousand French chefs he sowed in important positions around the world bore his influence. As they carried forth Escoffier's methods and theories a new style of public dining was established internationally.

In the mid-nineteenth century the illustrious name in French gastronomy was Marie-Antoine Carême, chef to Talleyrand, Czar Alexander I, George IV, and Baron Rothschild. Although born under Louis XVI, the great Carême died (in 1833) only twenty-six years prior to Escoffier's debut in his uncle's restaurant.

Carême's habitual spreading of fifty to a hundred dishes over an immense table laden with ornate silver was the prevailing mode for state banquets under the Second Empire and for aristocratic receptions in both France and England. The food, graced with highfalutin names, was manipulated into elaborate edifices: Carême specifically studied architecture to achieve ever more fanciful structures of fish, fruit, and fowl.

The seated guests were able to partake only of those dishes within arm's reach, no matter how tempted they might be by a delicacy two yards down the groaning board. As such dishes were all presented on the table at the same time, the appropriate temperatures ranging from hot to cold lost all significance.

Escoffier was hardly six months into his apprenticeship when he began to veer from the Carême line by devising well-composed menus that would stimulate the desire to savor a repast intelligently prepared and presented. In naming his dishes, he searched for agreeable phrases that nevertheless bore some relationship to the foods themselves. Menus were important documents to people in his native Provençal village of Villeneuve-Loubet. Those created for baptisms, marriages, and anniversaries were kept as "poems" commemorating hours happily spent.

Escoffier's menu planning was always dictated by common sense. He was the first to alter tradition for a new and prosperous business class unable to linger endlessly at table. He aimed for rapid, precisely timed service so that his dishes could be eaten at their correct temperatures. Stripped of gorgeous but inedible garnishes, each dish had to stand on its own in terms of flavor and quality. Typical of Escoffier's simple elegance was a shallow dish of fillets of sole encircling a mound of choice shellfish.

Without ceasing to be an art, cuisine, he decreed, would have to be viewed and executed scientifically, leaving nothing to chance. This may seem self-evident to us now, but it was a milestone in restauration in Escoffier's day.

His one celebrated lapse into distinctly non-scientific euphemism was a gala supper at the Savoy Hotel in London that featured *"Cuisses des Nymphes à l'Aurore"* (thighs of nymphs at dawn). Paris had been appreciating frogs' legs for two centuries, but no self-respecting Britisher would touch them. An exception was the Prince of Wales, who loved French cuisine, both rustic and refined. The prince had a good laugh watching his compatriots eat *"cuisses des nymphes"* with pleasure, blissfully unaware of what they were putting into their mouths.

Of the thousands of menus prepared and saved by Escoffier as a taste index of his clients and as a future reference for his colleagues, none more accurately mirrored the man than the breakfast he prepared on August 15, 1870. At the outbreak of the Franco-Prussian War, twenty-four-year-old *saucier* Escoffier of the fashionable Petit Moulin Rouge restaurant in Paris was recruited as cook for the 2nd Section of the general staff of the French Army of the Rhine.

His outfit encamped near Metz, in northeastern France, at 11 P.M., August 14. Escoffier, in charge of provisions and the horse-drawn supply wagon, had hastily obtained an enormous superior-quality cut of beef, which he was planning as the pièce de résistance for the morrow. He was too preoccupied to sleep. Should there be a sudden order to depart, what was he to do with the beef? There might not be enough time to cook it, and leaving it behind was out of the question. He decided to ready himself for an emergency.

"I'm roasting it now," he told Bouniol, his faithful sidekick. At once the two soldier/cooks hacked four stout branches from a hedge and drove them into the ground to form two X-shaped supports. A fifth branch was run through the meat to serve as the spit and propped over the fire. Onlookers converged from every tent, lured by the tantalizing aroma. Escoffier and Bouniol, sabers drawn, spent the rest of the night protecting their prize.

Escoffier's characteristic foresight paid off. Before seven in the morning the order came to have a "comfortable lunch" ready by nine, as it was possible that the day's events would not allow a second meal. The "lunch," which preceded the march to Gravelotte—France's only victory of the war—consisted of sardines in oil, sausages, soft-boiled eggs (procured from a nearby farm), roast beef (medium-rare), potato salad, coffee, and Cognac *fine champagne*.

The next meal was served up late that night, the actual eve of battle. This time the officers delightedly sat down to sautéed rabbit on a *fondant* of onion purée. (The ever-anxious Escoffier had been off gunning rabbits to provide some gastronomic variety.) *"Lapin de Gravelotte"* became part of culinary history as a result of this dinner.

The war made Escoffier realize that the usual methods of feeding an army on active service had become outmoded. Years later, in an article addressed to the military, he condemned the inefficiency of having herds of animals follow the troops. He furthermore criticized as heavy and cumbersome the packages of rice and bacon carried in the backpacks of the infantry. Instead he advised that every soldier should be equipped with four days' provisions, totaling 2.6 kilos: He recommended eight tins of stewing beef, which could be eaten hot or cold; eight squares of concentrated sweetened coffee; eight 80-gram tablets of concentrated vegetable soup; and twelve "emergency" pastilles made of cocoa and chocolate.

Around 1874 Escoffier, now head chef of the Petit Moulin Rouge, successfully experimented with the conservation of whole tomatoes and encouraged factories to can them for restaurants to use when the tomato was out of season. Thus was born an industry that flourishes today.

Not long ago, while I was driving from Nice up to the Château du Domaine Saint-Martin, a serene and attractive retreat above Vence, I noticed a discreet sign pointing to Villeneuve-Loubet and the Musée de l'Art Culinaire, Foundation Auguste Escoffier. The museum, situated in the house where Escoffier was born October 28, 1846, is the result of the commemorative effort of several disciples who loved and venerated the great chef: Paul Thalamas, who worked under him at the Savoy, and Eugène Herbodeau, a member of his *brigade* at the Carlton. Most of the money for the creation of the museum was donated by Joseph Donon, whom Escoffier sent off to America in 1912 to be the private chef of steel magnate Henry Clay Frick.

The little museum opened its doors in 1966. Packed with memorabilia, it is a mecca of the métier. The profession's homage to one of its greats includes a library; displays of sugar fantasies ranging from

Greek temples to Wild West towns and of kitchen utensils devised by Escoffier; portraits of such heroic toques as Carême, Urbain Dubois, and Alexandre Dumaine; and a host of mementos and such homely artifacts as the paring knife used by the famous Lyonnais restaurateur Mère Fillioux. Also exhibited is a 1929 hand-lettered illuminated testimonial to Escoffier from the chefs of Poznan, in Poland. Three-star chef Pierre Troisgros recently stopped by to add one of his own menus to the museum's collection; captivated, he prolonged his intended visit by four hours, missed his plane, and confessed he couldn't have cared less.

One entire room is devoted to Escoffier menus, and as such it becomes an à la carte survey of Europe. A menu from the Hôtel de Paris reveals how Monte Carlo coped with rationing in 1943. The London Carlton's dinner for 712 guests on the night of November 11, 1918, commenced appropriately with *potage de la victoire*. In Instanbul on June 28, 1902, Commandant Julien Viaud hosted the local French ambassador aboard his ship, *La Mouette*. The splendid dinner included *cannelloni au foie gras,* fillet of beef, roast quail, asparagus with a *sauce mousseline,* and pistachio ice cream. Commandant Viaud created splendid works of his own among the novels and travel books he wrote under the name of Pierre Loti.

One July afternoon in 1874 a letter was delivered to the Petit Moulin Rouge in Paris from the statesman Léon Gambetta (instrumental the following year in forming the Third Republic) reserving a private dining room for that evening. As long as a saddle of lamb Béhague and chicken in tarragon aspic could be served, the rest was up to the chef, the letter specified.

For Gambetta and his two guests, the future Edward VII and an unidentified foreign diplomat, Escoffier added cantaloupe filled with Tawny Port, *consommé Royale* (chicken consommé garnished with savory custard shapes), fillet of sole with soft roe, and a crayfish soufflé. The panoply of desserts included a *biscuit glacé Tortoni* (vanilla and pistachio ice cream layered with sponge cake), fresh green almonds, and the incomparable peaches of Montreuil. The accompanying wines were a Chablis; an 1864 Col d'Estournel; and an 1864 Veuve Cliquot. In Escoffier's opinion this dinner laid the basis for the eventual 1907

Entente Cordiale, or Triple Alliance, between France, England, and Russia. The Entente Cordiale of his own life is dated 1884, the year he and César Ritz joined forces.

The thirty-four-year-old Ritz, director of the deluxe Grand Hotel in Monte Carlo, had lost his talented chef Jean Giroix to the rival Hôtel de Paris. Convinced that a hotel's fame depended on its restaurant's cuisine, he was desperate for a replacement of equal stature. Without first-class cuisine in the dining room, the perfection of service that was his forte seemed to him an empty standard.

Ritz gave Escoffier the chance to develop fully his ideas. Henceforth and wherever they went the indefatigable pair would attract the most dazzling clientele in Europe. During winter they worked in Monte Carlo; in summer they moved to the Hotel National in Lucerne. "The National became a great hotel," wrote Ritz, "only after Escoffier took over the management of the kitchens."

In 1890 Richard D'Oyly Carte, the English operatic impresario, beguiled Ritz and brought him to London to salvage his foundering Savoy Hotel (which had opened in August of the previous year); part of the deal was Escoffier. The duo decided to attack first the reordering of the restaurant, which was in as much of a mess as the rest of the operation.

On arrival Escoffier discovered that, out of spite, the departing personnel had cleaned out the kitchens down to the last grain of salt. Escoffier remained calm. He called on a friend, Louis Peyre at the Charing Cross Hotel, to lend him supplies enough to be able to coast through the crisis, and the restaurant was ready for business on schedule.

In Monte Carlo both Ritz and Escoffier had observed that most of the English-speaking clientele could not read a French menu and had to rely entirely on the maître d'hôtel. The menus of London's Savoy, like those of most grand hotels on the Continent, were written in French as well, leaving the diner equally dependent on the headwaiter. In view of this the two men quickly decided to introduce a *prix-fixe* plan for parties of four or more. The system was simple: The headwaiter relayed to the kitchen the name of the host and the number of guests, and Escoffier devised a harmonious succession of dishes from items already on the menu. A duplicate of the order was kept in a special book so that return customers would be served no repetitions except by special request. Londoners loved the *prix fixe,* which left all the worrying details to the chef. They would have been crazy not to when an eight-course dinner priced at 12 shillings 6 pence (which works out to just under $40 today) offered

> *Melon Cocktail*
> *Velouté Saint-Germain*
> *Truite de Rivière Meunière*
> *Blanc de Poulet Toulousaine*
> *Riz pilaw*
> *Noisette d'Agneau à la Moelle*
> *Haricots Verts à l'Anglaise*
> *Pommes Byron*
> *Cailles en Gelée à la Richelieu*
> *Salade Romaine*
> *Asperges d'Argenteuil au Beurre Fondu*
> *Mousse Glacée aux Fraises*
> *Friandises*

In 1865, when Escoffier had first begun work at the Petit Moulin Rouge in Paris, the only women who dined in public were beauties of "easy virtue" or a free spirit like George Sand, who saw no reason to be deprived of all those good things being enjoyed by men. Toward the end of the century, however, society ladies moved out of their private-quarters-only status, and Ritz was one of the first to capitalize on the change. The grand staircase, where an attractive woman could be seen to advantage entering and taking her leave, became an essential of his décor, and flattering lighting at table was *de rigueur.*

To honor his new, female clientele Escoffier created one dish after another: *filets Mireille* and *filets Olga, fondant de volaille Louisette, glace Dora, fraises Sarah Bernhardt, salade Irma* and *salade Noémi, oeufs Magda, soufflé Hilda, bombe Miss Helyett,* and *potage Miss Betsy.*

To celebrate opera singer Nellie Melba's triumph in *Lohengrin* at

Covent Garden, Escoffier created a dessert of peaches poached in vanilla syrup and served on vanilla ice cream. The dish was presented to the singer between the wings of a majestic swan carved from a block of ice. A few years later the chef gave the famous *pêches Melba* their final definition by adding the now indispensable raspberry purée.

On another occasion the diva, resting at the Savoy after a strenuous American tour, was visited by her doctor, who prescribed a light diet that included toast. Escoffier helped her out by shaving the toast to an audacious thinness. Thus—after a trial tasting for Madame Ritz, who had complained that toast was always too thick for her liking—was born Melba toast.

Escoffier's seven years at the Savoy were punctuated with other projects. Luxury hotels were mushrooming, and the Savoy Society had interests in many of them. Ritz and Escoffier opened Le Grand Hotel in Rome, and Escoffier helped form a kitchen *brigade* for the Excelsior there. The pair went to Salsomaggiore for the Grand Hôtel des Thermes. They organized a coquettish chalet and restaurant on the heights overlooking Aix-les-Bains. In short they went, jointly, from one success to the next, for each man was a master in his field and both had the ability to select first-class personnel.

Not that setbacks never befell this talented team. A new hotel being built in Paris was absorbing too much of Ritz's time as far as D'Oyly Carte was concerned, and fur flew. The angry Ritz resigned from the Savoy in 1897, and his team followed suit.

The separation from the Savoy has been a clouded story. The management was said to have accused Ritz and Escoffier of taking percentages from their suppliers. Escoffier supposedly returned some of the take, although he does not mention it when later he wrote sadly: "We had put our whole heart into saving this place [the Savoy] from disaster, to raise it to the peak of glory, and to give the investors the satisfaction they had every right to expect. Without wounding anyone's pride, it would have been possible for these *messieurs* to arrange a reconciliation in the general interest. But they did nothing."

By fortuitous circumstance, however, what would soon be the even grander Carlton Hotel was at the time under construction at the corner of Haymarket and Pall Mall, and its administrators joyfully leapt at the chance to acquire the Ritz-Escoffier duo, even though the premises would not be completed for another two years. (The great hotel was bombed out of existence during World War II.)

This hiatus proved providential, for it allowed Ritz and Escoffier the chance to concentrate on Paris. A hotel on the Place Vendôme required their attention: The rooms and salons were yet to be decorated and the restaurants, kitchens, and cellars required organization.

Opening day of the Paris Ritz—June 5, 1898—was a crush, marvelous in its diversity. Among those present were Marcel Proust, the mysterious financier Gulbenkian, American publisher James Gordon Bennett, Brazilian aviator Alberto Santos-Dumont, the aged prince of gastronomes Emile Winter, plus the usual floating "cream" of society.

The fortunes of The Ritz did not falter for a day. Escoffier and Ritz stayed on until March of the following year, when they returned with easy conscience to London to assume the direction of the Carlton, which was to be Escoffier's headquarters for the next twenty years.

Escoffier continued to follow the principles that had helped make the Savoy the training school par excellence for the entire hotel profession. The restaurant client's waiting time was reduced to a minimum without detracting from the quality of the cuisine. To accomplish this, Escoffier—long before industry began hiring efficiency experts—divided his kitchen staffs of sixty to eighty into specialist squads responsible for sauces, fish, entremets, soups, roasts, pastries, ices, and confections.

Heretofore, for instance, eggs Meyerbeer took a single chef fifteen minutes to produce. Under Escoffier's system the eggs were cooked by the *entremetier,* the lamb kidneys were grilled by the *rôtisseur,* and the *saucier* prepared the truffle sauce. The completed dish was ready for serving in a fraction of the former preparation time.

Despite the inevitable rush and pressure, Escoffier's kitchens functioned in an atmosphere of tranquillity. Remembering the indignities and brutalities suffered in his youth, he forbade drinking on the job, swearing, shouting, and any other vulgarity. If a cook erupted into a fit of temper he was quietly admonished by Escoffier. "Here you are expected to be polite. Any other behavior is contrary to our practice." In the face of an unpardonable breach of such decorum, he habitually pinched his left ear and announced in a soft voice, "I am going out. I can feel myself getting angry."

A notable exception was the day the Carlton's director walked into the kitchens at the height of the "rush hour" and ordered a dish of spaghetti. A short time later he returned and abused a cook for being too slow. The invective grew stronger. The cook finally retaliated by hurling the spaghetti in the director's face. Escoffier stood fast by the cook, asserting his right to more consideration.

Always concerned about the social acceptance of his profession, Escoffier urged his staff—most of whom had left school at the age of thirteen or fourteen—to read and study. When going out onto the street, his cooks were advised to wear hats, collars, and ties, leaving behind their kitchen attire of white jackets and checked trousers. One's wardrobe, he told them, is the first step up the social ladder.

He never lost the respect for economy learned in his youth. Leftovers in his scrupulously clean kitchens were carefully saved for the Little Sisters of the Poor, who called on him each morning. With the provisions went Escoffier's directions for how to transform them into good, nourishing meals at the home for the elderly maintained by the order.

During the Carlton years, Escoffier and Ritz established their style of *prix-fixe* restaurants for the first-class passengers on three of the luxury liners owned by the Hamburg-Amerika Line. In 1910 the pair went to New York City to open The Ritz-Carlton, situated in midtown then and until the 1960s. (The present hotel, on Central Park South, opened on the premises of the former Navarro in the early 1980s.) During this visit Escoffier also spent fifteen days in Pittsburgh to organize the kitchens of the Grand Hotel. He made two subsequent trips to America, one in 1926 and another in 1930, when he presided at the inaugural dinner of New York City's Hotel Pierre on October 16.

Thalamas and Herbodeau have left an hour-by-hour account of a day at London's Carlton under Escoffier, who lived there in a fifth-floor apartment. He arose at six-thirty. He dressed elegantly, even early in the morning, adopting the style of the diplomat Pierre-Joseph Cambon, whose stature and build resembled his own. By seven he was in the kitchens, overseeing breakfast preparations.

At eight he went to his small first-floor office to draw up the day's menus after having looked over deliveries of fresh produce. He bought only the highest quality. What was unobtainable in London markets came from Les Halles in Paris. He had little confidence in cold-storage food, and apart from the famous preserved tomatoes no tinned food was used at the Carlton.

After a breakfast served in his office he went back to the kitchens to taste dishes in preparation. At eleven he was in the restaurant to chat with the manager and the headwaiters and to go over the list of expected clients, their likes and dislikes, their nationalities, the proportion of men and women. If not invited to lunch with friends among the clientele, he and Ritz lunched together before service began. Escoffier then returned to the kitchens for further sampling of dishes and supervision of their presentation. His staff, conscious of the privilege of working for him, did their very best and willingly submitted to the strict discipline he imposed without so much as raising his voice.

At three-thirty Escoffier retired to his office to read, write, and rest. Toward the end of the afternoon he left the hotel to call on various suppliers. He was a tireless walker with a rapid gait. The bobbies along his accustomed route recognized his impeccably dressed little figure and greeted him affectionately. Like a Rockefeller, he handed each of them sixpence.

By six he was back in the kitchens. The restaurant service continued without interruption from seven until one in the morning. When dining alone, he had a light evening meal of soup sprinkled with rice and a dessert of fruit. After a few more hours devoted to writing, he made a final tour of the kitchens around midnight.

This routine was broken by occasional nights at the theater, which he adored (he never missed a play in which his good friend Sarah Bernhardt performed); mass on Sunday mornings; and Sunday afternoon tea at the Ritzes' house in Golders Green after having supervised the Carlton's heavily attended Sunday lunch, for which he donned his chef's hat and jacket. (Escoffier had married sometime between 1873 and 1888—so little is known about his private life—but Delphine Escoffier, née Daffis, was unable to adapt to the English lifestyle and climate, and thus she lived in Monte Carlo with their three children, the family reuniting only during the chef's visits there.)

According to Herbodeau and Thalamas, Escoffier constantly helped young cooks make a good start in life. He could not bear poverty or injustice, and no one ever appealed to him in vain.

It was during the Carlton era that Escoffier brought forth his *Guide Culinaire*, a monumental opus still used in professional kitchens around the world. This project had been germinating for twenty years: While still in Monte Carlo he had met the vacationing Urbain Dubois, chef for the German court, and the renowned Dubois, author of numerous cookbooks, encouraged Escoffier to carry through to completion his idea of a small, comprehensive manual that would outline the principal elements of his recipes. This would serve as a guide to cooks and particularly as an aid to headwaiters so that they might be better informed about what they were suggesting to guests.

Never having written before, Escoffier was shy about putting his notes into publishable form. (He overcame his reticence in later years to the extent of writing *Le Carnet d'Epicure* in 1911, *Le Livre de Menus* in 1912, and *Ma Cuisine* in 1934. A British edition of *Le Guide Culinaire* was published by Heinemann in 1979 under the title *Escoffier: The Complete Guide to Modern Cookery* and is now in its sixth reprinting.) Given the pressures of his daily workload, the pile of notes grew ever larger, and it was only in 1900 that he finally began the codifying of more than five thousand recipes. Philéas Gilbert and Emile Fétu, two devoted colleagues, helped draft the introductions and the theories; other esteemed chefs—Appolon Caillet, Jean-Baptiste Reboul, Alfred Suzanne, and Charles Dietrich—added their grains of salt, and in 1903 *Le Guide Culinaire* appeared in print.

Escoffier did not consider the tome a definitive work and foresaw that modified future editions would be necessary to keep cuisine abreast of the inevitable changes in society. As Herbodeau and Thalamas, his literary executors, pointed out, "*Le Guide Culinaire* ended the age of empiricism in the kitchen. Everything was now weighed and calculated, and recipes classified, as in a real culinary encyclopedia."

Escoffier died in Monte Carlo in 1935 at the age of eighty-nine, after fifteen years of "retirement" that was more active than most people's working careers. His influential career spanned seventy-five kaleidoscopic years, beginning in the modest, crowded household of his grandmother in the hills above Cannes, where, as a little boy, he watched attentively and, later, put what he had absorbed and much more into practice for the pleasure of all. His name is still magic in the profession he did so much to ennoble.

October 1989

LUCIUS BEEBE: THE LAST MAGNIFICO

James Villas

On the evening of February 4, 1966, Mr. Lucius Beebe, in full formal dinner attire that included a magnificent pocket-watch chain specially crafted of large solid gold nuggets, welcomed six equally well-turned-out guests at his mansion in Hillsborough, California, and directed the butler to waste no time dispensing ample measures of sour mash whiskey, ice-cold gin Martinis, and single-malt Scotch.

Once appetites were adequately boosted, the party moved into the polished-wood paneled dining salon, where it commenced a heroic attack on baked salmon *en croûte;* roast haunch of venison with *sauce poivrade;* chocolate soufflé; and a richly veined Stilton—all washed down with ample sufficiencies of Krug '62, Haut-Brion '55 in magnum, and decanted Warre Tawny Port of the rare and exceptional '35 vintage.

Over coffee, Cognac, and illicit Cuban Montecristos #2 in the ornate drawing room, spirits remained high as Beebe proffered a boozy discourse on the mounting vicissitudes of maintaining a private railroad car and two Rolls-Royces, and, after his old friends took their leave around midnight, he retired—replete with food, drink, and bonhomie—to his bedroom, stepped into his custom-made Turkish bath, said good night to the butler, and dropped dead.

Longtime readers of *Gourmet* magazine might well remember Beebe's highly sophisticated column, "Along the Boulevards," which he conducted on and off for more than twenty years and where he expounded imperiously (and often hilariously) on such urgent matters of note as Scottish grouse and Southdown mutton, airplanes ("cartridges of death"), silly half-bottles of wine, expense-account show-offs, the idiocies of golf, and the social status of the waistcoat.

During his illustrious career, his name became legend: He was profiled in *The New Yorker*, made the cover of *Life*, and his last book, *The Big Spenders*, remained on the best-seller list for nearly a year. Today, however, Beebe is virtually and egregiously forgotten except by an almost extinct small breed of sybaritic souls like myself who, at a tender age, came under the dynamic influence of a man who not only epitomized gracious living and refined manners but also, from the early thirties till his death, captivated the imagination of readers everywhere with his felicitous stories of high society; pithy observations on gastronomy, travel, and hotels; unbridled opinions of restaurants and the theater; and his ribald prejudices against plastics in any form, easy credit, and the health police. Forever steeped in pristine nineteenth-century mores and ruthlessly at odds with the mediocrity of a modern society that he classified as "a major street accident," Beebe always adhered scrupulously to the philosophy that "If anything is worth doing, it is worth doing in style and on your own terms—and nobody goddamned else's!" Thus, as Charles Clegg, his literary collaborator and partner, was the first to warn, people who read Beebe (now as before) do so at their own risk.

I met Mr. Beebe twice. First as a guileless young blade with my father, when, through mutual acquaintances, we were invited to visit him in his palatial private railroad car, the *Virginia City*, and were forced to maneuver ourselves over a strapping 185-pound Saint Bernard known as Mr. T-Bone sprawled at the entrance. And second, when, on my way to board the old *Queen Elizabeth* to study in France, we dined together in New York City at Le Pavillon (on which occasion he advised that I would learn more in five days on the liner than after a year at any university). My foggy recall of him indeed confirms his turgid reputation as the millionaire boulevardier and dilettante, the impeccably dressed dandy, and the ultimate snob whose very presence (he was a towering six foot four) dominated any social arena. But I also remember an eminently polite, generous, witty, and kind gentleman who was not out to impress anybody and simply relished a civilized evening on the town over "a hot bird and a cold bottle."

Born into a wealthy Boston banking and mercantile family with as much blue blood as Pétrus flowing through its veins, Beebe had the early distinctions of being suspended from both Yale and Harvard for various behavioral and sartorial shenanigans (he once showed up in Monday morning classes still wearing formal evening clothes and carrying a monocle and cane) and of being, by age twenty-three, the youngest gent in the country to be listed in *Who's Who*.

Attired in a mink-lined topcoat with an astrakhan collar, the majestic rank swept into Manhattan in 1929 with the mien of a postpubescent archbishop, landed a reporting job on the *Herald Tribune*, eventually established himself as an arbiter of the good life in a column entitled "This New York," and, perched on the town's red velvet banquettes as if the Great Depression didn't exist, literally created Café Society.

And over the next two decades, this fulminating eccentric and *bon viveur extraordinaire* splashed ink with impunity across the pages of the *Trib, Gourmet, Holiday,* and *Town & Country,* extolling the virtues of all things Edwardian, his beloved Cunard Line and America's crack trains, the four-Martini lunch, superior London tailoring, four-legged animals (as opposed to "homo saps"), and long, florid sentences and paragraphs, while at the same time venting his spleen about progress, organized religion, Democrats ("moral lepers"), pusillanimous journalism, children on the loose, the gullible American public, milk (except with "a liberal infusion of proof spirits"), and confiscatory taxes.

Variously referred to as "Mr. New York," "Luscious Lucius" (by Walter Winchell), and "the orchidacious oracle of Café Society," Beebe, an indefatigable worker, strived as much to praise those persons, traditions, and institutions he believed were truly respectable and worthwhile as to expose shame and duplicity for what they are. In doing so, he not only flaunted a new epicureanism, with reverberations far into the future, but, by severing the jugulars of those parvenus and rubes perceived as obstacles to a life of quality on every level, he successfully exploited "political correctness" some forty years before the first smug moralist even thought of the peccant notion.

Some of Beebe's texts infuriate, others amuse and evoke nostalgia for better days, and still others teach important and timeless lessons about civility. What's for sure is that we simply don't read this sort of provocative, coruscating, free-wheeling journalism anymore, and that the prospect of another Beebe materializing in this spurious age is as unlikely as finding a bottle of Château d'Yquem '67 or hearing again the operatic brilliance of a Flagstad or Gigli.

Having determined in 1950 that New York was "showing soup stains on its boiled shirt front" and that it was best to "leave a party while it was still good," Beebe and Clegg (whose close, lifelong relationship nobody ever so much as dared to question) headed West and settled in Virginia City, Nevada (where there was "one saloon for every twenty men, women, and children"), in an enormous Victorian abode complete with a six-car garage, an oversized pool set up with cabana, heated dining area, full kitchen, and vistas that stretched two hundred miles. At once Beebe purchased his first railroad car (the *Gold Coast*) and vintage Silver Cloud Rolls-Royce, and, donning an appropriate claw-hammer coat, wide-brimmed black hat, string tie, and snakeskin boots, assumed his new role as a bespoke cowboy of the Comstock.

Next on the agenda was the acquisition of *The Territorial Enterprise*, a pioneer weekly on which Mark Twain had once worked and which Beebe enlivened with editorial invective aimed at any and every aspect of the human comedy. (When a local civic group, for instance, complained that a brothel was too close to a school, Beebe exploded, "Don't move the girls, move the school!") Concurrently, he also continued to contribute his keenly literate but breezy style of journalism to certain upscale periodicals and to produce books (most now out of print) on every topic from the Stork Club to Edwin Arlington Robinson to his beloved steam locomotives. And his public never stopped begging for more.

Offered a weekly column in 1960 at the *San Francisco Chronicle* entitled "This Wild West," and ready to escape Nevada's harsh winters, Beebe bought the sumptuous property in extremely conservative Hillsborough, south of the city, and, partly to transport Mr. T-Bone comfortably, invested in an even more resplendent second railroad car outfitted with an eye-popping Venetian chandelier, ceiling murals, woodburning fireplace, wine cellar, and Turkish bath.

Though he always considered California to be "an overcrowded nut hatch run by the inmates," he nonetheless relished San Francisco's decadent urbanity, outlandish history, and faded glory. When he was not entertaining on the grand scale at his home, staffed with a full battalion of servants, he held court at Jack's, Ernie's, the Sheraton-Palace, and other such grand, gilded venues with immaculate pedigree, gathering grist for his new columns at the *Chronicle* and at *Gourmet* and nurturing himself on a careful diet of Olympia oysters, kidney-spiked mutton chops, *faisan en cocotte à la périgourdine*, and strawberries Romanov.

Intermittently, he and a contingent of grandees would steam to the spread in Virginia City, or to New York, or to New Orleans, and a couple of times a year he boarded a Cunard liner for London to satisfy his "deep need for regional communion" with plovers' eggs, genuine Dover sole on the bone, and Sage Derby cheese and to replenish his collection of morning coats, striped trousers, and silk top hats.

When, after five kidney operations, chronic gout, and repeated flare-ups of a liver "with ducal dimensions," someone had the outrageous temerity to criticize his expansive lifestyle, Beebe, in his thundering voice, pronounced peremptorily, "Do you really expect me to face old age on a regimen of mere bread and seltzer?" followed by "It's the price one pays for civilized living."

As to how this blue-chip curmudgeon might have assessed the present generation, all I can say is heaven help us had he survived to witness such salient breaches of social and cultural decorum as designer jeans and sneakers, cellular phones, the Internet, wine by the glass, nosmoking bars and restaurants, and braggart "superstar" chefs executing their various and endless hybrid cuisines. What Beebe lacked in tolerance, however, he balanced by an ethical code of behavior and aesthetic standards that seem ruefully lacking today, a rescript that stands in stark contrast to a vulgarity on the verge of destroying not only what remnants of rugged individualism still exist but the very fabric of a bedeviled world.

Beebe was altogether unique, an anachronistic original who marched to a different drummer and deemed eccentricity, in both himself and others, the birthright of any free person determined to combat uniformity and shallowness. As he once told an interviewer, "I'd like my obit to say: 'Everything he did was made-to-measure. He never got an idea off the rack.'"

Over the years, I guess I've read the bulk of Beebe's opus but to this day there's still no passage that I find more trenchant and revealing of the magnifico's true personality than probably the last of many late-night notes that he was in the habit of writing to himself (usually "in wine") and that Charles Clegg was good enough to show me during a visit to Hillsborough:

I have not cared greatly for nor been impressed too urgently by people or what they do or want or think. I haven't known many people, but those I have, have derived from, I think, the better vintages of professional competence. This is what has most impressed me and may well be a shallow thing, but I have admired most of all expertise, the quality of being strictly professional. This must be understood to extend to every aspect of living within the individual purview so that the business of having lived has been done, in all directions, with competence, its obligations discharged without blemish, its satisfactions achieved in the knowledge of their excellence.

February 1998

MATTERS OF TASTE

A Very Late Confession

Joseph Wechsberg

Most reminiscences of the Prohibition era were written by people of authority—historians and experts—or by men desperately trying to get a drink. Some, as you can gather from Waverly Root's amusing account, showed ingenuity and perseverance, even bravery. My own contribution to the literature of that heroic epoch is in the minor key, I'm afraid, and you might stop reading right here. I wasn't trying to get a drink; I was trying to sell it. I didn't care for the stuff then. (I do now.) It's rather late to confess, but better late than never.

In the wonderful year 1928 I was twenty-one, a student at the Sorbonne in Paris. I also studied law at Prague University, which took some Continental commuting. To support myself I played the fiddle in obscure joints around the Place Pigalle, where I lived on the top floor of a small hotel, with a sign reading *eau chaude* that fooled many people. There was no hot water. On our floor the rooms were rented by the month; those on the lower floors were let by the hour. Physically and psychologically it was a salubrious experience, highly recommended, as they say in the guidebooks.

One day in July I was given a chance to see America first when I was offered the position of second violinist in the mini-orchestra of *La Bourdonnais*, a mini-steamer owned and operated by the venerable Compagnie Générale Transatlantique. There was nothing venerable about *La Bourdonnais*, whose name was mercifully unknown to most American travelers of the period. They would sail on the French Line's elegant ships, the wonderful (earlier) *France*, with her four funnels and at least forty old tapestries, the fashionable *Paris*, or the unforgotten *Ile de France*. Remember midnight sailings, Champagne corks popping, streamers, confetti? Very nice, but not for *La Bourdonnais*, of which the French Line executives must have been somewhat ashamed. They wouldn't let us sail from Le Havre. *La Bourdonnais* slipped out surreptitiously from Bordeaux at dawn's early light (when decent citizens are asleep in Bordeaux and elsewhere). We went straight south and southwest, making stops in Santander and Vigo in Spain, continued northwest to Halifax, Nova Scotia, and south again to New York City—eleven days of zigzagging, too long for most Americans who were in a hurry even then. Our long-suffering passengers were Spaniards and Canadians, who, I noticed, were not an ideal mixture. The two groups were openly antagonistic and had to be seated on different sides of the dining room.

I noticed other things too. *La Bourdonnais* seemed only slightly larger than the *bateaux-mouches* on the Seine, on which no one would ever want to go to Halifax. On my first trip we lost the upper part of the only funnel we had. The lifeboats were not tested, so far as I remember. It was common knowledge aboard that the ship was mystically held together by rusty nails and the nightly prayers of the elderly *femme de chambre*. It was rumored that *La Bourdonnais* was listed as a liability, not an asset, on the books of the French Line. Then why did I sail on such a decrepit boat? Because I wanted to see New York, which, I thought, was America. That's a perfectly good reason, and I am not ashamed of it to this day.

We sailed from the Quai des Chartrons in Bordeaux, where, I learned much later, *les aristocrates du bouchon*, the great wine merchants and well-known shippers, kept their offices and hundreds of thousands of bottles of vintage claret in large cellars. I couldn't have cared less. I'd never heard of claret, and I didn't know what a vintage was. I was only familiar with the *pinard* they served at my *prix fixe* restaurant near the Place Pigalle, along with the *raie au beurre noir* (skate with brown butter), *boudin blanc* (white sausage), and other good things. Today some people in the trade would call my *pinard* a *grand ordinaire*. And sometimes I go to three-star restaurants where they wouldn't serve such vulgar but wonderful things as *raie au beurre noir*, where all the wines are vintage, and where the sommelier might be shocked if asked for a *pinard*. But I fondly remember my little *prix fixe* at seven and a half very old francs, including plenty of bread and half a bottle. So much for all that snobbish talk about vintages.

My colleagues on this memorable trip were Maurice, a short, rotund, red-faced Alsatian cello player, and Dimitri, a tall, handsome, melancholy White-Russian pianist from Vladivostok. I don't remember the name of the first violinist, a Frenchman. He never played with us, and I became *the* violinist. The nonplaying fiddler was active in the bathroom of our small musicians' quarters down on C-deck, where he skillfully diluted the contents of bottles of gin, rum, Cognac, and whisky that Maurice had purchased on the musicians' account from the second-class barman at the fifty-percent reduced crew rate. Since we would be paid only after the return trip, the barman had to finance the operation. It seemed unusual to me, but Maurice said they always "did things that way." On the second day I asked the nonplaying French violinist what he was doing with all the bottles.

"Stretching the stuff. I can make three bottles of whiskey out of two. Even the king of England won't notice."

"But why?" I asked. He gave me a long, hard stare. I still remember his look though I cannot think of his name.

"Listen," he said. "Why did *you* take this job?"

"I want to see New York."

He almost dropped a precious bottle of Scotch. Fortunately, he caught himself, and the bottle, just in time.

"*Tu es fou*" (you're nuts), he said, shaking his head. Afterward he ignored me. I went to see Maurice, the cellist, whom I liked. He was the oldest of us. He said he worked on ships because he had a wife in America and *une petite amie* in Paris, eighteenth arrondissement, and he liked to keep them both happy. I asked him why the French violinist was working with all those bottles in our bathroom.

Maurice looked at me pensively. It was a nice soft look; he was a sweet fellow.

"*Écoute, mon petit,*" he said. "You are still young but you will learn by experience. Just enjoy yourself and don't worry. And please leave our colleague in the bathroom alone. He isn't much of a violinist, but he's a pretty good chemist, see?"

Looking back now, I admit I must have been a little stupid, but this was 1928, my age of naïveté. There were too many mysteries. Take the second-class barman who sometimes offered me a glass of brut Champagne that he charged to a tipsy Canadian passenger. Able and handsome, the barman, too, was an expert in diluting drinks. The lonely Canadian women admired him while they sat on the high stools, sipping their cocktails. Once I asked him why he didn't work on the *Paris* or the *Ile de France,* where he would make more money on tips, with all those American millionaires aboard. He stopped wiping a glass, winked at me, and said, "Are you kidding, *mon petit*?" After that I asked no more questions.

In those incredible days we musicians had no uniforms, no union cards, no steady working hours, and certainly no discipline. We played for the apéritif hour before lunch and dinner, and later there was an evening *concert classique,* followed by *le dancing,* when Maurice put the cello aside and performed miracles on the drums. It was a lovely era, with lovely songs. Remember "Always," "Tea for Two," "Ain't She Sweet," and all the others?

We would mingle freely, sometimes too freely, with the first-class lady passengers and had our meals in a corner of the first-class dining room, before the general service, in the company of noisy babies and their suffering mothers. Each of us was entitled to two bottles of wine with each meal, labeled "Rouge Supérieur" and "Blanc Supérieur." This was before the French wine laws known as Appellations d'Origine were passed, and I have no idea what was in the bottles. Maurice, our expert, said maybe wine from the south of France that arrived in Burgundy or Bordeaux in large tank trucks that looked like gasoline trucks. Occasionally (Maurice said) they mixed up the trucks and that was why the red wine sometimes had a slight aftertaste of not yet fully matured Mobiloil. Maurice forbade us to drink the white "superior" wine, which, he said, was almost as bad as water, and water "makes frogs grow in your stomach." After each meal we took all the bottles down to our staterooms and stored them under the beds. Occasionally we invaded the dining room after the main service and removed all the wine bottles that the Canadian passengers had left on their tables. Most of them disliked wine and drank water. The Spanish passengers unfortunately drank most of their wine, even the whites.

I don't want to convey the impression that we didn't work. We played Massenet's *Manon* and Tchaikovsky's *Nutcracker,* arranged for trio, and I played solo pieces of what the Viennese called *Salonmusik.* I had some success with Albéniz' *Pavane Espagnole,* Kreisler's *Caprice Viennois,* and especially Gounod's *Ave Maria,* which made some Spanish women cry. Maurice's great hit was Saint-Saëns' *Le Cygne* (The Swan), which made even some hard-boiled Canadians cry. Maurice said he had "studied" the piece with Pablo Casals. Maybe. Unfortunately he (Maurice, not Casals) was unable to play a legato after his fifth glass of wine, and he rarely had less than eight at dinner. Dimitri said it was "the situation" that drove Maurice to drink. "He always has to say good-by, either to his dear wife in America or to his dear *amie* in Paris. That's enough to make a man an alcoholic." Dimitri had neither a wife nor *une amie,* but he drank milk with vodka when he was depressed. He was often depressed because he was homesick for Vladivostok.

On the afternoon prior to our arrival in New York my three colleagues were getting quite busy. Dimitri swiped the mouthwash glasses from all unoccupied staterooms in the vicinity. Maurice, completely sober for a change, stored several bottles of sweetish *goût américain* Champagne in his second cello. It had a detachable back and contained his laundry and a collection of interesting photos, such as those offered to tourists by unshaved North African *types* around Pigalle. The chemist-violinist arranged his bottles in the bathroom, which looked like the barroom in a Marx Brothers farce. Maurice told Dimitri to get enough ice cubes, whereupon our pianist broke into tears. He said ice cubes reminded him of Vladivostok.

I was too excited to go to bed that night. Long before the pilot boarded the ship outside New York harbor I saw a reddish glow in the dark sky way ahead. Maurice, who was with me on the bridge, said it was the reflection of the lights of Broadway. He hadn't touched his wine at dinner. He said he never drank while in New York.

"There's too much to do what with all the business we're going to have. And my wife approves of Prohibition. In fact, she's quite strict about it."

We passed the Statue of Liberty and slowly sailed past Lower Manhattan: the Battery, Wall Street. It was very beautiful. The sun had just come up and was reflected in the windows of the tall buildings. A fine haze was hugging the tops of the skyscrapers. Maurice gave a low whistle and said it was going to be a very hot day, "good for business." I hardly listened. One arrives in New York for the first time only once in life. Nowadays I often watch my fellow passengers when we arrive by plane at Kennedy Airport. I'm afraid it's not the same thing. They miss most of the excitement. I was luckier that hot morning in July, 1928.

We passed the *Ile de France*, lying at the large French Line Pier 57 at the foot of West Fifteenth Street. The foghorn of *La Bourdonnais* greeted the *Ile,* but she didn't answer. She was audibly ashamed of her shabby relations. The second-class barman spat over the railing and said something terrible. There were other fine ships at various piers. We passed them all and continued north until we could go no farther. We stopped at the last pier, number 99, at the foot of West Fifty-ninth Street. The neighborhood was not very chic, with a row of tall chimneys belonging to the municipal garbage disposal plant. Pier 99 is still there, falling to pieces, but whenever I ride past it on the West Side Highway (which was not there in 1928) I have a warm feeling in my heart.

We docked quietly. A few Spanish-looking people stood down on the pier, gloomily awaiting the arrival of the dear relatives they would have to put up with now. The Canadians had disembarked in Halifax. A few American mongrel dogs barked. Two customs men down there waved at Maurice, and he waved back.

"They are our friends," he said. The second-class barman glared at the customs men. I said to Maurice the neighborhood was depressing.

"Don't be silly," he said. "It's the perfect setting. We are well concealed here. Only one customs man on duty at the gangway. Do you know how many there are at the *Ile de France*? Sometimes ten and more. Impossible to do any business there. Let's go down. Our friends will drop in."

The two customs men dropped in and were greeted with enthusiasm by my three colleagues. I was introduced. Even Dimitri stopped being melancholy. The chemist offered our friends two mouthwash glasses filled with Scotch whisky, straight. I noticed with amazement that he'd opened a new, undiluted bottle. Obviously the customs men were *very* good friends.

There was no time for questions, though. Maurice gave me my debarkation card and a piece of paper with a score of names and phone numbers.

"Now this is where you come in," he said. "*Écoute bien, mon petit.* You walk eastward, all the way to Columbus Circle. You'll find a drugstore there. They've got pay phones in it. You put one of these coins in." He gave me a handful of nickels. It's hard to believe now. Nickels!

"You dial and ask for the first name on the list. You'll get the secretary first. These are all important men and have secretaries. You tell the secretary you want to talk to Mr. So-and-So. If she asks you anything, you tell her, 'I'm from *La Bourdonnais.*' "

"But will Mr. So-and-So talk to me?" I asked. "He doesn't know me. Also, I cannot speak English."

"*T'en fais pas*" (don't worry), said Maurice. "Those *types* are waiting for your call. They'll be delighted to hear your voice, even if you talk Czech. All you say is, '*La Bourdonnais* is here, good-by.' "

By that time I should have guessed the facts of life, but I still didn't realize that I had just become a bootlegger's apprentice. I walked up to Columbus Circle and found the drugstore with the telephone booths inside. It was terribly hot. I dialed the first number on my list and got the secretary and then the important man himself. I said, "*La Bourdonnais* is here." He understood right away, for he emitted a yell and said something *I* didn't understand, but he sounded happy. My English vocabulary was extremely limited: a few dozen words, not all of them very elegant ones. But Maurice had been right. I had no problems. By the time I reached the last name on the list, I was soaking wet. New

York is perhaps a wonderful place, but not in a phone booth in a Columbus Circle drugstore in July. I had a few nickels and got myself a chocolate soda, asking for chocolate ice cream instead of vanilla.

"That's called 'all black,' sonny," the man said. I still remember the taste of my first American chocolate soda. I thought it had been worth it to come all the way to America for that soda.

I looked around Columbus Circle and ventured along Central Park South, all the way to Fifth Avenue, and then I walked down to Times Square and up Broadway. The heat got worse, but it didn't bother me. It was exciting. In Columbus Circle I thought of having another chocolate soda but one must not overdo a good thing, and I walked back to the ship. At the gangway Dimitri was welcoming two straw-hatted, prosperous-looking Americans. Dimitri told our friend, the customs man on duty, that the gentlemen were friends of the musicians.

The customs man nodded understandingly. "Music makes friends all over the world," he said. One of the two men laughed so hard that he dropped his straw hat.

"They look like millionaires," I said to Dimitri as we followed them on the way to our staterooms.

"They are," he said.

There were already a dozen friends of music downstairs, sitting on chairs and beds and cello cases and even on the floor. Some were fat and others were tall, some had hair and some hadn't, but each had a mouthwash glass filled with (diluted) liquor in his hand. All seemed happy and very thirsty. No wonder, on such a hot day. Almost all had taken off their jackets. In the bathroom our chemist was busy washing the glasses and filling them again, but he found time to make a check on a list with names every time he brought the friends of music another drink. I was now quite sure that he was no violinist. No fiddler ever kept a list like that. I asked Maurice why the second-class barman hadn't been asked to help out. He said the second-class barman had had some "trouble" and must not get "involved," and, anyway, didn't I know that the ship's bars were closed while *La Bourdonnais* was in the territorial waters of the United States of America?

More friends of music dropped in, and some brought along their friends, who didn't even know we were musicians. Maurice had said I would learn the facts of life, and I learned them that afternoon—very fast. Unpleasant ones, too. Some friends seemed in such a hurry to get down as much liquor as possible that they drank too fast. They had to catch "the five-sixteen for Chappaqua." That sounded like another code word to me. One friend was a powerful-looking, bald character; Maurice said he was the president of a large corporation as rich as half of Czechoslovakia. The president fell down flat on his stomach. Dimitri and I dragged him to a nearby stateroom, and Dimitri threw two glasses of water in the president's face, which seemed a strange way of treating a president. At last the president opened his eyes and said what he needed was something to make him *really* awake.

"Black coffee?" I asked hopefully.

"Nope, gin," he said. He turned over on the floor and was asleep again. We called for help. A few friends gave us a hand in carrying the president into another stateroom where they stored old mattresses, and we put him on top of them. He was sound asleep; he wouldn't make Chappaqua, or whatever it was called, that night.

By late afternoon there were at least three dozen presidents, board chairmen, and ordinary millionaires in our staterooms and in the corridors. I was sure I hadn't called all of them, but Maurice said it was always like that. The friends would bring along their customers and business associates, and, he said, "one hand's washing the other." Most of them behaved well, but there were a sad few who were, as Maurice said, "*pauvres types* who had never learned to drink."

The evening remains hazy in my memory. I know that Maurice asked the customers—he'd stopped calling them "friends"—to rinse their mouths with milk before going ashore. Then he would sniff each man's breath. If he detected a trace of liquor the customer was given a coffee bean and asked to chew. Don't ask me where the coffee beans came from. Apparently, my colleagues were great organizers who had thought of everything. Some customers hugged me before leaving and said they hoped I would come and have lunch with them *any*time, and they would be glad to do *any*thing for me. Here I was in America less than twenty-four hours and already I had a lot of friends in very important circles who would do *any*thing for me. America was certainly a wonderful country. Europe had never been like that.

One millionaire was stretched out flat on the floor and sat up only to drink some more. I indicated in my poor English that maybe he had had enough, but he pointed at his stomach and said, "Son, what you've got in here, no one can take away from you," and then he began to cry, very quietly. Maurice said, "Prohibition!" and spat contemptuously.

Our two customs men had left and there was a tough-looking man at the gangway, but he wasn't really tough. He had dinner with us and a couple of the presidents in our corner of the dining room. The presidents gave enormous tips to our steward, and everybody was happy. One of the presidents asked for more whisky and refused the wine. Wine, he said, was only for sissies. Whisky was for men, and, he said, "It's the only thing that goes with everything. Oops!"

We had a late visitor, the first violinist from the *Ile de France*. They were sailing for Le Havre at midnight. He looked at the happy customers all over the place, and he saw that Maurice and Dimitri had their pockets stuffed with American money. He was disgusted.

"I wish I were here," he said. "That damn *Ile de France*! Impossible to do something there with all those customs men watching each other. *C'est la barbe.* Would you care to take my place on the *Ile?*" he asked me.

"No, he wouldn't," Maurice answered for me. "He loves *La Bourdonnais.* He hates those luxury liners. Am I right, *mon petit?*"

I nodded emphatically. I had learned a great many facts of life on my first day in America. It had been an instructive day.

La Bourdonnais sailed from New York three days later. Our departure was anonymous and quiet, no good-by parties and very few passengers, mostly elderly Spanish-Americans. Maurice said they'd made some money in America and now they were going home to Spain to die. "There are good places in Spain to die," he said. Most passengers would come aboard in Halifax.

When we reached the open sea, we threw the empty bottles out of the portholes. Maurice gathered all the money, counted it, and divided it by five. The second-class barman was getting his share, too; he had certainly earned it. Each of us got over three thousand francs, which was more than three times our round-trip salary as members of the ship's orchestra. On several successive trips we made even more. Toward the end of the year I went back to Prague to continue my studies at the university. Everybody said it must be a great life to be a ship's musician, to see the world, and to get paid for it.

I said, sure it was, but I didn't tell them of my nonmusical activities in the territorial waters of the United States of America. My fellow law students might not have understood.

August 1974

Dining Alone

Mary Cantwell

A gray and muggy afternoon. The walker returning from an errand that was as dreary as the day is crossing a street near Times Square. Behind her two teen-age hookers are standing in a doorway; ahead there's a man selling funny hats. Beyond him is the man who sells incense, and beyond him the one who sells fake Vuitton bags. Beyond both a bag lady is perched on her usual branch, a fire hydrant, gumming something out of a cardboard carton.

The walker turns into a Japanese restaurant, sits at the counter, and orders *sushi* and Scotch on the rocks. Halfway through the Scotch and the third *tekkamaki* she suddenly realizes that she is happy. But it's not the food and drink alone that have lifted her spirits. It's watching the *sushi* chef wielding his knives and the customers wielding their chopsticks. It's picking up the threads of conversations, imagining the speakers' lives, and following laughter as it rises to the ceiling. The walker is, of course, myself, and when I leave that crowded, noisy room for that sad street I have been fed in more ways than are known to cooks.

There are people who bring books to restaurants, and who hide behind them, blind and deaf to everything beyond their pages. They hide behind menus, too, and order carelessly, and they never glance at the other diners. Maybe they're afraid the glance will reveal a hunger that has nothing to do with food. Or maybe they are so ashamed of being companionless that they court invisibility. But I am not one of them, because to me a restaurant is a theater, and my table a seat on the aisle.

The first time I ever dined alone—dined, that is, in a restaurant that had tablecloths, waiters, and large, stiff menus—was in London many years ago. I had gone there ahead of my husband for a few days of bookstores and museums, and I had not imagined that I would be lonely. But I was, and I saw the city with the eyes of someone who was peering through smoke. I lived on Wimpeys and Wipseys—pathetic versions of American burgers and shakes—at a nearby Lyons', and I went to bed early, believing that sleep would shorten the days until he arrived. But each night I woke around two o'clock, to stare at the ceiling and the thin line of light from the hallway under the door and the white curtains stirring in the sullen September air.

Early on the third evening, however, I passed a restaurant at which my husband and I had eaten on a previous trip. It was in Leicester Square and famous for its fish; I thought of Scottish salmon and Dover sole and, without thinking any further, walked right in.

The headwaiter was startled. I was young, I was alone, and besides the hour was ridiculous. Perhaps he thought I was there to see whom I could pick up, or perhaps he was simply trying to spare me the embarrassment I was bound to feel when I saw that ladies did not dine alone in so fashionable a place. In any case he put me in the back, by the kitchen door, and I, not realizing the insult, settled in happily and unfolded my napkin.

The salmon was as good as I thought it would be, and so was the sole, and I drank a white wine I remembered my husband once ordering. The restaurant filled with men who looked like Trevor Howard and women who looked like Celia Johnson, and I eavesdropped on two middle-aged couples discussing the Queen. "She likes hock, you know," one wife said while the others marveled, and I, citizen of a country in which a president's taste for bourbon, say, is interesting only if it drowns him, marveled too.

Outside, moviegoers were lining up for the old-fashioned picture palaces in Leicester Square, and buskers were assembling with their flaming torches and their golden balls and their tap shoes. And I, because I was eating the food of this particular country, listening to its dialogue, and spying on its entertainment, was part of its spin round the sun.

When I refused coffee the waiter, thinking it might be beyond my purse, leaned down and whispered, "It's all right. It comes with the meal." "No thank you," I said, "I don't like coffee," and paid the bill with a flourish. Then I sailed, rather than walked, out and if I had left a wake I wouldn't be surprised. Pleasure had transformed me from a leaking skiff into a three-masted schooner, and I was running before the wind.

When my husband finally got to London I was glad to see him, but I have never thought of that first evening I dined (in the grand sense of the word) alone as an evening I spent without him. Rather I think of it as the first I ever really spent with myself. We—that other person with whom one's conversation is perpetual and I—were free to concentrate on everything that was assaulting our senses, which is why the sensations are remembered so clearly now.

Since then I've dined alone a lot because I've traveled a lot and wouldn't think of incarcerating myself in a hotel room, captive to room service and fears I've read about but do not understand. Why should it take courage, as I'm told it sometimes does, to treat oneself as generously as one would a guest?

It wasn't courage, for instance, but a terrible hunger for lobster mayonnaise that once drove me to dinner in the garden of a restaurant in Dubrovnik. It was a romantic garden, I suppose, with rosebushes and leafy walls and candles on every table, and I was the only person there who was dining alone. But an old woman sitting in the second-storey window of the building that backed the garden watched my every move. When the light failed—it was summer and the sun set very late—and a younger woman came and took her away, I waved at her with that dippy bend of the fingers one gives to babies. I was saying good-bye because we had, in a sense, dined together.

Nor was it courage but an enthusiasm for the faintly seedy that took me to the dining room of a hotel in Istanbul. The hotel was respectable but run-down and past its prime, and the man who played old show tunes was as dusty as the potted palms that drooped over his piano. I, who might have been created by Mary McCarthy, stared at characters out of Graham Greene and wondered at our unlikely conjunction. Meanwhile the pianist played songs from *South Pacific*.

There was a time, though, when I did need a bit of courage: when all I had to wear for dinner in a rather fancy place in Ankara was a sweater and corduroy pants tucked into lace-up boots. But I stood very straight when I asked for the table, and there was no pause before I got it. Good posture, it seems, will take you far if what you have to navigate is other people's notions of propriety.

Nonetheless there is a restaurant to which I will never be brave enough to go by myself. It is close to the house in which I grew up, and its menu hasn't varied since it opened, which must have been when my parents were newlyweds. Its specialties are boiled live lobster and shoestring potatoes, the kind of coleslaw that isn't creamy, and a lemon meringue pie made by a woman who must be about 115 years old by now. I had my first mixed drink at that restaurant, a Martini, and drank it with what my father called policemen's sandwiches—oyster crackers split with one's thumbnail, heaped with horseradish, and closed again.

The restaurant is on a harbor and faces west, so my family and I try to get there in time for sunset. "Remember my daughter?" my mother is apt to say to any of her old friends who might be there. "She's all grown up now." Oh, how I am, with grown children of my own, but to her I am, as I suppose my daughters will be to me, a just-hatched butterfly still waiting for my wings to dry. This is no place for solitary dining. I couldn't see my fellow eaters for the memories.

But there is another place only a few miles away that belongs exclusively to me. It's on a raggedy waterfront street of spruced-up houses and tumble-down derelicts, of secondhand shops and aspiring *antiquaries*, and if the wind is right—or, more accurately, wrong—the smell of fish from the packing plant down the road can set one to staggering. I like that street; I walk it every weekend I am home to see if any of the shopkeepers are stupid enough to sell a treasure for a song (they aren't) and to peek into the windows of the latest restoration. Then I go to the restaurant, with its small patio and smaller bar, for fish chowder and a view of the town's businessmen, the occasional secretarial pool celebrating somebody's birthday, and those tweed-and-walking-shoes widows who march through New England ever on the alert for a new knitting yarn, a new decoration for the Christmas tree, and the ultimate Indian pudding.

Two hundred miles due south is its city counterpart, also on a raggedy street not far from the water. It's a new restaurant with a silly name and two small rooms. The first has a bar to the right and an elegantly programmed jukebox to the left. The second has small tables over which hang little stained-glass lamps and on which stand mustard pots filled with daisies. The waiters try hard to memorize the specials, the chef appears to be a serious striver, and the neighbors have taken to dropping by. So far I have been there only with friends but soon, I know, there'll be a night when I find myself deserving a kindness. When it comes, I'll take myself out for the calf's liver with Sherry vinegar, a glass of the house red, and a look at how life is being lived in one small restaurant on one small street in Greenwich Village on one night in 1985. And when I leave I'll be going home happy.

July 1985

JELLIED CONSOMMÉ: A REMINISCENCE

William Hamilton

Back down the cone of time to my fifth year you find me outraged by what jellied consommé turned out to be. Such pretty words from our most glamorous and important great-aunt were enough to make my brother and me mind our manners punctiliously as courtiers for a whole day. A whole day at that early age is a substantial portion of your entire life. To behave for the complete daylight period at age five is proportionally equivalent to a hitch in the army or a bad marriage.

"If you children are very good, you will have Pong's jellied consommé tonight. It is the best jellied consommé in the world," said our Auntie Alec, sitting and smiling as adults do in the presence of visiting children, looking us in the eye. Her skin was whiter than her perfect teeth, which were the color of the paper of engraved invitations.

What a woman! Even then I suspected she was superior to the ordinary member of the human race. She was beautiful, rich, kind, and very stylish. Her automobiles were never ready-made, and she never drove them herself. The roof of one of those limousines was a pebbly leather that felt almost paternal against a young cheek.

"Jellied consommé" sounded exotic and delicious, like the way she lived. Offered as a prize for model behavior, the words became an invocation with biblical divinity and authority. Nevertheless, an entire day of good behavior is a fierce, demanding expedition, not unlike that of the Spanish conquistadors heading in a hot and dangerous direction for two years or more, with no idea of what was there beyond the hope of riches and sainthood. Jellied consommé, Golconda, both glittered above and ahead of the sufferers present.

When I was five my brother was six and a half, an age I considered remote, powerful, and authoritative, but not as unsympathetic as, say, eight, twelve, thirty, and sixty-five. He had a policing relationship toward me. He told me we must not leave the pea gravel pathways of the garden, even when we were lured by the most fabulous-looking toad. He wouldn't even permit gravel thrown at the thing, not on a day that might be crowned by jellied consommé.

Perhaps sympathetic to our excruciating good behavior, our adolescent cousin offered us a game of badminton. There may be children who can play badminton at five the way some can plunge through Beethoven in velvet suits at a grand piano in Carnegie Hall, but I was no such prodigy. The racket was light and strange. It was pleasant to press the webbing of strings against your hand, leaving a trace on your palm, but that's the full use to which I was capable of putting the thing.

All we said to anyone, all day, was "Please thank you," and we didn't even say that too loud. Spasmodically we remembered the dictum "Sit up straight," even before it could be issued. I didn't wet my pants. We shared and passed whatever was going around and didn't get cranky. Our mother and father lounged unmolested in the distance on the lawn furniture. The complex and fragile maze of the adult world was never more imposingly present for us than it was on that long, long day of good behavior.

"Time for your nap, boys," said my mother, like Zeus telling Hercules it was time to clean the Augean stables. We didn't even balk at this provocative command. I did turn my head when I felt it start to wince, so she wouldn't know that anything but cheerful obedience abounded in her son's breast. We lay down like mummies under blue-gray cashmere afghans knitted in a waffle-like pattern. The shade was drawn.

The door was closed. With the reader's permission I'll render our nap-time dialogue in contemporary language:

"Sandy, what the hell is jellied consommé?"

"Oh it's great, fabulous stuff. I love it," answered my brother, rolling on his side out from under his cover.

"Really?"

"Yeah, it's incredible."

"Did you ever taste it?"

"Are you kidding? All the time."

"Where?"

"When I'm out playing with eight-year-olds."

"What color is it?"

"All kinds. Sort of orange sometimes."

"God."

"Yeah, it's really great."

Chastened, I actually did nap a bit. You can guess my dreams: jellied consommé, a brilliant, delicious radiant orange color, as good as Jell-O, jelly, and orange sherbet ice cream, a sublime elastic substance served by Auntie Alec borne on ivory wings in the tender, gravity-free billows of heaven.

We dressed for dinner. The hairbrush bit harshly, knocking aside my head as my mother fine-tuned my appearance for the children's table. My brother got the same. It was a glass table, under an awning in the garden. The grown-ups were having drinks on a terrace far away.

"Jellied consommé?" my brother asked Pong.

"Yeah, yeah!" responded Pong, an elderly, pastel Chinese with many buttons. He laughed and rushed inside the house to get the magic stuff. My heart was beating, a family of quail ran across the lawn like spilled marbles, the French doors between us and jellied consommé rattled.

"Napkin in your lap!" shouted my brother just in time for me to get it there.

"Jellied consommé," laughed Pong, putting in front of us sinister vessels of silver filled with ice in which the most unsympathetic to children substance I'd ever seen glittered and quivered. Sight already told us both we'd been robbed, but, with Pong hanging there watching us so urgently, we spooned into the slime. It tasted salty, bland, and creepy. We spit the outrageous stuff out in unison, and I burst into tears. It was useless to be crying, and my brother wasn't, so I didn't get beyond a few tears down hot cheeks. He stoically and majestically said, "No thank you," and the hideous apparatus were taken up and away into the house.

"Jellied consommé," he said, disgusted, and we both began to make faces and laugh bitterly, knowing you can't take back an entire day of good behavior. "Jellied consommé," we shouted, laughing derisively until the grown people had to break off their cocktail hour a lawn away. "Jellied consommé" followed by a Bronx cheer was what we had worked up to by the time my enraged mother had to invoke paternal authority itself to come over and stop our rebellion.

"Hey, Bill," whispered my brother during the night after lights out.

"Jellied consommé," I responded, correctly, starting us on piano duets of giggles.

Since then, many of my expectations have turned out like jellied consommé. I am grateful to my late Auntie Alec for providing such an early reference for such experience, and to Pong for, as usual, preparing it so perfectly.

August 1985

A Harried Cook's Guide to Some Fast Food

Laurie Colwin

Some time ago, when I was a young bride, I had endless time to cook and endless time to shop. Anyone delivering a package to my house on the afternoon of a dinner party back then might have found me in the kitchen dicing or slicing or tying up a chicken and rubbing it with a kind of pomade made of butter, garlic, and crushed herbs.

The morning of a dinner party I would curl up in an armchair and think about dessert. I made things like *crème brûlée* with a crackly sugar top, lemon mousse, and Bavarian cream. I turned out lemon curd for a lemon tart. I whipped egg whites in a copper bowl and made Elizabeth David's flourless chocolate cake.

Those days are long gone. There is nothing that puts a crimp in your cooking style like the arrival of a baby. It is hard to whip the egg whites wholeheartedly when at any moment your infant may wake up from her nap and require you. It's also not easy to stuff the chicken breast with something complicated when your darling is crawling on the floor at your feet. And it is impossible to concentrate on a recipe when your seven-year-old calls out a thousand times from the dining room, "Mom, what does this spell?"

Once you have a child, speed and convenience is the name of the game. It is my opinion that you can make a decent dinner speedily and conveniently if you go in for what I call *la cuisine de la "slobbe" raffinée,* or "the cooking of the refined slob."

Take, for example, ROAST CHICKEN, which is almost everyone's favorite dish. I have never seen a menu outside of a vegetarian restaurant that does not list some variety or other of it. In the old days I used to slip herbs and savory things like *porcini* mushrooms under the skin and baste the chicken constantly, but I have gradually come to know that none of these things is necessary.

The refined slob does not, for instance, even tie up her chicken. Her fancy imported linen kitchen string—which she bought at a snooty cooking shop at great expense and which was, she told her family, for trussing the chicken *only*—has been purloined by her child, who has used it to make spider webs by tying all the chairs together. Before I had a child, I would no more have cooked an untrussed chicken than I would have re-used the dead coffee grounds, but today I know an untrussed chicken is perfectly fine.

As for stuffing, half a lemon or some cloves of garlic works out swell. Wait till your child is in junior high school to make some wonderful mixture of chestnuts and diced prunes. I always dust my roast chicken with paprika. This is a family tradition. Paprika gives a chicken color and taste, and it takes under eight seconds to apply it.

Butter flavored with microscopically minced garlic is great if you have the time, but, if not, take an entire head of garlic, break it into cloves, and throw the cloves into the roasting pan. When the chicken is done, the garlic is too, and the cloves can be slipped out of their skins (the refined slob does not peel the garlic) and spread on bread or merely gobbled down.

If you are particularly harried, it is perfectly acceptable to cut up potatoes you have not bothered to peel along with some carrots and put them in the roasting pan too. Then you have not only roast chicken but also roasted vegetables. ROASTED VEGETABLES are about the easiest thing in the world to cook and are lovely to eat hot, cold, or lukewarm. People who want to avoid chicken fat can cook them in a companion roasting pan, preferably earthenware or ceramic. Slice the onions, cut up the potatoes quite thin, and slice some red peppers any old way. Put the vegetables in the pan and sprinkled them with salt and pepper (or merely salt, if you are serving this to a child). Drizzle the vegetables with olive oil and roast them next to the chicken for an hour.

I like to roast my chicken at 325° F. for about two hours. I do actually baste when I think about it, but I have also basted only at the last minute and all was well. Then it's just a matter of straining juices, skimming off the fat, carving up the bird, and there you are.

SCALLOPED POTATOES go wonderfully with roast chicken. In the old days I took great pains with these, and they never came out the way I liked them. I have since learned a trick from a now-unrecalled magazine article, and I make them in a trice. If you have a food processor you can make them in less than that. The potatoes—say about 2½ pounds—should be cut ⅛ inch thick and then plunged into cold water. Bring 2½ cups milk to a boil in a large saucepan, pat the potatoes dry, and boil them in the milk until they are barely tender. Add salt to taste and then tip the whole affair—the sludgy milk and the half-cooked potatoes—into a buttered dish. Add garlic if you like— if not, not—scatter bread crumbs on top, and bake the potatoes in a 400° F. oven for about fifteen minutes, or until they are bubbly and brown. (You will have to soak the saucepan for quite a long while— that's boiling milk for you—but it's worth it.)

When I was a little girl, making salad dressing was my chore, and it was an awesome one. Everything had to be measured out scrupulously, including the sugar (which my mother felt was essential). These days my method is to smash a clove of garlic, pour some olive oil on it, and add salt, pepper, and lemon juice. My daughter has now assumed this chore and performs it very well. For people who want kitchen help, I highly recommend children on the cusp of seven for such jobs.

If you eat a lot of salad you might want to save yourself time by expending about four minutes some afternoon and making yourself a jar of GARLIC VINEGAR, a substance I could not live without. Take a big head of garlic, separate the cloves, and quarter or smash them. You can leave the skins on, which, if the garlic is purple, makes for a nice color. Put the garlic in a jar that you will never use for any other purpose, cover it with the vinegar of your choice, and let the mixture stand for a few days. As you strain off the vinegar, replenish it. Garlic vinegar is wonderful in a green salad and good on beets, in corn salad, on fried fish, or in a salad made from diced leftover flank steak and lentils.

There are few citizens of this land who do not like a brownie. Even people on diets will nibble a small one if it is offered. Brownies are in many ways the ideal dessert. You can eat as many or as few as you wish. And brownies go well with so many things—ice cream, strawberries, poached pears, or whipped cream, for instance.

There are as many brownie recipes as there are flowers in the meadow. Some are fancy, some are plain. Some have nuts, which I consider a bad idea, because children seem to hate them and end up picking them out and getting brownie crumbs all over everything. I also have several friends with fatal nut allergies, and so I leave nuts out. I have been served brownies with chocolate chips and brownies with raisins, but what most people want is plain old brownies. Some people like their brownies on the cakey side, and some feel they should be more like fudge. I myself like brownies that are what I call "slumped" and the English call "squidgy," which means slightly undercooked but not quite runny in the center.

The best recipe I have for brownies comes from a friend who got it from a magazine article about Katharine Hepburn. It is, apparently, her family's recipe. If there were no other reason to admire Katharine Hepburn, this pan of brownies would be enough to make you worship her.

KATHARINE HEPBURN'S BROWNIES

1. Melt together 1 stick butter and 2 squares unsweetened chocolate and take the saucepan off the heat.
2. Stir in 1 cup sugar, add 2 eggs and ½ teaspoon vanilla, and beat the mixture well.
3. Stir in ¼ cup all-purpose flour and ¼ teaspoon salt. (In the original recipe, 1 cup chopped walnuts is added here as well.)

4. Bake the brownies in a buttered and floured 8-inch-square pan at 325° F. for about 40 minutes.

You can cut these brownies into squares, once they have cooled, and eat them out of the pan, but it is so much nicer to pile them on a fancy plate, from which people are going to eat them with their hands anyway. If you want to smarten up your act you can put a square of brownie on a plate with a little blob of *crème fraîche* and a scattering of shaved chocolate.

A dinner of roast chicken, roasted vegetables, scalloped potatoes, salad, and brownies is a festive meal. In certain lights it might even been seen as *elegant*. And as you sit with your feet up, listening to the hum of the dishwasher (or perhaps of some person other than yourself washing the dishes), you can pat yourself on the back for having produced such a feast with a minimum of work. Everyone will think you are wonderful for having made this monumental effort on their behalf. And when they tell you this, you can lean back with a wan smile and say, with some truth: "It was nothing."

February 1992

I, Bon Vivant, Who, Me?

George Plimpton

The other day a friend of mine telephoned—my literary agent actually—and remarked cheerily, "Well, how's the *bon vivant* today?"

At the time I had just come off the last week of jury duty and had ridden uptown in a dense and damp crowd on the Lexington Avenue subway. Out on the street it was raining slightly. The pavement was wet. Because of small holes in the soles of both shoes I walked along on my heels to avoid the water getting through and permeating my socks. The rain increased, and I took refuge in a Häagen-Dazs ice-cream parlor long enough to feel I should purchase something. I bought a chocolate ice-cream bar. Outside, I bit down on the bar, which had been frozen so hard that I broke off a tooth—one of the incisors. Unbelieving, I felt the gap in the front of my mouth, first with my tongue and then with my finger. No doubt at all. I had lost a tooth to the Häagen-Dazs ice-cream bar! In a rage I took the offending bar by its stick, and, like skipping a stone, I scaled it down the length of the sidewalk. It behaved beautifully. Just off the pavement it went sailing by a man walking a dog.

"I lost a tooth," I said to my agent.

"Defending your honor, no doubt."

I've forgotten what else we talked about that day. But later on, sitting in the dentist's chair having the tooth replaced, I began pondering being referred to as a *"bon vivant."* Did I fit? I got to thinking about those I would consider *bons vivants* (besides myself, of course), some of whom I've known over the years. The name Serge Obolensky kept coming to mind. Needle-thin, always impeccably dressed, possessed of a trimmed mustache and a rather high, nasal, aristocratic voice, he seemed to me the embodiment of elegance and grace. A great party-goer and giver, he was in the business of tonying up some of the great hotels of New York—among them The St. Regis, The Plaza, and The Sherry-Netherland.

A Russian-born prince (he claimed to be a descendant of Rurik, an early ruler of Russia), he preferred to be called "Colonel." He was a cousin of Prince Felix Youssoupoff, in whose Saint Petersburg palace Rasputin was assassinated. In fact, Colonel Obolensky was there at the time. He described his involvement to me as we were driving down Park Avenue in a taxicab. I was particularly intrigued by the colonel's description of the conspirators pretending to hold a dance upstairs while, in a room below, Rasputin was being plied with Madeira laced with poison. The conspirators (the colonel among them) pounded their boots on the floor in time to the music from the windup phonograph machine, playing the same record over and over again.

"The poison didn't work, and we shot him as he came up the stairs," the colonel said. He was hard of hearing and he announced this in full cry. The cab gave a lurch, and I realized the driver had been listening. It is not often that one has a self-proclaimed murderer riding in the back seat.

The dentist took a wad of cotton out of my mouth. I said, "Not much glamour in losing a tooth to an ice-cream bar, is there? Should have had it knocked out in a barroom brawl. Hey, guess what? I knew the man who killed Rasputin."

"Open," the dentist said.

The novocaine began to take effect. I closed my eyes. Who else might fit the part of *bon vivant?* Cole Porter, certainly. He had lived the good life until that riding accident on the grounds of the Piping Rock

Club on Long Island largely muzzled it. Born of wealth, which always helps, he had lived a most cultivated and adventurous life, at one point joining the French Foreign Legion. Afterward, he epitomized the Roaring Twenties (surely an era of *bon vivantisme*), as the titles of his hit shows suggest—*Anything Goes, Gay Divorce, Dubarry Was a Lady, Silk Stockings*. When I was a boy, I was trying to learn his haunting "Love For Sale" by heart on the piano. I was far too young to know what the song was about. My grandfather, a somewhat austere and difficult gentleman, overheard my attempts from the library and rang for the parlormaid. She was instructed to go to the music room and tell me to cease and desist. No more "Love For Sale." My grandfather never came to tell me himself. Perhaps he thought he might have to explain *why* the song was unsuitable for a young boy.

I rinsed out into a porcelain sink. "Cole Porter," I announced. "Right at the top."

I sat back again and began thinking of Venice. When Cole Porter and his wife, Linda Lee Thomas, stayed at Venice's Rezzonico Palace, they entertained lavishly there, thinking nothing of inviting the Monte-Carlo ballet for their guests' enjoyment. An elderly friend of mine once described a treasure hunt the Porters had arranged throughout Venice, the guests searching out the clues by gondola. I can't recall the particulars of the hunt, but I do remember her telling me that her gondolier had become quite caught up in the spirit of the chase and in rounding a corner had lost control of his oar in the darkness and tumbled into the canal.

Who else? A somewhat more sinister vision of the *bon vivant* came to mind. A few days before I went on jury duty I met a gentleman in his thirties, quite worldly, sleek-haired, sharp-featured, designer jeans, a soft white shirt. I was seated next to him on a banquette in a fancy late-hours bar in New York called Morgans—a place lit entirely by votive candles. In their light his shirt seemed to glow. He reminded me of a boulevardier dressed for a duel. Oliver Stone, the filmmaker, was in our party. So were two or three young models, one of them a beautiful Russian girl. Her jeans were worn through at the knees so her pale skin showed, which was the fashion, of course. She spoke very little English.

At one point I asked the gentleman seated next to me if he minded my asking what he did. His reply was delivered slightly contemptuously, as if he *did* mind being asked. He said, "Well, I like the resort places when they are in season. Biarritz, Cannes, Monte-Carlo, Aspen. I like small amounts of very good food." He had a faint Continental accent. "I like nightclubs, the best of them, like this, candles, dark. I like to seduce very young girls." He said this last without a trace of humor, as if speaking about something quite sacred to him. I was tempted to ask him if the beautiful young Russian girl was young enough for his designs. Instead, I said, "My, quite the *bon vivant.*"

"I would think so," he said.

It occurred to me that this fellow would have fit quite nicely into the Regency period. Perhaps he would end up like the duke of Queensberry, known as "Old Q," a great rake of the time—a familiar sight in his seventies, sitting on his London balcony; below, a servant was kept on alert to hop on a horse and take after anyone "Old Q" especially fancied.

"Rinse, please."

I thought of Beau Brummell, of course, the leader of the London beaux ... that fraternity of reckless, gay, adventurous, dissipated, witty men around town. Lord Byron was a great admirer of Brummell's. Indeed he once said that the three great men of his time were Brummell, Napoleon, and himself. Brummell, of course, was especially noted as a fashion plate; it was said that he had two makers for his gloves—one for the thumbs, the other for the rest of the hand. He spent two hours daily—after cleaning his teeth and shaving—in scrubbing himself with a pig's-bristle brush and working over his eyebrows and whiskers with a dentist's mirror and tweezers before he ever considered getting into his clothes.

Neckwear had to be starched, tied, and creased perfectly or it was discarded. A story went the rounds that Brummell's valet, coming down the staircase from his master's dressing room, remarked on the armful of ties he was carrying as "our failures." Three barbers were on hand to do Brummell's hair, and his boots—including their soles—were polished with the froth of Champagne. On his daily walk he never took off his hat because replacing it exactly as it had been, just so, was unlikely. He was so fastidious at his dress, and knew so much about fashion, that the Prince of Wales was once reduced to "blubbering" when told that Brummell did not like the cut of his coat.

Much of this is probably exaggeration. One felicitous observation about Brummell was that he escaped notice because he fitted the landscape with delicate exactitude. Somebody once remarked to him that an acquaintance was so well dressed that people turned around to gaze after him. "Then," said Brummell, "he is *not* well dressed."

A minor thing I remembered about Brummell was that among the items on his dressing table was a spitting dish made of silver, as porcelain was too déclassé. It crossed my mind to tell the dentist this, but I resisted.

"Open wide. Turn this way a bit."

My favorite peer of that time, and certainly a candidate in the *bon vivant* business, was Henry de la Pier Beresford, the marquis of Waterford, often known as the "Mad Marquis." He was not only interested in the usual pleasures of life but for reasons best known to himself he had a strong desire to see two locomotives smash into each other. He wrote the following letter to the officials of the London and Greenwich Railway Company:

> Sirs:
>
> I am anxious to witness a train smash. If you will allow two of your engines to collide, head on, at full speed, I will contribute a sum of 10,000 £s to your funds.
>
> Waterford

The London and Greenwich officials wrote back and refused, implying in their letter that Waterford belonged in an institution. The peer was not deterred in the slightest. He managed to buy a pair of decrepit engines, and on a friends' estate, which included a spur of track, he built a small pavilion for friends and for the bestowing of Champagne and so forth. The day of the smash was fine, the marquis's elegant guests in good form; but, alas, at the appointed moment the empty engines drew toward the pavilion at different speeds. One of them, its throttle fixed too far forward, sped by; there was a fine bonging sound back behind a hill, and all Waterford and his friends got to see was a distant plume of steam.

The dentist's assistant appeared. She was perhaps a bit old for my boulevardier friend of the nightclubs, but very pretty nonetheless, and I felt vaguely embarrassed as she bent close and peered into my open mouth.

"Aaargh," I said.

As I looked up at her, it occurred to me that one does not often speak of the *bonne vivante*, the female representative of the species. A few names came to mind as I sat back. Surely toward the top of the list would be the late Marjorie Merriweather Post, heiress to the Post cereal fortune and noted especially for her years as a hostess. In Washington, invitations to her parties were second only to those from the White House. One synopsis of her life described her as a "financier, philanthropist, horticulturalist, hostess, square-dance enthusiast, and former amateur boxer." She got an enormous pleasure out of life. People said of her that when she walked into a room, everyone else looked exhausted. Years ago I went to one of her dances at Mar-A-Lago in Palm Beach. Sure enough, there was an instructor to tell us how to line up for the Virginia reels and so on. I barely remember Mrs. Post. It seems to me she was sitting in a large chair and didn't join in. If I'd known then about her boxing past, I would have gone over and asked about it.

I would suppose Perle Mesta is a good candidate. When she was very young, growing up in Oklahoma City, she was given a birthday party to which no one came. She often said that back then she had vowed, weeping, that she would eventually give parties to which "the mostes'" people in the world would come. And indeed they did— sometimes as many as eight hundred to her Washington estate, Les Ormes. She had her detractors: A rival hostess referred to her as "The Thing." But a friend, the writer Louis Bromfield, described her as "one of the gayest people I know—she could give you a good time if she had only a five-cent beer."

Mesta's counterpart in New York was Kitty Miller, the wife of Gilbert Miller, the theater producer. She gave sought-after New Year's Eve parties. I remember going to one in the fifties. I had a little tin trumpet. At the stroke of midnight I noticed that Salvador Dalí was standing next to me in the crowd. He was famously distinguished by a waxed mustache that curled up at both ends. Undoubtedly invigorated by the Millers' end-of-the-year Champagne, I bent down on impulse and, placing the bell of the little trumpet over one tip of his mustache, I blew a blast. What I remember about that moment is that Dali didn't flinch. When I pulled away, it was evident that the mustache had not been affected in the slightest.

The dentist snapped off his gloves. "I wouldn't recommend eating for a few hours," he said.

Most people equate the *bon vivant* with eating—with gourmandising, the love of good fare. To pick a name at random I would suppose Edward VII makes the roster. After all, on one of his visits to Monte-Carlo he supposedly presided over the invention of a dish whose name combined quite nicely his love of both food and women: crêpes Suzette—Suzette being one of his favorite mistresses.

So how does one arrive at a notion of the *bon vivant* from the above? The idea suggests wealth, a bit of time on one's hands, an ability to get along on three hours' sleep at night (or during the day, so that the night is free for carousing), a zest for good food, a knowledge of fine wines, and, most important of all, a supercilious manner that suggests there is absolutely nothing special about this style of life at all. It can be dangerous: Witness one of the eulogies at Truman Capote's funeral (surely a practitioner himself of the good life), namely the statement that Capote had died from living.

It helps, of course, to be endowed with above-average energy and vim, what the French refer to as élan. My favorite exemplar of this was Augustus the Strong of Saxony, a suitably named German prince of the early eighteenth century, said to have been famous for two parlor tricks. The first was to ride a horse bareback into a barn and chin himself on a crossbeam, gripping the horse between his knees. The second was to appear before the lady of his choice, holding a bag of gold in one hand and crushing a horseshoe with the other. He reputedly had 367 illegitimate children (among them a future *maréchal* of France), which would suggest that the latter stratagem was extremely successful.

Now, what do I have in common with these worthies? I have no intention of dashing into a barn and chinning myself on a crossbeam, with or without a horse between my knees. I have very little interest in clothes and have been known to wear a seersucker suit in the dead of winter. I have never murdered a monk.

Perhaps *bon vivantisme* is only in the eye of the beholder. So the other day I called my agent.

"Hey," I said. "It's the *bon vivant*."

"Of course," he said. "Who else?"

February 1998

ON FOODS AND COOKING

The Mixing of the Green

Louis P. DeGouy

Since time immemorial, whenever that was, but certainly ever since history began to be recorded, the world has treated itself to a fantastic succession of food fads. A few of these, to be sure, have been most beneficial to the human race and its collective stomach, but the majority have had nothing but dire effects, these running the full gamut from ludicrous to lethal. Some few of these weird flights of gastronomic imagination were propagated by well-meaning crackpots who felt it their mission to cure the world of all its ills nutritionally, but most of them were sponsored and promoted for the sole purpose of monetary gain. Which of the two causes of origin is the more deadly is of little importance; the results are the same. There were the days when all red meat was considered a short-cut to an early grave, and there were others when pepper was thought injurious to the human system; and now we have a set of medicos who claim that it is downright harmful to drink milk. But never fear, there'll be more fads tomorrow—not necessarily new ones, however.

One of the oldest and most frequently recurring subjects of culinary superstition has been the collection of the raw greens that we like to eat singularly or collectively in the form of green salad. These greens have been blessed and blamed for everything and anything that might reasonably or unreasonably be reduced to the modern slogan: You are what you eat. Lettuce, for instance, during the Middle Ages was considered a necessary part of the diet of all monks and nuns, "for it has the hallowing influence that makes one oblivious of love and all its fevers"; while celery was—and still is—supposed to have the opposite reaction. An old French proverb speaks to the effect that "if a wife only knew what a loving charm there is in celery, she would send to Rome for it every day to provide a salad for her husband." Well, you pays your money and takes your choice.

However, no matter what promising charms may be hidden in the greens, we prefer to eat them for the sole reason that they are the most pleasing adjunct to almost any dish.

Now, what constitutes a green salad? It may be anything from just lettuce to a fanciful conglomeration of from two to ten greens, all depending on what is available. The beauty of the thing is that all salad greens go together in any imaginable combination; so we need never be at a loss for that real delight of all salads, the mixed green. Its composition is well-nigh without limitation or rules. In it belong the various types of lettuce, Boston, iceberg, or cos; the frizzle-topped escarole should be part of it, as well as the curly endive—also called the Batavian endive, the leaves of which look as if they'd been treated for a permanent wave—or water cress, garden cress, and sorrel leaves. However, don't be too particular in your tastes and overlook young, green nasturtium leaves or young dandelion—picked, of course, before the plant has bloomed—or even spinach leaves or beet tops, that is, if they are very young and tender. For a still different flavor you might add a few leaf stalks of the Belgian endive, the pale, ivory-colored, cigar-shaped plant, or green peppers, carefully cleaned of white ribs and seeds and cut into thin rings.

But one fruit that is only too often encountered in a mixed green, and has no place in it whatever, is the tomato. There is good reason for this dictum, for the juice that runs from a quartered tomato will dilute the salad dressing and completely alter the taste of, let's say, the simple French dressing which you took great pains to compose in its proper ingredients. We do not mean to sneer at a tomato salad as such; but a tomato salad is one thing, and a mixed green another, and never the twain should meet.

When getting the salad greens ready for the bowl, never let them soak in water. Wash them, instead, leaf by leaf under cold running water, and lay them on a towel to drain. During the washing, remove all hard and coarse parts, such as the heavy center ribs or the dark green outer leaves. Of the frizzly escarole, only the center leaves should be used, which in all likelihood will be a pale, yellowish green; of the cos lettuce, also called romaine, only the leaves without the heavy stalks should find their way into the salad bowl. However, these coarse parts need not be thrown away, since they have pleasant uses in cooking.

After all the leaves are well washed and drained, they should be broken into pieces of the desired size with the fingers. Never cut salad greens, not even with a silver knife. No matter how sharp a knife, it will invariably bruise the cut spot and cause the greens to bleed, particularly in the case of Boston and cos lettuce.

After the salad is well picked over, the towel on which the greens were drained will be well moistened. Wrap the wet towel tightly around the green, tucking in all corners to cover them completely. Set this bundle on a large plate, and put the plate in the mechanical refrigerator or on top of the ice. Chill the greens for at least one hour, though a longer time won't hurt, since they may even be left in the refrigerator overnight as long as a towel covering them is kept very moist, but not dripping wet, at all times.

After having been thoroughly chilled, the greens are ready for their final benediction, the dressing, the choice of which is necessarily a matter of taste. But a really fine mixed green salad calls for more than just a good dressing. It needs what the French call the *fournitures pour salade*. These are the various salad herbs that lend that final snap of good flavor to the greens. If no others are available, finely chopped parsley alone will have to do—and that's a must—but a good salad will be improved many fold if chopped tarragon or chervil are also added, preferably both. To digress for a moment—chervil seems difficult to get this year, even in the big cities; so if you are fond of its fleeting anis flavor and can't find the herb, substitute for it sweet cicely, which you may know better by its Biblical name: myrrh. But if even cicely cannot be procured, all need not be lost. To each four ounces of French dressing, add four—and no more—drops of Anisette liqueur. Incorporate the liqueur well into the dressing; the little green flecks of chopped chervil will be missing, but the faint whiff of anis is sure to lessen the disappointment.

The missing tarragon flavor, if that herb, too, should be scarce, can be simulated by using tarragon-flavored vinegar in the dressing, but the real thing is much better, even if it is only the dried herb. However, when using dried tarragon, use only half the amount you would of the fresh, and before adding it to the salad, soak it well in a little vinegar for at least an hour.

Although green salads have been eaten for many centuries, it was only at about the end of the nineteenth century that we learned to appreciate the pleasures of "dressing" a salad properly. As in many other lines of the culinary art, the French here lead the way. It is a wise salad maker who lets himself be guided by the French in his efforts. And one quality will stand out immediately in the Gallic treatment of the greens. Simplicity is the keynote of all French salads and salad dressings, together with the proper use of garlic. Garlic should be used with the respectful reticence it deserves. Kettner wrote in 1877 on salads, "Some of the most successful compounds owe their excellence to an unsuspected undertone of garlic." It can't be said any clearer; the words "undertone of garlic" cannot be improved upon.

The most satisfactory manner of employing garlic in mixing a green salad is with the *chapon*. This is a piece of dry, stale bread, usually the heel of a long French loaf, that is rubbed with a cut clove of garlic. When the salad is being mixed, the *chapon* is added to the greens with the dressing and tossed about during the mixing. When the salad is ready, the *chapon* is discarded. A subtle undertone of garlic is the result.

Recently, however, many people have taken to rubbing the salad bowl with a cut clove of garlic. This custom has its drawbacks. First of all, the danger of overdoing it is great, and secondly, this method should be applied only to certain kinds of salad bowls. And with those ponderous words we have arrived at a most precarious salad subject, the utensils. Much fuss is being made that a green salad can be tossed properly only in a wooden bowl, and much has been written about how the wood is "seasoned" by frequent use; but only too little has been said about the types of bowls that lend themselves to that kind of treatment. A wooden salad bowl must be of excellent quality. The bowl must be well finished, like fine furniture. Only such bowls will survive the frequent attacks of the vinegar contained in salad dressings. The finish on cheap and badly made bowls will soon crack, the oil will seep into the crevices and eventually go rancid, and if garlic is rubbed frequently over the surface, the desirable faint undertone will soon become an objectionable odor that can only be described as a stench. Therefore, use only well-made wooden salad bowls, and if these should prove too high for the budget, forego the supposed elegancy of the wooden bowl and be content with porcelain, glass, earthenware, or one of the heavily lacquered Chinese-type bowls.

This about concludes our warnings and hints anent the mixed green salad, and leaves only one more subject, the application of the dressing. A salad should be anointed with the dressing only at the last possible moment, and certainly not longer than ten minutes before it is served; preferably, in spite of what H. Allen Smith had to say in "The Padded Kitchen," the dressing and the greens should be mixed at the table. If a salad is "dressed" too soon, the greens will become limp and unappealing.

The amount of dressing to be used is of equal importance. Never apply more of it than absolutely necessary to cover the leaves. The greens should be well covered, but should not float in dressing. As Fred Allen puts it: A salad should be dressed like Dorothy Lamour— adequate but lightly.

This, then, is the green salad in its simplest form. That there are many variations, and good ones, on this theme goes without saying; but before a mixed green is dolled up too much, the *saladier* had better ask himself about each addition: Is this bit necessary? In most cases he will forget about cream cheese, pimiento, tomatoes, grapefruit sections, or—the horror of horrors—marshmallows. Radish roses, however, or thinly sliced young cucumber, shredded cabbage, Chinese cabbage, asparagus tips, artichoke bottoms, palm hearts, crisp, thin slivers of celery or carrots, and even crunchy, raw cauliflower flowerettes are fitting and well-blending additions.

With such ornamentations the salad maker begins to enter the mysterious realm of a group of salads that are collectively known as chef's salad. With care and reticence, wide vistas are opened in the fields of salad making. To make a plain and somewhat rash statement, a chef's salad is any salad that combines the mixed greens with shredded meats. Cold cooked or roasted chicken cut into long, thin strips and tossed with a mixed green is an epicure's delight, particularly if the accompanying salad herb is chervil, or the aforementioned few drops of Anisette. Tongue cut up in a like manner mixes well with curly endive and water cress, and finely slivered cold roast veal blends well into a mixed green salad with the added embellishment of one filet of anchovy for each serving.

In the beginning of this dissertation we voiced strong objections to the addition of tomatoes in any form to a green salad. However, to prevent any misunderstanding, let's admit that a tomato salad *per se* is a fine component of salad-dom; it is merely the mixture that meets our objection. That we are not alone in our opinion may be seen from Nathaniel Gubbins' remarks on the use of tomatoes as salad:

> Four large tomatoes and one Spanish onion, cut into thin slices, mix a spot of mustard, a little white pepper and salt, with vinegar, in a tablespoon, pour it over the love apples, etc., and then add two tablespoonfuls of oil. Mix well and then sprinkle over the mixture a few drops of Worcester Sauce. For the fair sex, the last part of the programme may be omitted, but on no account leave out the breath of Sunny Spain. And mark this well. The man, or woman, who mixes tomatoes with lettuce or endives in the bowl is hereby sentenced to translate the whole of this book into Court English.

The same may be said for beets. Sliced beets are much better by themselves, and at their very best when the dressing is applied while they are still lukewarm. Only oil, lemon juice, and a few grains of sugar should be used.

March 1945

The Marrowbone Matter

Kenneth Roberts

Years ago, when my duties as a foreign correspondent in Europe took me to London, I made two pleasing discoveries. I learned that "digs" in the extensive Berkeley Square section are far superior to any room in the most expensive London hotel; and English friends taught me that few restoratives anywhere, at the end of a hard day's work, can equal a Scotch or two, accompanied by six boiled marrowbones, each bone primly wrapped in spotless napery (as our British cousins call culinary diapers).

"Proper digs," as they are known and as I was long in learning, is or are a suite of rooms, or even one comfortable room, in an old-fashioned house in a once-fashionable neighborhood. If the digs are extra proper, a capable manservant appears each morning with breakfast. He then presents a dinner menu and asks solicitously if madame wishes dinner served, how many persons are to be present, and if madame will be kind enough to indicate the dishes she prefers and the wine she would like him to purchase when he does his shopping for the day.

After London visits of previous years, during which I had spent long weeks of writing in the purgatory of bleak and dreary hotel rooms, those Berkeley Square digs seemed almost paradisiac to my wife and to me, and in them I was able to write and write in almost ineffable peace. Nothing marred our pleasure in those London digs—with the exception of a slight contretemps over a brand of Burgundy which had been suggested to us by that helpful manservant who so admirably served our dinners before a tarrily-fragrant sea-coal fire.

When the man had queried us as to wines, I had said loosely, "Any good Burgundy; it's up to you."

He had replied almost deprecatingly, "Some of our guests have spoken most highly of an Empah' wine—Austrylian, sir—Emu."

Having none of a Briton's low opinion of colonial products, I told him to bring on his Empah' Burgundy. It arrived shortly before dinner in a distressingly chilled state; and I, unskilled in the consumption of Empah' wines, set a bottle on the floor near the sea-coal fire without—and let this be a lesson to you—without either unwiring or uncorking it. The bottle promptly exploded. Only the fastest of footwork with bath towels saved the pearl-gray rug of our digs from being soaked by a flood of Empah' Burgundy—which, when the chill was taken off another bottle, proved to be as sound and fruity a wine as anyone could want.

Lord Clive is said to have occupied the dwelling that housed our digs on Berkeley Square—and had, for reasons still unknown, hanged himself obtrusively in the front hall. Perhaps he'd had a premonition that an American would one day transgress so far as to try to take the chill off a bottle of Empah' Burgundy, not only before a fire, but—horror on horror!—without first drawing the cork.

I have no apologies for this seeming gaucherie. I was brought up in a tough school, as are most reporters and newspaper correspondents, and I am accustomed to getting results with no more frills than necessary. The experts on wine tell us that red wines must never be served cold and must furthermore achieve room temperature without artificial assistance—but most experts haven't been around enough. I refer such wine experts as doubt my words to the delightful four-volume *Life of William Hickey*. Hickey spent his most fruitful, hilarious, and profitable years in India, where he and his titled guests drank incredible amounts of claret. The claret was not brought to the temperature of India's stifling dwellings by natural, or any other, means. It was iced—carefully and invariably iced.

There was, in spite of their charm, one minor drawback to our London digs. After I'd been working half the night on material laboriously garnered from the Public Record Office or from Oxford's Bodleian Library, we couldn't arouse the house by calling for a dozen boiled marrowbones. If we wanted them, we had to venture forth to one of the glittering underground restaurants near Piccadilly Circus, and this we often did. So far as we could tell, no good London restaurant or London club ever has run out of marrowbones or ever will.

They are, I gathered, as essential to the health and well-being of cultivated British clubmen, late at night, as are kippers and a spot of tea in the early morn. I base this opinion on the enormous number of British silversmiths who hammered out marrow spoons as regularly as they hammered out coffeepots—and in the ratio of forty spoons to one pot. I have three marrow spoons, each one with the hallmark of a different silversmith, but they are almost identical. Their average length is eight and a half inches; at one end is a shallow bowl three-quarters of an inch wide and two to three inches long. At the other end is an even narrower bowl—more of a scoop than a spoon—only a quarter of an inch wide and three to four inches long. The larger bowl is, of course, for spooning marrow from large-tubed marrowbones. The smaller is for poking marrow past the osseous obstructions that frequently and irritatingly crop up in even the best and largest marrowbones.

The dates of these spoons, as revealed by their hallmarks, are significant. The smallest was made by R.S. in 1750; the largest, by I.M. in 1765; the medium-sized one by William Marshall of Edinburgh, Scotland, in 1817.

So, on the evidence of the spoons alone, the British have been spooning away at marrowbones for more than two hundred years, and since the British have never been in the habit of suddenly adopting fads, the idea of marrow spoons must have been germinating in the minds of British silversmiths long before 1750. Indeed, it is my considered opinion that the British were sedulously attacking marrowbones long before America was discovered.

Yet in all those years the possibilities of the marrowbone have never been explored by American cooks or American gourmets or by the compilers of American cookbooks—or even by persons gravely in need of a nourishing food at minimum expense. Thus the marrowbone as treated in the United States is a splendid example of American waste. Marrowbones are scorned and thrown into the bone barrels by most large chain stores, along with ribs, backbones, and other scraps. All that delicious marrow, uncooked and unappreciated, is hauled off to the bone yard to be made into fertilizer!

In case there is a question in the minds of readers as to the virtue of marrow, I digress momentarily to the subject of baked beans. In my boyhood days in Maine and in New Hampshire, I had an enormous capacity for baked beans. I looked forward to Saturday night when I could almost eat my fill of beans—almost, but not quite. The obvious determination and apparent ability of a small boy to outeat grown males three times his weight and double his height was viewed with austere alarm. So I never quite had my fill of beans, and in my co-matose after-supper state I always looked forward to Sunday morning and the possibility of gaining access to the remaining beans before my grandfather and my uncles attacked them.

So beans interested me from an early age, and I made a study of their preparation: of their all-night soaking, the scoring of the succu-lent pork slabs, the early morning simmering, the half-hourly addition of salted water which prevented the separation of fats and liquids. We never called them Boston baked beans, but by a sort of osmosis I gath-ered that baked beans and pork had originated in Boston, where the early settlers had been taught to cook them in the Indian manner at Thanksgiving time by their lovable Indian neighbors.

Not until the writing of novels taught me to separate hearsay from fact did I wake to the true state of affairs: that early Indians in the vicinity of Boston possessed no ovens, no bean pots, and no salt pork, and were seldom inclined to spend all day Saturday baking beans so that Sunday could be devoted to religious ceremonies.

It was this same need to pry into facts that led me, while I was writ-ing *Lydia Bailey,* to the discovery that baked beans, instead of being a Boston institution, originated with the Jewish population of North

Africa and Spain; that the salt pork which accompanies baked beans in New England is a corrupt substitute for beef marrow; and that Yankee sea captains brought the whole baked-bean concept to New England—just as they brought tomato seeds and tomato ketchups to their adoring families—from Spanish and Mediterranean ports.

In 1815 an Ohio sea captain, James Riley, was shipwrecked on a far-off shore, as a result of which he produced a book loosely known as *Riley's Narrative* and sometimes listed as *The Loss of the Brig Commerce.* Its full, verbose title is *An Authentic Narrative of the Loss of the American Brig Commerce, Wrecked on the Western Coast of Africa, in the Month of August, 1815, with an Account of the Suffering of the Surviving Officers and Crew, Who Were Enslaved by the Wandering Arabs, on the African Desart, or Zahahrah; and Observations Historical, Geographical, &c., Made During the Travels of the Author, While a Slave to the Arabs in the Empire of Morocco.*

Some years later Captain Riley made a second trip to Africa and wrote another book, to which he gave the stark title *Sequel to Riley's Narrative.* Riley could not, as the saying goes, write a lick, but his word-pictures of life on and around striking the "Desart of Zahahrah" were far more striking than some of the admired passages of more modern and more famous literary lights.

In both books Riley refers feelingly to the baked beans he encountered in the Jewish sections of Morocco. In his *Sequel to Riley's Narrative,* he wrote:

"After passing Saturday as a Sabbath of rest from our journey, we ate with the Jews their hot baked beans, swimming in marrow from the bones of beeves, called *skanah,* with roasted meats and eggs, which had lain in the oven since Friday afternoon, all fat and savory (the constant Sabbath dinner of all Jews in this country)...."

In the *Narrative* itself, writing of the year 1816, he expatiates on this delightful Jewish dish, but he refers to the beans as peas.

"The Jews' Sunday begins on Friday evening at sunset, after which time no Jew can even light a candle or lamp, or kindle a fire, or cook any thing until Saturday night, at the same hour; so that they heat their ovens on Friday; put in their provisions before night, for their next day's meals, and let it stand in the ovens until Saturday noon, when it is taken out, and set on the table, or on the floor, by Moors, whom they contrive to hire for that purpose. Every Jew who can afford it has brass or silver lamps hanging up in his house, which are lighted on Friday and not extinguished until Sunday morning: they burn either olive or argan oil. Their principal and standing Sunday dinner is called *skanah*; it is made of peas baked in an oven for nearly twenty-four hours, with a quantity of beeves' marrow bones (having very little meat on them) broken into pieces over them: it is a very luscious and fattening dish, and by no means a bad one: this, with a few vegetables, and sometimes a plum-pudding, good bread, and Jews' brandy, distilled from figs and aniseed, and bittered with wormwood, makes up the repast of the Jews who call themselves rich. The poor can only afford *skanah* and barley-bread on their Sunday, and live the rest of the week as they can."

So much for Boston baked beans.

Although I had frequently enjoyed cooked marrowbones in London during that chilly winter, I had foolishly neglected to find out how they were prepared for the table. All I knew was that they are the large leg bones of a beef "critter," that each end of the bone is sawed off to expose the marrow, that a container filled with cooked marrowbones—standing upright, each swathed in a napkin—can always be produced by a first-class London club or restaurant within ten minutes after it is ordered, and that the delicious, jellylike marrow is almost impossible to remove from the bone without the help of a marrow spoon.

If, on my return to Maine, I hadn't embarked on the writing of *Northwest Passage*, perhaps I would have been content to wait for another voyage to England before taking up the study of marrowbones in a more scientific manner. In *Northwest Passage*, however, I delved a little into old-time London, as well as into the lives of Rogers' Rangers at the period when they almost died of starvation. As I wrote and corrected and revised those scenes, late at night, I found myself reverting, mentally, to the succulent, meltingly tender marrowbones that had warmed me in London. Vicariously I became a starving Ranger and was almost overcome by a gnawing craving for marrow, "all fat and savory," just as Captain Riley had said.

The members of my household, conscious that I was under a strain, were eager to humor me. "All right," they said, "just take it easy. You go get the bones, and we'll cook 'em as soon as you tell us how to do it."

"If anyone," I thought, "can tell me how to cook marrowbones in the British manner, Mrs. Beeton can."

Mrs. Isabella Beeton's *Book of Household Management* is the queen of British cookbooks—England's Fanny Farmer. My earliest edition of Mrs. Beeton is dated 1864, and on the title page are the impressive words "Sixty-fifth Thousand." I also have an 1888 edition, but in both editions the recipe for cooking marrowbones is the same. It reads:

902.—Boiled Marrow Bones

Ingredients.—Bones, a small piece of common paste, a floured cloth.

Mode.—Have the bones neatly sawed into convenient sizes and cover the ends with a small piece of common crust, made with flour and water. Over this, tie a floured cloth and place them upright in a saucepan of boiling water, taking care there is sufficient to cover the bones. Boil them for 2 hours, remove the cloth and paste, and serve them upright on a napkin with dry toast. Many persons clear the marrow from the bones after they are cooked, spread it over a slice of toast, and add a seasoning of pepper; when served in this manner, it must be very expeditiously sent to table, as it soon gets cold.

Time.—2 hours. *Seasonable* at any time.

Note.—Marrow bones may be baked after preparing them as in the preceding recipe; they should be laid in a deep dish, and baked for 2 hours.

As soon as I read Mrs. Beeton on marrowbones, I knew that something was wrong. No British club or hotel had ever made me wait two hours for marrowbones. They had been produced in minutes.

I followed Mrs. Beeton's instructions, however, and, surrounded by flour paste, floured cloths, and binding twine, I fatigued myself by tying up the bones as directed. They were a pretty spectacle, standing like little soldiers in a pan of water, but at the end of the specified two hours all the marrow within the bones had melted and leaked through and around the paste and through the floured cloth, turning to a bright yellow crankcase oil in the process. The bones were completely empty.

Undiscouraged, I skimmed the crankcase oil into a container and placed it in the ice chest, where it eventually hardened into a snowy-white cake which, softened again by warming, blended admirably with anchovy paste and lent itself pleasantly to use as an hors-d'oeuvre spread.

I can't imagine where Mrs. Beeton picked up her abysmally incorrect information on the cooking of marrowbones, or why she has been permitted to disseminate it for so many years.

I discarded Mrs. Beeton and went to other cookbooks. Fanny Farmer coldly ignored marrowbones. Oscar of the Waldorf knew about them. "Take the bones from two legs of beef," Oscar wrote, "and saw them into pieces about four inches long. Scrape them well to clean them and put them in cold water to soak. Place them in a saucepan side by side, not standing up, cover with good stock, boil up quickly and then remove to the side of the fire and cook slowly for an hour and a half. Take out the bones, drain them, place on a napkin spread over a dish, and serve with slices of hot toast."

I did this, and got another batch of bright yellow crankcase oil, but no marrow.

I turned to *Everybody's Cookbook.* "Marrow," said *Everybody's,* "is the soft fat found inside large bones. It is considered a dainty in many parts of Europe, but not very frequently served in this country. To cook, the bones containing the marrow are cut in 2- to 3-in. lengths. Cover end of bone with a little paste of flour and water, boil slowly about 1 hour in salted water (1 teaspoon to 1 qt.). If the bones are from corned beef, do not add salt. (Each bone may be tied in a piece of cloth to make sure that no marrow escapes.) Drain bones, remove the paste, wrap in a napkin to keep hot and serve at once with hot toast. The marrow is picked from the bone with a fork. It may, of course, be removed after cooking and served on the toast, but the first method is better, because the marrow cools quickly when removed from the bone."

I tried this and got more crankcase oil.

So I threw away the cookbooks, held firmly to the thesis that London clubs produced marrowbones in ten minutes, and started all over again with a fresh batch of unchilled marrowbones. I tied them in a dishcloth, set a kettleful of water to boiling vigorously, and lowered the bundle of bones into the water. At the end of ten minutes I removed the bundle, dropped the bones into a bowl without wrapping them in napkins or adding furbelows of any sort, and went at them with a marrow spoon. They were delicious: perfectly cooked, "all fat and savory," to quote Captain Riley once more.

That renewal of my acquaintance with marrow led to the invention of a canapé or sandwich filling that I believed to be without a peer as an accompaniment for cocktails. In the beginning I produced small batches, but they vanished with such unbelievable rapidity that I was forced to make them larger and larger. I pass on the recipe willingly, for the good of the human race, which has too long suffered from canapés that either adhere distressingly to the roof of the mouth or result in unsightly toothpicks scattered on the floor.

MARROWBONE CANAPÉS ROBERTS

Have the ends sawed from three marrow bones in such a way that the marrow is exposed at both ends. Wrap them in a cloth, lower the cloth into a kettle of boiling water and boil the bones for 10 minutes. Into a large warmed bowl, put two cloves of garlic, finely chopped, ½ pound—two large packages—soft, fresh cream cheese, one tube of anchovy paste and the hot marrow from the three bones. With a fork mash the ingredients until they are blended, then chill the paste until firm. Spread ¼ inch of the mixture on a thin slice of bread, place another slice on top and cut the sandwich into four strips.

I could eat a million of 'em if I weren't insistent on keeping my weight below 185.

My research into the mysteries of marrowbones led me into an intricate correspondence with dietitians and experts on fats. What was the relationship, I wished to know, between marrow and the ordinary fat around the edges of a steak or a chop? The dietitians couldn't tell me. Some thought there was little difference. Some thought marrow was less fattening than ordinary fat. Some thought it might possibly be less nourishing. In my opinion, the dietitians, like the compilers of American cookbooks, had never eaten marrow and didn't quite know what they were talking about.

By degrees my correspondence led me to the two most sympathetic of all the experts—Colonel Edward N. Wentworth, director of Armour's Livestock Bureau in Chicago, and Vilhjalmur Stefansson, the arctic explorer, now doing work in the Dartmouth College Library. Both are ardent advocates of the nutritious and appetizing aspects of marrow fat, and encouraged me to make further researches into its possibilities. Both gentlemen have written on the high value of fats as food—Colonel Wentworth in a book describing the use by early Americans of *Jerky and Pemmican, Frontier Rations* (as the book is called); and Stefansson in his books *Not by Bread Alone* and *My Life with the Eskimos,* among a score more. Mr. Stefansson, irritated by bills of fare that celebrate pastry and pastry cooks, wrote me solicitously and eloquently concerning a Marrowbone Foundation:

"How about a non-profit educational and scientific foundation to study the possibility of a return to sound eating habits? Or how about just founding a hilarious club for banquets of the Homeric type, featuring marrowbones and ale?"

As far as I'm concerned, all that's necessary is for prospective members of the Marrowbone Club to supply themselves with a badge— that essential and almost forgotten piece of tableware, the marrow spoon!

November 1955

THE GUMBO CULT

Eugene Walter

On the subject of appetite in general, Monsieur de Saint-Just had this to say in the *Almanach des Gourmands* of 1807:

> *C'est un plaisir, c'est le dernier qu'on quitte.*
> *Est-il éteint? bientôt il ressuscite.*

(A pleasure 'tis; the last that we surrender/Is it impaired? a little time's its mender.) How precisely this describes my feeling for gumbo—a dish I have always considered special, indeed, ritualistic! It was in my grandmother's kitchen that I first saw gumbo prepared, at her table that I first ate it and joined the gumbo cult for life.

My grandmother was a tiny, plump woman, passionately interested in flowers. I really remember little about her, save that she wore clanking amethyst beads and that she smelled good, rather like lemon verbena. At that time there were still a few Indians living in the woods around Mobile, Alabama, remnants and revenants of the tribes that had been moved west by the government. A few old women among these Indians were "boboshillies," who came to town once or twice a week with their herbs, barks, and remedies. The boboshilly who came to my grandmother was tall and thin, and wore a muslin headcloth almost like a turban. She was completely noiseless as she came and went with a market basket full of this and that: I remember bay leaves, bird's-eye peppers, and the important gumbo filé.

This filé is a preparation of dried ground sassafras leaves that have been pounded in a mortar, sifted through a hair sieve, and bottled. It is a thickening agent and is used in many Southern variants of gumbo and jambalaya. It is always added just before serving and is never cooked. It is the ingredient often missing when these dishes are prepared away from the South. But there's no excuse for lacking gumbo filé if you belong to the cult. The specialty food shops have it or can get it for you.

Okra is often used to impart to gumbos a special smoothness, a kind of figured-bass accompaniment to the piquant spices. Okra is the seedpod of a plant belonging to the mallow or hibiscus family: the rose madder and marshmallow are its cousins. Sassafras is native, but okra was brought from Africa by slaves. Sometimes, to confuse things, okra is called *gumbo* (or *gumbo plant*)—both are African words. *Gumbo* means "everything together"—for example, *gumbo ya-ya* means "everybody talking at once." The most subtle gumbos employ okra and filé.

I remember one occasion when a grand or state gumbo was being prepared in my grandmother's kitchen. The boboshilly had come and gone, and my grandmother and two Negro servants were busy washing and chopping and boiling. One was Rebecca, who had been my father's nurse; the other was Estelle, who was mine. It was a cloudy day, and when thunder suddenly crashed and a downpour began, the yard man, Edward, came inside to sit in the corner by the stove and have a cup of coffee. Edward was very religious and, in imitation of Old Testament prophets, he wore long hair and a curly silken beard. I think his origins were either East African or Coptic. I had been given the task of picking pecans for pie and was sitting under the kitchen table.

Father Seydell of St. Joseph's Church was coming to dinner, and the gumbo was to contain crab, shrimp, and chicken. The crabs were banging about in a box under the sink, the lid held down by a brick. Suddenly there was a huge crash of thunder and a blinding yellow-green light. Then a rose-colored globe of fire rolled through the room. Lightning had struck the pecan tree growing in the yard. Rebecca screamed, Estelle crossed herself, and my grandmother looked under the table and said, "Are you there, Humbug?"

But then everybody began to laugh madly, and since I couldn't see what they were finding so amusing, I crawled out and stood up. The electricity had caused Edward's hair and beard to puff out in the most extraordinary way. His head had become an enormous puffball, like a human dandelion puff. He was confused and sputtering. The funny thing was that he couldn't make his hair and beard go down, and they stayed puffed out for the rest of the day. I had been afraid of Edward before this episode; afterwards, we became friends.

This is my grandmother's state gumbo:

SHRIMP AND CRAB GUMBO

In a large soup kettle combine 1 large bunch of celery, chopped, 12 allspice berries and 3 peppercorns, all cracked, 6 cloves, 2 bay leaves, a few sprigs each of thyme and parsley, 1 blade of mace, the peel from ¼ lemon, 1 red pepper pod, free of seeds and chopped, and 1 gallon of water. Salt the water liberally, bring it to a boil, and let it boil for a few minutes. Add 4 dozen whole large shrimp. When the water returns to a boil remove the kettle from the heat and let the shrimp cool in the court bouillon. Remove the shrimp and shell and devein them. Bring the court bouillon to a boil. Plunge 6 or 8 good-sized crabs into cold water and then into the boiling court bouillon and cook them for 10 minutes. Remove the kettle from the heat and cool the crabs in the liquid. When they are cool enough to handle, pick the meat from the shells but leave the claws intact. Strain the bouillon.

In a heavy iron skillet combine 2 tablespoons each of melted bacon fat and flour and cook the *roux,* stirring, until it is a rich dark brown. Stir in gradually 1 cup boiling water and 6 ounces concentrated tomato paste. Add 1 bay leaf, 6 allspice berries and 6 peppercorns, all cracked, 3 cloves, a good pinch of cayenne, and a dash of Tabasco. Turn the mixture into a soup kettle and add 2 quarts of the strained court bouillon. Add 3 green peppers, 3 tomatoes, 2 medium slices cooked ham, and 2 stalks of celery, all chopped. Brown 4 onions, sliced, in 4 tablespoons butter. Add 2 garlic cloves, chopped, and a 3-pound chicken, cut into serving pieces. Brown the chicken on all sides. Add the chicken and onions to the soup pot. Pour 1 cup stock into the pan the chicken was cooked in, stir in all the brown bits, and add this to the gumbo. Cook for 30 minutes. Add ½ pound fresh okra, chopped, and simmer the mixture for 1 hour, or until the chicken is tender. Salt to taste. Reheat to serve. Add the reserved shrimp and crab meat and claws 10 minutes before serving. In 5 minutes, stir 1 tablespoon filé powder into 1 cup of the gumbo stock. Remove the kettle from the heat and add the filé and stock. Serve the gumbo with rice and hot buttered French bread. Serves 12 to 16.

Well, that gives you an idea, doesn't it? People are always asking me what gumbo is. As you see, it's not a soup exactly, it's not a stew, not a ragout, it's uniquely and incomparably gumbo! It is as dark and as thick as river mud, unctuous, spicy, and satisfying.

Thackeray, when he came to New Orleans, decided that he liked gumbo even better than the bouillabaisse he had hymned in Marseille. But it was Lafcadio Hearn who went about sampling and jotting down recipes. This nineteenth-century exotic, born of mixed European parentage on a Greek island, lived long in New Orleans, though he settled at last in Japan. He compiled a book of Creole *recettes* which appeared anonymously under the auspices of the New Orleans *Times-Picayune*. He reported dozens of gumbo variations, among them, simple okra *gombo* and *maigre* oyster *gombo*. Which reminds me that although *gumbo* is now the universal spelling, old family manuscript cookbooks in the South spell it *gombaud, goumbaud, goumbo*. One excellent cook but poor speller living near Vicksburg, with its memories of the Civil War, jotted down for me her formula for shrimp *gunboat*.

Here are Lafcadio Hearn's recipes:

Simple Okra Gombo

Chop a pound of beef and half a pound of veal brisket into squares an inch thick; slice three dozen okra pods, one onion, a pod of red pepper, and fry them all together. When brown pour in half a gallon of water; add more as it boils away. Serve with rice as usual.

Maigre Oyster Gombo

Take 100 oysters with their juice, and one large onion; slice the onion into hot lard and fry it brown, adding when brown a table-spoon of flour and red pepper. [Caution with that red pepper! He means a tablespoon of flour to which has been added a pinch of cayenne.] When thick enough pour in the oysters. Boil together twenty minutes. Stir in a large spoonful of butter and one or two tablespoons of filee [filé], then take the soup from the fire and serve with rice.

The Aleutian Islands, of which the Andreanof Islands are a part, are quite grand and strange. Nobody knows how many thousands of is-lands and islets make up this chain, since this is the part of the globe which is geologically the youngest, bearing out the contention that the moon was born of the Pacific ocean. There are earthquakes daily, and some of the islands have the habit of sinking into the sea for unpre-dictable periods, then rising again just as nonchalantly. There are no trees, only the thick wind-flattened tundra grass which springs up in May and June and dies down in September.

The landscape is without doubt the saddest on earth, shrouded in fogs and snow. The wind, called williwaw, really does blow horizon-tally from the North Pole, and one can lean into it until one is walking almost horizontally. Since I came from Alabama and had never seen snow in my life, I was bewitched by the Aleutians. But many of the other World War II soldiers found the absence of trees depressing. Some of them made a tree of wood, chicken wire, and burlap, and put a little fence around it with the sign: "Aleutian National Forest." When the bulldozers were pushing earth and rock and ice to make an emergency landing strip on the island of Atka, the mounds piled up by the bulldozer had grotesque shapes which seemed to yearn to change into faces and figures. I thought of the rock peak Pavel Tchelitchew designed for the ballet *Apollon Musagète:* at the end of the ballet, in the calm light, it is seen as the heroic head of a sleeping Apollo. But there was no calm light here; the sun showed itself only five times, and then fitfully, in the three years I spent on the islands. The ravens seemed to hover on the brink of human speech. I used to imagine astonishing exchanges between them. With little effort I had taught them to say "hello" and "hi, doc" and several satisfying obscenities. As I strolled, furred and booted, along the black Bering sands with a pet caribou and two dogs, listening to the ravens cry greetings and oaths through the thickly swirling snow, it is not surprising that I longed nostalgically for the reassurance of a good spicy gumbo and the conviviality it implies.

So I learned to cook on the islands, since the food in the Air Force mess was usually inedible. By dint of much stealing, bargaining, and scrounging of various sorts, and making use of occasional food packages from the States, I was able to provide, for some of my gourmet buddies, one or two interesting suppers a week. A pilot friend of mine who made a regular run down the Aleutian chain brought us gin and other things we required to exist. I kept begging him to bring a can of okra, but he said it was too hard to find. I was longing to try a gumbo. I remember well the night he finally turned up with the okra. The snow was deep and the williwaw was blowing. The runway had been cleared and I waited by the hangar with dogs and caribou. My friend arrived frozen, but smiling.

"You and your okra," he said. "You know what it's really called? Ladyfingers!"

But he had found a tin of okra at Edmonton, in the Alberta province of Canada. I have never heard it called ladyfingers before or since; ladyfingers in the South are a kind of spongy tea cake in the shape that the French call *langue de chat* (cat's tongue). The next day, caribou and dogs and I went to dig clams on the black shores of the Bering Sea, and I made a gumbo of fresh clams, dried onion flakes, tomato paste, celery salt, lemon peel, and the blessed okra, alias ladyfingers. The gumbo was somewhat ersatz, but we enjoyed it anyway.

One winter day in New York after the War, I felt again a persistent, mystical, and not-to-be-denied hunger for a big bowl of gumbo. It's interesting that in New York one can find authentic food of every country on earth, save of the South. What is advertised as Southern fried chicken is usually an ancient fowl encased in a cement mixture and tormented in hot grease for an eternity. Southern biscuits à la New York are pure cannon wadding. Gumbo they've not even heard of. In the summer I lived on Ninth Street where there was a little garden back of the apartment, but when the steam heat came on in October I moved to an unheated flat on Tenth Street for the winter. I hate steam heat; it makes me think I have a brick on my head. It keeps me awake at night and I hear the spines of old leather books cracking open in the nasty, smothery heat. Crack! There's Ovid. Snap! Oh, poor Beddoes! Creak! Pop! Alas, the little two-volume Herrick.

Later on, the composer Donald Ashwander came from Alabama to live in the same building on Tenth Street, and he made his excellent corn bread—baked in an iron skillet—but at first I was quite alone in my nostalgia for Southern dishes. I went over to the Bleecker Street markets to look for okra, and got nowhere. But while shopping for paprika bacon on Third Avenue, I saw garlands of tiny okra festooning the window of a food shop run by an Armenian.

"I want some okra," I began, but that wasn't the name he knew. When I pointed, he said, "Oh, those are Greek peppers."

"But they're neither Greek nor peppers," I protested, adding to myself, "just as the Harmonious Blacksmith is neither harmonious nor blacksmith; as the City Center is neither city nor center; and red sable brushes are made of squirrels' tails." But I took home a garland of the precious pods, which had been strung on cotton thread and dried in the sun, and made a nice

CHICKEN GUMBO

Have a tender 3½-pound chicken cut into serving pieces and brown them in 2 tablespoons bacon fat. Add 1 chorizo (garlic sausage), cut in pieces, and 2 medium slices ham, diced. Add enough additional fat to cover the bottom of the soup kettle and add 2 bunches of celery, 2 onions, and 1 green pepper, all chopped, and 1 pound fresh okra, sliced. Cook, stirring, until all the ingredients are nicely browned. Add 2½ cups cooked tomatoes, 2 bay leaves, and the grated rind of 1 lemon. Cover the kettle and simmer the gumbo slowly for 30 minutes. Do not let it boil. Add ½ cup chopped parsley, several cracked peppercorns, and dashes of Tabasco and cayenne. The gumbo should be very highly seasoned. Add 2½ quarts chicken stock, cover the pan, and simmer the gumbo for 1½ hours. Correct the seasoning and serve with rice.

When I went to live in Paris, I intended to stay only temporarily at the Hôtel Helvétia in the rue de Tournon. It was run by Monsieur and Madame Jordan. He was from the Jura, she from Provence. The woodwork in the entry hall was painted exactly the same color as their yellow cat Nounouche, who was perfectly camouflaged when he sat on the radiator. Since I never succeeded in finding an apartment in Paris, I remained for five years at the Helvétia, which was not without its charms. It was a remodeled eighteenth-century *hôtel particulier* kept well scrubbed and polished by the Jordans. The problem was that cooking was forbidden in the rooms. There was a marble-topped commode in my room, and in it I hid a two-burner alcohol stove, pots and pans, tableware, and other necessary tools. The iron screen of an unused fireplace concealed my modest cellar. I gave rather elaborate dinner parties in this room not much larger than a refrigerator crate. Each guest had to take away a neatly packaged bit of garbage, to prevent discovery of my culinary activities and to discourage mice. One Italian princess, unused to such procedures, left a trail of coffee grounds and *langoustine* shells from my third-floor room to the street. But usually all went well. What with the Riesling cooling in an ice-filled bidet, and candles burning in ormolu candelabra, I managed to create a small oasis against the dire Paris climate. The most memorable dinners centered around a chicken cooked in *vin jaune de Jura* for Jack and Gurney Campbell; a soup of leeks and *merlan* for the Pakistani actress Roshann Dhunjibhoy and the Dutch photographer Otto van Noppen; and shrimp in a fondue sauce for a Finnish darling named Renata Vitzthum von Eckstädt. I'll tell you about these plates another time. What I'm getting at is the time I planned a particular dinner party at which gumbo was a must, since I had three serious eaters coming to dinner: Sally Higginson, Theodora Keogh, and Celestino Mendès-Sargo—all of whom had heard just about enough on the subject of gumbo and demanded to taste it. As usual, the quest for okra began. I hopped into a bus and rushed to Hédiard's, back of the Madeleine.

"Okra?" demanded the fat pink clerk in white apron. *"Qu'est-ce que vous voulez dire?"* He offered mangoes and *loukoumia,* but the magic pods were unknown to him. My gumbo dinner might never have materialized if, shortly after this initial failure, I had not dined in a Greek restaurant with some African friends. The first plate we attacked was a mound of okra.

"Comment s'appelle ce plat equis?" I asked cautiously.

"Ça? Mais, ce sont les bamias."

"Ah, oui, bamias," I observed knowingly. But I sought out the head chef to learn his source of supply. He confided that there was a grocery in the rue Hautefeuille that stocked enormous quantities of tinned okra or *bamias.* Next day, armed with a string bag and hope, I set out for the rue Hautefeuille, a narrow, short street off the Boulevard St. Germain. I entered a low-ceilinged, dark *épicerie.*

"Bamias," I mumbled, receiving an uncomprehending glare in return.

"Bamias," I repeated, but then I saw them, rows of fat tins with baroque lithographs of the okra plant. I pointed an adamant, triumphant forefinger.

"Ça? Mais, ce sont les cornes grecques." (Greek horns.)

"That which we call a rose ..." I muttered, and gave my order.

Anyway, I had my okra, and made for Sally, Theodora, and Celestino a

GUMBO IMPROVISÉ DIT DE PARIS

In a large saucepan, sauté 4 leeks and 1 stalk of celery, all chopped, in 2 tablespoons butter. Stir in 2 tablespoons flour and add ¼ cup chopped parsley and a few sprigs of thyme. Continue cooking for

1 minute. Scrub 3 dozen mussels, trim off the beards, and steam them open in a little water. Reserve the mussel meat. Add the mussel liquid to the saucepan with enough water to make 1 quart. Add 6 cracked peppercorns, 2 bay leaves, and a good dash each of cayenne and Tabasco. Cover the pan and simmer the gumbo for 1½ hours. Add 8 *langoustines* (or 4 pounds cut-up lobster), 4 tomatoes, skinned and quartered, and 1 large can okra, drained, and cook for 15 minutes. Add 1½ pounds shrimp and cook for 3 minutes. Add the reserved mussels and cook them for a few minutes until their edges curl and the shrimp turns pink. Correct the seasonings and stir in 1 tablespoon butter. Serve with rice.

When I moved to Rome and lived in a tiny house with a pocket-handkerchief terrace and garden, I immediately had okra seeds sent from America. I lovingly tended the green seedlings in the center of a flower bed until a helpful gardener took them for weeds and snatched them out. I gave seeds to Italian farmers at Latina on the Pontine plain, and the plants flourished, but the farmers refused to pick the pods until they were longer then the regulation inch and a half, with the result that when I cooked them they had the texture and flavor of boiled tree trunks.

But down in Calabria, in the neighborhood of what once was Sybaris, okra is cultivated and used in many a savory country dish. It is called Greek pepper there. The okra is a staple of diet in Greece under its name of *bamia*. It has other names—African, Turkish, and Slavic—which I've not yet learned. But okra or ladyfinger or *bamia* or Greek horn or Greek pepper or gumbo or African mallow or what you will, it's a delightful vegetable and will survive the conspiracy to consign it to oblivion. It just occurs to me that I have mentioned okra only in connection with gumbo; actually, it has a fame and career in its own right. If you have a little water boiling in a pot with a little salt, a pinch of sugar, two or three cracked peppercorns, and a twist of lemon peel, you can toss in a peck of okra pods, cook them until they are succulently just right, then drain, butter, and serve them. One picks up each pod by the stem and eats all save this stem. Fried okra is also fine.

Fried Okra with Green Tomatoes

Slice 1½ pounds okra and 2 large green tomatoes. Dredge the vegetables in ½ cup corn meal seasoned with salt and pepper, and brown them in 3 tablespoons bacon fat, stirring from time to time. Drain on absorbent paper and sprinkle with salt. Serve immediately.

April 1962

Cooking with James Beard: Pasta

James Beard

Contrary to romantic legend, pasta was not brought to Italy from China by Marco Polo. It actually dates back to the ancient Romans, whose equipment for making, cooking, and serving *laganum*, an early form of *tagliatelle*, is preserved in the museum at Pompeii. Certainly by the thirteenth century there was much mention of the macaroni and noodles turned out by skilled pasta cooks.

Although Italy is the great homeland of pasta, it is fairly popular in France, where noodles, usually homemade, are widely used. The Provençals eat a great deal of macaroni and nearly always serve it with their *daubes* to absorb the delicious juices that have cooked along with the meat. And I suppose the *Spätzle* so dear to the Austro-Hungarians and Czechs could also be included under the heading of pasta.

With this country's large Italian population, I find it strange that the average restaurant here serves rather poor pasta. Only occasionally do you get it memorably prepared. Oddly enough, in England you are much more likely to get a good dish of pasta—not sticky or mushy—that tastes freshly cooked and bears a properly prepared sauce rather than one that has deteriorated from overcooking.

At home there is no excuse for having anything but excellent pasta. In some cities—we in New York are truly blessed—there are shops where pasta is made in sheets to be cut wide or thin, according to your particular whim or needs. Because it is not dried this fresh pasta cooks in a very short time, but it will not stay fresh for very long. For best results it should be bought, cut, and cooked at once. Only the ribbony types of pasta such as *fettuccine, tagliatelle,* and lasagne can be bought this way. The tubular pastas are put through a machine that shapes them into cylinders, and they are almost always sold dry. There are some five or six hundred types and shapes of pasta, and to eat them all would require considerable ambition and effort, especially if each was served with a different sauce.

When it comes to the commercial packaged pasta, you'll find that there is a tremendous difference among those of the various manufacturers. It's advisable to experiment with imported and domestic kinds of pasta until you find the one that best suits your palate and bite.

If you like, you can make your own pasta. Recently machines have been introduced to the market that are a delight to use because they do away with so much of the drudgery and muscular effort that were formerly necessary. I can well remember watching a darling old woman in the kitchen of the Fenice in Venice making spinach pasta one morning for the day's specialty of green *cannelloni.* It seemed to me that she was blanching and kneading and rolling and cutting for hours, but the end result was certainly worth it—a steaming plate of excellent, remarkably tender green pasta with a ruddy sauce and a generous dusting of freshly grated cheese.

The pasta machine I mentioned is a neat little gadget, not large or unwieldy. It clamps onto the table and has two sets of two cylinders— one set that can be regulated to roll various thicknesses and the other that can cut the pasta into several widths after it is rolled. You may cheat a little and use it to knead the dough, too, running the pasta in and out through the rollers, decreasing the distance between them as you go along and the pasta becomes thinner. This does the same job as the hands and wrists. You will then have long strips of rolled dough and, by switching the handles from the rolling to the cutting cylinders, you can cut the pasta to any width you want. Hang the pasta strips up to dry or cook them at once without drying and you'll find that they are thoroughly good.

Here is my favorite recipe for homemade pasta, or *pasta fresca*, which I use for noodles, lasagne, and *cannelloni*—all a matter of how wide the pasta is cut.

Pasta Fresca
(*Fresh Pasta Dough*)

In a bowl combine 4 cups hard-wheat or all-purpose flour with 3 eggs and 1 teaspoon salt. Add about ¼ cup water—due to the great difference in flours you may need more—and blend the ingredients with the hands. Knead the dough, turning and pushing it with the heel of the hand, for about 10 minutes, or until it is very stiff. If you have a machine, divide the dough in quarters and run each piece through the rolling cylinders, setting them rather far apart. Continue to put the rolled dough through the machine until it is well amalgamated and comes through in long, even ribbons without any breaks or holes. Let the strips rest on paper towels until all the dough is rolled. Transfer the handle to the cutting cylinders and cut the dough to the desired width.

If you are not using a machine, divide the dough in half and roll each half on a floured cloth with a rolling pin into a rectangle of the desired thinness. Roll up the rectangles like jelly rolls and cut them to the desired width. Toss the rolls of cut pasta lightly to loosen them into strips and either hang them up to dry or cook them at once.

Fresh Spinach Pasta Dough

Wash 1 pound spinach in several changes of water. Remove and discard the heavy stems and steam the leaves in the water that clings to them until they are wilted. Run the leaves under cold water, drain them, and squeeze out as much moisture as possible. Chop the leaves finely and press them through a sieve. Prepare *pasta fresca* dough, knead in the spinach purée, and continue to knead and roll the dough until it is a delicate green. Roll and cut the pasta according to the directions given in the recipe for *pasta fresca*.

Fresh pasta should be cooked in a very large kettle with a large quantity of boiling well-salted water. It needs plenty of salt, so don't be afraid of overdoing it. Taste the water to see if the salt content is satisfactory. Bring the water to a full rolling boil, add the pasta, and let it boil at the same seething, rapid bubbling rate. I usually add a few dashes of oil to the water to prevent the strands from sticking together. Test the pasta often, by fishing out a strip and biting it, until it has reached the special degree of doneness and firmness you like. I prefer it in the Italian fashion, *al dente* (to the tooth), with a fair amount of bite to it, not at all soft or mushy.

Drain the cooked pasta in a colander or sieve and return it to the pan for saucing or serve it forth on a serving dish or plates—it is my belief that rather shallow soup plates are ideal for pasta.

If you are cooking commercial pasta, read the cooking directions on the box, for they all seem to differ slightly. Cook the pasta in a large quantity of boiling salted water, as before, and test it for doneness after 6 to 8 minutes. Do not let the water drop below a rolling boil while the pasta is cooking. Drain the cooked pasta and arrange it on a serving dish or in individual plates to be sauced.

How much pasta does one cook? This depends entirely on who is going to eat it. As the late Alice B. Toklas was wont to say, "How do I know what appetites they will have?" How true. I know people who will cook a half pound of pasta for two, and others who will stretch it to serve three or four. This is a situation in which you should make your own decision.

Certainly the simplest and in many ways one of the most satisfying preparations of pasta is just to give it some melted butter and grated cheese. Whenever I feel rather bored with food, I can always regain my appetite by cooking a dish of *spaghettini* or *fettuccine* or macaroni *al dente* and tossing it with butter and cheese.

PASTA AL BURRO
(*Pasta with Butter and Cheese*)

Cook ¾ to 1 pound pasta—any type of homemade or commercial pasta you wish—in a large quantity of boiling salted water. Be sure to keep the water at a good boil and after about 5 minutes start moving the pasta about with a fork or pasta lifter. Taste it after 8 or 9 minutes and continue testing it for bite until it is done the way you like it. (I find that cooking times are quite fickle, so I'm prone to frequent testing.) Drain the cooked pasta well and return it to the pot. Add 1 stick or ½ cup butter, melted or softened, and toss the pasta well. Add ½ to ¾ cup freshly grated cheese (Parmesan, Romano, *pecorino,* or Asiago), toss the pasta well with the cheese, and add a few grinds of black pepper. Serve the pasta in heated deep plates or soup plates and pass additional grated cheese and the pepper mill. Serves 4.

If you're having the pasta as a main course, you might start with some *prosciutto* and figs to continue with a good salad. Drink a pleasant Valpolicella.

You can vary this dish by using half shredded Gruyère and half Parmesan or Romano for the cheese. Or add about ½ cup slightly warmed heavy cream after adding the cheese and continue tossing the pasta until it is well mixed. Freshly ground pepper is needed here as well.

For garlic lovers, here is a delicious and pungent mixture.

SPAGHETTI AGLIO OLIO
(*Spaghetti with Garlic and Oil*)

Cook ¾ pound pasta in a large quantity of boiling salted water until it is done to taste. While it is cooking, heat 1 cup of the best olive oil until it is barely warm. Add as many garlic cloves, finely chopped, as suits your tolerance for the flavor—I usually gauge 1 clove per person and 1 or 2 for the pot. Let the garlic soak in the warm oil for 2 or 3 minutes. Drain the pasta and toss it with the oil and garlic and freshly ground pepper. Serves 4. If you prefer, you may strain the garlic from the oil, but in so doing you lose the whole point of the dish. Cheese is superfluous with this combination, but chopped parsley and a bit of fresh basil or thyme are wonderful. Drink a robust Barolo and have some crisp bread and a salad—preferably without garlic.

For another version of this dish, sauté 4 or 5 garlic cloves, coarsely chopped, in ¼ cup olive oil until they are lightly colored. Combine the garlic and oil with ½ teaspoon crushed dried hot red pepper and ¾ cup heated olive oil. Toss the mixture with the cooked pasta as before.

Still another variation on the garlic and oil theme adds 8 to 10 anchovy filets, coarsely chopped, to either of the preceding recipes. Toss the sauce with the pasta and garnish it with chopped flat-leafed Italian parsley.

The next pasta sauce is a most unusual one that I first ate in Sicily. I found it highly intriguing and I have used it frequently since then as a surprise for my pasta-loving friends. It is best served with either *spaghettini* or *tagliatelle.*

Spaghettini o Tagliatelle alla Siciliana
(*Pasta with Pine Nuts and Raisins*)

Cook ¾ pound *spaghettini* or *tagliatelle* in a large quantity of boiling salted water until it is tender. Drain it well and return it to the pot. Combine ¾ cup heated olive oil with 4 garlic cloves, finely chopped, and pour it over the pasta. Add ½ cup each of pine nuts and Sultana raisins or currants, and toss the sauce well with the pasta. Add several grinds of pepper and about ⅓ cup chopped parsley, preferably the flat-leafed Italian variety, toss the dish again, and serve it without cheese but with additional pine nuts if you wish. Serves 4.

For a variation of this dish, add 10 to 12 anchovy filets, coarsely chopped, to the mixture.

Serve either dish with crisp toasted French or Italian bread and a salad of *rucola* or, failing that, Bibb lettuce, and drink a California Zinfandel.

Tomatoes are to pasta as chocolate is to ice cream. However, I found out when I was very young that tomato sauces cooked long and lovingly with many ingredients and improvisations usually turn out to be one hundred percent boring and overpowering. The less cooking most of these sauces get, the better they taste—that is, of course, if you have ripe tomatoes at your command.

SALSA DI POMIDORO FRESCO
(*Fresh Tomato Sauce*)

Peel 8 to 10 very ripe tomatoes and cut each one into 6 wedges. In a skillet sauté 2 garlic cloves, finely chopped, in ¾ stick or 6 table-spoons butter over medium heat for 1 minute. Toss in the tomatoes, increase the heat slightly, and add 1 teaspoon salt and ½ teaspoon freshly ground pepper. Cook the tomatoes briskly for about 5 minutes. Add 2 or 3 fresh basil leaves or 1 teaspoon dried basil and correct the seasoning. Serve the sauce over ¾ pound freshly cooked *tagliatelle* and pass copious amounts of freshly grated Parmesan or Romano cheese. The delicacy of the tomato flavor will astound you.

If you can't get really ripe tomatoes, the canned Italian plum tomatoes are the next best thing.

QUICK TOMATO SAUCE

In a heavy saucepan sauté 3 garlic cloves, finely chopped, in ¼ cup olive oil over medium heat for 1 minute. Add one 32-ounce can Italian plum tomatoes and cook them over rather high heat for 10 minutes. Add 1½ teaspoons salt, a few grinds of pepper, and 1 or 2 fresh basil leaves or 1 teaspoon dried basil. I also like to add about 1 teaspoon grated orange zest and 1 tablespoon tomato paste and let the sauce cook for another minute or two.

Pour the sauce over a dish of cooked pasta or ladle it over individual servings and pass plenty of freshly grated Parmesan, Romano, or Asiago cheese, or a selection of them.

Either of these tomato sauces may have other ingredients added to them. Here are two suggestions.

Tomato Sauce with Mushrooms

Prepare fresh tomato sauce or quick tomato sauce. In a skillet very lightly sauté ½ pound mushrooms, sliced, in 4 to 5 tablespoons butter. Add them to the tomato sauce and simmer it for 2 to 3 minutes.

Tomato Sauce with Mushrooms and Sausages

Prepare fresh tomato sauce or quick tomato sauce. Cut ½ pound Italian sausages into small pieces and cook them in a heavy skillet for 4 minutes. Drain them on paper towels and add them to the tomato sauce with ½ pound mushrooms, sliced and lightly sautéed in 4 to 5 tablespoons butter. Cook the sauce for 6 or 7 minutes and season it to taste. This sauce is extremely good with *fettuccine* or *tagliatelle*.

A more traditional, but less fresh-tasting, tomato sauce may be used for most pastas, for meats, and for other Italian dishes.

Traditional Tomato Sauce

In a heavy saucepan combine 2½ pounds ripe tomatoes, unpeeled and cut into sections, 1 medium onion, finely chopped, and 1 rib of celery and 2 medium carrots, both finely sliced. Add 2 or 3 fresh basil leaves or 1 teaspoon dried basil, 1 or 2 sprigs of parsley, 1½ teaspoons salt, and ½ teaspoon freshly ground pepper. Bring the sauce to the simmering point over low heat and let it simmer for about 45 minutes, or until it is well blended. Correct the seasoning and rub the sauce through a fine sieve. Return it to the saucepan, add ½ cup tomato paste, and reduce the sauce for a few minutes, or until it has some body.

If the sauce seems too thick after being sieved, add a small amount of broth, tomato juice, or white wine and cook it for a few minutes more. Serve the sauce with any pasta and pass a bowl of freshly grated Parmesan or Romano cheese.

While visiting friends in a tiny village not far from Milan, I encountered a fascinating variation of the pasta-tomato partnership. Their cook had served it to them the previous summer with such success that they had immediately adopted it for their guests. It's an especially delightful combination for hot days and is best when made with vermicelli or *spaghettini*.

PASTA WITH TOMATO AND ONION SALAD

Cook ¾ pound vermicelli or *spaghettini* (or 1 pound if your guests have large appetites) in a large quantity of boiling salted water until it is done to taste and drain it. Combine 6 ripe large tomatoes, peeled and cut into wedges, 1 red Italian onion, finely sliced, 2 or 3 finely cut fresh basil leaves or 1 teaspoon dried basil, 6 tablespoons olive oil, 1 tablespoon wine vinegar, 1 teaspoon salt, ½ teaspoon freshly ground pepper, and 2 tablespoons chopped parsley. The tomatoes and onion should be chilled until the last minute before being tossed. Combine the salad with the hot pasta and toss them together—the contrast is a delight. With this dish serve crisp rolls and a chilled rosé wine. Follow it with some kind of summer fruit—perhaps lusciously ripe cherries in a bowl of ice water. Serves 4.

Summer brings basil, and basil is one of the most provocative of all herbs. Its delicate scent and flavor are robust yet subtle and, to most people, mouthwatering. Perhaps the greatest of all pasta dishes, as far as I am concerned, is *spaghettini* or *trenette* or vermicelli *al pesto. Pesto* may be made in a mortar but in these days of laborsaving appliances I find the blender an ideal instrument.

PASTA AL PESTO
(*Pasta with Basil Sauce*)

In the container of a blender put ½ cup each of olive oil and pine nuts, 3 garlic cloves (or more to taste), and about 1½ cups basil leaves, rather tightly packed. Add 1 teaspoon salt and whirl the mixture on the "blend" setting for about 1 to 1¼ minutes, or until the ingredients are reduced to a paste. Add ½ cup grated Parmesan, Pecorino, or Sardo cheese (or a combination of the three) and blend the mixture again for just a moment. Toss the *pesto* with ¾ pound freshly cooked *trenette, tagliatelle,* or *spaghettini* and serve it with additional grated cheese. Serves 4.

To make *pesto* in a mortar, crush the basil leaves and garlic with the pestle, add the nuts and grated cheese gradually, and grind the mixture to a smooth paste. Work in ¼ to ½ cup olive oil. Sometimes a quantity of broad-leafed Italian parsley is added to the *pesto.* Some people have been known to use walnuts instead of the traditional pine nuts, and I've even heard of substituting sunflower seeds— shelled ones, of course.

Pesto keeps well in the refrigerator if you pour a film of olive oil over the top and cover it with plastic wrap. You can also freeze it in small containers, each holding enough for a meal, and it will keep for months and retain its color. *Pesto* isn't confined to pasta—you can use it with rice or *gnocchi* or other starches, including potatoes, with which it is truly sensational.

Probably the most famous of all sauces for pasta is the *bolognese,* which, as its name implies, is native to Bologna, supposedly the center of great food in Italy. I usually cast my vote for Venice, but certainly Bologna has great traditions. This *ragú,* as it is often called, has been a standard for centuries, and you'll often find it used as a filling for lasagne.

RAGÚ BOLOGNESE
(*Bolognese Meat Sauce*)

In a heavy skillet or saucepan sauté gently ½ pound bacon, cut into small pieces, in 2 tablespoons butter until it is lightly browned. Add 2 medium onions, finely chopped, and 2 medium carrots and 2 ribs of celery, both chopped, and cook the vegetables until they are lightly colored. Add 1 pound ground beef and cook it until it is browned, breaking it up with a fork so that it browns evenly. Add ½ pound chicken livers, chopped, and sauté them for 2 or 3 minutes, or until they are blended with the sauce. Add 1½ cups beef stock, 1 cup white wine, ¼ cup tomato paste, and salt and freshly ground pepper to taste. Simmer the sauce, covered, very gently for 35 to 40 minutes more. This sauce, possibly with the addition of some chopped parsley, is fine for any pasta. Try it on the small seashell pasta and sprinkle it plentifully with grated cheese.

LASAGNE ALLA BOLOGNESE
(*Lasagne with Meat Sauce*)

Prepare *ragú bolognese* and béchamel sauce.

Cook 1 pound lasagne in a large quantity of boiling salted water until it is done to taste. Spread a little of the *ragú bolognese* on the bottom of a baking dish, 6 by 9 inches, and cover it with strips of the cooked lasagne. Spread the lasagne with a layer of the béchamel sauce, well seasoned with nutmeg, and sprinkle it with freshly grated Parmesan or Romano cheese. Repeat the layers until all the ingredients are used, ending with a layer of béchamel sauce. Sprinkle the top liberally with grated cheese and bake the lasagne in a moderate oven (350° F.) for about 15 to 20 minutes, or until the pasta is heated through and the sauce is bubbly. Serve the lasagne cut in oblong sections, and accompany it with crisp rolls or bread and a Bibb lettuce and watercress salad with a garlic dressing. Drink a good Beaujolais.

Chiocciole, the pasta shaped like seashells, is excellent to eat, most attractive to serve, and thoroughly different from the usual run of spaghetti and *linguine* and the like. A favorite way to prepare seashells is *alla carbonara*, which requires a deft hand in the mixing.

CHIOCCIOLE ALLA CARBONARA
(*Seashell Pasta with Cheese, Bacon, and Eggs*)

In a skillet cook 5 or 6 thick slices of well-smoked bacon, cut into strips, until they are crisp but not dried up. Drain them on paper towels. Combine 4 or 5 eggs with ¾ cup grated Pecorino or Parmesan cheese. Cook ¾ pound seashell pasta of any size in a large quantity of boiling salted water until it is tender. Drain the pasta, transfer it to a deep bowl, and combine it with the eggs and cheese. Add the bacon and toss the mixture well, adding a little freshly ground pepper as you toss. Continue tossing the mixture until the egg has coagulated with the cheese and adheres to the pasta. Serve the dish at once, with additional grated cheese if you wish. If the mixture seems too thick, add a little melted butter.

Thin strips of *prosciutto* or, better yet, Smithfield ham make a remarkably good substitute for the bacon.

A similar hearty dish, made with *tagliatelle*, is especially well suited to a Sunday luncheon in winter.

TAGLIATELLE ALLA PAESANA
(*Pasta with Pork and Mushrooms*)

In a skillet cook 5 or 6 thick slices of well-smoked bacon, cut into strips, until they are crisp but not dried up. Drain them on paper towels and transfer them to a skillet. Add 1 onion, finely chopped, and 1 or 2 garlic cloves, chopped. Sauté the mixture for a minute or two and add 1 cup finely cut cold roast pork and 2 to 3 ounces dried Italian mushrooms that have been reconstituted in warm water and cut into small pieces. Mix in 2 tablespoons chopped parsley and 1 teaspoon dried basil.

Cook ¾ pound green or white *tagliatelle* in boiling salted water until it is *al dente*, drain it, and mix it well in a bowl or the pan with 4 eggs, lightly beaten, the pork mixture, and a generous amount of freshly grated Parmesan or Pecorino cheese. If desired, add ½ cup white wine. Pass more cheese with the pasta.

I used to think that I would be the most delighted person in the world if I could have all the pasta with fresh white truffles that I wanted. Then I found that the imported canned white truffles have great quality and are excellent with pasta. Naturally, they are not up to the fresh ones, which may be ordered here in season from Italy, but the very expensive canned truffles are amazingly good. I think white truffles are best with freshly made noodles, *linguine,* or vermicelli and I prefer them rather coarsely shredded with a goodly amount of melted butter. No cheese—only the shredded truffles, the butter, and some freshly ground pepper. Simply toss the truffles and butter with the pasta and serve it piping hot. Be as extravagant as you can because the better the truffle, the better the dish.

LINGUINE CON TARTUFI BIANCHI
(*Pasta with White Truffles*)

Cook ½ pound *linguine* or any preferred ribbon pasta in a large quantity of boiling salted water until it is done to taste. Melt 1 stick or ½ cup butter and shred 1 large can (about 2 or 3) white truffles—more if you like—it's really a question of how many you can afford and how much you like them. Toss the pasta with the butter, the truffles, and their juice. Or, if you want to make a great impression, toss the pasta with the butter and serve it on a platter topped with the truffles, either shredded or shaved with a truffle shaver. Pass more melted butter. No matter how you present it, this is a dish of great distinction. Serves 2.

Occasionally you find special French pasta dishes from the South of France that are closely related gastronomically to those of Italy. But this one must have been created in the north, for the name is by no means Provençal. It uses macaroni or the largest kind of *ziti.*

MACARONI À LA PARISIENNE
(*Macaroni with Chicken, Ham, Tongue, and Truffles*)

Skin 2 whole chicken breasts and in a skillet sauté them in ¾ stick or 6 tablespoons butter over fairly high heat for about 10 minutes, or until they are just lightly colored on both sides. Reduce the heat and continue cooking the breasts for about 3 to 4 minutes, or until they are just cooked through. Add ⅓ cup Madeira and cook it for a minute. Remove the chicken breasts and reserve them and the pan juices.

In a heavy saucepan melt 3 tablespoons butter and blend in 3 tablespoons flour. Cook the *roux* for 2 or 3 minutes, stir in 2 cups chicken broth, and continue to cook the mixture, stirring, until it is thickened. Add ¾ cup heavy cream, the reserved pan juices, and ½ cup shredded Gruyère cheese and stir the sauce until it is thoroughly blended. Season it with salt and pepper to taste and a sprinkling of freshly grated nutmeg.

Cut the chicken into julienne and combine them with ¼ pound each of cooked tongue and ham or *prosciutto*, both cut into julienne. Cut 1 medium black truffle into matchstick strips. Chop another truffle very finely and chop a little of the tongue very finely.

Cook 1 pound macaroni or large *ziti* in a large quantity of boiling salted water until it is *al dente* and drain it well. Arrange the pasta in a buttered rectangular baking dish, 11 by 14 inches, or a buttered round baking dish, about 12 inches in diameter and 3 inches deep. Combine the julienne of chicken, tongue, and ham and the matchstick pieces of truffle with the sauce and spoon it over the pasta. Sprinkle the top with the finely chopped truffle and tongue and a generous amount of grated Parmesan cheese. Bake the dish in a moderate oven (350° F.) for about 15 minutes, or until the top is delicately brown and the sauce is bubbling. Serve the macaroni as a buffet dish with perhaps a green bean salad with onion rings, some hot rolls, and a pleasant Meursault or Bâtard-Montrachet, nicely chilled. Serves 8.

I remember vividly the first time I had *maccheroni con quattro formaggio*. It was in Naples, high up on a hill, and it was a delight to watch the careful preparation—almost a rite—in which the different cheeses were blended with the pasta. This is a dish that should be done at the table and there should be a certain flair to the blending.

MACCHERONI CON QUATTRO FORMAGGI
(*Macaroni with Four Cheeses*)

Cut ¼ pound mozzarella cheese into small strips. Cut ¼ pound Gruyère cheese into very small dice. Dice ¼ pound Edam cheese. Grate enough Parmesan cheese to make 2 cups. Reserve 1 cup of the Parmesan and blend the remaining cheeses together.

Put 1½ sticks or ¾ cup butter in a bowl and put the bowl in warm water so that the butter softens but does not melt.

Cook 1 pound macaroni, *ziti,* or seashell pasta in a large quantity of boiling salted water until it is done to taste, drain it well, and transfer it to a shallow bowl or deep platter. Toss it well with the butter and mixed cheeses until the mixture is just creamy—do not let it get overmixed and stringy. Sprinkle the dish with the reserved Parmesan cheese and serve it at once on hot plates. With crisp bread, a hearty salad of greens with some thinly sliced red onions, and a husky red wine—a Barbera or a red Hermitage—you will have a feast.

All too often a dish of spaghetti with clam sauce turns out to be a disastrous thing because the clams are overcooked and tough and the sauce is heavy and overly rich. For years I have been making a recipe that I learned in Florence from a friend who had made it in various parts of Europe with canned clams rather than fresh. I find that the best grade of minced clams serves the purpose admirably.

TAGLIATELLE ALLE VONGOLE
(*Pasta with Clam Sauce*)

Drain well 2 cans minced clams, either razor clams or the East Coast variety. Reserve the clams and their juice.

In a saucepan heat 3 tablespoons olive oil, add 2 garlic cloves, finely chopped, and let them "melt" into the oil over very low heat until they are just transparent. Add the reserved clam juice, 1 scant teaspoon salt, and 4 or 5 grinds of pepper. Let the sauce come to a boil and simmer it for 5 minutes.

Cook ½ pound *tagliatelle* in a large quantity of boiling salted water until it is *al dente* and drain it well. Return the pasta to the cooking pot, add 2 tablespoons olive oil, and toss it well. Add the re-served clams to the sauce in the pan with ½ cup finely chopped parsley and let it boil up. Divide the pasta among 4 serving plates, spoon the sauce over it, and eat it at once—no cheese with this, please, just some good bread and a chilled dry white wine, perhaps a Verdicchio. Serves 4.

Another simple and delicious way to sauce *tagliatelle* or *fettuccine* is with thin strips of *prosciutto,* cheese, and heavy cream.

FETTUCCINE CON PROSCIUTTO
(*Noodles with Ham, Cheese, and Cream*)

Cut ½ pound *prosciutto* into thin shreds. Rather coarsely shred 1½ cups Gruyère cheese. Grate enough Parmesan cheese to make ½ cup. Gently heat ½ cup heavy cream.

Cook 1 pound freshly made *fettuccine* (or *tagliatelle*) in a large quantity of boiling salted water until it is *al dente*. Drain it well and return it to the pot. Add the *prosciutto* and cheeses and toss the mixture until it is well blended. Add the cream and a few grinds of pepper and toss it briefly. Serve the pasta immediately, passing ad-ditional grated Parmesan cheese if you wish. Have an onion and tomato salad for a first course. Serve crisp bread and drink a cooled Valpolicella or a chilled Soave.

Baked macaroni is not, as you might think, a typical American dish, but an old Roman way of preparing the pasta.

MACCHERONI AL FORNO
(*Baked Macaroni with Cheese*)

Cook 1 pound macaroni of any preferred shape or thickness in a large quantity of boiling salted water until it is *al dente*. Drain it quickly and well.

Butter a 3-quart baking dish and arrange a layer of the macaroni on the bottom. Sprinkle it lavishly with grated Gruyère or Fontina cheese, add another layer of macaroni and another layer of cheese, and pour over it 1½ cups béchamel sauce. Sprinkle the sauce with cheese, add another layer of macaroni and another sprinkling of cheese, and top it with about 1 cup more béchamel sauce. Top the sauce with the remaining macaroni and a final sprinkling of cheese and top it with ½ cup buttered bread crumbs. Bake the dish in a moderate oven (350° F.) for 10 minutes, or until it is beautifully brown and bubbly on top. Serve it with Italian whole-wheat bread and fresh peas buttered and sprinkled with chopped parsley. The baked macaroni is a superb dish for a buffet or late supper. Drink a Riserva Ducale Chianti.

The following recipe for *rigatoni* requires a good deal of work, but I think you'll find the result unusual and well worth the trouble. It is a rather different approach to the subject of pasta.

RIGATONI CON SALSICCIE
(*Pasta with Sausage*)

In a skillet cook 14 large sweet or hot Italian sausages, skins removed, in 3 tablespoons each of butter and oil over medium heat until they are lightly browned. Add ¾ cup beef broth and cook the sausages slowly, turning them often and adding more broth as it cooks away, for about 10 minutes, or until the sausages are cooked through. Keep the sausages warm.

Cook 1½ pounds *rigatoni* in a large quantity of boiling salted water until it is about half done. Drain the pasta and transfer it to a large skillet. Cover the pasta with well-seasoned beef or chicken broth, cover the skillet, and cook the pasta slowly until it is tender and the broth is absorbed. Add ¾ stick or 6 tablespoons butter, about 1 cup freshly grated Parmesan cheese, and 8 of the reserved sausages and blend the mixture well. Cook it for 5 minutes and turn the heat very low. Lightly beat 4 eggs, season them with ½ teaspoon each of salt and freshly ground pepper, and spoon them over the pasta, making indentations with a fork to the bottom of the pan so that the eggs run down and cook lightly with the pasta and thicken the broth. Garnish the dish with the remaining reserved sausages and sprinkle it with a bit of chopped parsley, preferably the broad-leafed Italian type. Serves 6 to 8.

November 1970

Pueblo Indian Breads

Caroline Bates

In the *piki* house, the smoke from the cedar fire became denser as Lucille Talaswaima, sitting before a blackened slab of sandstone, went through the slow, timeless motions of making *piki,* the crackly, tissue-thin "paper bread" that is the ancestral bread of the Hopi. Dipping her hand into a pottery bowl of blue-cornmeal batter, she wiped it on the side and then smeared the batter with her fingers in a graceful, sweeping motion over the hot *piki* stone, covering it with a thin film. In a minute or two the edges began to curl and the sheet looked shiny and transparent. Peeling it off deftly, she put it on a newspaper on the dirt floor and immediately smeared the stone again. While the second sheet of *piki* was baking she lay the cooked sheet on top for a few seconds so that the steam would moisten it slightly, then folded in the ends and rolled it up. The process was repeated again and again. One sheet stuck slightly to the stone, a sign that the surface needed greasing. With a piece of sheepskin Lucille carefully rubbed in a little beef brain until the stone once again took on the sheen and smoothness of marble. Slowly but steadily, rolls of blue-gray *piki,* thinner than the sheets of newspaper on which they rested, began to accumulate.

Eyes smarting from the smoke, I went outside to get a breath of air and sat on a ledge near Terrance, Lucille's son and the director of the museum at the Hopi Cultural Center. The *piki* house and many other stone dwellings were built on a high escarpment in Shipaulovi, a village in Second Mesa, Arizona, in the heart of the Hopi Reservation. We had stopped there on the first leg of a trip that would take us to New Mexico to eat Indian foods and to see firsthand how bread is baked in the large beehive ovens of the pueblos, and it was fitting that we began our search for the Indians' breadmaking traditions where the heritage is oldest and purest. The prospect from the heights of Shipaulovi, which rises four to five hundred feet above the desert plains, is awesome. The dirt paths combing the cliff-top village are so steep that I got dizzy every time we climbed them; but Lucille, a woman twice my age, had been up and down with no visible fatigue between her dwelling and her *piki* stone all morning preparing the fire for baking. The clean, dry air smelled of dust and sage, and the only sound was of wind rushing through the stones. Occasionally a strong gust scattered dust and scraps of paper, causing a dozing dog to open one eye briefly, and then the wind stilled as suddenly as it had begun. A hawk appeared over a cliff—a young ferruginous by the looks of its white underparts, but I wasn't sure—and soared out of sight. Far below us the rabbit-brush plains stretched to the horizon and the cornfields lay fallow now in early winter. The light snow that had fallen the evening before had melted, but some eighty miles to the southwest there was a mantle of white, the season's first, on the sacred San Francisco Peaks where the kachinas (benevolent spirits who bring rain) dwell. From the stones of First, Second, and Third Mesas, which form the nucleus of the old Hopi villages, Hopi have watched the hawks wheel and the seasons change over that expanse of desert for some seven hundred years. We, rootless and recent arrivals to the land our European ancestors called America, can hardly comprehend the continuity and sweep of the vision.

Terrance Talaswaima is an artist, a writer of children's stories, and, like all traditional Hopi, a farmer, who says more in a few short, pithy sentences than most people can convey in paragraphs. He spoke of the crops, the fields, and some tribal customs, and always the talk centered around corn, which the Hopi attribute to divine origin and invest with a profound sacramental nature. It is Mother, sustenance, inseparable from life itself, and it permeates art, stories, dances, rituals, and ceremonies. The Hopi cultivate red, white, blue, and yellow corn and many strains of each, which are passed down within individual families; but the important varieties are the white and the blue, the stubby ears of midnight-blue kernels that have earned the Hopi the epithet "the people of the short blue corn." That extraordinary corn with its unique toasty taste and ancient lineage is the most sacred of all corns, and it typifies the flavor of the Indian Southwest.

The Talaswaimas have long grown their own corn, as each Hopi household does, on plots miles away in the valley without benefit of large-scale irrigation. There are no rivers to channel in this hard land. Rarely growing higher than five feet, the corn is nurtured by the snowmelt of spring, the infrequent summer rains that fall on the high desert, and water from the springs and natural seeps at the base of Black Mesa, an extensive sandstone plateau drained by four great washes. The corn has adapted to these conditions in several unusual ways. One is the development of a single long root, instead of several seminal roots, to reach the underground moisture.

Corn is prepared in ways that probably have not changed in centuries. Terrance described a delicacy called *pikami*, a fresh corn pudding made in the fields when blue corn is harvested. The kernels are scraped off the ears and ground to a paste, enclosed in cornhusks, and baked in hot ashes in an earthen pit covered with stones and sand. The Navajo make something like it called "kneel-down bread." *Somiviki* is a similar primitive tamale made with sweetened blue cornmeal wrapped in dried cornhusks and boiled, numberless variations of which can be found among the Indians of the Southwest and of Mexico.

For as long as there have been Hopi there has been *piki*, which used to be the basic breadstuff. It no longer is, although just about every woman in Shipaulovi has a *piki* stone and young girls are still taught how to make it. *Piki* is always made for ceremonies, however, and because the Hopi calendar is marked by many of them the paper bread is around most of the time. On dance days one may see red and yellow *piki* made from white cornmeal colored with vegetable dyes and folded into flower shapes, which are gifts to children from the kachinas.

Returning to the *piki* house, I saw that Lucille had nearly emptied the bowl of batter. The baking had occupied two and a half hours, and she still sat stoically, breaking the rhythm of dipping, smearing, pulling, and folding only to wipe her smoke-reddened eyes. Her fingertips looked almost raw from repeated contact with the heat of the *piki* stone. Earlier in the morning we had been privileged to watch her mix the batter in her sky house, which clings to a cliff top with sheer sides and has a view that seems to take in all of northern Arizona. Some Hopi women still stone-grind their own corn by hand, using a *mano* and a *metate*, but Lucille had reduced her dried blue corn to a meal as fine as flour in a small electric grain grinder. She began making the *piki* batter by pouring boiling water into a bowl of the blue cornmeal, which precooked it and filled the room with a fragrant roast corn aroma. After mixing the batter with a stick, she kneaded it vigorously with her hands, gradually adding cold water until it achieved its characteristic soupy consistency and high sheen. The last step was straining in a liquid of greasewood ashes to give the bread a better flavor and keep it bluish-gray, for blue corn takes on a pink cast when subjected to heat.

By the time the batter was gone the floor was covered with at least fifty rolls of *piki* in neat rows. Lucille gave me one to try. It was dry and crackly with an indescribably delicious flavor. It tasted more profoundly of corn than any corn bread I've ever eaten. Lawrence Durrell once described the black olives of the Mediterranean as having "a taste as old as cold water." *Piki* is like that, reaching back into the mists of prehistory to the essence of America.

Although *piki* may be the oldest corn bread of all, it was but one of dozens of corn-based foods being made in the pueblos of the Southwest when the Spaniards arrived on the scene. Coronado set out from Mexico in 1540 to find the treasures of the fabled Seven Cities of Cíbola and discovered goldless Cíbola in the land of the Zuñi in southwestern New Mexico. "They eat the best cakes that ever I saw....," he wrote. "They have the finest order and way to grind that we ever saw in any place. And one Indian woman of this country will grind as much as four women of Mexico." Unfortunately, neither Coronado nor subsequent observers described in depth the variety of "cakes," making it impossible to put together anything like an accurate picture of the Indian diet soon after the advent of the Spanish. Few of the voluminous studies of Pueblo peoples in the last hundred years devote much thought or space to cookery, although the basic food-stuffs and techniques of Indian agriculture are well explored. The re-searchers who became interested in Indian cooking in more recent times were almost too late: Many of the old ways and the old dishes had been lost in the continuing process of acculturation.

An outstanding exception is the remarkable *Zuñi Breadstuff* by Frank H. Cushing, who lived with the Zuñi as an adopted member from 1879 to 1884 and recorded everything he learned and observed about their food. Nothing escaped his attention, from the growing and harvesting of the crops with their accompanying rituals to the construction of bake ovens and stones and the laying out of the table. Cushing exemplified the best of that breed of enlightened, nineteenth-century man who approached new experiences with an open mind and threw himself into his work with prodigious energy and dedication. His monumental 673-page study is the most exhaus-tive account in English of old Pueblo cooking, which by that time in-cluded many breads and puddings based on the Spanish-introduced wheat and on *chile* dishes of less certain origin, for *chile* was not grown in ancient New Mexico. One suspects that Cushing romanticized as-pects of Zuñi life and accepted on faith everything he was told, but, nonetheless, what emerges is an extraordinary account of a rich and varied cookery based on corn, far more complex than is generally ap-preciated. But perhaps it isn't surprising that a sophisticated cookery evolved among a people whose ancestors built multistoried apartment houses as early as the eighth century, created a tradition of making baskets and pottery of high artistry, and developed a beautiful, esoteric religion rich in symbolism and ritual.

Among the Zuñi and—it is safe to infer—other Pueblo peoples, green corn was boiled, roasted, baked, stewed, and fried; ripe corn was toasted and parched. There were corn dumplings, sweet corn pud-dings, and corncakes in infinite variety, thick and thin, leavened and unleavened. Cushing describes the subtleties of each in meticulous, loving detail. A great delicacy was "salty buried-bread," which called for a batter of corn flour and white corn samp layered sandwich-fashion between cornhusks and stones in a sealed hearth, where it baked all night. Without salt but sweetened with honey, licorice root, and dried flowers, a similar bread reminded Cushing of a New England Indian pudding. In cold weather Zuñi liked to eat a curious concoction made by freezing a boiled corn paste spread thinly between stones. Among the Navajo a variation of this Indian ice cream and a popular breakfast dish is frozen corn milk mush. Wheat-flour "fire loaves" leavened with lime-yeast and kneaded and shaped into thick cakes were baked on hot coals with frequent turning; the same dough buried deep in hot ashes produced "ash bread," and each had an entirely different taste. For feasts it was customary to bake many loaves of bread at a time in the domed earthen ovens now universally called *hornos,* a practice that survives unchanged in the present-day Rio Grande pueblos. During his life among the Zuñi Cushing's "favorite luxury" was "contorted cakes"—thin, round patties of flour, water, and salt deep-fried in suet to a golden-brown. (These are none other than fry bread, a favorite snack at state fairs in the Southwest that has come to be identified as much with the Navajo and Apaches as with the Pueblo Indians.)

Near the end of his long chronicle Cushing describes a typical Zuñi feast that was "as extensive ... as that of the most luxurious of civilized dinners." It goes on for several pages, but among the highlights are dumpling soup with blue-corn balls, a meat and hominy soup that sounds like *posole,* skewered meats, Zuñi-style haggis, and small game cooked in a rich gravy of squash-seed meal, and bowls of a "superior sauce" made at the height of the *chile* season with green *chiles,* onions, coriander, and salt. Dry *chile* is represented by boxes of toasted powdered *chile colorado* and salt, which "looks and smells like snuff; but tastes like the wrong end of a lighted cigarette (until you get used to it)!" The meats are supplemented by vegetables such as corn on the cob, fried squash, milkweed pod greens, and dried melon coils simmered with dried peaches. The breads rival a bakery's wares with wheat rolls, loaves of skinned-corn paste (hominy) wrapped in cornhusks, red-corn tamales, and always *he´-we,* the Zuñi word for *piki,* which accompanied every meal the Zuñi ate. The Zuñi made several kinds of *he´-we*—one of red corn was sweetened, the batter for another was thinned with milk—using six varieties of corn ground together or separately. Cushing believed that paper bread was "the most perfect of all known corn-foods."

In the cookery of the Zuñi a century ago one can recognize comparable dishes made in the present-day Rio Grande pueblos; but with modern cooking appliances there is little reason to bake breads between stones or in pits, and part of a rich heritage is receding into the past. Paper bread—some New Mexicans call it "sheet bread" or "stick bread"—is made occasionally, but only by very old women, and mastering the techniques of baking it is no longer a womanly art to which most Pueblo girls aspire. That it exists to the extent it does among the Hopi can be explained by the relative purity of their culture and their dependence on corn instead of wheat. By contrast, three centuries of close contact with European ways has profoundly changed the New Mexican pueblos.

The bread invariably associated with the pueblos is the crusty, densely textured, round white loaf baked in the outdoor stone-and-adobe *hornos* that resemble large beehives. Indian women bake all manner of quick breads and corn breads in their modern kitchen ovens, but never leavened pueblo bread. The *horno,* prefired with juniper or piñon, is considered essential for achieving a hard, crackly crust and the subtle flavor imparted by wood and clay that no electric or gas oven can duplicate. It is used for roasting corn for *chicos* (steamed dried green corn) and baking sweet sprouted-wheat puddings as well. Many anthropological texts refer to the *horno* as a "Spanish oven," the presumption being that the Pueblo Indians had only a griddle comparable to the *piki* stone for baking until the Spanish introduced the oven of their homeland. Cushing, who had a different opinion, wrote how the Zuñi oven evolved from a stone-lined pit in the ground or a stone granary—an ideal natural oven with a slab to cover the opening—to the efficient dome shape with a smoke hole. A more persuasive argument for the *horno* as a native Indian design appears in the journal of Gaspar Castaño de Sosa, a conquistador on an expedition that followed Coronado's. According to archaeologists at the University of New Mexico, he described seeing a beehive bake oven on a roof in San Ildefonso. The *horno,* in any event, is a permanent and picturesque feature of just about every Spanish village and Indian pueblo in New Mexico, and eating bread still warm from the oven is one of the great pleasures of traveling in the Southwest.

The best time to see *hornos* in use is two or three days before a dance or fiesta, when virtually every Indian woman in a pueblo bakes twenty-five to fifty pounds of bread to give as gifts. By luck more than design we had the chance to visit Jemez, a large pueblo about forty miles northwest of Albuquerque, just before the annual corn dance and Fiesta de San Diego on November 12. Jemez occupies nearly ninety thousand acres along the Jemez River in an area of compelling natural beauty with striated flat-topped mountains that resemble a layered red and mauve cake. In late autumn the great golden cottonwoods, the noble trees of Southwestern riverbeds, had half shed their leaves and the cornfields bordering the compact houses of the village were the color of straw. The Jemez, we had been told, are the only Pueblo peoples who speak the Towa dialect, and the women have a special knack for bread making, a fact that our noses quickly verified. The entire pueblo village that day smelled of burning piñon and baking bread, one of the most aromatic combinations on earth. Everywhere we went we saw bread in tinfoil pans entering ovens on long peels or, browned and puffy, being emptied into washtubs and lugged back into houses. About an hour before they intend to bake, the women build a roaring fire on the oven floor, then rake out the hot embers and ashes and swab the floor with a wet mop. Various materials are used to test oven temperature, but at Jemez dried cornhusks and crumpled newspaper seem to be favored. If they scorch too quickly, the wet mop comes into play again to cool the floor. Besides the breadmaking activity, there was a flurry of housecleaning in progress. Windows were being washed and houses given a fresh coat of plaster in preparation for the pueblo's most important fiesta, which would attract thousands of visitors.

On the outskirts of the village near some cornfields we stopped to admire a crib of blue corn extending half the length of an adobe whose walls, like those of many houses in Jemez, were hung with wreaths and *ristras* of drying red *chiles.* The owner materialized, introduced himself as George Shendo, and seemed pleased to talk about his harvest with these interested Anglos. He said that when the blue corn was thoroughly dry it would be ground into flour for tortillas. As I was imagining how many women and *metates* would be required to carry out this formidable task, he explained that a truck machine comes around—a modern, motorized gristmill, in effect—and grinds hundreds of pounds at a time. The unhusked ears that were spread on the roof would be roasted in a *horno,* dried to make *chicos,* and then cooked with meats in a stew. The quantity of stacked corn seemed enormous to us, but Shendo shook his head and said it made a poor showing; there had been too little snow the previous winter. In a good growing year the corn crib would be filled almost to the rooftop.

We had a note of introduction to Juanita Fragua, a Jemez potter, whom we found just about ready to put a batch of bread in her oven. She took a few minutes to show us a wedding jar and other examples of her impressive work. Much of the Jemez ware is unfired and decorated with poster paints, and it is frankly created for the curio trade. Serious artists like Juanita work with what she calls "commercial ware using white man's paints" and make pottery in the traditional Indian way, grinding rocks to obtain natural earthen colors. Her bowls, in subtle shades of tan and rust, are collectors' pieces. Her beautifully rounded bread, some thirty-five loaves, looked outstanding too, and it took up every available tabletop and floor space in the kitchen. We formed a relay to carry it outdoors to the oven down the street. After determining the temperature with a few cornhusks (they browned evenly and slowly), Juanita arranged the loaves on the oven floor and propped a sheet of tin against the opening. She looked weary, and with good reason. Kneading more than twenty-five pounds of dough—Indian women never seem to make pueblo bread in smaller amounts—is a Herculean labor. The dough had been mixed the evening before, using two pounds of lard and just one cake of yeast to twenty-five pounds of flour, and set to rise all night. During that period Juanita had punched it down twice. I asked her why Indian bread makers use so little yeast, and she said it was simply the custom, perhaps because too much yeast would produce an undesirable sour taste and make the bread spoil sooner. It occurred to me that at the altitudes of the pueblos, which usually are between five and seven thousand feet, more yeast might also make the bread rise too quickly. The lard—the secret flavor ingredient in many Indian dishes—contributes to the bread's fine texture.

After the loaves had baked for about an hour we helped Juanita remove them from the oven, a hot but rewarding job, cart them into the house, and spread them out on sheets on the floor to cool. They made an impressive sight with their perfect, golden-brown crusts, and the aroma was heavenly. Juanita looked relieved and more relaxed now. The most tiring part of the fiesta preparations was finished. The next day would be spent cooking red *chile* with meat, a traditional feast-day dish. And because she was one of the pueblo dancers, in the evening she would go to the kiva (ceremonial chamber), as she had done for weeks, to practice the intricate steps.

Just before we left, Juanita, with characteristic Indian generosity, presented us with a loaf of her bread. I don't know whether it was the admiration we felt for this warm and gifted woman or the intrinsic goodness of her bread or both, but to us it seemed the best of all possible pueblo breads. "Juanita's bread" became the measure by which all subsequent pueblo loaves were judged and found wanting, and for the next week we began each day with a thick slice of it. It remained crusty and fresh to the end.

Unless one is invited into a pueblo home on ceremonial days to share traditional dishes, the opportunities for eating Indian foods and breads in the Southwest are limited, though much improved from a few years ago. The only restaurant I know of with *piki* on its menu is the Hopi-owned establishment on Second Mesa that is operated in conjunction with a motel and an adjacent museum and arts and crafts center. When I was there a year ago they served not only rolls of *piki,* which are made by village women, but blue-corn griddlecakes tinted a startling turquoise; the Hopi equivalent of *posole* (meat and hominy soup, here made with beef instead of the customary pork), which is a Southwestern Indian staple; and puffy pillows of fry bread that were closer in concept to the *sopaipillas* that accompany every meal in Hispanic restaurants in and around Santa Fe. Skilled women also make *piki* at various state fairs and Indian crafts exhibitions held throughout Arizona and New Mexico. A special bakehouse with a *piki* stone in use is one of the attractions of the Hopi crafts festival held annually in early July at the Museum of Northern Arizona near Flagstaff. At such fairs and shows the most popular area is frequently where Indian women, usually Navajo, set up their kettles of boiling lard and turn out puffed rounds of fry bread.

Driving through the Isleta Pueblo, about fourteen miles south of Albuquerque, one sees *hornos* alongside nearly every farmhouse and frequently "bread for sale" signs. We followed one up and came away with a just-baked loaf and a bagful of fresh green *chiles* that a farmer pressed on us as a gesture of friendliness. Islet's best-known baker is Felicita Jojola, who turns out superior pueblo bread and Indian fruit pies in the bakery on the plaza. Pueblo bread is also sold on occasion in various other New Mexico pueblos, Taos for one. And there is usually one woman selling bread at the Indian market on The Plaza in Santa Fe. However, the loaves there are wrapped in plastic, a practice that satisfies local health ordinances but contributes nothing to the crust.

The best place to sample Indian dishes along with a broad spectrum of Indian culture is at the Indian Pueblo Cultural Center in Albuquerque, which we visited shortly after it had opened. This unique establishment, a living museum, educational center, and research facility all in one, is owned and operated by the tribes that make up the nineteen New Mexico pueblos. It represents a landmark achievement—the first time there has ever been anything so comprehensive and ambitious presenting Pueblo history and culture from the Pueblo point of view. Among its attractions are Indian dances in the plaza, artists at work, exhibits demonstrating the distinctive ways of life in each pueblo, and an outstanding arts and crafts store with the largest collection of Zuñi jewelry in the Southwest for sale. The main building is constructed in a semicircle inspired by Pueblo Bonito in Chaco Canyon, one of the greatest examples of Pueblo architecture. On the grounds is a replica of a Pueblo house and two *hornos* that eventually will bake bread. The Center's attractive Pueblo Kitchen Restaurant, staffed by Indian cooks, has an informal menu of authentic foods along with such ingenious compromises for visitors as hot dogs and hamburgers served between fry bread and topped with red or green *chile*—both improvements on the originals in my opinion. It was there that I developed an insatiable craving for fry bread spread with hot red *chile,* a combination that a San Juan Indian told me he ate every morning for breakfast. The restaurant also serves *posole;* corn, squash, and *chile,* one of the best vegetable combinations ever created; and exceptional Indian pies, little square tarts made with a flaky lard pastry and filled with dried peaches or prunes. On one evening a week during the winter—by reservation only—the restaurant prepares a Pueblo feast, with bowls passed around the table as is the custom in pueblos on feast days. The dozen or so dishes include red *chile* and green *chile* stews made, respectively, with mutton and beef; blue-corn tamales filled with red *chile* and meat; fry bread and pueblo bread; and such ancient Indian foods as *hi-yan-ynee,* a blue-cornmeal gruel seasoned with wild celery, which is the only food taken at most pueblos during the fasts preceding religious ceremonies. In early spring there is Acoma *wa-ku,* simmered wild spinach from the desert around Acoma. (Traditionally the juice left from the cooking is saved to make paint for pottery.)

The Pueblo feast offers a rare opportunity to experience one of the most interesting and least known indigenous cuisines in America. We went to the Southwest in search of Indian breads and discovered a culinary heritage far richer than we knew.

The following recipes include Indian dishes that have hardly changed in centuries and hybrids derived from Indian sources. Save for *piki,* which is beyond the ken of any but certain Indian cooks, most Indian breads can be made at home, although pueblo bread baked in a modern oven won't taste like pueblo bread from a *horno.* The basic seasoning in Indian dishes comes from a large New Mexican *chile* relished in both its fresh green and dried red stages. In late autumn in New Mexico *ristras* of drying *chiles* brighten roadside markets throughout the state; the Chimayó variety grown in the Espanola valley north of Santa Fe is highly esteemed. The same *chile* in California is called "California" or "Anaheim," but in California's cooler climate it is milder and lacks the characteristic deep flavor. These dried *chiles* are exported to cities around the country and may be found in Mexican markets. Out of season, green *chiles* are sometimes found frozen. Blue cornmeal is ground finer than commercial yellow or white cornmeals, and there is no substitute for it in texture or in flavor.

PUEBLO BREAD

In a large bowl proof 1 envelope active dry yeast in 1 cup lukewarm water with 1 teaspoon sugar for 10 minutes. Stir in ¼ cup lard, melted and cooled, and 1½ teaspoons salt. Beat in 8 cups flour alternately with 3 cups warm water, beating vigorously with a wooden spoon until the dough is fairly smooth and shiny. Beat in 1½ cups more flour, or as much as the dough will hold. Turn the dough out on a lightly floured surface and knead it gently but thoroughly, gradually working in 1 to 1½ cups flour, for at least 20 minutes. Put the dough in a bowl, lightly greased with lard, and let it rise, covered airtight, in a warm place for 1 hour, or until it is double in bulk. Punch down the dough and knead it on the floured surface for 5 minutes. Return the dough to the bowl and let it rise, covered airtight, in a warm place for 45 minutes to 1 hour, or until it is double in bulk. Punch down the dough, knead it briefly to expel the air bubbles, and shape it into 3 round loaves. Put the loaves in 8-inch round cake or pie pans, greased with lard, brush the tops with melted lard, and let the loaves rise, covered, for 30 minutes. Bake the loaves in a preheated moderately hot oven (375° F.) for 1 hour, or until they are golden brown and sound hollow when the bottoms are tapped. Turn the loaves out on racks and let them cool. Makes 3 loaves.

Blue-corn marbles, an ancient Hopi breakfast dish, have a fundamental corn flavor enhanced by red *chile*.

HOPI BLUE-CORN MARBLES

Put 1 cup blue cornmeal in a mixing bowl and add 1 cup boiling water in a stream, stirring with a wooden spoon until the cornmeal is thoroughly moistened. The batter should be a very stiff paste. Between the palms of the hands roll small pieces of the batter into 1-inch balls. Drop the balls into a wide saucepan of boiling salted water and boil them for 15 to 20 minutes, or until they are puffed slightly and cooked through. Transfer the balls with a slotted spoon to paper towels to drain. Serve the marbles with a bowl of red *chile* purée. (Or serve a quick red *chile* sauce, made in the Hopi manner by crumbling 3 or 4 dried large red *chiles,* seeded, into a skillet and sautéing them in oil or bacon fat just long enough to heat them through.) Makes 15 blue-corn marbles.

RED CHILE PURÉE

With a sharp knife cut off the stem ends of 45 dried large red *chiles,* preferably New Mexican *chiles.* Wearing rubber gloves remove and discard the seeds and rinse the *chiles* under running cold water. In a large saucepan cook the *chiles* in boiling water to cover for 5 minutes, or until they are soft. Drain them in a colander and refresh them under running cold water. In a blender in batches blend the *chiles* with 6 small garlic cloves and 4½ cups water at high speed for 2 to 3 minutes, or until they form a smooth purée. Strain the purée through a sieve into a bowl. The purée keeps, chilled and covered, for about 1 week. Makes 6 to 7 cups.

The following fry bread recipe comes from Ed Marcus of the San Juan Pueblo, who owns The Indian Oven Restaurant in Albuquerque and ran the restaurant at the Indian Pueblo Cultural Center in its opening months. Fry bread is descended from the Spanish *sopaipilla.* Lard is essential to the texture and flavor.

FRY BREAD

Into a bowl sift together 2 cups flour, 2 teaspoons double-acting baking powder, and 1 teaspoon salt and cut in 1 tablespoon lard until the dough resembles fine meal. With a fork mix in lightly ⅔ cup warm water, a little at a time, or enough to form a dough that just holds together. Form the dough into a ball, turn it out on a very lightly floured surface, and knead it slowly and gently for 5 minutes, or until it is smooth. Let the dough rest, covered with plastic wrap, for 15 minutes. Divide the dough into 6 pieces, shape each piece into a ball, and let the dough rest, covered with plastic wrap, for 10 minutes.

In a deep heavy 9- to 10-inch saucepan melt enough lard (2 to 3 pounds) to measure at least 1½ inches and heat it until it is very hot (380° F.). Roll 1 ball of the dough into a 6- to 7-inch round and cut a 3-inch slit in the center with a sharp knife. Drop the dough into the oil and fry it, turning it once, for 2 to 3 minutes, or until it is puffy and golden. (Never let the temperature of the lard drop below 375° or exceed 390° F.). Transfer the bread with a slotted spatula to paper towels to drain. Roll out and fry the remaining dough in the same manner. The breads may be kept warm in a preheated slow oven (200°F.). Serve the bread spread with honey or red *chile* purée or use it as a taco-style base for Indian red *chile* with meat. Makes 6 breads.

INDIAN RED CHILE WITH MEAT

Cut into small dice 1½ pounds boneless beef, pork, or lamb, or use lean ground beef. In a large heavy saucepan brown the meat in 1 tablespoon oil, adding ¼ onion, minced, when the meat is almost browned. Add 1 teaspoon salt and stir in 6 to 7 cups red *chile* purée. Cook the stew over very low heat for 45 minutes to 1 hour, or until the meat is tender and the stew is moderately thick. Serves 4 to 6.

BLUE-CORN CHILE BREAD

Into a large bowl sift together 1½ cups each of flour and blue cornmeal, ¼ cup sugar, 4 teaspoons double-acting baking powder, and 1 teaspoon salt. In a bowl combine well 2 eggs, beaten, 1¼ cups milk, 6 tablespoons lard, melted and cooled, and ¼ cup red *chile* purée or 5 teaspoons chili powder. Add the milk mixture to the cornmeal mixture, stirring until the cornmeal mixture is well moistened. Stir in ½ cup grated Longhorn cheese and ¼ cup each of minced green sweet pepper and minced onion. Pour the batter into a well-oiled

9-inch-square baking pan and bake it in a preheated hot oven (400° F.) for 30 to 35 minutes, or until the top is light brown and a cake tester inserted into the center comes out clean. Serve the bread hot, cut into squares. Serves 6 to 8.

The following version of tamale pie comes from Stella Teller, a gifted potter at the Isleta Pueblo.

TAMALE PIE STELLA TELLER

Into a bowl sift together 1½ cups blue cornmeal, ½ cup flour, 2 teaspoons double-acting baking powder, and ½ teaspoon salt. Stir in 2 tablespoons melted lard or vegetable shortening and ¾ to 1 cup water, or enough to make a fairly stiff batter. Spread a ¾-inch layer of the batter evenly in the bottom of an oiled 8-inch-square baking pan, spoon 2 cups Indian red *chile* with meat over the batter, and top it with the remaining batter. Bake the tamale pie in a preheated moderate oven (350° F.) for 25 to 30 minutes, or until the topping is lightly browned and no longer sticky. Serve the tamale pie, cut into squares, with additional Indian red *chile* with meat. Serves 6.

POSOLE
(*Pork and Hominy Soup*)

Soak 2 cups dried *posole* corn (dried whole hominy) in cold water to cover overnight, drain it in a colander, and rinse it under running cold water. In a saucepan combine the corn with enough water to cover it by 2 inches, bring the water to a boil, and simmer the corn for 3 minutes. Drain the corn in a colander and rinse it under running cold water. Put the corn in a kettle with a 1-pound fresh ham hock, split into 3 pieces, 1½ pounds pork shoulder, cut into chunks, 1 onion and 2 garlic cloves, all minced, and 4 teaspoons salt and add 3 quarts water. Bring the water to a boil, cook the mixture, covered, over very low heat, adding water when necessary to keep the meat and corn well covered, for 4 to 5 hours (traditionally it cooks all day), or until the meat is very tender and the corn has burst.

Transfer the pork with a skimmer to a cutting board, remove and discard the bones, and cut the meat into small pieces. Return the meat to the kettle, chill the soup, and remove the fat. Heat the soup until it is hot and add salt to taste. Ladle the soup into heated bowls and stir in red *chile* purée to taste. Serves 6 to 8.

Hi-yan-ynee, which resembles the Mexican *atole*, is a healing dish made with the sacred blue corn. Conventional celery leaves may be substituted for wild celery, a Southwestern herb.

HI-YAN-YNEE
(*Blue-Corn Gruel with Celery*)

In a heavy saucepan bring 4 cups water to a rolling boil. Pour in slowly ½ cup blue cornmeal combined with 1 cup cold water. Sprinkle the mixture with ½ cup chopped celery leaves and 1 teaspoon salt and simmer it, undisturbed, for 4 minutes. Stir the gruel once and serve it hot or chilled in cups. Makes about 5 cups.

Green *chile* stew is one of the Pueblo feast dishes served at the Pueblo Kitchen Restaurant.

SAN FELIPE GREEN CHILE STEW

Cut into small dice 1½ pounds boneless beef or pork. (Rabbit or venison may also be used.) Coat the bottom of a large flameproof casserole thinly with oil and in it brown the meat over high heat. Add 2 tablespoons rendered beef or pork fat or oil and 1 onion, minced, and cook the onion until it is golden. Stir in 2 cups roasted, peeled, and coarsely chopped New Mexican or California green *chiles*, 4 cups water, and salt to taste and cook the stew, half covered, over very low heat for 1 hour, or until the meat is tender. Serves 4 to 6.

To Roast and Peel Green Chiles

Arrange large fresh New Mexican or California green *chiles* in one layer on a baking sheet and prick each one with a fork. Bake the *chiles* in a preheated very hot oven (500° F.), turning them frequently with tongs, until the skins are blistered and blackened on all sides. (Do not let the meat of the *chile* turn black or it will be bitter.) Transfer the *chiles* to a dampened tea towel, cover them with another dampened towel (the moisture generated as they cool will make peeling easier), and let them rest for 15 minutes, or until they are cool enough to handle. Just before peeling the *chiles,* coat the hands thoroughly with vegetable shortening, or wear rubber gloves, to protect the skin from the volatile oils. (Never touch the face or eyes while handling fresh *chiles* and scrub the hands afterward with soap and water.) Peel the *chiles* by pulling up a section of skin close to the stem and peeling down toward the tip. Remove and discard the stems and seeds. Eight to 10 *chiles,* chopped, make 1 cup.

Indian Capirotada
(*Indian Bread Pudding*)

Cut 12 slices of white bread, toasted, into 1½- to 2-inch squares. Or use 8 or 9 slices of pueblo bread, cut ¼ inch thick from the center of the loaf, toasted, and cut into squares; or use 6 fry breads, cut into squares of comparable size. Have ready 1 cup each of raisins and grated Longhorn cheese and ¾ cup pine nuts.

Scatter one third of the bread squares in a buttered 2½-quart baking dish, sprinkle them with one third of the cheese, one third of the raisins, and one third of the pine nuts, and top the mixture with a generous sprinkling of cinnamon sugar. Continue to layer the remaining ingredients and cinnamon sugar in the same manner.

In a large heavy skillet heat 1½ cups sugar over low heat, stirring constantly with a wooden spoon, for 25 minutes, or until it is a golden caramel. Add 1½ cups boiling water in a stream and cook the mixture, stirring, until it is clear. Pour the mixture very slowly over the entire surface of the dish and bake the pudding in a preheated slow oven (300° F.) for 30 to 40 minutes, or until the syrup is absorbed and the pudding is brown but not crisp. It should remain moist. Serves 6 to 8.

CINNAMON SUGAR

In a bowl combine 1 teaspoon cinnamon with 1 cup sugar. Makes about 1 cup. Keeps indefinitely.

November 1977

Notes on Contributors

Naomi Barry wrote for *The International Herald Tribune* from Paris and contributed regularly to *Gourmet*.

Caroline Bates joined *Gourmet* in 1958. She moved to California in 1967 and in 1974 became the magazine's restaurant critic there. She's been covering California and the West Coast for *Gourmet* ever since.

James Beard wrote more than twenty books on food and cooking, including *Delights and Prejudices* and *The New James Beard*.

Ray Bradbury has written more than fifty books. His most recent novel is *From the Dust Returned: A Family Remembrance*.

Mary Cantwell, the author of three memoirs, was an editor at *Mademoiselle* and *Vogue*, and later a member of the editorial board of *The New York Times*.

Richard Clark Cassin contributed occasionally to the magazine.

Robert P. Tristram Coffin was a Maine poet and writer. His books include *Strange Holiness*, which was awarded a Pulitzer Prize for poetry, and *Maine Cooking: Old-Time Secrets*, among dozens more.

LAURIE COLWIN was one of *Gourmet*'s best-loved contributors in the eighties and early nineties. A collection of her *Gourmet* articles appears in *Home Cooking* and *More Home Cooking*.

PAT CONROY is best known for his novels, which include *The Great Santini* and *The Prince of Tides*.

Books by ELIZABETH DAVID include *French Provincial Cooking* and *An Omelette and a Glass of Wine*.

LOUIS P. DEGOUY was a professional chef, cooking-school owner, and a member of *Gourmet*'s founding editorial team. He wrote more than a dozen cookbooks, including *The Gold Cookbook*.

LOUIS DIAT popularized French cooking both in *Gourmet* columns and in cookbooks, including *Cooking à la Ritz* and *Gourmet's Basic French Cookbook*.

DON DRESDEN was a journalist who lived in Paris both before and after World War II.

M.F.K. FISHER redefined food writing throughout her more than sixty-year career. Her fifteen books include *The Gastronomical Me* and *The Art of Eating*.

RUTH KIM HAI wrote for the magazine in the forties.

WILLIAM HAMILTON, a cartoonist and writer, contributed to *Gourmet* in the eighties and early nineties.

RUTH HARKNESS attracted widespread attention in 1936 when she became the first person to bring a live giant panda from China to the United States. She is the author of *The Lady and the Panda* and *Pangoan Diary*.

ELIZABETH HAWES is a New York City–based food writer.

JAY JACOBS was *Gourmet*'s New York restaurant critic from 1972 to 1986 and wrote about other aspects of New York under the pseudonym Hudson Bridges.

MADHUR JAFFREY is an actress and the author of several cookbooks, including *Madhur Jaffrey's World Vegetarian*.

IRENE CORBALLY KUHN served as a foreign correspondent for newspapers in Singapore and the Far East during the twenties.

ANITA LOOS was a Hollywood screenwriter and the author of the book *Gentlemen Prefer Blondes.*

A. J. MCCLANE was the longtime editor of *Field & Stream* and the author of more than twenty books, including *The Encyclopedia of Fish Cookery.*

EDNA O'BRIEN was born and raised in Ireland. Her eighteen novels include *Wild Decembers.*

GEORGE PLIMPTON is an editor of *The Paris Review.*

E. ANNIE PROULX is the author of many books, including *The Shipping News,* which won a Pulitzer Prize and a National Book Award, and *Close Range.*

KENNETH ROBERTS was a journalist and novelist whose books include *Northwest Passage* and *Arundel.*

CLAUDIA RODEN was born and raised in Egypt and is the author of *The Book of Jewish Food: An Odyssey from Samarkand to New York* and *The New Book of Middle-Eastern Food.*

FRANK SCHOONMAKER wrote about wine for *The New Yorker* before covering the topic for *Gourmet.* He was the author of *Encyclopedia of Wine.*

JANE and MICHAEL STERN have written more than twenty books about American food and pop culture. Their most recent book is *Blue Plate Specials and Blue Ribbon Chefs.*

PAUL THEROUX, a novelist and travel writer, is the author of many books, including *The Mosquito Coast* and *The Great Railway Bazaar.*

JAMES VILLAS first wrote for *Gourmet* in 1973. He was the food and wine editor of *Town & Country* for more than twenty-five years and is the author of several books, including *My Mother's Southern Entertaining.*

EUGENE WALTER was a novelist and authority on southern food. His books include *The Untidy Pilgrim* and *American Cooking: Southern Style,* which was part of the Time-Life Foods of the World series.

JOSEPH WECHSBERG was a Czechoslovakian-born journalist, violinist, and author of a dozen books, including *Blue Trout and Black Truffles.*

About the Editor

RUTH REICHL, former restaurant critic of *New West* magazine, *California* magazine, the *Los Angeles Times,* and *The New York Times,* is now editor in chief of *Gourmet* magazine. She is also the author of the bestselling memoirs *Tender at the Bone* and *Comfort Me with Apples.* Reichl lives in Manhattan with her husband, her son, and two cats.

THE DELECTABLE

Modern Library Food Series

Edited by Ruth Reichl

Life à la Henri
Henri Charpentier
and Boyden Sparkes
Introduction by Alice Waters
0-375-75692-2, $13.95/C$21.00

A rediscovered classic: a delightful memoir by the first celebrity chef.

High Bonnet
Idwal Jones
Introduction by
Anthony Bourdain
0-375-75756-2, $11.95/NCR

"Exciting and entertaining
. . . it titillates most if not all
of our overworked senses."
—M.F.K. Fisher

NATIONAL BESTSELLER
Clémentine in the Kitchen
Samuel Chamberlain
0-375-75664-7, $13.95/C$21.00

"A minor masterpiece. . . .
I wish the book to stay with
us forever."—M.F.K. Fisher

Katish
Wanda L. Frolov
Introduction by
Marion Cunningham
0-375-75761-9, $11.95/C$17.95

The unforgettable memoir
of how an irrepressible Russian cook transformed an
American household.

Perfection Salad
Laura Shapiro
Introduction by Michael Stern
0-375-75665-5, $13.95/C$21.00

"Delightful. . . . There are
two stories here, one about
American cooking and one
about American women."
—*The New York Times
Book Review*

The Supper of the Lamb
Robert Farrar Capon
Introduction by Deborah Madison
0-375-76056-3, $11.95/C$17.95

"Awesomely funny, wise,
beautiful, moving . . .
delicious . . . an extraordinary book."
—*The New York Times
Book Review*

Cooking with Pomiane
Edouard de Pomiane
Introduction by Elizabeth David
0-375-75713-9, $13.95/C$21.00

"I know of no cookery
writer who has a greater
mastery of the captivating
phrase."—Elizabeth David

The Passionate Epicure
Marcel Rouff
Introduction by Jeffrey Steingarten
Preface by Lawrence Durrell
0-375-76080-6, $11.95/C$17.95

A French novel, described
by Lawrence Durrell as "a
little masterpiece"; perfect
for anyone with a passion
for food, wine, and love.

For more information visit
www.modernlibrary.com/seriesfood